DISCARD

The End of Philosophy,
the Origin of "Ideology"

The End of Philosophy, the Origin of "Ideology"

*Karl Marx and the Crisis of
the Young Hegelians*

Harold Mah

University of California Press / *Berkeley, Los Angeles, London*

University of California Press
Berkeley and Los Angeles, California

University of California Press, Ltd.
London, England

Library of Congress Cataloging in Publication Data

Mah, Harold.
 The end of philosophy, the origin of "ideology."

  Bibliography: p.
  Includes index.
  1. Marx, Karl, 1818–1883. 2. Bauer, Bruno, 1809–1882. 3. Ruge,
Arnold, 1802–1880. 4. Philosophy, German—19th century. I. Title.
B3305.M74M326   1987   193   86–11418
ISBN 0–520–05848–8 (alk. paper)

Printed in the United States of America

1 2 3 4 5 6 7 8 9

*To the memory of
my father, Edward Mah.*

Contents

Acknowledgments

I have incurred many debts in the course of writing this book, and I welcome this opportunity to acknowledge them. The book began as a doctoral dissertation in the Department of History at Stanford University. Peter Paret was an influential teacher who led me to think about the complex interaction of social and intellectual life. I benefited from Paul Robinson's critical reading of the dissertation, his concern for felicitous prose, and his contagious good humor. Felix Gilbert generously shared with me his knowledge of German history and philosophy. I am very grateful to these scholars for their sound advice and unfailing encouragement.

Jim Sheehan, Gary Steenson, and Frank Eyck also read the manuscript, and I very much appreciated their comments. Parts of the manuscript were presented to the Humanities Symposium at the Ohio State University and to faculty colloquia in the Departments of History at the University of British Columbia and the University of Illinois at Champaign-Urbana. I thank my colleagues at those institutions for their interest and ideas. For their support and suggestions, I am indebted to Ron Imhoff, Eric Nellis, Chris Friedrichs, June Fullmer, John Rule, Alan Beyerchen, John Rothney, David McGinnis, Jeremy Cohen, John Burnham, Alan Wildman, Warren Van Tine, and Marilyn Waldman.

Research and writing were aided by grants from the Social Sciences and Humanities Research Council of Canada, the Mrs. Giles M. Whiting Foundation, and the Vancouver Foundation at the University of British Columbia. I thank Stan Holwitz at the University of California Press for his efficient and sympathetic handling of the manuscript.

Columbus, Ohio   H. M.
June 1986

Introduction

Philosophy and Ideology

In the preface to his doctoral dissertation of 1841, the young Marx defended the dignity of philosophy against those who wanted to subject it to the requirements of religious belief. Although he was a recent convert to Hegelian idealism, he sought support for his cause in the writing of an eighteenth-century empiricist. Marx quoted David Hume:

'Tis certainly a kind of indignity to philosophy, whose *sovereign authority* ought everywhere to be acknowledged, to oblige her on every occasion to make apologies for her conclusions and justify herself to every particular art and science, which may be offended at her. *This puts one in mind of a king arraign'd for high treason against his subjects.*[1]

Marx's appeal to Hume illuminates a premise that had long been held by philosophers—namely, the idea of philosophy's "sovereignty." Since the waning of the Middle Ages, philosophy had again come to be thought of in ancient terms as the "queen of the sciences." It was the discipline that, directed by its own internal principles, would ultimately provide a secure foundation for the sciences and a reliable guide to ethics and politics. Philosophy was thus "sovereign" in that it was both autonomous from contingent worldly interests—it recognized no standards but its own rational criteria—and authoritative for worldly action and thinking. Uncontaminated by the particular, ephemeral concerns of mundane society it postulated universal and timeless truths that could then be applied to everyday life.

At the beginning of the 1840s, the young Marx believed in the traditional notion of philosophy as autonomous and authoritative mental activity. But in the course of the decade, he and other thinkers came to question that notion and ultimately asserted its opposite: that philosophy was not the sovereign but the servant of worldly concerns. Marx wrote in 1845: "The ruling ideas [of an epoch] are nothing more than the ideal expression of the dominant material relations, the dominant material relations grasped as ideas."[2]

Philosophy appeared to be autonomous and authoritative, but in actuality it was dependent on social and political conditions. To explain this disjuncture between the autonomous appearance and the derivative reality of philosophical abstraction Marx and these other critics of philosophy postulated an inverse relation between philosophical thinking and reality: a bad reality, they argued, generated its opposite in abstract thought. Philosophy compensated for and justified adverse social and political conditions by presenting a distorted representation of them. It deluded itself into believing that contingent worldly conditions were derived from timeless and universal abstract truths.

This new way of thinking about the relation between philosophical thought and social and political reality is conventionally called the theory of ideology. That theory, as it was first formulated in the 1840s, and as it is still formulated today,[3] is the direct converse of the traditional idea of philosophy. Whereas philosophy assumes that it clarifies and masters reality, the theory of ideology asserts that abstract, philosophical thinking misrepresents the reality from which it is derived. On the theory of ideology, systematic abstraction justifies particular social and political interests and/or compensates in abstraction for the deficiencies of reality.

The theory of ideology that appeared in the 1840s dramatically changed the nature of philosophy and social theory. It inaugurated a radical reappraisal of abstract thinking that continues today. Since its advent, intellectuals have had to deal with the suspicion that systematic abstract thought is not pure and high-minded mental activity but a cloak for vulgar material interests or psychological dysfunctions.[4]

This study attempts to elucidate the intellectual and historical origins of this extremely cynical and highly influential way of thinking about abstract thought. It examines the transition in the 1840s from the traditional notion of the sovereignty of philosophy to the theory of ideology. Such a study must necessarily consider the development of the young Marx, who is well-known for his formulations and applications of the theory. But the study also examines the thought and experiences of two of Marx's contemporaries—the religious critic Bruno Bauer and the political thinker and activist Arnold Ruge. These three were the leaders of the Prussian wing of the radical Hegelian movement—the so-called Young

Hegelians. At the end of the 1830s these Prussian luminaries of radical Hegelian theory believed in the sovereignty of philosophy. But in the course of the next decade, their encounter with a hostile social and political reality discredited their views of politics, society, and philosophy. Their efforts to find a way out of the ruins of their beliefs resulted in a wrenching reversal of the traditional notion of philosophy, in the first formulation of the theory of ideology. In short, I argue that the emergence of the theory of ideology was the culmination of a crisis of radical Hegelian philosophy in Prussia in the 1840s.

By considering not only the development of Marx but also that of his fellow thinkers Bauer and Ruge, I hope to show further that the crisis of Hegelian philosophy and the resulting formulation of the theory of ideology were products of the uneasy and incomplete shift from "traditional" to "modern" social forms in Prussia. The Prussian Young Hegelians' overturning of traditional philosophy and their framing of a theory of ideology implicitly registered the social, political, and intellectual dislocation that accompanied the uneven consolidation of "modern" market society and popular politics in Prussia.

In asserting that these three thinkers were responsible for the emergence of the theory of ideology, I do not mean to say that they produced fully articulated versions of the theory. Not all of them presented the theory as a formal theory, as a systematic set of explicit general propositions about the relation between thought and society. Marx alone attempted to give the theory such a form, and, even in his case, much was left unarticulated. Bauer, Ruge, and Marx until the mid-1840s did not so much delineate formal general principles of a theory of ideology as construct operational prototypes of the theory. They made investigations of philosophies and philosophers—investigations that often assumed a theory of ideology. In a word, their theory of ideology was frequently *implicit;* its general principles were embedded in specific analyses of particular thinkers.

To recognize the underdeveloped nature of their theory of ideology is not, however, to preclude the Prussian Young Hegelians from a significant role in the creation of the theory. Entirely coherent, self-consciously systematic social theories do not spring forth whole like Minerva from the head of Zeus. Rather, their emergence is frequently obscured by false leads, inconsistencies, and subterranean principles that need to be unearthed. What is important is that in their critiques of German philosophers, the Prussian Young Hegelians were continually developing the general character of the theory of ideology—namely, its notion of how abstract thought justifies and compensates for particular social conditions. Indeed, as we shall see, Marx's attempt in the mid-1840s to formulate an explicit systematic theory was the logical extension of his earlier implicit applications of the theory. His formal theory of ideology was drawn from his polemical attacks against philosophers.

The articulation of a theory involves not only the formulation of a set of general principles but also an attempt to deal with possible objections to the theory. In this respect as well, the approach of the Prussian Young Hegelians was implicit. The standard objection to the theory of ideology is that it logically issues in relativism. If the theory holds that theoretical reasoning is entangled with particular social and political conditions and hence lacks universal validity, then this must also be true of the theory itself. In short, the theory cancels itself out.

This problem of the theory's apparently self-negating relativism was directly addressed by such notable social commentators as Karl Mannheim. But in the Prussian Young Hegelians' rudimentary formulations of the theory the problem was not posed and dealt with explicitly. Rather it was implicit in their writings and actions. It manifested itself in the intense fear that their own ideas were caught in the ideology that they denounced. This transformation of the theoretical issue of relativism into a question of personal authenticity gave the need to resolve the issue not only a logical but also a psychological urgency. Indeed, as we shall see, their anxiety about their complicity in what they identified as ideology was the propelling force of their intellectual and political developments. The notion that abstract thought legitimizes and/or compensates for particular social and political conditions, the problem of the theorist of ideology being entangled in ideology—these defining characteristics of the theory of ideology are thus to be found, albeit sometimes implicitly, in the thought of the Prussian Young Hegelians. Their writings provide sometimes incompletely formed but nonetheless recognizable models of the theory of ideology.[5]

My contention that the theory of ideology emerged out of the social and political experiences of Prussian Young Hegelians in the 1840s needs to be defended against the possible objection that it defines the origin of the theory too narrowly. For several studies have argued that the sources of the theory of ideology are to be found in earlier periods of European thought. Francis Bacon pointed out that "idols" or prejudices were derived from social fears.[6] Machiavelli linked an individual's ideas to his political interests.[7] Enlightenment thinkers criticized religious belief and derived ideas from sense experience and self-interest.[8] The term *ideology* was in fact first coined by the early nineteenth-century heir of the Enlightenment, Destutt de Tracy. He used that term to refer to his "science of ideas," which, in keeping with the Enlightenment, attempted to find the origin of ideas in sense perception.[9]

But although these thinkers recognized that ideas might be affected by prejudice and self-interest, they should not, I think, be considered the originators of the theory of ideology. In one crucial respect they would not go along with that theory: they still believed that abstract thought was by nature capable of raising itself above immediate worldly concerns to produce universal and timeless truth. They still believed in the sovereignty of philosophy. Indeed, like his eighteenth-century predecessors, the figure who first used the term *ideology* thought that his science of ideas would provide a secure foundation for the moral and natural sciences.[10]

The term *ideology* first obtained an antiphilosophical meaning when it was used by Napoleon to criticize de Tracy and his followers. The French emperor ridiculed their attempt to work out the guiding principles of human thought and behavior. Ideology, Napoleon asserted, was abstract speculation divorced from reality.[11] With Napoleon the term *ideology* thus acquired a pejorative meaning that challenged philosophy's traditional sovereignty. To call philosophy "ideology" was now to say that it was ineffective in the world. It operated in a dream world of abstraction.

Yet despite Napoleon's criticism of the idea of philosophy's worldly efficacy, he too should not be considered the originator of the theory of ideology. His passing criticism of de Tracy's "ideology" can scarcely be considered a systematic theory of how philosophy operates. His contempt for philosophy seems to be merely a variation of the conventional prejudice of the practical-minded Realpolitiker against intellectuals.

Moreover, Napoleon's criticism of philosophy bears only a superficial similarity to the theory of ideology. Although both question philosophy's ability to affect the world, they have incompatible views about how it is related to the world. For Napoleon, it is detached from reality; it dwells in its own abstract realm. But according to the theory of ideology, philosophical thought is not divorced from society but is a slave to it. The workings of philosophy are, on the theory of ideology, intimately bound up with the workings of the mundane world.

One commentator has asserted that the origin of the modern theory of ideology is to be found in the Young Hegelian movement as a whole,[12] not principally, as I contend, in the thought and experiences of its Prussian members. On the surface, this argument is well taken. The non-Prussians David Friedrich Strauss in his *Life of Jesus* (1835) and Ludwig Feuerbach in *The Essence of Christianity* (1841) argued that Christianity was a form of human self-alienation. Frustrated in the real achievement of their hopes and desires, human beings sought recourse in fantasy. They projected their own hopes and desires into an imaginary world of fulfillment. God, Jesus, the afterlife—these were the products of human wish fulfillment. Once created, these projections then appeared to be "sovereign": they seemed to be autonomous of worldly determination, yet authoritative for worldly affairs. God was a human creation, yet appeared to govern humanity. Feuerbach later extended his criticism of religion to a criticism of philosophy. He argued that the abstractions of speculative philosophy were also unreal; they too were projections of human nature. Philosophy, Feuerbach concluded, was the last refuge of theology.[13]

Young Hegelian religious criticism thus seems to have provided the general model for the theory of ideology. Both are concerned with the deceptions and self-deceptions of human consciousness. Yet the religious criticism of the non-Prussian Young Hegelians remains in one essential respect removed from a theory of ideology. The non-Prussian Young Hegelians were never interested in the relation between philosophy and politics and society. Their views of the alienation of consciousness continued to be philosophical: the generation of religious and philosophical abstractions, they argued, was the necessary product of the autonomous evolution of human consciousness.[14] Karl Löwith astutely noted that the content of Feuerbach's theory—that is, its concern with sensuous humanity—might be concrete, but its form was idealistic.[15] Like Strauss, Feuerbach's explanation of why consciousness alienated itself in abstraction was itself a philosophical abstraction.

The Prussian Young Hegelians were exceptional in attempting to extend their radical religious criticism to a criticism of specific social and political forms. It was this linking of philosophy and concrete social and political processes that generated the theory of ideology, the theory of how mundane reality determines abstract thought.

Different isolated aspects of the theory of ideology might be traced back to a variety of thinkers and intellectual movements. But to understand why all the essential ingredients of the theory appeared and played thereafter an important role in the development of modern social theory, one must consider the evolution of Young Hegelian thought in Prussia in the 1840s.

The next part of this study outlines the intellectual, social, and political background of Hegelian theory in Prussia. It sketches the general character of Hegelian theory and the development of a Hegelian school in the context of European, and especially Prussian, social and political history. This analysis of Hegelian theory determines the organization of the subsequent main parts of the study.

Those parts focus on the leaders of the Young Hegelian movement in Prussia. The chapters on Bruno Bauer, Arnold Ruge, and Karl Marx show how their Hegelian loyalties were formed in the 1830s and then fatally undermined in the 1840s by social and political changes in Prussia. For each philosopher, the outcome of the collapse of Hegelian theory was social and political dislocation, and the theoretical result of that dislocation was a radical reevaluation of the relation between thought and reality. Out of the crisis of Hegelian philosophy in Prussia emerged the theory of ideology.[16]

Part I
The Reality of Spirit: Hegelian Philosophy Between Tradition and Modernity

1

Spirit as Subject:
The Phenomenology of the Philosopher

1

Hegelian theory is conventionally divided into two periods: an era of
social and political opposition lasting until the late 1790s, and a subsequent era of reconciliation with society. Like many young German
intellectuals who lived during the period of the French Revolution, the
young Hegel was in conflict with his world.[1] During and after his university education in the early 1790s at the Tübingen *Stift*, he attacked the
dominant social, political, and religious values of the age. These, he
believed, had failed to satisfy humanity's spiritual and political needs. In
his early essay, the so-called "Positivity of Christianity," he argued that
Christianity had rendered humanity the servant of an alien being. Human
beings were forced to obey laws that were not of their own making.[2] The
politics of the age were equally oppressive. Since the demise of the Greek
polis, European society had collapsed into the degraded form of a collection of alienated, atomized individuals. In such a form, the majority of
people could no longer express themselves in politics. Greek democracy
had given way to modern oligarchy and tyranny.[3]

For the young Hegel the pressing problem of the age was how to regain
spiritual freedom and political community in a situation that denied them.
Initially, the young man was determined to change the existing world.
With his Tübingen friends Schelling and Hölderlin, he embraced the
French Revolution as the beginning of a new and better era[4] and, in
1795, while a tutor for a patrician family in Bern, he engaged in mildly
radical activity. He secretly translated into German a French political
polemic that denounced as tyranny the political hegemony of his employ-
er's social class.[5] The young Hegel's conception of philosophy at this
time was consonant with his political radicalism. Philosophy, he thought,

should not be content with interpreting the world. Rather, as he said in a letter to Schelling in 1795, it is in duty bound to change the world, to oppose what is with what should be.[6]

In the first half of the 1790s, Hegel was thus estranged from his world, and he sought to change it. But in the last years of the decade and in the first years of the new century, the young man dramatically altered his thinking. He reversed his earlier relation to society. Where he had formerly opposed the existing world, he now sought a reconciliation with it, a unity with the present age.[7] This change in attitude did not mean that he repudiated his criticism of society. On the contrary, he continued to find alienation and division in the existing world,[8] but he now regarded those defects in a different light: they were historically and spiritually necessary for the establishment of a free and harmonious spiritual life. The present age, he said in a major essay of the period, was not a product of contingent circumstances: it was "as it ought to be."[9] With this new point of view Hegel redefined the role of philosophy. It should not engage in what he now considered to be wishful thinking: it should not seek to overcome the present.[10] On the contrary, the task of the philosopher was to recognize the necessity of the existing world and demonstrate how it already contained the conditions for freedom and harmony.

This momentous reorientation in Hegel's thinking was made theoretically possible, according to Charles Taylor, by his turn to metaphysics. Where the subject of Hegel's earlier philosophy had been humanity, it was now a metaphysical entity. *Geist* or spirit became the object of concern, the principal character, in Hegel's writings after 1800.[11] Defining the nature of Hegel's spirit has been the source of much controversy. At times, Hegel calls spirit "God,"[12] but it is clearly not the God of Judeo-Christianity. It is not a supreme being who exists before time and space and who is greater than humanity. Rather, spirit develops by embodying itself in the forms of this world.[13]

This embodiment is a process that occurs in two ways. There is, in Charles Taylor's terms, an increasing internalization and externalization of spirit.[14] Spirit evolves internally by developing an increasingly sophisticated and ultimately free self-consciousness. This increasing articulation of *Innerlichkeit* is the formation of spirit as a personality, as a self or subject. The development of spirit as subject must take place in an embodiment that can allow for an evolving consciousness. It occurs, that is, in the human mind. Spirit emerges as subject in the collective consciousness of humanity.

The formation of spirit as subject goes hand in hand with the increasing externalization of spirit. At the same time that it develops into a free self-consciousness, it also embodies itself in the external objective world as the world's underlying substance. Spirit as substance increasingly determines the form and content of nature and society until it establishes the social and political institutions necessary for a free and unified community.[15]

The idea of the evolution of spirit as subject and substance into a condition of existing freedom and harmony is the keystone of Hegel's mature philosophy, and it was of critical importance to his followers. The rest of this chapter considers in more detail the notion of spirit as subject and its implications for Hegel's followers. The subsequent chapter looks closely at the notion of spirit as substance in Hegel's mature political philosophy, its fate in the 1820s and 1830s, and how it determined the thought and experiences of the Young Hegelians in the 1840s.

2

When spirit reaches its highest manifestation as subject, it attains, in Hegel's theory, freedom and unity. This ultimate condition of spirit does not exist only in the abstract but is also realized in the existing world. Hegel's notion of the reality of spirit as a free and unified subject can be clarified by considering first his notion of freedom and then the evolution of spirit in the *Phenomenology of Spirit* (1806).

Defined negatively, to be free is to be neither determined nor limited by an external agency. Otherwise one is dependent on something outside of oneself. Freedom is in other words the condition of being entirely self-determining. To use Hegel's technical expression, it is the *Bei-sich-selbst-sein*, self-contained existence, the state of being-at-home-with-oneself.[16] Hegel defines this condition of self-unity in his *Lectures on the History of Philosophy*:

Spirit is *self-contained existence* [*Bei-sich-selbst-sein*]. Precisely this is freedom, for if I am dependent, then I relate myself to an other that I am not; I can not be without an external agent [*Äusseres*]. I am free if I exist through myself.[17]

Stated in this manner, Hegel's notion of freedom does not significantly differ from that of other schools of philosophy. Proceeding from a different set of presuppositions, an empiricist philosopher can argue that the individual is free only if he is unimpeded in the pursuit of his interests. But this resemblance is superficial.

For the empiricist, the individual is a sense-perceiving ego. This ego obtains knowledge solely through its sensuous perception of an external object. To have knowledge there then must first exist an outside object that can be perceived. The sensuous ego needs and, in cases of complex arrangements of sense perceptions, desires sensuous objects. Freedom for the sensuous ego is hence the unrestrained ability to fulfill its needs and desires.

Such a view is entirely at odds with Hegel's notion of freedom. On his theory, to need or desire objects is to rely on something external to oneself. Whether one actually obtains the object one needs or desires—the only criterion of the empiricist's notion of freedom—is unimportant to Hegel. Merely needing or desiring are already signs of one's subjection to an alien authority. They are conditions of dependence. Freedom is therefore impossible in an immediate, sensuous relation between the individual and the natural, empirical world. Indeed, Hegel considers freedom to be possible only when one's natural or sensuous needs and desires are overcome.[18]

The proper field and mode of freedom is thought. The object that I am thinking of need not exist externally for me to think of it. Like the thinking process that apprehends it, the object of thought can be solely a product of thought itself. Both thinking and the object of thought share the same essence. Hegel writes in the *Phenomenology:*

In thinking, I *am free*, because I am not in an *other*, but remain simply and solely in communion with myself, and the object . . . is in undivided unity my being-for-myself; and my activity in conceptual thinking is movement within myself.[19]

Freedom as thought is in Hegel's terminology "infinite." Because it is wholly self-defining, because it therefore encounters only itself and meets no external boundaries, it is limitless.[20]

The highest form of freedom is logically that which corresponds to the purest form of thought. This form must be that which is furthest removed from natural, sensuous, and consequently delimiting objects. It is therefore introspective thought, thought thinking about itself. The thinking self attains freedom when it thoughtfully, that is, rationally recognizes its own nature: the thinker thinks of himself as thinking. The thinking self attains, in a word, self-consciousness. "This self-contained existence of spirit," Hegel momentously announces, "is self-consciousness, the consciousness of itself."[21]

In the *Phenomenology of Spirit*, Hegel provides an account of how spirit attains a condition of freedom or rational self-consciousness. To reach that state, it must undergo an arduous development in human consciousness. In its first manifestation it exists in a rudimentary unity with itself. It dwells in pure, undifferentiated being. There is, strictly speaking, no real consciousness at this level for there is no distinction between subjects and objects of perception. But this crude unity is unstable and disintegrates into fragmented entities.

At the first level of differentiation, spirit has at most an embryonic sense of itself: it perceives without mediation and consequently tends to lose itself in the natural object it perceives. Only when more conscious analysis enters this closed world does spirit as a distinct self truly emerge. When one attempts to describe an object, one must use words like *here* or *now*. In some form one must say, "That object is here." But this apparently simple description of a unified reality contains a complex paradox. For in recognizing a discrete object's particularity, one applies to it universal categories ("hereness," "nowness"). Any object can be here or now, not just that object. In arriving at a consciousness of particularity one therefore simultaneously denies it. Particularity, in other words, can only be described by universality.[22]

Merely trying to describe an object thus tears apart one's unity with it. In fact, a three-way division occurs. First, one recognizes the particularity of the object: it is a discrete entity separate from oneself. Second, one recognizes at the same moment one's own consciousness as a discrete entity separate from the object. It too has particularity. Finally, one recognizes but does not understand universality. Describing particularity necessarily entails ascribing universal qualities, but exactly what those qualities are or how they function remains mysterious. With this fragmentation, spirit thus emerges as a distinct self and begins a process of development. It passes through ascending forms of perceiving and knowing until it attains a form of consciousness in which it reestablishes an identity between self, object, and universality.

The movement from one mode of consciousness to another is a movement from outer to inner, from the natural to the spiritual. Once spirit has emerged as a self cognizant of the existence of external objects, it sets out to understand them. First, it tries to comprehend them on their own terms—according to empirical laws of nature. But time after time, it is thwarted in reaching full comprehension. Finally, it recognizes that there is not after all a complete separation: its own consciousness necessarily influences the analysis of the object. The truth behind the object lies in the perceiving subject.

At this point in the *Phenomenology*, the merely conscious spirit becomes self-conscious—but at a crude level. To reach its highest stage it must go through more trials. It enters into social conflicts; it works its way through human history, passing through Christianity, the Enlightenment, and the French Revolution. The character of this Bildungs-process continues to be one of disintegration and reconstitution, then further disintegration. At the same time, there is a constant inward movement toward a more spiritual and abstract consciousness.

After traveling through nature and history, spirit finds its home. The final and highest mode of self-consciousness is systematic philosophy, what Hegel calls *Wissenschaft*, the rational cognition of what is rational. As systematic philosophy, spirit at last knows that reason constitutes all: the world, itself, and the link between the two. It is the subject and object of perception and the unifying, universal medium that connects them. And by recognizing that what it had faced was not something external but itself, it reappropriates all that once seemed alien and domineering.[23] As Hegel put it in another work:

In thinking an object, I make it into thought and deprive it of its sensuous aspect; I make it into something which is directly and essentially mine. Since it is in thought that I am first by myself, I do not penetrate an object until I understand it; it then ceases to stand over against me and I have taken from it the character of its own which it had in opposition to me. . . . The variegated canvas of the world is before me; I stand over against it; by my theoretical attitude to it I overcome its opposition to me and make its content my own. I am at home in the world when I know it, still more when I have understood it.[24]

To reappropriate what was part of itself yet appeared separate thus requires that spirit rationally comprehends that separation as rationally meaningful and necessary. In other words, the defining act of fully developed spirit—of spirit as self-consciousness—is the recapitulation of its development in purely conceptual or philosophical terms. The evolution of spirit culminates in a philosophical demonstration of the rationality of that evolution.[25]

The first such demonstration of the necessary, rational progress of spirit is the *Phenomenology* itself: Hegel and his book are the hitherto highest manifestations of spirit. In this sense the *Phenomenology* is not simply concerned with the evolution of spirit in the abstract. Free and unified self-consciousness, the rational knowing the rational, must be actual: it is Hegel himself.[26]

3

In the Hegelian scheme of things, spirit as a cosmic subject finds its highest embodiment in the mind and writings of the Hegelian philosopher. From this identification of spirit's fulfillment with the Hegelian philosopher an important conclusion could be drawn: namely, that the formation of the individual philosopher was part of spirit's purpose. If spirit necessarily manifested itself in the cognitive processes of the Hegelian philosopher then it had to provide for individuals who could think in Hegelian fashion. It had to ensure that it would have the proper embodiment. The individual Hegelian philosopher could thus regard his personal development as part of spirit's providential plan.

Hegel suggested such an equivalence between the life of spirit and the prosaic development of an individual in the first address that he gave as a professor at the University of Berlin in 1818. In the course of that lecture, he raised the question: Why does one become a philosopher?

The conventional response, Hegel noted, is that one is led to philosophy out of personal interest or by an external authority such as a parent or teacher. But Hegel was dissatisfied with this common-sensical answer. The urge to philosophize, he said, has a more profound source: it is the culmination of an individual's necessary development.

He went on to describe that development which has the same general pattern as that of a phenomenology of spirit. A person, Hegel said, originally is entirely bound up with the external, sensuous world. Sense perception constitutes the basis of knowledge; sensuous desires and drives (*Triebe*) determine action. But as one matures, one finds this direct relationship with the sensuous world to be unsatisfactory. The rational element in a person directs him or her to investigate the origins of contingent, sensuous appearance and to seek behind it an eternal, universal principle.[27]

The individual thus strives to understand and transcend nature, and in doing so passes into new forms of awareness. These forms range from religious faith to mechanistic natural science, but in all cases they are inadequate. They contain contradictions. A person might, for example, find that he or she can understand the objective world only as a confusing mixture of contingency and necessity. The underlying unity that one seeks is then rendered an empty abstraction. One might also find oneself caught in a contradiction between freedom and objectivity. One might feel both materially constrained by the world yet spiritually above it. Finally, an individual might internalize this conflict with nature. An exhilarating sense of liberty could flow from the pursuit of one's natural desires and interests, yet at the same time one could recognize that feeling as incompatible with one's rationality, which requires a renunciation of instinct.[28] The experience of contradiction drives a person to other ways of thinking. Ultimately, to restore wholeness to oneself and to one's relations with the world, one engages in speculative philosophy.

The making of a philosopher thus has the same structure and significance as a phenomenology of spirit. Like spirit, the individual passes from an initial condition of natural unity, through alienated or contradictory states of mind, to the unity-restoring coherence of self-conscious philosophy. The philosopher thus undergoes a personal development equivalent to the cosmic development of spirit. The ontogeny of the philosopher recapitulates the phylogeny of spirit.[29]

4

In the first chapter of each of the subsequent parts, I attempt to show how the identification of spirit with the individual philosopher was crucial in turning Bauer, Ruge, and Marx into devoted followers of Hegelian philosophy. They converted to Hegelian theory because they came to identify the course of their lives with the development of spirit as subject. To demonstrate how these thinkers arrived at this transfiguring recognition, I have constructed for each what might be called an "empirical phenomenology." Each account is empirical in that it is justified not by an a priori logic of development but by its ability to do justice to the explicit empirical record and to the philosopher's actual concerns. The accounts are phenomenological in the Hegelian sense of the term: they describe the individual's development as a progression from an initial condition of unity, through conflicting or contradictory states of consciousness, to the final harmonious state of self-conscious Hegelian philosophy.

The propelling contradictions that drove each figure to Hegelian theory can be seen to be variations of those described in Hegel's Berlin address. In chapter 3, I argue that Bauer was led to Young Hegelian religious theory by his growing dissatisfaction with the empty and forced abstractions of orthodox Hegelianism, which, in Bauer's view, confused historical contingency with philosophical necessity. In chapter 5, I try to show how Ruge was driven to Hegelian theory by a contradiction between freedom and objectivity. As a political idealist, the young Ruge fell into conflict with the political authorities of early nineteenth-century Germany. In chapter 7, the young Marx is shown to have been deeply troubled by an internal conflict. He was torn between the pursuit of Romantic passion and loyalty to the Enlightenment reasonableness that was the legacy of his father.

These young men resolved the contradictions of their lives by becoming Hegelian philosophers. As such, they believed that their conflicts were spiritually necessary and productive. They embraced Hegelian philosophy because they came to think that spirit determined not only the general character of the world but also the specific character of their individual lives. This transfiguring realization was, moreover, reached in proper Hegelian fashion. Each recognized that he was an embodiment of spirit when he reappropriated his past philosophically, when he rethought his life in purely conceptual and rational terms. Like spirit's development in the *Phenomenology*, the development of each figure culminated in the formulation of his development as a phenomenology. For the Hegelian, the defining act of his self-consciousness was his philosophical demonstration of the rational necessity of his evolution to that moment. He became a philosopher when he showed that the travails of his past had a purpose: they issued in his free, rational self-consciousness, in his assumption of Hegelian philosophy.

2

Spirit as Substance:
The Emergence of the Rational State

Spirit as subject attained freedom and wholeness in the self-consciousness of the philosopher. But if the self was to be entirely free and reunited with the world, its freedom and unity could not be confined to the cognitive processes of the philosopher. The philosopher also lived under specific social and political conditions, and therefore, following Hegel's definition of freedom, for the philosopher to be free, those existing conditions also had to be free. Rational spirit was at home in its world only if the external, objective world was rational. Reason thus had to manifest itself not only as subject but also as substance, as the underlying essence of existing social and political institutions.

To understand Hegel's mature political philosophy one must then consider both his a priori philosophical principles and the social and political institutions and problems that he immediately confronted. The first section of this chapter broadly outlines the existing social and political issues that he attempted to resolve in his mature philosophy. That section first deals with general trends in European history and then focuses on the specific situation in Prussia—the center of Hegelian philosophy—at the beginning of the nineteenth century. The second section considers the general philosophical principles of Hegel's mature political thinking. The third section examines how Hegel used those principles in his *Philosophy of Right* (1820) to resolve theoretically the social and political issues outlined in the first section.[1] The fourth section investigates Hegel's search for a practical realization of the theoretical program in the *Philosophy of Right*. It examines his relationship with the Prussian state and his belief that Prussia was the embodiment of spirit as substance. The final section discusses the fate in the 1830s and 1840s of the Hegelian notion of spirit as substance and its identification with the Prussian state. In the decade and a half after Hegel's death in 1831, those beliefs within the Hegelian school were challenged by social and political changes in Prussia. This challenge was the propelling crisis of Young Hegelian development.

1

As commentators have noted, Hegel was among the first social theorists to address one of the most troubling problems of the modern age: the separation of the state from society.[2] This division between a public political realm and a private social realm was the result of a long historical development.

In the late Middle Ages, a condition of political decentralization prevailed throughout Europe. Territorial princes were generally too weak to challenge the self-governing authority of regional and local estates, or *Stände*.[3] Given the social order of Europe at the time, the dominant estate was the aristocracy, but other members of society also had a measure of political power. Burghers and guildsmen, for instance, generally controlled the towns.[4] In a large sphere of society there was thus no distinction between social and political power. Social status was identical with political authority.[5]

Between 1300 and 1600, the power of princes increased but not to the extent that they could unify their states under a single political authority. Rather, the increasingly strong prince entered into an arrangement with the territorial estates, producing what historians have conventionally called the dualistic state, or *Ständestaat*. In this political system, the prince shared political authority with the estates organized into a territorial diet—called Estates or *Landtage*. Just as in society at large, so in the Estates, the nobility was politically predominant.

The prince exercised legitimate political authority only in council, that is, by periodically consulting the assembled Estates.[6] He and the Estates shared, according to Otto Brunner, common assumptions about a "good old law" which enshrined the particular social privileges that defined each group in society.[7] A prince's attempt to violate the law of tradition could result in what the Estates regarded as legitimate armed rebellion. In this sense, not the ruler was sovereign but the ancient law: it was the source and guide of political authority.[8]

In the early dualistic state, the prince was more powerful than before, but not sufficiently powerful to monopolize political power. The Estates and the law preserved the political power of other groups in society. But after the fifteenth century, as the princes built standing armies and more sophisticated administrative systems, the balance of the dualistic system was radically disturbed. Until the eighteenth century, princes claimed in theory to obey traditional law, but in practice they rendered the estates of society defenseless and deprived them of their traditional self-governing authority.[9]

By the eighteenth century, the dualistic state—with the exception of England—existed only as a shadow of its former self. The centralized absolute state had become the dominant political form on the continent, while, deprived of their political authority, the estates were left with only their social and economic privileges. The dualistic state had collapsed into a dualism of state and society. The political authority of the monarch stood opposed to the subordinated members of society.[10]

In the course of the eighteenth and the beginning of the nineteenth century, the opposition between the state and society was further complicated by the consolidation of new social forms. In the decaying dualistic state, society was organized according to prescribed social and economic privileges. One's social role was defined by one's legal claim to particular rights, dues, offices, monopolies, or membership in a closed group. These privileges might or might not be heritable. In the eighteenth century this system of privilege began to break down in several ways.

First, middle-class capital penetrated the once-closed havens of the nobility. Noble seigneuries fell into non-noble hands. At the same time, many of the rural nobility began to apply modern capitalist techniques to agriculture and hence became less interested in preserving traditional modes of labor.[11]

Second, Enlightenment social and political theorists severely criticized the organization of traditional society. Liberal thinkers such as Adam Smith and the Physiocrats called for the abolition of social privilege and economic monopoly, which they believed were both economically inefficient and morally insupportable. They demanded the replacement of traditionally ascribed status with social equality. Each person should participate in society as an equal individual; social status and economic reward would then be determined by free competition.

Third, the traditional form of social organization was being undermined by state bureaucrats who had been won over to the liberal theories of the Enlightenment.[12] By abolishing the order of traditional privilege and establishing instead a society of free and equal individuals, these officials could at once fulfill the Enlightenment's ethical mission and enhance the power of the centralized state. An unfettered and vigorous individualism was, they argued, a source of social and economic power that could be tapped by the state.[13]

Both in theory and to a lesser extent in practice, society's traditional form was being dissolved into a "modern" market society of free-floating individuals. This development tended to intensify the opposition between the state and society; in modern society, one ceased to confront the state as a member of a long-established social group with ancient privileges. Rather, one now opposed the state as an atomized individual. All mediation between the person and the state was effaced.[14]

In France the eighteenth-century attack on privilege and the traditional social order culminated in the events of 1789. The Revolution did away with prescribed rights, dues, and venal offices. Declaring tradition to be invalid, it reconstituted society as an order of equal individuals.[15] The collapse of Prussia before Napoleon's army allowed the reformers in that state's bureaucracy to attempt their own renovation of the old order. The edicts of 1807, 1811, and 1816 ended servitude, opened trades to all, and dissolved the legal barriers dividing the estates of society.[16]

But while the economy and the society were liberalized, the power of the traditional nobility was largely untouched. Even though many opposed social reform, noble landowners tended to benefit economically from the agricultural emancipation. Their landholdings grew, and they no longer owed obligations to emancipated peasants. They also retained much of their traditional social authority. They continued to exercise patrimonial justice, commanded the local police, and selected from their own ranks the local representative (*Landrat*) of the crown.[17]

Early nineteenth-century Prussia was thus a perplexing mixture of traditional and modern social systems.[18] The state bureaucracy attempted to bring about the creation of a new social order, but the strength of the old order forced the bureaucracy to carry out its plans in ways that preserved the power of the traditional social elite. The bureaucracy's desire to create a liberalized society was in part a desire economically to revitalize the defeated Prussian state. But the need to establish a modern social system was also related to pressing political problems that were direct results of the separation of state and society.

In the course of the eighteenth century, members of society had become extremely critical of their exclusion from politics. Both notables of traditional society and spokesmen of the embryonic new social order demanded a voice.[19] Both groups played a part in the French Revolution: the Parlements of Paris wanted a resuscitated dualistic state; all the constitutions of the Revolution were based on some conception of popular sovereignty.

In early nineteenth-century Prussia, enlightened bureaucrats in the government recognized that with the French Revolution the reunification of state and society, the establishment of representative institutions, was a historical necessity.[20] But the problems that reform entailed were formidable. How could reform be reconciled with the absolute state and the mixed nature of Prussian society? The option favored by conservatives was a return to the Ständestaat in which representation would be based on traditional social groups. As the most powerful of those groups, the nobility would exercise political hegemony.[21] The liberal reformers in the bureaucracy preferred a modern representative constitution—one that would turn a broad range of subjects into politically active citizens.[22]

The liberal reformers recognized that such a political change required the social transformation of Prussia. The existing society offered little opportunity for political renovation: the middle class was economically and politically lethargic; the peasantry was dominated by the nobility.[23] To be made suitable for political participation, the Prussian subject had to be freed from traditional constraints, allowed to develop as an individual, and educated in politics. The reformers' plan for reuniting the state and society thus presupposed the successful creation of a society of free individuals.[24] But, as we have seen, the attempt to establish a free-market society in Prussia had the paradoxical effect of strengthening the enemies of political liberalization, the traditional nobility. By 1819 the plan to establish a modern representative constitution had collapsed. Conservative aristocratic resistance had brought about the defeat of the reform movement.[25] A statewide constitution was promised but never implemented by Frederick William III, while in 1823–1824 provincial assemblies (Landtage) were founded in the form of traditional Estates.

The failure to bring about a modern representative state constitution meant not only the perpetuation of the opposition of state and society but also the intensification of that opposition. The conservative aristocracy was now politically aroused against reform. Liberal aims had been frustrated but were still alive in the bureaucracy and in the intelligentsia, and they were seeping into the middle class. Moreover, the new social groups created by the economic liberalization of society were crystallizing—groups that had no place in traditional society and hence directly confronted the state.[26]

In the *Vormärz*, Prussia was thus rent with extreme tensions and contradictions. It was undergoing economic liberalization while its traditional social elites were still powerful. The separation of state and society had become untenable, but their reunification had become complicated by the contradictory nature of society. Demanding a restoration of traditional Estates in which they would be politically preeminent, the aristocracy had blocked the establishment of a modern representative constitution. This confluence of conflicting social and political forces was the complex situation that Hegel faced in the first decades of the nineteenth century.

2

The evolution of spirit as substance is guided by the same general principles as the evolution of spirit as subject. Spirit develops as substance by manifesting itself in a series of social and political institutions that are progressively removed from the natural, sensuous world as they are increasingly constituted by reason.[27] For Hegel, the highest form of spirit as substance is the rational state. Such a state has a constitution that is constructed according to purely rational principles and is concerned with the welfare of the citizenry in general.[28]

Hegel's ideal of a free rational state placed him at odds with other early nineteenth-century conceptions of political organization. He was in conflict with the various conservative political theories. Before the French Revolution, the theory and practice of the centralized monarchy stood opposed to the idea of representation according to traditional status and privilege. Absolutism was against the Ständestaat.[29] After the French Revolution, both theories were judged to be hostile to the new theory of popular sovereignty. The two were now considered conservative.

Hegel rejected both absolutism and the traditional Ständestaat. The absolute centralized state functioned, he thought, with all the sensitivity of a machine. It sapped the soul of its subjects. Hegel wrote in *The German Constitution*: "How dull and spiritless a life is engendered in a modern state where everything is regulated from the top downwards, where nothing with any general implications is left to the management and execution of interested parties of the people."[30]

To revitalize the life of the state, its citizens had to be given a measure of political representation. But not just any form of representation would do. Some had negative political results. Hegel explicitly attacked the conservative conception of representation according to privileged estates. He criticized in 1817 the Wurtemberg estates and in 1832 the English elites that supported the Reform Bill for advocating traditional constitutions. Both groups, he believed, sought to impose their selfish, antiquated interests on the entire state.[31] For the philosopher, the traditional form of political representation had been rendered obsolete by the French Revolution. And to persist in calling for it was to engage in wishful thinking, to "demand that the present be changed into the past and reality into unreality."[32]

Politics had been irrevocably altered by the French Revolution. Indeed, for Hegel the significance of the Revolution was precisely that it stripped away the past. It rendered untenable traditional social and political forms, the old order's "mass of positive law and privileges."[33] The Revolution announced that the social and political world was henceforth to be constructed strictly according to rational, abstract principles. Or as Hegel said grandiloquently in his lectures on the philosophy of history:

Never since the sun had stood in the firmament and the planets revolved around him had it been perceived that man's existence centres in his head, i.e., in thought, inspired by which he builds up the world of reality.[34]

The French Revolution thus signaled the beginning of a new era—one in which politics was to operate according to rational principles. But although Hegel welcomed the decline of tradition and the advent of a rational order, he was at the same time critical of the Revolution for pursuing its mission too thoroughly. The Revolution had become fanatical about bringing reason to the world. In its frenzy for rationality, it had rendered the social and political world overly abstract, divorced from concrete reality.[35]

Hegel's aversion to the excessive abstraction of the Revolution is seen in his consideration of the liberal and democratic theories of sovereignty that emerged in the eighteenth century and that were given powerful force in the Revolution. The underlying principle of those theories is the abstract concept of the sensuous self-interested individual. Liberal theory isolates the individual: it treats one as a being without family, community, religion, morality, or culture. The living person who is enmeshed in many different situations is thus rendered an abstraction: one is made into an individual who is concerned with nothing but the fulfillment of one's immediate sensuous interests. This abstract fiction is the keystone of liberal social and political theory. It is, for a liberal, the source and limit of the state's authority. The state is identified as the guardian and representative of self-interested individuals.[36]

In Hegel's view, the liberal view of the state is untenable. A rational, universal state cannot be based on the contingent, particular interests of empirical egos. The sensuous needs and desires of self-interested individuals would overrun the state, canceling out its rational, universal purpose.[37] Hegel was extremely fearful of all types of liberal and democratic constitutions. Suffrage limited by age and a property qualification produced "inorganic aggregates" of isolated individuals.[38] The idea of democratic representation threw him into a panic. It would create, he believed, an assembly that was "a formless mass whose commotion and activity could therefore only be elementary, irrational, barbarous, and frightful."[39] To give each empirical ego the vote was to deliver the state to an irrational rabble.[40]

Spirit as substance manifested itself in a free, rational state that was in keeping with modern developments in society and politics. Such a state could not, then, conform to the backward-looking principles of the restoration. It could neither be absolutist nor allow representation according to a resuscitated system of privilege. The French Revolution had shown that those political organizations had been irrevocably superseded. The state was to be a rational construct.

But although the Revolution had introduced this valid general principle, it had done so in ways that had distorted it. Liberal and democratic theories of sovereignty, based on an abstract notion of selfish individualism, were inadequate to establish a rational, universal state. The problem for Hegel was to find a rational ordering of existing, post-Revolutionary institutions that circumvented the problems of liberalism, yet avoided the nostalgic illusions of the restoration.

3

In the principal text of his mature political theory—the *Philosophy of Right* of 1820—Hegel attempts to deal with both real and theoretical issues. His procedure is first to acknowledge the existing problems of social reality and political theory and then to overcome them by subsuming them into a larger rational framework. Each social and political form gives rise to a higher form, until the structure of the rational state is fully articulated. Hegel's dialectic of substance integrates, in other words, the conflicting currents of existing society and elements of liberal and conservative theory. These are brought together in such a fashion that each is recognized as logically necessary, but none is regarded as final or absolute. Each is shown to lead to the formation of fully realized spirit as substance.

Hegel begins his book by accepting the advent of modern society and the liberal conception of the individual. He tells us that the basis of modern society is "the immediate or natural will."[41] Each individual will is driven by its impulses and desires, and thus behaves arbitrarily. Its actions and existence are determined by its fluctuating, contingent sensuous appetites.[42] This immediate natural will, Hegel further tells us, is "abstract." It is defined as a simple self-relation: it is concerned only with itself.[43] The original empirical ego is exempt from all real contexts—from family, custom, society, history, religion, and politics.[44] Indeed, Hegel later identifies the moment that an abstract will emerges as the time when its family life has disintegrated. For to become an abstract will, the individual enters the marketplace, and doing that "tears the individual from his family ties, estranges the members of the family from one another, and recognizes them as self-subsistent persons."[45]

From this first principle—that the will is individual, natural, and abstract—Hegel goes on to derive the necessity of social equality, private property, simple commodity exchange, and the institution of contract. He thus accepts and legitimizes as logically necessary the constituent elements of liberal theory and modern society.

But he is not content to establish a political community on these principles. On the contrary, at the same time that he legitimizes the empirical ego, he also attempts to transform it. As the abstract will expresses itself, it generates and is caught up in increasingly rational and ethical social formations. The merely immediate, empirical will is thus increasingly changed into a mediated, rational will.[46] In developing the institution of contract, for example, the will must also of necessity formulate a notion of obligation and with that of crime, punishment, and conscience.

When Hegel follows the abstract will into a fully developed market society—what he calls "civil society"—he argues that even in this sphere of apparently unrestrained sensuous activity and hence total contingency the will is educated and elevated. Hegel makes creative use of classical political economy to show how civil society, as a field of interacting particular interests, brings about an enhanced sense of a rational universal order.

To satisfy its sensuous needs the empirical individual must work in the external world. Labor is the means through which one appropriates nature. As relations of labor (and exchange) develop, a "system of complete interdependence" arises. A division of labor emerges in which "the livelihood, happiness, and legal status of one man is interwoven with the livelihood, happiness, and rights of all."[47] In attempting to satisfy one's own needs, one is thus automatically entangled in the life of all society. Particular self-interest is wedded to the universal interest of the whole. The abstract individual merges with a society of interconnected abstract individuals. Even though one likely does not recognize that in producing for oneself one produces for all of society, that interconnection can still be grasped self-consciously by some; namely, by theorists of classical political economy.[48] Thus a rudimentary self-consciousness arises with the rudimentary interconnectedness or universality of civil society.

Once civil society emerges it generates further institutions that moralize the abstract will, that render it less abstract, by fitting it into extraindividual groups. On Hegel's theory, civil society naturally divides itself into three large classes defined by their relation to nature and their function in society. The "substantial" or agricultural class tills the land and hence directly works with nature. The business class reworks natural objects into commodities; it includes those engaged in crafts, factory production, and trade. The "universal class" does not labor in nature, but devotes itself to the welfare of all society. It is, in short, the class of civil servants.

The mentality of each class is determined by the character of its labor.[49] Because of their close connection to nature, members of the agricultural class have a passive, intuitive sensibility. They respond directly to nature, showing little reflection and independent will.[50] Members of the business class are engaged in refashioning and exchanging the products of nature, and consequently they bring to bear "reflection and intelligence" both on nature and on their relations with the rest of society.[51] The members of the universal class are freed from dependence on nature—their direct needs are supplied by the community—so they devote all their time to the general interests of society. In this sense, the universal class is doubly liberated from nature. It neither takes anything directly from nature nor gives anything directly to it.

The importance of these classes to Hegel's plan for politics is twofold. First, in varying degrees, they develop the rationality of the empirical will, and second, they socialize it. With the formation of classes, the self-interested individual will moves beyond itself, identifies with other wills, and senses thereby its relation to a universal, to the welfare of the whole.[52]

Two other institutions emerge in civil society that are designed to render the abstract will still more rational and ethical—namely, what Hegel calls the "police" and the "corporation." These social forms appear in response to the self-destructive effects of civil society.

As civil society grows, it produces "a spectacle of extravagance and want."[53] In the free play of the market, some individuals accumulate great wealth, while many more are driven into poverty. In other words, the "inner dialectic of civil society" necessarily produces a rich minority and an ever-growing rabble (Pöbel) of poor.[54] Although both suffer from "physical and ethical degeneration"—both are preoccupied with their material existence—the emergence of a rabble, the creation of mass poverty, is a particularly serious threat to the continued existence of society.

Before entering civil society, an individual is economically supported by his or her family. But as noted earlier, once one enters the marketplace one's connection to one's family is severed. Consequently, if society is not to destroy itself, new institutions must arise to maintain the impoverished and redirect them back to economic self-sufficiency.

There are, for Hegel, two agencies that act as substitutes for the family in civil society.[55] First, the police or public authority exercises some control over trade in order to mitigate conflicting interests and to ensure fair trade.[56] As the economic polarization of civil society takes place, it intervenes to aid the poor by providing not welfare but work.[57]

The second agency that aids the poor is the corporations that arise in the business class. Their membership is determined by skill and "rectitude," and is fixed in number by the "general structure of society." Their purpose is to provide their members with education in the craft and economic aid in periods of adversity.[58] The corporations are, in a word, modernized guilds.

Integrated into classes and corporations and guided by the occasional intervention of the police, the empirical ego begins to transcend itself. It senses the necessity of a higher order, of a community not determined by natural needs and desires.[59] The abstract will develops a political sensibility, an awareness of the rational state.

In the organization of the *Philosophy of Right,* the abstract, isolated individual and civil society are shown to be logically prior to and independent from the state. Hegel thus gave theoretical recognition to the historic separation of state and society. Yet such a situation, he further acknowledged, could no longer prevail. The events of the age dictated that civil society had to be joined to the state. Yet to be consistent with his own philosophical purpose the unification of civil society and the state could not allow the former to exert its contingent particularity over the latter's free rationality. The empirical will needed to be connected with the state, but in a way that negated the disruptive force of its self-interested sensuousness.

In determining the locus of sovereignty, Hegel makes no attempt to unite the state and society. He rejects all liberal and democratic theories that identify the source of the state's authority with the collection of individuals in society. Sovereignty resides in a hereditary monarch. That is the only securely rational foundation for the state because it is impervious to the claims of civil society. In the "'majesty' of the monarch," Hegel writes, "the unity of the state is saved from the risk of being drawn down into the sphere of particularity and its caprices, ends, and opinions, and saved too from the war of factions round the throne and from the enfeeblement and overthrow of the power of the state."[60] With sovereignty invested in the crown, the state's ultimate authority is preserved from the pressures of particular social interests. Those interests can now be safely brought into the state. This is done in several ways.

Composed of the universal class, the police, and the judiciary, the executive has the purpose of "subsuming the particular under the universal."[61] It brings rational universality to particular interests by enacting general laws in society and by regulating the particular interests of society so that they are compatible with the "higher interests of the state."[62]

Legislation is made by the crown, the executive, and the Estates. The last are composed of representatives of civil society. These representatives are not chosen according to liberal or democratic principles. They are selected from those social groups that are most suitable for participation in the life of the state.[63] One Estate is composed of that section of the agricultural class that has its position and capital fixed by birth and so is not vulnerable to the "uncertainty of business, the quest for profit, and any sort of fluctuation in possession." In other words, the first Estate is the landed aristocracy defined by primogeniture.[64] The other Estate is constituted by deputies from the "fluctuating element in civil society"— namely, the business class. In its unmediated atomized form as a set of empirical egos, it is inadequate for politics. Only the more mediated, organic occupational groups or corporations that emerge in this class are suitable to send representatives.[65]

Political representation in Estates is the most important element in reuniting a civil society and the state. The Estates, Hegel writes, are "the middle term" that prevents "both the extreme isolation of the power of the crown, which otherwise might seem a mere arbitrary tyranny, and also the isolation of the particular interests of persons, societies, and Corporations."[66] By giving some of society political representation the conflict between the state and society is then canceled out. The possibility of the revolt of civil society against the state is circumvented. Or, as Hegel put it, "individuals" are prevented "from having the appearance of a mass or an aggregate and so from acquiring an unorganized opinion and volition and from crystallizing into a powerful *bloc* in opposition to the organized state."[67]

Hegel's mature political philosophy is an attempt to reconcile tradition and modernity.[68] It seeks to resolve the historical tensions between the absolute state and society, as well as to sort out the confluence of social forces that had emerged in early nineteenth-century Germany. Hegel rejects the traditional view of society as the predominant social reality. Prescribed privilege and status have irrevocably given way to a modern society of equal, self-interested individuals. The abstract will dominates in a civil society. This society is, moreover, logically separated from the state. Abstract individualism competing in the market is logically distinct from politics.

But this is not the final situation for society. Hegel argues that the dynamic of civil society generates other social forms that allow for a reconnection of the state and civil society. Some of those forms—classes, police, and corporations—domesticate the empirical ego and invest it with a sense of belonging to a group, with a rudimentary awareness of the universal. Once this sense is cultivated, particular interests are then taught to find a place in the state itself. They become the concern of the executive and, most important, they obtain representation in the Estates.

With his opening analysis of the abstract will, Hegel appears to an- nounce, even advocate, the demise of traditional society. But in his passage from civil society to the state, we find that he reintroduces the institutions of traditional society. Guilds reappear as corporations that educate and offer support to the victims of civil society. The absolute sovereignty of the hereditary monarchy is accepted because it preserves the autonomy of political authority in the face of the divisive particular interests of society. The political power of the aristocracy, the principle of primogeniture, and the political representation of corporations are justified because they offer representation to civil society yet circumvent the takeover of the state by the atomized interests of society.

Thus after initially abolishing the institutions of traditional society, Hegel then proceeds to rehabilitate them, providing them with a new, modern raison d'etre: they provide the means of reuniting public and private life, the state and modern civil society. Traditional institutions are denied from the point of view of their traditional social justifications, but then reaffirmed from the point of view of modern politics. In this sense, Hegel fulfills in the *Philosophy of Right* what he suggested in 1817: namely, "to bring the lower spheres [of traditional society] back again into respect and political significance, and, purged of privileges and wrongs, to incorporate them as an organic structure of the state."[69]

Hegel's mature political philosophy is an attempt to harmonize the social, political, and intellectual tensions of the day. It strives to integrate conflicting social and political forms into a rational order. In the final analysis, Hegel sanctions neither a fully modern nor a fully traditional society. He accepts liberal over conservative social principles, but then, to mitigate the adverse political effects of the liberal principles, he reintroduces conservative principles.

4

Spirit as substance reached its fulfillment when it embodied itself in a real set of social and political institutions similar to those in the *Philosophy of Right*. Fulfilled substance required, in other words, that the theoretical plan in the *Philosophy of Right* have an actual, existing manifestation.

In an 1820 letter to the reformer and head of the Prussian government Karl August von Hardenberg, Hegel described the purpose of his political treatise. That book, he wrote to the minister, sets out "to demonstrate the unity of philosophy with those principles which the nature of the state requires" and especially with those principles established by his enlightened majesty King Frederick William III and by the first minister—Hardenberg himself.[70] Hegel here explicitly identified his mature political philosophy with the reality of the reformed Prussian state.

In the previous sections, I have argued that Hegel devised the theoretical plan of the *Philosophy of Right* to resolve some of the general tensions of European, and especially Prussian, history. Several studies have made detailed comparisons of specific institutions described in Hegel's treatise with the institutions of reformed Prussia. The match between Hegelian theory and Prussian reality is far from exact. There are some points of agreement—notably, between Hegel's ideal bureaucracy and the enlightened Prussian bureaucracy—but there are also important points of divergence.[71] The most significant disagreement is immediately apparent: when the *Philosophy of Right* appeared in 1820 Prussia did not have a constitution.

This discrepancy might seem to disqualify the Prussian state from being considered the fulfillment of spirit as substance. But for several reasons Hegel resisted such a conclusion. First, when he was composing his book the establishment of a constitution was still being debated and even when a constitution clearly was not going to be granted, it was nonetheless still promised by the crown. Hegel might then have thought that, given the other specific and general affinities between his theory and Prussian reality, the Prussian state was still in the process of generating a modern constitution. Moreover, in addition to the indeterminateness of the constitutional situation in Prussia there were other conditions that drove Hegel to seek spirit's fulfillment in that state.

In his opening address at the University of Berlin, he told his audience that now, in the period after the French Revolution, Prussia had made "the formation and the flowering of the sciences [*Wissenschaften*] one of the most essential moments in the life of the state."[72] Hegel was referring to the remarkable reforms of Wilhelm von Humboldt and others that transformed the Prussian educational system in the first decades of the century. Those reforms involved not only the establishment of new institutions of higher learning, including the University of Berlin; they also involved the vigorous promotion of a new ethos in the universities. Where eighteenth-century universities emphasized corporate and community duties and responsibilities, the new Prussian institutions were to be havens of pure learning. University professors were now expected to engage in *Wissenschaft,* or pure research and scholarship, for its own sake.[73] The Prussian reformers thus institutionalized the late eighteenth-

and early nineteenth-century notion of *Bildung*—of the intrinsic value of spiritual self-development.[74] The showcase of this new notion of the university was the University of Berlin, and it was thus the ideal place to practice philosophy, as Hegel acknowledged in his first lecture there.[75]

Hegel felt at home in the state that cultivated Wissenschaft. Indeed, the minister in charge of education, Karl von Altenstein, and his senior official Johannes Schulze acted as patrons of Hegelian philosophy.[76] They deflected criticism of Hegel—primarily from Romantic conservatives and Pietists—and they gave university posts to his followers.[77] Throughout the 1820s, Hegel found a firm friend and ally in the Prussian state.

In addition to the positive affinities between Hegelian philosophy and the Prussian state, Hegel also had negative reasons for turning to that state. First, it did not have what he regarded as the serious defects of other nations. Unlike Austria and Bavaria, its predominant religion was not Catholicism, which for Hegel was a backward, authoritarian form of spirituality.[78] And unlike Britain, where the traditional aristocracy continued to assert its privileges, the Prussian state had established, especially under Frederick II, rational legal codes that opposed irrational privilege.[79]

The Prussian state also rejected what Hegel considered to be the retrograde forces of the age. It was a bulwark against political Romanticism. It had suppressed Romantic extremists in the nationalist student organizations, the *Burschenschaften*. And although Romantic conservatives had gained important friends in the state—including the crown prince—and in the growing Pietist groups, the bureaucracy as a whole resisted their intrusions. Altenstein and Schulze even attempted to block the academic appointments of some of the more mystical of Romantics.[80]

Further, the Prussian state had stood aloof from liberal and democratic movements. In enshrining the sensuous particular interests of the individual, those movements were for Hegel incompatible with rational politics. He viewed with alarm their political advances in the 1830s. The liberal revolutions of France and Belgium, he feared, might spread to Germany and interfere with the consolidation of his rational political scheme.[81]

The 1832 Reform Bill also caused Hegel some anxiety. He not only wrote a polemic against it but also suggested in that polemic how the political situation in Prussia was superior to that in Great Britain.[82] The Reform Bill disturbed Hegel because it was a historical monstrosity: in its suffrage plans it perpetuated traditional privileges, but then justified them by appealing to the liberal principles of the abstract will, popular sovereignty, and public opinion.[83] Such a paradoxical mixture was unstable and could issue in a violent social uprising, for by appealing to and hence legitimizing liberal principles, the English elite gave liberals a means of arousing the masses.[84]

The Prussian state thus seemed to stand on the side of philosophy. It had significant affinities with the theoretical plan of Hegel's mature political philosophy; it benevolently cultivated the practice and diffusion of philosophy; it opposed the irrational forces of the period. The Prussian state was the reality of spirit as substance, the necessary counterpart to spirit as subject, to Hegelian philosophy itself.

As Hegel became increasingly anxious in the last years of his life about the seemingly retrograde developments of the age, he also became more and more reliant on the Prussian state. Hegel called himself "an old heart," who worried that his hopes were coming undone.[85] He died before he witnessed the full collapse of his plan for the realization of spirit. That experience was left to his followers.

5

In the 1820s, the dissemination of Hegelian philosophy with the benevolent support of the Prussian *Kultusministerium* brought about the rise of an academic Hegelian movement. Hegel won converts in other faculties and universities, and his students obtained academic appointments. In 1826 the leading journal of Hegelian philosophy, the *Jahrbücher für wissenschaftliche Kritik,* was founded. By the late 1820s, Hegelian philosophy was at the height of its influence. In 1828, against the wishes of the conservative legal theorist Friedrich Karl von Savigny and the crown prince, Hegel's follower Eduard Gans was made a professor in the law faculty at the University of Berlin—an appointment that led Savigny to withdraw from all University business.[86] In the next year Hegel was elected Rector of the same institution.[87] By 1830, the philosopher seemed to exercise a tyranny over German philosophy.[88] The transformation of Hegelian philosophy into a powerful academic movement was rapid and, it seemed, complete. But the decline of that movement after Hegel's death in 1831 was also rapid and overwhelming.

In the early 1830s the unity of the Hegelian school disintegrated because of internal disputes over philosophy's relation to politics and Christianity. Some philosophers, such as Eduard Gans, were sympathetic to the liberal revolutions of 1830 and, inspired by the new upsurge of liberalism, they argued that further political reform in Prussia was necessary to realize the fully rational state. These reformists fell into conflict with the more conservative Hegelians who accepted the most reactionary of existing institutions and regarded any liberal reform as anathema.[89] By the end of the 1830s the reformists dominated the Hegelian school, but, as John Toews has noted, this shift in the Hegelian school should not be considered a movement toward political radicalism. Although critical Hegelians wished to reform the Prussian state, they still considered it to be the most advanced form of spirit as substance.[90]

The religious dispute among Hegelians in the 1830s proved to be even more divisive than the political controversy. Already before Hegel's death in 1831 there was considerable controversy over the religious implications of his philosophy. Critics argued that the Hegelian notion of an immanent, developing God was incompatible with Christian theism. If God as spirit developed by embodying itself in the mind of humanity and the institutions of the present, then this was entirely at odds with the Christian notion of a transcendent God who promised fulfillment in an afterlife. The debate over Hegel's supposed pantheism and whether or not his philosophy disallowed the possibility of immortality raged throughout the 1830s.[91] In 1835, the publication of David Friedrich Strauss's *Life of Jesus* radically transformed the controversy. Up to then, Hegelians had attempted to reconcile Christianity and philosophy, a transcendent God and immanent spirit.[92] But Strauss asserted that reconciliation was no longer possible, in two respects. First, he said that Christianity was an inferior form of consciousness and should be abandoned for philosophy. Second, he suggested that insofar as spirit developed in the mind of humanity, it should be considered to be nothing more than humanity itself. Strauss's book, in short, threatened to do away with God.

As Strauss himself later noted, the controversy over his book brought about yet another alignment in the Hegelian school. Orthodox or "right" Hegelians continued to cling to the conventional Hegelian view of the substantive compatibility of Christianity and philosophy. "Center" Hegelians tried to reach a compromise, asserting that some aspects of the two forms of consciousness could be reconciled. "Left" or Young Hegelians accepted Strauss's rejection of Christianity and his humanism.[93]

Interpreters of the development of Hegelian theory have generally assumed that the Young Hegelians' radical religious criticism naturally developed into the radical social and political criticism of the 1840s. We are told that the attack on the Christian values of restoration Germany was a subtle, implicit form of political rebellion which soon led to an explicit criticism of the political values that were supposedly linked to the religious ones.[94] This view of the political significance of Young Hegelian religious criticism oversimplifies the set of movements and institutions that constituted the political reality of Germany in the late 1830s and 1840s. Moreover, it ignores the explicit views of the Young Hegelians themselves. No Young Hegelian religious critic initially believed that his religious radicalism made him a political radical. On the contrary, as we shall see, some thought at first that it strengthened their ties to the Prussian state. And, as already noted, Strauss and Feuerbach were never interested in politics. Strauss withdrew as a contributor to Arnold Ruge's philosophical journal, the *Deutsche Jahrbücher für Wissenschaft und Kunst*, when it began to become politically controversial. Ludwig Feuerbach resisted attempts to involve him directly in politics.[95]

Young Hegelians became politically and then socially radical in Prussia. That happened not because of the innate character or necessary internal development of religious criticism but because of external factors. The continued radicalization of Young Hegelian theory was closely related to the further development of the historical forces that troubled Hegel in the 1820s.[96] In the 1830s and early 1840s first political Romanticism and then the welling up of the particular sensuous interests of society undermined the reconciliation of Hegelian theory and the social and political reality.

In the first years after Hegel's death in 1831, the Kultusministerium continued to support Hegelian philosophy. Against the fierce opposition of conservatives and Pietists, Altenstein forced through the appointment of a Hegelian as Hegel's successor.[97] But in the course of the decade the cause of Hegelian philosophy was severely weakened by the loss of doctrinal unity in the Hegelian school and by the growing infirmity of the aging and ill Altenstein. At the same time, the Romantic opposition to Hegelian theory became increasingly influential in the state.[98] The troubles that all of the Prussian leaders of the Young Hegelian movement experienced in obtaining or holding academic positions and in dealing with Prussian censors indicated a changing balance of power in favor of the enemies of Hegelian theory.

Romantic conservatism ascended to the throne with the 1840 accession of the Pietist King Frederick William IV. Reform liberals in the bureaucracy were now replaced by conservatives.[99] An enemy of Hegelian theory, Johann Albrecht Friedrich Eichhorn, was made Kultusminister, and soon academic positions once held by Hegelians were given to Romantic conservatives. Friedrich Stahl filled the professorship vacated by Gans upon the latter's death in 1839.[100] Two years later, in order to eradicate the "dragon seed" of Hegelianism, Frederick William invited Friedrich Schelling to take up the chair in philosophy that had once been Hegel's.[101] At about the same time, the new King also instituted a program of censorship and political persecution that drove the Prussian Young Hegelians out of public life. They were dismissed from or passed up for academic positions, and their newspapers were suppressed.

Thus in the early 1840s the belief in the unity of spirit as subject and substance, in the harmony of Hegelian philosophy and the Prussian state, fell into jeopardy. The Prussian Young Hegelians found themselves in what was by Hegelian standards an impossible contradiction: spirit had attained its highest manifestation as subject in the free self-consciousness of the philosopher, but its necessary, corresponding manifestation as substance had become retrograde—the state had become the enemy of philosophy. The symmetrical unity of subject and substance, of philosophy and politics, had collapsed. The rational state had given way to an irrational politics.

The Young Hegelians attempted to adapt their theory to this perplexing situation. But their efforts to adjust theory to reality were further complicated by changes in Prussian society. As we have noted, the Prussian reformers had liberalized the economy by freeing the peasantry and by opening up crafts and trade. But the reform legislation was designed and enacted in a way that was generally to the disadvantage of peasants and craftsmen. The result of the agricultural reforms was to increase noble land holdings and local authority while freeing noble landlords from traditional obligations to their former peasants.[102] Peasants who previously owed dues and services were now free, but many had also been dispossessed of land and support from the landlord. There consequently emerged in eastern Prussia a growing number of landless workers who tended to sink into poverty.[103]

The implementation of free trade in the towns had a similar result. Prussian craftsmen resisted the liberalization of crafts and trades. For much of the nineteenth century, they called for the restoration of controls on entry into trades, and they attempted to circumvent state policy.[104] But their efforts did not prevent dramatic increases in the numbers of craftsmen in the first half of the nineteenth century.[105] The outcome was more craftsmen than the essentially preindustrial economy could support, and consequently many were forced into poverty.

The problem of poverty in Prussia was further exacerbated by an unprecedented growth in population. Between 1816 and 1846 the population in the eastern provinces grew from ten to sixteen million.[106] Social and economic reform coupled with the swelling population turned the Vormärz into what one historian has called the "Age of Pauperism."[107] Another historian has estimated that in the 1840s half the population of Prussia was affected by poverty.[108]

The ever-growing mass of mobile, displaced poor was the great social problem of the 1840s.[109] Indeed, it was a problem of such proportions that conventional social categories were considered inadequate to describe it. A new term for the poor gradually replaced the standard *Pöbel*. The mobile mass of displaced poor came to be called the "proletariat."[110] The proletariat was made up of individuals who had fallen out of the traditional order and who felt excluded from a changing world.[111] As the historian Reinhart Koselleck has observed, their relation to the rest of society was that of being society's negation.[112]

As we have seen, Hegel discussed in the *Philosophy of Right* the tendency of civil society to generate a mass of impoverished individuals. To mitigate this tendency without disturbing the essential principles of civil society, he proposed several countervailing measures; but as commentators have pointed out, none of these measures was very effective.[113] In his mature philosophy, Hegel recognized the problem of mass poverty in a liberalized economy, but provided no real remedy for it.

This deficiency in Hegelian theory became of pressing concern to the Prussian Hegelians in the course of the 1840s. The reality of mass poverty signified the rising up of brutalized nature, of atomized sensuous needs and interests in their most degraded form. And such a development was, according to the Hegelian scheme of things, retrograde, inexplicable, and insoluble.

Shortly after they were faced with the inexplicable surge of political Romanticism, the Prussian Hegelians were thus confronted with social developments that Hegelian philosophy could not deal with. Bauer saw in the rise of the "masses" the end of civilization. Ruge attacked socialism and communism, the political movements derived from the new social groups. Marx discovered the proletariat. Given this second challenge—the surging forth of sensuous self-interest—there was little chance of rescuing

Hegelian theory. The notion of spirit as fulfilled substance was for the Prussian Young Hegelians rendered nonsensical.

6

The second chapter of each of the subsequent parts follows in detail the unfolding of the crisis of Hegelian theory in the thought and experience of Bauer, Ruge, and Marx. Each chapter can be seen as an "antiphenomenology," a reversal of each figure's coming to philosophy. For where a phenomenology describes a development from contradiction and alienation to rational unity and freedom, the development of each Hegelian in the 1840s followed the opposite course. The consolidation of political Romanticism and the increasing intervention of degraded sensuous interests undermined the Hegelian ideal of spirit unified as subject and substance. Each thinker attempted to adapt Hegelian theory to the altered circumstances—Bauer advocated "pure criticism," Ruge became a radical democrat—but they were unsuccessful. Yet despite their growing dissatisfaction with the validity of Hegelian philosophy they continued to cling to Hegelian principles and standards. Their fate was isolation and disorientation in an adverse social and political world.

Marx too fell from the unity of Hegelian theory into alienation and opposition. At different times, he was an advocate of Bauer's theory of pure criticism and of Ruge's democratic radicalism. But unlike his fellow philosophers, Marx did not remain with those alternatives. His "antiphenomenology" progressed one step farther. He not only recognized the disturbing intrusion of sensuousness; he embraced it. The hegemony of atomized, sensuous self-interest and the formation of a mass of displaced and impoverished workers became the foundation of his new theory of historical materialism. The end point of the young Marx's development—namely, his reliance on the immediate, sensuous world—is the beginning point of a Hegelian phenomenology. In reaching that point, Marx accomplished what his fellow thinkers could not bring themselves to do: he completely rejected Hegelian theory.

The fall from a complex rational unity to alienation and then, for Marx, to a new, simpler unity of sensuousness reversed the trajectory of a Hegelian phenomenology. In another important sense, as well, the development of the Young Hegelians in the 1840s constituted an "antiphenomenology." As they entered into conflict with their state and society, they became increasingly critical of Hegelian philosophy. They felt more and more that Hegel had misled them about the nature of the world. To comprehend why this had happened, each Prussian Young Hegelian engaged in a self-reflective recapitulation of the development of Hegelian theory. Each attempted to recover meaning from his experience of dislocation. The result of their recapitulations of philosophy's troubled development was directly opposed to the result of spirit's recapitulation at the end of the *Phenomenology*. The Prussian Young Hegelians' recovery of their past did not, as did spirit in the *Phenomenology*, end up exalting philosophical self-consciousness. On the contrary, they concluded that philosophy had deluded itself about the liberating and redeeming power of abstract thought. Philosophy, they said, compensated for an inadequate reality by creating a fantasy world of unity and freedom. Hegelian theory was, in a word, ideology.

The crisis of Hegelian philosophy, its antiphenomenology, thus issued in the emergence of the theory of ideology. That theory registered the Young Hegelians' experience of alienation from society and their disillusionment with their master's philosophy. What for Hegel was the highest manifestation of free spirit—namely, autonomous and authoritative philosophy—was on the theory of ideology an unwitting pawn of narrow and unreasonable sensuous interests. The theory of ideology was the expression of a self-negating philosophical self-consciousness. It was a self-awareness that denied the validity of an autonomous and authoritative self-consciousness. It was the suicide of spirit.

Inasmuch as Marx was alone in fully accepting the sensuousness of society and in trying to work it into a new unified theory of history and society, he was also the Prussian Young Hegelian who produced the most rigorous understanding of ideology. All acknowledged, but Marx was exceptional in producing a formal, systematic theory of the social limitations of abstract thought.

Part II

Bruno Bauer and the
Crisis in Religious Theory

3

Biblical Criticism and the
Search for Redemption

1

On September 6, 1809, Bruno Bauer was born into the family of a Thuringian porcelain painter. Bauer spent his early childhood in Thuringia, but in 1815 the family moved to Berlin, where the father had been offered employment in the Prussian state's expanding luxury trade.[1] Bauer's father apparently prospered in the service of Prussia. When he retired in 1853, he was one of the shop directors in the factory where we worked.[2]

Bauer's parents hoped that their children would find even greater success in reformed Prussia. As pious Lutherans, they at one time wanted the favored son Bruno to become a minister.[3] They encouraged their children to obtain the instruction that they would need to advance in society. Bruno and his brother Edgar obtained university training and became, respectively, an academician and a writer. A third son Egbert became a printer and publisher. But what the sons actually did with their educations went against traditional notions of social mobility: in the 1840s all three became political and religious dissenters.[4]

We do not know how the father reacted to his sons' radicalism, but the mother had invested too much hope and love to withdraw her goodwill. As Edgar reported to Bruno in 1841, their mother anxiously followed the latter's career in philosophy. She had given up novels for philosophical treatises, and she predicted that Bruno would attain even greater fame than David Friedrich Strauss, the author of the controversial *Life of Jesus.*[5]

The young Bauer attended the Friedrich-Wilhelm Gymnasium where he received a classical humanistic education. In 1828 he entered the University of Berlin as a theology student. He first studied with August

Neander, the conservative Pietist theologian, and then with Friedrich Schleiermacher, the famous liberal theologian. At this time, Bauer was searching for an intellectual guide, but he found the theology of feeling that these two professors offered to be philosophically "unsatisfying."[6] He did not gain a sense of being spiritually at home until he visited the lectures of a philosophy professor.[7] Indeed, he later reverentially described his first encounter with Hegel as a kind of conversion experience. He felt himself possessed by a palpable truth, a truth that originated as much from within as from without:

Hegel alone has given back peace and certainty to my unsteady spirit. From the first moment I heard them, his lectures held me chained and seemed to present nothing new but only the explanation of that of which knowledge is inherent in each of us.[8]

After this experience of "peace" and "certainty," Bauer was permanently won over to Hegelian philosophy. Regardless of the personal and social upheavals that he would pass through his philosophical career would be firmly anchored to this event.

The Hegelian convert excelled at the university. In 1829 he won a prize in an essay contest. His essay, a critique of Kant's aesthetic theory, obtained the approval of Hegel himself, who was one of the judges.[9] In the Department of Theology, Bauer gained the patronage of its most eminent Hegelian member, Philipp Conrad Marheineke. Through the latter's intervention, he became a regular contributor to the most important organ of Hegelian philosophy, the *Jahrbücher für wissenschaftliche Kritik*.

Bauer's reputation as a promising young scholar was crystallizing at the same time that the unity of the Hegelian school was disintegrating because of internal disputes. Bauer was never involved in the 1830s controversy over political reformism, but he did become a major participant in the controversy over philosophy's relation to Christianity.

The young Hegel, as we have seen, was a critic of Christianity. But the mature Hegel had reached a reconciliation with religious belief. For him, philosophy did not preclude Christian faith. The absolute truth of philosophy, he believed, merely presented itself in another form in the absolute faith of Christianity. Common to both his philosophy and Christian faith was the teaching of one ubiquitous, unifying spirit that ruled nature and history.

Hegel had believed that this principle of substantive identity had resolved the long-standing antagonism between religion and philosophy.[10] But as we have seen, more orthodox Christian critics disagreed, asserting that his immanent, this-worldly spirit was irreconcilable with the traditional Christian idea of a transcendent, infinite God. Throughout the early 1830s, the issue of the compatibility of Hegelian philosophy and Christianity came to preoccupy theologians in the Hegelian school. In 1835, the debate was raised to a new level by David Friedrich Strauss. In *The Life of Jesus,* he argued that Christianity and philosophy were radically different forms of consciousness. He asserted that the founding documents of Christianity, the Gospels, were largely mythological creations, and hence Christian belief was far removed from the rational self-consciousness of philosophy.[11] Philosophy's proper relation to religion, he concluded, was to separate itself from the crude mythological consciousness of Christianity:

Faith, in her early stages, is governed by the senses . . . what she holds to be true is the external, ordinary event. . . . But mind having once taken occasion by this external fact, to bring under its consciousness the idea of humanity as one with God, sees in the history only the presentation of that idea; the object of faith is completely changed; instead of a sensible, empirical fact, it has become a spiritual and divine idea, which has its confirmation no longer in history but in philosophy. When the mind has thus gone beyond the sensible history, and entered into the domain of the absolute, the former ceases to be essential; it takes a subordinate place, above which the spiritual truths suggested by the history stand self-supported; it becomes as the faint image of a dream which belongs only to the past, and does not, like the idea, share the permanence of the spirit which is absolutely present to itself.[12]

Strauss's *Life of Jesus* created new divisions in the Hegelian school. At one extreme were those who agreed with Strauss and attempted to develop the implications of his ideas. These left or Young Hegelians came to embrace atheism and humanism. At the other extreme were the right or orthodox Hegelians who continued to deny the mythological nature of the Bible, asserting instead the identity of traditional religion and modern philosophy.[13]

At the same time that religiously orthodox Hegelianism faced this challenge from within its ranks, it met strong opposition from without. Since the Wars of Liberation, Pietist fundamentalism had been aggressively gaining influence in the universities and government.[14] Its leaders—

men such as Ernst Hengstenberg at the University of Berlin and August
Tholuck at the University of Halle—insisted on the literal truth of the
Bible and therefore objected to the presumptuous interpretations of
rationalists and Hegelians. Reason, Pietists said, could not penetrate the
Bible. Faith alone obtained entry to its mysterious truth. As early as
1830, Hengstenberg sensed the challenge that Hegelian philosophy posed
to Pietism. He wrote in a letter to Tholuck: "The Hegelian philosophy
will in the near future develop into a much more diabolical force than
the declining rationalism. . . . It is our holy duty to watch out and to
attack immediately."[15]

In the early 1830s, Bauer's philosophical loyalty lay with the orthodox
Hegelians. He was the protegé of one of the group's leaders, Marheineke, who had been instrumental in having him made a *Privatdozent*
at the University of Berlin. From 1836 to 1838, Bauer edited the short-
lived orthodox Hegelian journal, the *Zeitschrift für spekulative Theologie*.
With the publication of Strauss's *Life of Jesus* in 1835 and 1836, he was
chosen to defend Hegelian orthodoxy in the *Jahrbücher für wissenschaftliche Kritik*.[16] He also wrote in 1838 a two-volume study of the Old
Testament, *Die Religion des Alten Testaments in der geschichtlichen
Entwickelung ihrer Principien*,[17] which he intended to be a more comprehensive refutation of *The Life of Jesus*. In *Die Religion* he hoped to
show that the Bible's contradictions, which Strauss had so skillfully
exploited, were not flawed manifestations of an inferior consciousness
but necessary embodiments of spirit's development. He argued that in
the Bible one witnessed an immanent ascension of spirit through its
contradictions to a point where all contradictions disappeared, a point
where religion became identical with philosophy.[18]

Shortly after dealing with the philosophical left's attack on the principle
of the identity of religion and philosophy, Bauer set out to defend the
same principle against the criticisms of the theological right. In opposition
to the Pietists who believed that philosophy was inferior to religious
faith, he wrote in 1839 another study of the Old Testament, *Herr
Dr. Hengstenberg: Kritische Briefe über den Gegensatz des Gesetzes und
das Evangelium*.[19] Because his two Old Testament studies share essentially
the same view of religious consciousness, the following analysis treats
them together, concentrating however on *Die Religion*, the more comprehensive and systematic of the two works.[20]

In *Die Religion*, Bauer wanted to show that the consciousness that
revealed itself in the Bible possessed the same character as Hegel's spirit.

Biblical consciousness therefore had to fulfill the requirements of Hegel's notion of freedom as self-determined existence. But Bauer found that this controlling principle of Hegelian thought was contradicted by the principle of biblical revelation. For if God gave revelations to human consciousness, then they were not part of the "free process of the human spirit."[21] They came from without. They were forced upon the human subject by an external God and thus violated the autonomy of free self-consciousness.[22] Strauss solved this contradiction by giving everything to humanity, by rendering all revelations, including those of Jesus, products of human consciousness. But Bauer at this time sought to demonstrate that spirit's evolution united man and God without injuring the integrity of either.

In his methodological preface to the first volume of *Die Religion*, Bauer outlined the stages of spirit's development in the Bible. The lowest form of spirit or human consciousness was "feeling" (*Gefühl*), in which humanity and God were still entirely bound up in nature. In feeling human consciousness directly identified God with nature, and then lost itself in this emotional worship of nature. Indeed, in this state of primitive unity with nature, a human being did not have a sense of being a discrete "self."[23]

Humanity acquired a perception of itself as an entity distinct from nature and God in the following stage of consciousness, namely "intuition" (*Anschauung*). Human intuition distinguished between the subject and object of perception. To the intuitive consciousness, God appeared as an "other," an object external to subjective human consciousness.[24] But this differentiation from God was rudimentary. The self, not yet strong and autonomous, continued to surrender itself unconsciously to God and nature. It felt that it was different from but also united with an external God. Its unity with God thus seemed to be imposed externally by God.[25]

In the next stage of consciousness, "representation" (*Vorstellung*), the subject and object of human consciousness were more thoroughly separated. Each acquired more abstract features and complexity, more integrity and awareness. God appeared in the Bible for the first time as a universal and purely spiritual being,[26] while human consciousness had developed to the point where it could perceive those qualities in God. Humanity saw that God's revelations were universal and eternal, that they were, in other words, entirely spiritual.[27] Representation was thus defined by an increased differentiation and a heightened spirituality, and it therefore allowed for a unity superior to those found in the lower forms of consciousness. The representative consciousness felt that its unity with God did not come from without but from itself: it recognized that it was part of one inner unifying spirit.

But despite representation's enhanced abstract nature, it was still inadequately spiritual. It ultimately remained tied down to nature. For example, it represented its spirituality in the sensuous form of one physical person—Jesus. This and other contradictions forced it to reevaluate its relation to God.[28] And by reflecting rationally on the nature of God and human beings, it raised itself to the level of the "concept" (Begriff), or conceptual thinking.

In this stage, humanity recognized that it and God were part of the same universal, eternal, and unified substance—namely, thought. The entirely free subject, that is, the thinking subject, attained self-consciousness: the thinker thought of God, who was nothing but thought itself.[29] Moreover, the concept of religion carried spirit or human consciousness beyond the word of the Bible: according to Hegel, the concept of religion had a real, historical correlate, which Bauer called the "idea" (Idee) of religion. For Bauer in 1838 the idea of religion, the union of the real and the rational, was the existing universal Christian community. It embodied an expanded self-consciousness: all knew that divine spirit was located within them, God's children.[30] Throughout his biblical studies Bauer conformed to this basic pattern of development, but the way in which he interpreted the stages of consciousness would change as he moved from the Old Testament to the New. The "concept" and "idea" of religion would obtain radically new meanings as he reevaluated the relation between religion and philosophy.

Spirit's long climb from the natural to the spiritual, from outer to inner, from feeling to reason, was the story told in the Bible. The Old Testament was about the interaction of two kinds of consciousness, intuition and representation.[31] The former, as a sensuous, particular consciousness, tended toward a natural religion. The latter, as a more general abstract consciousness, made for a universal, spiritual religion— the worship of an unworldly, eternal entity by an independent spiritual subject. Given the incompatibility of these two forms of consciousness and their derivative forms of worship, their interrelation was necessarily one of conflict. Indeed, according to Bauer, the Old Testament was the record of spirit's struggle to transcend intuition and natural religion and to gain the higher level of representation and spiritual worship.

The Old Testament began with spirit's fragmentation: humanity fell out of a primal unity with God.[32] In its fallen condition, it entered history as a differentiated entity, but, at this first level, its awareness of God and self remained obscure. The self was still too bound up with nature to perceive God except in sensuous forms such as a voice or as angels.[33] Because these natural manifestations constrained the emergence of spirit's true character, it compelled itself to forsake natural intuition for the more spiritual and universal representation. Thus it eventually appeared against itself. It manifested itself as a coercive agency: the Law.

The Law made its historical appearance when the Jews were enslaved in Egypt and were entirely subservient to a natural religion. They worshipped natural objects like the stars and made gods out of animals.[34] Against nature's particular, sensuous powers, the Law claimed to be a manifestation of a single all-embracing truth. It was the command of one God, Jehovah.[35]

Because of their submergence in nature, the Jewish people were unable to apprehend God except as an external determining force that annihilated the underdeveloped self. "The lawful consciousness," Bauer wrote, "can do no less than give up its self-consciousness, if it makes the Law its content. For the Law appears to the Hebrew as the will of an other and not as the determination of his own, personal will."[36]

This disjuncture between a spiritual God and a human subject lacking in *Innerlichkeit* resulted in a peculiar situation. The Law strove to endow human beings with spirituality, but because they were still so close to nature, it could make itself intelligible only in sensuous, particular ways. In the Hebraic consciousness, there was no afterlife. The Law's reward was direct and sensuous. Jehovah, for instance, smote down the chosen people's existing enemies.[37] The Law's universal will could find only particular, sensuous embodiments—in specific statutes and as the deity reserved for one people.[38]

Presenting what was spiritual in sensuous ways resulted in more than just a paradox. As a method of inculcating the spiritual, it was ultimately self-defeating. By using a sensuous, natural medium, the Law constantly referred humanity back to nature, so that the power of nature was consequently reaffirmed at the same moment that it was denied by the Law. Nature thus continued to exert a powerful influence: the chosen people were repeatedly guilty of backsliding, of abandoning the Law to worship natural gods.[39]

Seeking a way out of this paradox, spirit forced itself to yet a higher stage, to a consciousness more removed from nature and closer to pure representation. This stage, Bauer argued, appeared in the Old Testament with the prophets. Here the gap between humanity and God was partially reduced: the former had a stronger sense of self and consequently produced the desire for an earthly king,[40] then the rule of David,[41] and finally the idea of the Messiah. The last of these developments showed that there had been indeed a great advance in humanity's self-consciousness, for the idea of the Messiah was the first intuition of a spiritual union with God.[42]

But even with this "prophetic" consciousness, the ascension to representation was not complete. The prophets continued to lose themselves in Jehovah, and they continued to nurture much the same limited and paradoxical view of the spiritual. While they proclaimed, for instance, the universality of Jehovah more forcibly than before, they still could not extend his blessing to other peoples.[43] A truly universal and spiritual representative consciousness would not emerge until human beings improved their understanding of God and themselves.

2

Bauer wrote his two Old Testament studies while he was a Privatdozent at the University of Berlin. In 1839 an associate professorship in theology became available at the University of Bonn. Bauer and his mentor Marheineke saw in this a chance for the former's promotion, and both consequently wrote to the Kultusminister Karl von Altenstein.

Bauer also thought that a move to the University of Bonn would give him an opportunity to take stock of his beliefs and renew his intellectual vigor.[44] Despite the praise that his writings had received from orthodox Hegelians, he had come to feel increasingly uneasy as their apologist. Indeed, suggestions of a disengagement from orthodoxy were evident in the same works that had won the approval of traditional Hegelians.

Although Bauer's two Old Testament studies pursued the same purpose—namely, to reconcile religion and philosophy—there existed significant differences of tone and emphasis. Unlike the serious academic form of *Die Religion*, the later *Herr Dr. Hengstenberg* was Bauer's first outrightly polemical work. It was the prototype of the bitter, sarcastic style that would later prevail in so many of his writings. And while he argued in both that a mixture of the natural and the spiritual characterized Old Testament consciousness, he gave predominance to the spiritual in

Die Religion and to the natural in *Herr Dr. Hengstenberg.* In the former, the Law was nature's mortal enemy,[45] but in certain passages in the latter, Bauer presented the Law as almost another kind of natural consciousness.[46] And if the Law in *Herr Dr. Hengstenberg* was less spiritual, it was also more removed than in *Die Religion* from the free consciousness of philosophy. In *Die Religion* Bauer consistently emphasized the drawing together of religion and philosophy. In *Herr Dr. Hengstenberg,* he implied at times a potential parting of ways.

A disengagement from orthodox Hegelianism was also apparent in Bauer's social life. Sometime in 1839, he began to drift away from orthodox Hegelian circles. His life became more bohemian. He frequented the *Doktorklub,* about which little is known except that it was an informal discussion group composed of Privatdozents and students. Reputedly critical and iconoclastic in thinking, it was a crucible of emerging Young Hegelian thinking.[47] Bauer's involvement with this group was ambivalent. Even if he became a good friend of some of its members—notably, Karl Marx and Carl Friedrich Köppen[48]—he hesitated to embrace their beliefs or their style. When he later obtained a clearer view of the issues that bothered him, he reflected on his ambivalence at this time. He admitted in 1840 to his brother Edgar that, until he left Berlin, the "left wing" there had aversely "appeared to him as an extreme."[49] He was, in short, both attracted to and repelled by this new-found radicalism. In 1839 he was floating in a limbo between the right and left wings of the Hegelian school.

In the first half of the nineteenth century, clergymen in Prussia suffered from extreme underemployment: there were between 120 and 150 clerical vacancies a year, while theology students in the Prussian universities numbered yearly around 1,600.[50] And for those students who pursued academic careers, secure positions in universities were exceptionally rare. In the combined theological faculties of Halle, Berlin, Breslau, Bonn, and Königsburg Universities, there were no more than thirty to thirty-two tenured professorships.[51]

Bauer's entry into the University of Bonn was all the more difficult because of the character of its Department of Theology. Made up of Pietist, rationalist, and Schleiermachean *Vermittlungs* theologians, it had never been comfortable with Hegelian theory. And after the publication of Strauss's *Life of Jesus,* its discomfort turned into alarm. All Hegelians were thereafter suspect, and Bauer especially so because he had gained a reputation for arrogance in his reviews for Hegelian journals.[52] Regardless of these impediments, Altenstein managed to arrange a Privatdozent position for Bauer in the Department of Theology at Bonn. This was presumably the preliminary maneuver in a campaign aimed at obtaining for him a tenured professorship,[53] and hence a secure place in Prussia's intellectual and bureaucratic elite.

Bauer arrived at the University of Bonn in October 1839. He was greeted with suspicion. Right away he was confronted by a faculty member who wanted to know if he was going to cause trouble with his godless Hegelianism. When Bauer reported this incident to his brother Edgar, he revealed the depth of his personal confusion and theoretical uncertainty. He told Edgar that he had tried to make his colleague aware of his intention to avoid public controversy. What he hoped to accomplish in Bonn was of a more personal and contemplative nature. His last five years at the University of Berlin, he admitted to his brother, had left him with a sense of "incompleteness," an incompleteness caused by constantly bearing a feeling of "conflict." He was in fact so troubled by this anxiety that he felt the need to withdraw from what had been up to then his sphere of life, "in order," he said, "to compose myself peacefully and to work out all the more clearly and securely the principle—take note!—the principle to which I have committed myself."[54] Thus he envisioned his stay in Bonn as a chance to undertake a philosophical clarification that would be at the same time a self-clarification. He sought to reappraise the principle that had ordered his life.

Despite the hostility, penury, and isolation that he was to suffer during his years in Bonn, he put his stay there to good use. For by the beginning of 1841, he did indeed attain a new confidence, a more focused view of the principle that ruled his life and that would thereafter hold his loyalty. This process of philosophical and existential clarification was reflected in his studies of the Gospels. By continuing his analysis of how spirit represented itself in the Bible, he worked out a clearer sense of the relation between religion and philosophy and in doing so emerged with a clearer sense of self. He at last found fulfillment in a philosophical apprehension of Christianity, although, as we shall see, the nature of this fulfillment differed greatly from his original orthodox Hegelian faith.

3

Bauer conceived his Old Testament studies as refutations of the "tradition" hypothesis of Strauss and Hengstenberg. By asserting that a single continuous tradition—and therefore, consciousness—existed in the Bible, they set in motion the larger argument that religious belief was a unique kind of consciousness and that this consciousness—mythological for Strauss, mystical for Hengstenberg—was distinct from philosophical consciousness. Bauer, however, demonstrated that the Old Testament contained an evolving consciousness that assumed qualitatively different forms and that became increasingly abstract and spiritual. In this way, faith merged with reason, and religion became identical with philosophy.[55]

In *Die Religion* Bauer showed how a higher form of consciousness, representation, struggled with a lower form, intuition, for supremacy. But representation's struggle proved to be unsuccessful, for it was too entangled in nature and consequently caught in a repetitive pattern of transcendence and retrogression. The Old Testament consciousness found itself fluctuating between nature and spirit. This condition was overcome in the New Testament, in which consciousness successfully freed itself from nature. In the Gospels, there appeared for the first time a purely representative consciousness, a consciousness richer than ever before in subjective and universal awareness, in Innerlichkeit.

To demonstrate the workings of a qualitatively new consciousness Bauer needed a medium that would take into account both its new content and its new form. In the first of his New Testament studies, *Kritik der evangelischen Geschichte des Johannes* (1840)[56] he tells us that he had decided to change his method. Rather than consider "revelation" his topic as he had in *Die Religion*, he would approach the Gospel of John through an investigation of how the direct perception of the Messiah, found in the Old Testament prophets, had become in John a mediated "concept of reflection."[57] He wanted, in other words, to treat the new consciousness of the Gospels in a way that would reflect its more subjective, abstract, and mediated form (self-reflection) and content (concepts). He therefore chose to deal with John by analyzing the role of the author in its composition.[58] He asked the question: To what degree has the author's own consciousness conditioned the form and content of a supposedly factual record?

Proceeding from this point of departure, Bauer found that signs of the author's personal intervention filled the Gospel of John. The meaning and order that were given to events, the motives attributed to Jesus, the intelligibility (or unintelligibility) of events—all these were direct results of John's sensibility and purposeful design.[59] His powerful prologue ("In

the Beginning was the Word. . . . ") set down, for example, the concept
of God as the philosophical Logos, which then determined the following
narrative and invested it with a particular meaning.[60] John's Logos principle mirrored the state of Christianity at that time and the peculiar
mixture of ideas—Greek, Jewish, and Christian—that formed the intellectual environment of Ephesus, the city where he lived and wrote.[61] His
Gospel was thus a product of his self-reflection, the intentional working
of the ideas of the day into the story of Jesus.

John's presence seemed to permeate the entire Gospel. Indeed, all
of Jesus' speeches showed his tampering.[62] The Gospel was, in fact, so
thoroughly determined by a personal vision that it could not be distinguished from that vision. In this respect, Bauer argued, John had nothing
in common with the Synoptic Gospels, which were not entirely personal
creations. The latter, Bauer concluded at the end of *Johannes*, were about
real history.[63]

By the next year, however, Bauer renounced this view. In the first
volume of his three-volume study of the Synoptic Gospels, *Kritik der
evangelischen Geschichte der Synoptiker* (1841–1842), he admitted that
further investigation had proved him wrong.[64] By applying the same
method of analysis that he had used in *Johannes*, he had arrived at the
same conclusion: each Gospel had a "literary origin."[65] Each was a con-
sciously formed work of art. They were not "literary versions of a
tradition, but literary inventions."[66]

From the biblical critics Christian Weisse and Christian Wilke, Bauer
accepted the view that Mark was the original Gospel, followed first by
Luke, who drew on Mark, and then by Matthew, who drew on Mark
and Luke.[67] Writing at a time when the Christian community was just
forming, Mark, according to Bauer, was a purer artist than the others.
He had written a simple story uncluttered by dogma. But Luke and
Matthew composed their Gospels as spokesmen for a more consolidated
Christian community. They sought to justify the practices of that community, presenting the life of Jesus in such a way that it conformed to
the community's orthodoxy and established its legitimacy. Bauer consequently called them "pragmatists."[68]

But despite their many "pragmatic" considerations, Matthew and Luke
remained, like Mark, individual purveyors of a new consciousness, of
accomplished representation.[69] In this stage of spirit's development, the
separation between humanity and God had been further mitigated.
Human consciousness had attained a heightened, more articulated spiritu-

ality: individuals, rather than one *Volk,* recognized the divine spirit that dwelt within them. God also attained a more abstract and universal character. His spirituality was no longer reserved for one people: he was the God of all humanity. The image that represented this identity of man and God was the figure of Christ, who was at once the son of man and God.[70]

Unlike the Old Testament consciousness, in which nature retained a strong, if ambiguous, influence, the purely representative consciousness had cast off nature. It understood that spirit made and ruled the world and that humanity was itself a creature of spirit. Christianity was thus an advanced form of self-consciousness: human beings as God's creatures reflected upon and thereby recognized the presence of God in themselves. Each Gospel, Bauer concluded, in its form as a self-reflective artistic creation and in its content as the story of Christ, the man-God, thus testified to the emergence of a new and higher manifestation of self-consciousness.[71]

But even though it was an advanced form of self-consciousness, representation was not free self-consciousness. It still contained contradictions. It allowed for an internal identity of human and divine consciousness, but that identity embodied itself in only one corporeal individual— namely, Jesus.[72] Moreover, within this identity the preponderance was given to divine consciousness, for one merged with God because one recognized oneself as God's creature. A person's existence and meaning were thus derived from an outside force. In short, spirit or human consciousness was still alienated.[73]

The state of free self-consciousness was accomplished when human consciousness recognized that spirit originated from within. It became free when it acknowledged that it was spirit itself and not that spirit was placed in it. But to come to such an understanding required that it understand how spirit operated—it had to comprehend the nature of spirit. And to comprehend the nature of spirit it first needed to pass into a different mode of perceiving: rational thinking or cognition. In other words, it had to forsake representation and attain the level of the "concept."[74] Inasmuch as the nature of spirit changed through time— it passed through the forms of feeling, intuition, and representation— a rational understanding of that nature necessarily entailed a rational understanding of its development. Rational human consciousness had to recount the history of spirit before it could know what spirit was. Such a process of recollection and reintegration of the various stages of spirit's development—an act of remembering by spirit as rational human consciousness—did not take place in the Bible, but in the interpretation of the Bible. That is to say, the stage of consciousness that followed the highest level of consciousness in the Bible was the consciousness that revealed spirit's development in the Bible. The whole development of spirit in the Bible aimed, in other words, at a form of consciousness that would understand that development: the consciousness of rational biblical interpretation and criticism. Free, rational self-consciousness, spirit recognizing its own development, was philosophical criticism.

This form of criticism was the kind that went on in the present. Bauer's own time was the age of spirit's fulfillment. He wrote in *Johannes:*

our age is preeminently that in which the historical spirit turns inward from its previous development and expansion, composes itself, collects in memory all its previous moments, and works them into a spiritual unity.[75]

Bauer also played a personal role in the critical recovery of the evolution of spirit. By telling the history of spirit, he showed himself to be a manifestation of its highest form: Bauer, the philosophical critic of the Bible, was the necessary product of the spiritual striving that the Bible recorded. As a philosopher of religion, he was free self-consciousness incarnate, the fulfillment of biblical consciousness.

Bauer had thus returned to his point of departure. He started his philosophical studies of the Bible with the Hegelian aim of demonstrating the identity of religion and philosophy by showing how spirit evolved through the forms of religious consciousness represented in the Bible to attain a state of freedom, of complete self-consciousness. He ended by showing that this state of freedom was precisely the philosophical investigation of the Bible. The points of origin and conclusion were thus the same: philosophical criticism of the Bible. In this way, his biblical studies constituted, in form and content, a complete and sealed self-consciousness. His philosophical inquiry into the nature of biblical consciousness formed an internal identity in which the author and the investigation merged with the object of investigation.

Bauer's biblical investigation followed the same circuitous structure as Hegel's *Phenomenology*. And just as spirit in the *Phenomenology* finished where it began, but transfigured, so had the nature of Bauer's philosophical criticism transformed itself. Its essential principles had been transformed, for no longer did he believe in a reconciliation of religion and philosophy. In the *Synoptiker* he had lost his faith.

4

Bauer had left Berlin with distressing questions about his faith. He had looked upon his move to Bonn as a way of working himself out of his theoretical and existential quandaries, of restoring the peace and certainty that he had originally discovered in Hegel. In his isolation, he would challenge his own beliefs and, he said, force the contest to a final resolution.[76]

Bauer spent his first year (autumn 1839 to autumn 1840) in tormented self-reflection. He felt himself almost demonically possessed. In a letter to his brother Edgar, he described his interest in religion as that "which allows no peace to him who is once grasped by it until he has fought through all opposition and rescued the truth."[77] But even though he regarded religion as his nemesis, he was not yet fully alienated from it: "I cannot completely consider it," he wrote to Edgar, "as something alien."[78]

Around this time, Bauer began to work on *Johannes*, which was half-finished by 15 March 1840. He then reported to Edgar that he was beginning to find his way through the issues that worried him. The move to Bonn, he said, had acted as an intellectual catalyst: "I am glad I left Berlin. . . . Here in my solitude, it required only a light push in order to remove a barrier that would perhaps have fallen somewhat later in Berlin." He predicted an imminent resolution of a six-year process, a resolution that would be a cataclysmic and decisive reversal of his previous views: "I see it coming—that I resolutely confront the entire theological world."[79]

In the following year, Bauer finished *Johannes* and started the *Synoptiker*. He completed the first volume by 10 March 1841, the second around 11 July 1841, and the third sometime after the end of March 1842.[80] As he proceeded through these New Testament studies, his mind became increasingly settled, his identity as a philosophical critic ever more clear and certain. With the first volume of the *Synoptiker*, he believed that he had finally reached a breakthrough. "With that," he told his brother, "I have absolutely fulfilled criticism."[81]

Before he went to Bonn, Bauer was what one could call a moderate or liberal Christian. He attacked Strauss's radicalism at the same time that he criticized Pietist orthodoxy. He was as much opposed to Hengstenberg's annihilation of humanity in a mystical union with God as he was to Strauss's reduction of God to man. Like other traditional Hegelians he believed that God was united to humanity in a way that preserved the integrity of each.

Against Strauss's derogation of God, Bauer argued in 1838 that the biblical record of God's deeds in history was a record of real events. To defend this view he appealed to the writings of Hegel. Even if Hegel had not pursued the question of the Bible's factual truth in specific biblical exegesis, he had, Bauer asserted, left a philosophical "proof." According to Hegel, form and content constituted a necessary unity: how spirit appeared was necessarily tied to the kind of spirit that appeared. Therefore if spirit made a real historical appearance as representation or Christian belief, then how it appeared—in the form of Jesus—had to have been equally real.[82]

Bauer's criticisms of Strauss were, as Bauer himself seemed to recognize, transparent sophistries.[83] A comprehensive and systematic response—a response that both criticized and offered an alternative to Strauss's interpretation—was still needed. To make such a thoroughgoing defense of Hegelian orthodoxy was the purpose of Bauer's studies of the Old Testament and the Gospels.

Bauer stated in his programmatic preface to *Die Religion* that God evolved in history. He became increasingly universal and spiritual as he developed through the biblical forms of consciousness and, like humanity, he attained his highest form when he recognized that what stood opposed to him was an emanation of his own nature. Such a recognition was self-consciousness.[84] Bauer's God was, in other words, this-worldly and dynamic: "The absolute spirit is not beyond the finite and its limits. . . . On the contrary, it is itself this movement of experiencing its own nature in the finite."[85]

According to Bauer, God assumed a higher form of self-consciousness in the New Testament than in the Old. In the Gospels, he no longer coerced humanity through nature, but thought of himself as part of the same spirituality as humanity, of a communal spirituality embodied in Christ.[86] But even at this level of heightened self-awareness, a contradiction persisted: God as pure spirit knew his union with humanity in only one man. To attain full self-consciousness, he needed to know himself as the God of a universal Christian community.[87] This final manifestation of God, Bauer believed in 1838, had been accomplished in his own time.

Throughout *Die Religion* there was the presence of two distinct embodiments of spirit—the Jewish Volk and Jehovah. But in *Johannes,* when Bauer switched from the point of view of the Volk to that of the individual author, this differentiation disappeared. To analyze the Gospel of John from a point of view suitable to the new kind of consciousness that it represented, Bauer considered the question of to what degree the author's personal, self-reflective consciousness conditioned the form and content of the text. In *Johannes* and again in the *Synoptiker,* he found the authors' mediations pervasive. Thus he ceased to believe that one could identify elements that were not artificial products of the authors' consciousness. One could not be certain that the events recorded in the Gospels were real, independent events. All one could know with confidence was the consciousness of the authors:

> If the form is of a thoroughly literary origin and if the Gospel of Mark has the character of an "artwork," if, however, an "artistic composition" is not only an influence on the content but even creates the content, then can we stop with the recognition of a determined positivity? . . . can we hope to find directly in the description of such a Mark—of such an artist—such a supposed positivity—the purely given and naked reality? No![88]

Bauer concluded that the record of God's coming to self-consciousness in the Bible was nothing more than a record of the development of human consciousness. The divine father and his son were creations of human imagination.

At the beginning of his biblical investigations in 1838, Bauer would have been shocked by this conclusion. But in 1841 he welcomed it and its implicit atheism as the solutions to his philosophical problems. Indeed, he proceeded to draw from his biblical investigations even more radical implications than those of Strauss, who believed that Christian history could be reinterpreted and reintegrated into humanistic philosophy. According to Strauss, the story of Jesus, once divested of its claims to factual truth, could be reformulated as a history of humanity, or more precisely, as the coming together of the individual and the species. Religion might thus continue to have a meaning for philosophy.[89] But for Bauer one could not reappropriate Christianity so easily. His struggles with the Christian faith had convinced him that it was a profoundly flawed form of belief.

In *Die Religion,* he acknowledged the inevitability of some alienation, or a surrender of man to God, in Christianity, but the advantage of merging with God made up for this.[90] Nature, at least, no longer tyrannized humanity. "Religion," Bauer wrote in 1838, "is this process that overcomes the alien being and the otherness in man and constitutes in him the self-consciousness of God."[91] But once God was revealed to be a construct of human consciousness worshipping him became for Bauer a form of self-deception and a loss of freedom. It gave what belonged to humanity to an external entity. Religion was "absolute alienation," a "vampire" that consumed the autonomy of the "self."[92]

In 1835 Bauer had condemned Strauss for being unreasonably negative. His style of criticism, Bauer asserted, refused to accept the object of study on its own terms. Instead, Straussian criticism assumed that everything outside it was hostile and threatening. Hence it sought to negate and absorb the alien object into itself.[93] But Bauer's attempt to disprove Strauss paradoxically resulted in Bauer taking an even more radical point of view than Strauss. In his *Synoptiker* he claimed to have gone beyond Strauss by liberating criticism from all "positive claims," from all connections to existing religion.[94] He described his own method of criticism as the fulfillment of critical thinking, the "final act of a determined philosophy."[95]

4

Philosophy in a Perverted World

1

In 1842 Bruno Bauer believed that he had resolved the contradictions in Hegelian religious theory. By elucidating the evolution of spirit in the Bible, he thought that he had clarified the relation between religion and philosophy. Moreover, his biblical investigations had dispelled the tensions in his philosophical identity. The renunciation of religious belief had purified and strengthened his allegiance to Hegelian philosophy. His writings had demonstrated that as an atheistic Hegelian philosopher he was the highest manifestation of spirit.

But Bauer also thought that reason's present embodiment was not confined to the mind and the writings of the Hegelian philosopher. Like his master, he believed that the philosopher's fulfillment of spirit as subject had a counterpart in existing social and political institutions. And with other Prussian Hegelians, he identified the reality of spirit as substance with the reality of the Prussian state.

In the late 1830s, his sense of affinity with Prussia was reinforced by the support that he had received from the Kultusminister Karl von Altenstein. The latter had secured for Bauer a lectureship at the University of Bonn, a position that presumably was to lead to a tenured professorship. Yet once Bauer left the center of state power, his apparently strong connection with the government became increasingly tenuous. At Bonn he had to fend for himself in an unfriendly world of academic intrigue. As a Privatdozent his sole means of support were student fees and a meager fellowship that Altenstein had obtained for him and that was too small to live on.[1] To survive Bauer had to sell part of his library. When he helped edit the second edition of Hegel's *Lectures on the Philosophy of Religion*, he was forced to accept the honorarium, while the other editors renounced theirs in favor of Frau Hegel.[2] Bauer sent anxious petitions to Altenstein about his promised promotion and he had his friends and contacts in Berlin do the same,[3] but they were unsuccessful. By March 1840, he began to express his dissatisfaction with the supposed benevolence of the government.[4]

At the same time that his attempts to improve his financial standing failed, his relations with the Bonn theological faculty deteriorated. As his religious views became increasingly radical, he encountered more and more hostility from his colleagues. The situation became unbearable: "I have never known," he wrote to Marx, "people in such filth as now."[5] Reflecting on how he had to humble himself before state and faculty, he began to question his ideal view of the state. While he continued to acknowledge the close tie between philosophy and the state, he now suspected that such a tie constrained, even "chained," philosophy.[6] This emerging ambivalence was reinforced by the uncertain political climate of the time. In the early summer of 1840 Altenstein lay on his deathbed, and Frederick William III was seriously ill.[7] Bauer feared that in the new regime attacks on the Hegelian school would be allowed to intensify. He sensed an approaching crisis, although he was sure of its happy outcome: the triumph of philosophy.[8]

From such views, one would presume that Bauer was prepared to break with the new government. And after Frederick William IV ascended the throne in June 1840, he made an overture to just such a move. He came to feel that he and the philosophy that he represented could no longer tolerate the humiliation of the government's indifference. He swore to his brother that to save the honor of systematic philosophy (Wissenschaft) he would give up his job in November. "What there is in me of Wissenschaft," he wrote, "I cannot allow to become a spectacle and scandal before these people: I must rescue it."[9] Yet Bauer failed to follow through on this gesture. By August 1840 his resolve had collapsed into his former ambivalence. He continued to wait for the government to fulfill its promise and he continued to despair.

In part this reversal might have occurred because Altenstein's successor, Adalbert von Ladenberg, was actively considering Bauer's promotion. But unknown to Bauer a member of the Bonn theology faculty submitted to the new Kultusminister a negative appraisal of Bauer that effectively put an end to these stirrings.[10] Still thinking the government was on his side, Bauer sent a petition in October to Johann Albrecht Friedrich Eichhorn, who had been appointed by the new king in Ladenberg's place.

In this petition Bauer showed a willingness to compromise: in return for a promotion to associate professor, he offered to restrain his radicalism by limiting the subject of his lectures to church history.[11] But when they met at the end of October 1840, Eichhorn refused Bauer's request. Instead, he proposed that in return for a year of financial support Bauer should remain in Berlin where he could do research. After some consideration, Bauer rejected the offer. He could not, he said, withdraw to the private sphere. As he told Eichhorn, he now believed that he was duty-bound to show that his Hegelian philosophy was the "correct development of theology."[12]

2

Since his arrival at Bonn, Bauer's relations with the Prussian state had become increasingly strained. He had become increasingly skeptical of its rationality and hence affinity with Hegelian philosophy. Yet he could not bring himself to break with it—the habits of loyalty and the desire to succeed in his society were still too strong. During this period of ambivalence Bauer wrote two works on the Prussian state, a book on the state church, *Die Landeskirche Preussens und die Wissenschaft* (1840), and an article, "Der christliche Staat und unsere Zeit," for the *Hallische Jahrbücher*.[13] Both these works showed signs of Bauer's ambivalence and of the disrepair into which the Hegelian identity of reason and reality had fallen. The *Landeskirche* was written after *Johannes*, before the first volume of the *Synoptiker*, and when Altenstein was dying and Frederick William III was seriously ill. The book was a polemical piece that praised Prussia, welcomed the imminent accession of the crown prince, and exhorted him to do his duty—namely, to rule according to the rational standards of Hegelian philosophy. But beneath Bauer's optimistic heralding of a new age one can detect an irrepressible fear: that Frederick William was the enemy of philosophy.

The *Landeskirche* opened with a proclamation of the triumph of systematic philosophy, or Wissenschaft, in Prussia. "Wissenschaft, the power of thought, the eternal, unweary Wanderer," Bauer wrote, "had for the past century made its home among us in Prussia." It had gradually penetrated the schools, the government, and the everyday thought of the people. It had been raised onto the throne.[14] After this paean to the reality of reason, Bauer described the recent history of philosophy in Prussia, which was actually his own history. He related how the last years had been ones of ferment in which philosophy had fallen into conflict with itself. But even though it had experienced a schism, it ultimately emerged stronger than before, for it had thrown off the vestiges of a lesser consciousness.[15]

Thus Bauer established the controlling principles of his study of the Prussian state church, namely, the entry of philosophy into the Prussian state and the recently accomplished purification of philosophy. He further asserted that science or systematic philosophy in its purified form was irreconcilable with religion, just as the modern state was irreconcilable with the church.[16] He then concluded that because science and the rational state had materialized, religion and the church must have essentially disappeared. Bauer's study of the state church was an attempt to corroborate historically this logical development.

In the period after 1815, Frederick William III wanted to make spiritual life in Prussia more harmonious by uniting the Reformed and Lutheran Confessions. To accomplish this he had to establish a common liturgy and convince local congregations to forfeit their autonomy to the state. Both confessions naturally resented this assault on their independence and resisted Frederick William's order enacting the union, the so-called *Agende* of 1822. After a long *Agendenstreit* and after compromises by both sides, a united state church came into existence in the late 1820s.[17]

Bauer's interpretation of the state church was generated from a simple irony: that the fears of the religious opposition to the state church had been well founded. The state had indeed forced the two confessions to give up their defining characteristics—their unique sets of symbols—and to merge with the state.[18] The union had reduced the church to mere "religiosity." This derogation of the church, Bauer asserted, was an inevitable historical development, for the state's absorption of the church was the necessary counterpart of the passing of religion into philosophy.

Bauer's polemical interpretation of the condition of religion in Prussia is remarkably unconvincing. The reality of the state church was just the reverse of his presentations. Throughout the first half of the nineteenth century, the most conservative of religious groups—Pietist theologians and "awakened" aristocrats—had effectively infiltrated the centralized state and its institutions. Consequently, the state church was rapidly becoming an instrument of conservative theology, not of systematic philosophy.[19]

Bauer was himself not fully persuaded by his own view. For however much he argued for the triumph of philosophy in the *Landeskirche,* he showed at the same time a paradoxical awareness of the true nature of religion in Prussia. His post-mortem examination of religious life occasionally gave way to an incongruous acknowledgement of religion's continued vitality.

In his introduction, for example, Bauer stated that reason had permeated Prussia and that philosophy had entered a condition of purity, while religion and the church were on the wane. But after rejoicing in the decline of religion, he added something anomalous:

Earlier the Protestant churches could punish with civil death and expel their heretics from the state; now they make the state mistrustful and suspicious of science and bring it about that the state abandons its own rationality.[20]

How a thoroughly rational state allied with a powerful philosophy could now succumb to the blandishments of an enervated superstition Bauer never explained. Before returning to his main argument, he merely added that the state, misled by the church, might forsake science, but science would never forsake the state.[21]

At the end of the introduction, where Bauer asserted once more philosophy's steadfast hostility to the church, another anomaly appeared. "The state," he wrote, "can still err, become suspicious of Wissenschaft, and grasp coercive measures; reason however belongs to its [the state's] inner being and its activity is much too animated for it to err long."[22] Bauer again added that science would defend the state, even, if need be, from the state itself.

Bauer wrote as if of two minds. He seemed to doubt his own argument about the decline of religion in Prussia, and thus he inserted remarks that compromised his message. Philosophy might have purified itself, but his assertion that the state was rational and the church enervated was undermined by the author's own contrary suggestions. Although one can only speculate about how conscious Bauer was of these contradictions in the *Landeskirche,* the feeling one has is that he wrote the book in bad faith. He fluctuated between preserving a lost ideal and frankly admitting its loss. He lacked the resolve to reassess critically his philosophical and personal relations with Prussia.

In his later article, "Der christliche Staat," he displayed the same ambivalence but now tried to come to terms with it. His opening argument in the "Christliche Staat" was similar to that in the *Landeskirche.*

The state, he said, was the appearance of freedom in the world, it was rational self-consciousness in political form; and he added that Prussia was precisely that kind of state.[23] But he then pointed to an "error" committed by the Prussian state: it had allied itself with the church against science.[24] Thus, as in the *Landeskirche*, the present was and was not what it should have been. Bauer wanted to show that reason and reality inevitably merged, forming a simple, direct relation, a one-to-one identity. Instead, he was forced to admit that although reason existed, the existing world was on the whole irrational. The relation between reason and reality was, in truth, an inverse one.

Bauer now attempted to explain this incongruity by distinguishing between a "government," which was the mechanism of rule, and the pure "state," which was the political reality of reason. These two, he said, were not always the same:

In the dialectical flow of its becoming, the state is not identical with the government as long as the self-consciousness of its infinity, as it has historically developed, is not recognized by the government.[25]

In other words, an incongruity or a disjuncture could appear in the steady evolution of spirit. But Bauer did not explicitly explain why an anomaly could appear. Instead he appealed to a transcendent and mysterious logic. In the quotation just cited, his reference to a "dialectical flow" implied the natural necessity of a dissonance between the government and the state. In a latter passage, this appeal to historical necessity was even more explicit:

At the first moment when Wissenschaft establishes the realm of self-consciousness in theory and thereby transcends [*aufhebt*] the limits of the existing relations in the higher form of ethical spirit . . . it has to experience the reaction of a government, a specific determination belonging to an earlier form of consciousness. Thus begins the time in which it [Wissenschaft] must stand the test of oppressive relations and persecutions. The government mistrusts self-consciousness . . . it [the government] flees to the church, whose principle it itself does not acknowledge, and now supports its determinateness by binding itself to the church's abstract universality.[26]

In some respects, this passage appears to be a perceptive description of the situation of philosophy and politics in Prussia. But it is more than a statement of "fact," of what is. It is also a statement of necessity: spirit's first appearance as full self-consciousness necessarily placed it at odds with the existing state. Bauer converts a descriptive statement into a prescriptive one: existing events, he implies, are required by a historical or logical necessity.

In his biblical studies, Bauer rarely failed to support this kind of assertion, this conversion of description into prescription. But in "Der christliche Staat," he left such assertions standing alone. He merely assumed that an initial incongruity was a necessary development, part of the logic of history. He did not justify this assumption because he could not. Hegelian theory did not allow for such disjunctures or incongruities in the existing reality of reason. On the contrary, the whole point of Hegel's philosophy was to establish a harmony between existing philosophy and existing institutions.

Bauer's solution to the misaligned reality of his day was to force it into a dialectical scheme, arbitrarily to make an inverse relation between philosophy and the state the necessary prelude to a direct one. In this sense his response to the failure of philosophy to merge with the state was merely to advocate the truth of his philosophy more emphatically than before, to turn his philosophical adherence to Hegelian theory into a dogmatic act of faith.

Another consequence of the dissonance between reason and reality was to postpone the final reconciliation of reason and reality. Unity was still to be accomplished. This delay in the full realization of Hegelian philosophy now enhanced that philosophy's eschatological element.[27] With the other Prussian Young Hegelians who experienced an inverted reality, Bauer anxiously waited for an imminent apocalyptic fulfillment.

Although he could now admit in "Der christliche Staat" that the existing state had failed to merge with philosophy, he still could not separate himself from that state. He explained that the state acted as it did because it had to, and he nervously waited for history to raise it to the same level of reason that philosophy had already attained. But at the same time that he expected a final unity to come about, he suffered from a nagging fear of unfulfillment. He ended "Der christliche Staat" with a vigorous proclamation of philosophy's certain victory over religion, but in the paragraph before he spoke of a possible "occurrence" "so unnatural and unbearable" that it could not happen. What if the state should always embrace the "defeated principle" of religion and permanently expel

Wissenschaft from its domain? What if, in other words, there should come about a "monstrous anomaly": that Wissenschaft be rendered a "private concern"?[28]

3

Throughout 1841 Bauer's relations with the Bonn faculty continued to deteriorate. In May, Johann Augusti, his only friend and ally in the Department of Theology, died.[29] In July his fellowship was arbitrarily cut off for the following year.[30] He continued to petition the government to fulfill Altenstein's promise. At first, the government remained as apathetic as before,[31] but when he sent Eichhorn the first volume of the *Synoptiker*, requesting an official academic evaluation of his work, the Kultusminister decided to take action.

On 20 August 1841 Eichhorn ordered a review of his work from the six theological faculties of the Prussian universities. He put to them two questions: first, how were the views of the *Synoptiker* related to Christianity, and second, should the author of the *Synoptiker* be allowed to teach in a Prussian university, especially on a theological faculty.[32] When the results of the evaluation came in during the autumn and winter of 1841, they showed no unanimity—some faculties split over the nature of the *Synoptiker* and some over the principle of academic freedom. But the Bonn faculty voted as a bloc: it condemned Bauer's book outright and urged his removal.

Even before the tally, the government was already predisposed against Bauer. In September 1842 the famous south German liberal Karl Welcker visited Berlin and was feted by Berlin liberals. Bauer had joined in the celebrations, even if as a Hegelian he was less than sympathetic to Welcker's liberal politics. At the dinner party for Welcker, Bauer toasted Hegel's conception of the state. "On this toast," Bauer wrote to Arnold Ruge, "which I intentionally proposed, Welcker choked badly."[33]

The apparent support that Berliners showed for Welcker's views alarmed Frederick William IV, who set out to punish the participants in the celebration. Ironically, Bauer was one of those whom he singled out for investigation. In October 1841, Frederick William ordered the Minister of the Interior to see to Bauer's dismissal,[34] and on the prompting of Eichhorn, the judge of the University of Bonn sent for Bauer in December 1841 to explain his association with Welcker.[35]

In the spring of 1842, Eichhorn ordered the Bonn theological faculty to dismiss its radical Hegelian. In Bauer's last letter to Edgar from Bonn, he described how the University had revoked his teaching credential, his *licentia docendia*. Reproducing for his brother letters from two professors on the faculty, he showed that he had been dismissed because of his religious views and his political "affiliation," namely, his association with Welcker.[36] Bauer's worst fear had become a reality: philosophy was now a "private concern."

Once back in Berlin, Bauer wrote a pamphlet, *Die gute Sache der Freiheit und meine eigene Angelegenheit* (1842), in which he denounced the Bonn faculty and the Prussian state.[37] As the title indicates, Bauer continued to equate monumental historical developments with personal events. He identified his dismissal as a world-historical break, the decisive separation of philosophy from the Prussian state:

The government, which allows itself to be determined according to the judgement of the faculties, declares that its existence is incompatible with the freedom of thought; the public, which takes the side against criticism, cannot bring itself to admit that its indolence does not want to be troubled by free research and that it lacks the courage that is needed to give up old, rooted prejudices.[38]

The break thus clarified Bauer's relation to Prussian politics. The present, he said, was a distortion of what ought to be: humanity's essential or rational nature was subjected to the whims of superstition. A religious deception governed the state.[39] Prussian reality was an inversion of the true order of things: appearance dominated essence.[40]

What could philosophy do? How could an inverted world be set right? Despite the failure of his philosophy to master the political reality or even to stand up to the attacks of the church, Bauer did not abandon its essential principles. He still believed in the Hegelian notion that the activity that brought about freedom was critical, rational thinking. In March 1841 he told Marx, "It would be absurd if you should devote yourself to a practical career. Theory is now the strongest practice."[41]

Bauer had held that philosophy, which in Hegelian theory was the practice of freedom, lived in harmony with a rational reality. Both were manifestations—one as subject, the other as substance—of an existing uniform spirit. But once a disjuncture between reason and reality appeared, he was left with a paradox: spirit as subject had evolved into its highest form while spirit as substance was still at a lower plane of development. Bauer could not explain this paradox in any specific way. At most, he called it a necessary development, and waited for history to resolve the paradox. This dissolution of existing spirit resulted in what seemed to be disunited and independent forms of spirit: a mature theory worked beside a backward reality that was trying to catch up. The dissolution of what should have been an integrated spirit led to a contradictory adherence to both a voluntarist and a determinist view of historical change. Bauer could say that the practice of critical theory was the necessary means to a more universal freedom and that history would on its own inevitably realize complete freedom:

Theory, which has helped us so far, remains even now our unique means of succor, in order to make ourselves and others free. History . . . will overthrow the appearance and raise freedom to the power that gives the world a new form.[42]

Although Bauer, as a voluntarist, continued to look to theory as the sole means to freedom, he recognized that theory could not proceed as it had in the past. The present "friction" between philosophical criticism and the "feudal-Christian state" was a "warning" that criticism had to free itself from all the "unjustified presuppositions" that entangled it with the existing state.[43] Philosophy's imperative was therefore to purify itself of all the elements of the present; for Bauer, to purify philosophy was to reinterpret Hegel.

In *Die gute Sache*, Bauer explicitly attacked orthodox Hegelians, including his former patron Philipp Marheineke, for making philosophy a "handmaiden" of religion. Their belief that religion and philosophy could be reconciled had fettered philosophy with the presuppositions of the existing theological tyranny.[44] Elsewhere, Bauer acknowledged that the orthodox Hegelians were legitimate heirs of Hegel. Even Hegel, he admitted, had sought to demonstrate the unity of religion and philosophy. He too had tried to appease the theologians by compromising his philosophy. But, as events after Hegel had shown, conciliation was impossible. The only way to deal with theology was to refute it. Hegelian philosophy had to release its critical power.[45]

Bauer started his project of reinterpreting Hegel while still at Bonn. In the autumn of 1841, after he had finished the second volume of the *Synoptiker*, he wrote *Die Posaune des jüngsten Gerichts über Hegel den Atheisten und Antichristen*.[46] Like so many of his polemics, the *Posaune* was eminently ironic. Bauer assumed the guise of a fanatical Pietist theologian and mimicked an odiously righteous voice. Aside from mocking the theologians, this device served the tactical function of disarming his opponents. He simply agreed with his enemies. They were absolutely correct, he said, to think Hegel an "atheist" and an "antichrist," or, in short, a radical.[47]

The *Posaune* contained two basic arguments for Hegel's latent radicalism. First, Bauer presented the atheism that was implicit in the *Synoptiker*. Spirit passed through various stages—including religion, which was a stage of alienation—to arrive at self-consciousness. This development was not a divine, immanent unfolding of God. Spirit was nothing more than human consciousness. "The world spirit," Bauer wrote stating Hegel's view, "has its reality only in the spirit of humanity."[48]

Conceiving of Hegel as a humanist, Bauer then took to task those philosophers who misinterpreted Hegel's philosophy as a divine pantheism. For them, spirit was the unifying substance that permeated all history. Thus all historical phenomena were equally valid and acceptable, for all were manifestations of the same substance.[49] But according to Bauer, this view of spirit was unfaithful to Hegelian philosophy. It flattened out Hegel's ascending scale of stages of consciousness. If spirit was substance then each stage of consciousness was merely a different form of the same content. Against this emphasis on substance, Bauer argued that Hegel believed in the importance of qualitative differences among stages of consciousness, without which there could be no real change and hence no progress. Hegelian philosophy, Bauer asserted, had a role for substance, but ultimately it negated substance and elevated it to a higher form, to self-consciousness. Unlike the notion of spirit as substance, which made all equally holy, the view of spirit as self-consciousness deified only one kind of consciousness: rational human cognition.[50] If a reconciliation occurred in Hegel's philosophy, it did not take place in the form of substance as a reconciliation of religion and philosophy, but in the form of self-consciousness as a reconciliation of human being and human being, or more precisely, of thought and thought.[51]

The second way in which Bauer tried to make Hegelian philosophy more radical was to show that Hegel's philosophy was inherently critical, even revolutionary, or, to use Bauer's melodramatic expression, that Hegel "hated the existing."[52] According to Bauer, Hegelian philosophy was a systematic whole, a carefully articulated rational scheme of absolute truth. In this sense, Hegel's philosophy necessarily looked beyond existing, contingent conditions, measuring existing conditions by absolute standards of rationality. Thus Hegelian theory had a built-in critical impulse, for by subjecting existing conditions to standards that they could not meet, it acted as a dissolver of present reality. To show, for example, that serfdom was an inadequate form of free spirit was to say that serfdom should not exist.[53] And from the point of view of systematic philosophy, to say that something existing failed to live up to free spirit was to say that it would soon exist no longer. In other words, by apprehending the "whole," philosophy showed what inevitably lay beyond the inadequacies of the present. It thus sounded the death knell of the existing.[54]

Bauer intended his reinterpretation to achieve two ends, to demystify Hegelian philosophy and to render it more radical. He tried to divest the master's philosophy of its more metaphysical—and to Bauer, more religious—elements by recasting them in human form. Divine substance gave way to human self-consciousness. At the same time, Bauer argued that Hegelian method was necessarily critical in both voluntaristic and deterministic senses: philosophy provided an immediate weapon of criticism and an assurance that present evils would inevitably be expunged.

The above discussion has made a distinction between an internal and an external crisis, between Bauer's loss of faith in Christianity and his conflict with the Bonn theological faculty and the Prussian state. I have tried to show how a paradoxical relationship developed: just when Bauer gained a new-found clarity, a profound sense that spirit was embodied in his own writings and in his own mind, he found himself an outcast from what should have been the larger context of that personal reality of reason, namely, the Prussian state. An inverse relation thus displaced an ideal direct relation: reason became a private affair, while superstition governed the public domain. These two crises can be seen as autonomous movements of events that converged at a point of inversion. On this same point Bauer then constructed a more radical interpretation of Hegel.

But I have not yet asked if these two lines of development ever intersected before reaching the point of inversion, if the external crisis had an impact on Bauer's religious views. Did a conflict with the university and the state contribute to making Bauer an atheist? In one sense, this question was already implicitly answered when we recognized that Bauer's atheism can be reconstructed as a wholly internal development. But more explicit evidence also supports this view. Bauer arrived in Bonn with doubts about religion on his mind but with no obvious doubts about the nature of the Prussian state.[55] He wrote *Johannes*, which adumbrated the full atheism of the *Synoptiker*, before he completely despaired of the government, and even when writing the first volume of the *Synoptiker*, he showed a fluctuating loyalty. Bauer only turned against the state decisively when he recognized that it would not support his hard-won atheistic philosophy. He was an atheist before he was a political radical.

Even if he had never come into conflict with the state, his turn to atheism would have been just as certain. What might have differed, however, was the tone of his atheism. His disbelief might have been less hysterical and brutal. Although by 1840 he enjoyed assuming an ironic, condescending writing style with which to mock his enemies, he could still display a genuine sympathy for his subject of study. The first two volumes of the *Synoptiker* exhibited, for example, a benevolent understanding of the apostles', especially Mark's, accomplishments. As self-reflective artists they were, after all, genuine manifestations of self-consciousness and therefore part of humanity's ascent to freedom. But beginning with the third volume of the *Synoptiker*, completed just as Bauer was dismissed, a fierce hatred for religion appeared displacing what sympathy he had for religious expression. In *Hegels Lehre* (1842), he appraised anew the writings of the apostles. With the ambiguous exception of Mark, he now considered them to be theologians, and as such they were necessarily untalented propagandists who compromised their writing to fit their dogma.[56]

Bauer's conflicts in Bonn had taught him that religion was still powerful even though its time had long passed. Continuing in its decadence, it could only act, he felt, as a great evil—it deformed reality. Hence he could not say with Strauss that religion might be reappropriated in human form. As he argued in the *Posaune*, it had to be completely negated. One had to purge philosophy of the assumptions that it still shared with the existing religious reality. From about 1841, Bauer's attacks on religion became relentlessly vicious. Identifying religion with Christianity and both with the modern church, he called them at various times "shameless" and "hypocritical," "decadent," forms of "total passivity," and of course, "total alienation." He accused them of "self-deception," of suffering from "hypochondria" and "indolence," and of thriving on hate, fear, and human suffering. Theology was a "death chamber"; religion enslaved humanity.[57] All of these characterizations could be summarized in a word: perversion. Religion twisted essence into appearance, and conversely it made what was worst in human beings into their dominating aspect. It constructed a *"verkehrte Welt"* in which the rational fell prey to the irrational.[58]

In early 1842, when still at Bonn, Bauer formulated this characterization of religion as having "perverted" the rational into the form of the Christian state. After he had returned to Berlin in the same year, he set out to put the world right with his refined Hegelian criticism. But in the years that followed his return, he continued to be frustrated in his attempt to reconcile philosophy and reality. The world turned out to be "perverted" in more ways than he had imagined in 1842.

4

Bauer's dismissal in 1842 was the prelude to a major wave of political repression. At the end of the year the state closed several liberal and radical newspapers, including two Prussian Young Hegelian organs to which Bauer contributed, the *Deutsche Jahrbücher* edited by Arnold Ruge and the *Rheinische Zeitung* edited by Karl Marx. Ruge and Marx, like many other German radicals, then decided that they could no longer publish in Germany and both eventually emigrated to Paris.[59] But Bauer elected to remain in Germany. After his dismissal he returned to Berlin where he eked out a precarious living as a writer. When he had left Berlin in 1839, he was a reluctant associate of Berlin's radical intellectuals, but after his return in 1842, he became the leader of one of Berlin's most iconoclastic groups, the *Freien*. Men such as Eduard Meyen, Ludwig Buhl, "Szeliga," Max Stirner, Bauer's brother Edgar, and others adopted Bauer's theory of philosophical criticism and helped to propagate it in their short-lived journals, the *Norddeutsche Blätter für Kritik, Literatur und Unterhaltung* and the more important *Allgemeine Literatur-Zeitung*, edited and published by Bauer himself.[60]

Marx and Ruge, Bauer's friends and allies during his Bonn period, found his affiliation with the Freien disturbing. They thought that the group's style of criticism was recklessly provocative and theoretically sloppy. Ruge also felt that its cliquish bohemian way of life was offensive: important matters, he believed, demanded a tone of moral seriousness.[61] Marx hoped at first that Bauer would exercise a sobering influence on the Freien's hot-headed radicals.[62] But Bauer continued to draw closer to the Berliners. Marx's friendship with Bauer steadily deteriorated, and after 1843 the former attacked the latter in increasingly nasty polemics.[63] This unseemly disagreement among Prussia's radical Young Hegelians was occasioned by more than just disagreements over styles of protest.

At the root of the conflict were opposing interpretations of contemporary Prussian society.

As we have seen, in Germany during the first half of the nineteenth century, social and economic reform combined with a huge increase in population resulted in the swelling presence of an urban and rural poor. One historian has noted, for example, that in Berlin the social immobility and increasing impoverishment of the work force (except for skilled artisans in the luxury trades) generated a "comprehensive, objectively demarcated, and deeply hostile working class."[64]

By the 1840s, the "social question" had become a serious concern of German intellectuals. In 1842, Lorenz von Stein's *Socialism and Communism in Modern France* made French utopian thinking more widely known in Germany. Like Ruge and Marx, Bauer and the Freien sought to comprehend and solve the new social problems. In the *Literatur-Zeitung* few articles dealt with religious issues, and while many addressed themselves to politics in Prussia, just as many focused on the condition of Prussian society. There were analyses of pauperism in Berlin, of the different types of socialism, and of political issues that were related to the social question, such as the English debates over the corn laws.[65]

The social analyses of the *Literatur-Zeitung* were, moreover, serious studies that did not, as Marx and Engels made it seem in *The Holy Family* (1844–45), turn concrete concerns into abstractions. The authors of these studies displayed a keen understanding of modern political economy. The writer Carl Reichhardt called on social analysis to abandon forced abstractions for "naked reality."[66] One had to recognize, he said, that workers were entangled in a web of social relations—they were subject to the law of the market.[67] Bauer's brother, Edgar, uncovered the inherent contradiction of modern political economy—that wealth and poverty were inextricably linked.[68] And yet another social critic, Carl Jungnitz, argued that brute material interests interconnected by market relations—an interconnection epitomized by money—had dissolved traditional society.[69]

The dissolution of traditional society was a leitmotif in the *Literatur-Zeitung*. But this development was not enthusiastically received by the Berlin iconoclasts, as it was by Marx and other radicals. On the contrary, the Freien looked on the end of traditional society with some horror. For them, a modern world was a world governed by egoistic material interests which could have but one consequence: the annihilation of culture, intelligence, and morality. Money, they agreed, consumed all human values.[70] In the world of markets human beings were valued not for their rationality, but, as one writer lamented, for their utilitarian value.[71] The term that the Freien used to describe modern humanity emptied of meaning was the pejorative "the masses." They used this concept casually throughout various articles,[72] but Bauer officially and systematically presented it to the public in his article, "Die Gattung und die Masse."[73]

The masses, Bauer wrote, were a result of the dissolution of traditional institutions. Corporate wholes in Germany had decomposed into a welter of atomized individuals. Without higher moralizing loyalties or interests, the sole impetus of individual behavior was brute self-interest, sensuous need and desire in its rawest form. Modern society was consequently nothing more than a set of competitive relations among self-interested egos.[74] The aggregate of these colliding selfish individuals constituted the "masses."

Bauer used the notion of the masses to distinguish between traditional and modern society, not to make distinctions within modern society. Indeed, for him modern society possessed a terrible, unrelieved uniformity. Though the rich appeared to live according to a rational system (namely, political economy), their lives were actually predetermined by their capricious, sensuous activity, and hence "the possibility of a type of spiritualization was taken from them."[75] The poor lacked even the consoling appearance of rationality. They were totally mired in their sensuous labor, resistant to thought or rebellion:

The slave of manual labor does not even have the suspicion of a spiritual slavery to a universal competition; he feels only elementally its oppression without being able to interpret or explain it—what he cannot suspect, cannot bring to consciousness, he is also not capable of struggling against.[76]

To use an earlier distinction, Bauer's society of the masses was the realization of the empiricist notion of freedom: the sensuous ego pursued its interests without constraint, and the result, according to Bauer (following Hegel), was the denial of true, spiritual freedom. Human beings in mass society were utterly dependent on material objects. Their spirituality consequently remained untapped, impeded. In this sense, modern society was a return to the relations of dependency that characterized humanity's most primitive natural consciousness. Indeed, from the point of view of Hegelian theory, "modern" society could only be considered retrograde. Resurrected in the form of market relations, nature ruled over human beings, thereby blocking the emergence of a fully free spirit and threatening the vitality of the spirit that already existed.

At the turn of the 1840s, Bauer had reluctantly come to the recognition that, contrary to his Hegelian expectations, the existing state was retrogressive. In the early 1840s, as the social crisis unfolded, Bauer's Hegelian sensibilities thus experienced a second shock: society too was running backwards. Civil society had burst its restraints, letting loose its capricious and brutalizing sensuousness. Bauer's recognition of the political irrationality of the existing state had made him a political radical, an opponent of the existing state. As such, he had worked with other political dissidents, even arguing in the *Rheinische Zeitung* for the establishment of a German republic.[77] But his recognition of the surging irrationality of existing civil society had the opposite effect: it turned him against other political dissidents and reformers. The ally of political radicalism attacked the political radicals when he came to identify them as creatures of modern mass society.

Bauer's antipathy to the radical spokesmen of mass society was already evident at the beginning of the 1840s, when he entered the debates over the political status of Jews. Unlike other critics of the Prussian state, he did not favor granting Jews full political rights. On the contrary, in two essays on the so-called Jewish Question, he argued that Jews were rightfully denied political equality.[78] His argument was consistent with his atheism in that he sought to show that giving a religious group political rights should not be equated with human liberation. Inasmuch as political emancipation allowed that group to continue practicing its religion, it perpetuated servitude. It supported religious alienation.[79] To achieve true human liberation, Jews should not ask for the political rights of Christians but should demand instead that all religion be abolished.[80] Bauer's objection to Jewish emancipation was also consonant with his earlier biblical investigations. In those, he had identified Judaism as a form of consciousness that was inferior to Christianity, which was itself flawed. As Bauer had earlier argued in *Die Religion* and as he now reiterated, the Jews were still bound up with nature; they were servants to natural needs and desires.[81] To grant legal equality to this consciousness would thus be to sanction an inferior, unspiritual state of mind.

Bauer's rejection of Jewish emancipation flowed logically from his radical atheism and his earlier ideas about the evolution of spirit. But there was another concern that conditioned his attack on this measure of political reform: giving Jews political equality would tear apart one of the restraints of civil society and thus encourage the welling forth of brutal sensuous need.

Bauer explicitly draws a connection between the formation of mass society and the emancipation of the Jews in his first essay on the Jewish Question. At the beginning of that piece, he tells us in classic Hegelian terms that civil society is powered by natural, egoistic need and hence is characterized by uncertainty and sharp divisions between rich and poor. In the past, however, these natural tendencies of civil society had been mitigated by estates and corporations, which had domesticated the natural ego, trained it to seek not only its own selfish interests, but the interests of all society.[82] European Jews, Bauer goes on, never took part in these moralizing institutions. They had always associated with the "insecure element" of social life. Indeed, they excelled at profiting from capricious, egoistic need. Civil society was their "domain."[83] That Jews succeeded so well in the realm of unrestricted natural need and contingency was not, for Bauer, merely because they had been excluded by Christians from estates and corporations. Rather he tells us that the Jews themselves chose civil society as their own proper domain, seeing themselves as a people distinct from others. Further, their attachment to nature predisposed them to an existence defined by natural necessity.[84]

Bauer's writings on the Jewish Question reflected his growing concern about the consolidation of mass society and the collapse of Hegel's scheme for a rationally controlled social order. The demand for Jewish emancipation signaled the surging forth of base natural need, the triumph of chaotic civil society over traditional moralizing institutions. Bauer's dread of the forming mass society led him to oppose in 1842 and 1843 a basic demand of political reformers and radicals in Prussia, causing, in turn, his one-time allies to attack him. In 1843 his former friend and fellow radical Marx vigorously criticized Bauer's interpretation of Jewish emancipation in his own polemical consideration of the issue.[85]

Bauer's fear of mass society did not drive him into the fold of the traditional Prussian state but it did result in his falling out with other opponents of the state. After his essays on the Jewish Question he became increasingly alert to the consolidation of mass society and increasingly hostile to reformers and radicals for flirting with that society. As a Hegelian, Bauer had never been comfortable with liberals, because they championed the supremacy of atomized self-interest and contingent civil society. They were for Bauer representatives of atomized civil society. But he was surprised and greatly dismayed to find his colleagues and friends aligning themselves with the retrograde tendencies of modern society. Just when they had purged themselves of their remaining loyalty to religion and the state, they now surrendered themselves to the masses. Indeed, they made a deity out of what was for Bauer the most degraded aspect of the modern world. They converted the mundane reality of the masses into an abstraction that could be worshipped.

The masses became for Feuerbach the "species," the ideal essence of humanity to which all concrete, individual human beings were subordinated.[86] Ruge and the democrats made the atomized rabble of modern society into a rational state and Volk.[87] Marx and the communists transformed the poorest members of the masses into the instrument of world-historical change.[88]

In *Vollständige Geschichte der Partheikämpfe in Deutschland, 1842–46* (1849)[89] Bauer sought to explain the source of his fellow radicals' surrender to the existing reality of the masses by reflecting on the evolution of Young Hegelian radicalism over the past decade. In this recapitulation of the development of radical Hegelian theory, he attempted to clarify that theory's relation to the world. Before the 1840s, Bauer wrote, the Young Hegelians had looked to the state for support, believing that it was philosophy's ally.[90] In the early 1840s, to the shock of these young intellectuals, the state turned against them, systematically closing their papers and ejecting them from its institutions.[91] The radicals had difficulty adjusting to the state's actions. Even by 1842, when Prussia had clearly and repeatedly displayed its hostility, the radical Prussian Hegelians could not stop appealing to it. They began to criticize it, yet continued to call on it for support. Such behavior, Bauer argued, was perverse. The radicals had become entangled in a compulsive pattern of appeal and challenge, of submission and rebellion. The more they demanded of the state, the more their sense of dependency on it grew, until they raised "dependency" to a "pure principle."[92]

In their falling out with the state, the radical Hegelians had been revealed as lacking independent will and vision. They had grown to be dependent on the state and could not bring themselves to break from it. Only after suffering through increasingly intense waves of censorship and political persecution did they uneasily separate themselves from the state.[93] But even though they detached themselves in the years after 1842, they still could not escape the psychopathology of Prussian politics, their irrational need for an external authority. They continued to suffer from an inadequacy of self. Their need to be dependent led them to turn to a group that was similarly outcast and that could fulfill the role of historical agent which the state had rejected. The radicals came to rely not only on the masses, but in some cases on its most submerged group, on the impoverished declassé, the proletariat.[94] Feuerbach's species, Ruge's state and Volk, Marx's proletariat—these were all projections of a wretched aspect of existing social reality, the masses, into something utopian.

Bauer's analytic recapitulation of the fate of Hegelian theory in the 1840s amounts to an indictment of the traditional notion of philosophy. The events of the 1840s had revealed the philosopher to be psychologically weak. He had to anchor his place in the world by attaching himself to an external authority. Because the world was itself inadequate, the philosopher then had to make of it something that it was not. In other words, he compensated for his lack of self and the insubstantiality of reality by creating and then worshipping an abstract glorification of that bad reality. Before 1840, the intellectuals had made obeisance to an illusory image of the Prussian state; after 1840, they made themselves the servants of an illusory image of the masses.

Bauer's condemnation of Hegelian theory was an extension of his religious criticism. Like Strauss and especially Feuerbach, Bauer had earlier argued that religion compensated for the deficiencies of humanity by creating an abstract world of fulfillment.[95] But Bauer went his own way in applying that theory of religious alienation to the immediate social and political circumstances of Hegelian philosophers. The result of his recapitulation of the development of Hegelian theory in the 1840s was an implicit formulation of the theory of ideology: Hegelian theory and Young Hegelian radicalism were abstract forms of compensation for the inadequacies of a self mired in a correspondingly deficient social and political reality.

Just as Bauer had believed that religious alienation was pernicious to humanity, so he now criticized philosophical alienation. The abstract compensations of the philosophers threatened to aggravate the social problem, to bring about utter social collapse. By fashioning the masses into the species—an entity whose essence was supposedly "love"—Feuerbach set down a standard that the real masses were not able to meet. But their attempt to live up to Feuerbach's standard could mobilize their base passions. The ideal of the universal love of the species, Bauer wrote, "will give to their fear a great power. Helping them out of their sluggishness, onto their feet, it will set into motion their hatred of spirit."[96] Demagogues could also use Feuerbach's ideal of universal love to control the masses, enslaving them with delusions of grandeur.[97] The communists' utopian rendering of the masses was also potentially tyrannical. Since they believed that the essence of humanity was its sensuous activity and that it therefore fulfilled itself in physical work, they would subject human beings to a mechanical life of labor. A communist state would thus turn a rational spirit into a sensuous, ordered animal.[98]

Bauer's hostile analysis of the Young Hegelians' dangerous reliance on existing mass society brought about his final negative judgment of Hegelian theory. At the beginning of the 1840s he had distinguished between a critical and an uncritical Hegel. To the conservative philosopher who emphasized substance over subject and who conformed to the existing reality, Bauer had opposed a critical theorist who emphasized subject over substance and who held uncompromising standards of reason. In other words, Bauer had tried to disown the conformist Hegel, asserting that the true Hegel was a radical. After formulating his interpretation of Hegelian philosophy Bauer hoped that it would soon win over other Young Hegelians. He was quick to lash out at those still caught up in retrograde thinking. He attacked Strauss for committing the error of substance; Strauss, he said, employed the principle of substance to reintroduce Christianity into his system after he had ousted it in his criticism. By the end of 1841, Bauer was confident that his particular view of a radical Hegelian theory was winning the day.[99]

This hope for the radical possibilities of Hegelian theory collapsed in the course of the 1840s when Bauer proceeded with his analysis of mass society and its Young Hegelian spokesmen. He learned that his former friends and colleagues continued to adhere to, and indeed propagated, the wrong view of Hegelian philosophy. They carried over the notion of substance from religious philosophy into social and political theory. Bauer demonstrated how Feuerbach used a notion of substance to deify the masses, and his characterization of Feuerbach could have just as easily fit the other wrong-headed Young Hegelians.[100] Strauss, as it turned out, was not a single deviation but the harbinger of a concerted movement.

That so many disciples of Hegel could follow the conformist elements of Hegelian philosophy falsified Bauer's interpretation of Hegel as a radical theorist of critical subjectivity. The compelling features of Hegelian theory seemed to be those that rendered one a slave to existing reality. Confronted with contrary evidence, Bauer repudiated in 1844 his view of the inherent radicalism of Hegelian theory. Hegel, he now said, was a pantheist, a theorist of substance, a philosopher reconciled to the existing world. He was not against the conformism of theology, but had cleverly preserved it by giving it a philosophical form.[101]

The persistence of a conformist tendency in Hegel's disciples showed Bauer that conservativism and weakness were the dominant aspects of Hegelian philosophy. For Bauer in 1844 Hegelian theory was ideology: it was a cloak for a bad reality and for the insubstantiality of the philosopher; it justified the persistence of an intolerable world.

Bauer's development in the 1840s led him increasingly into isolation. He had made himself an enemy of the state, yet he refused any association with other outsiders—with either the mass of the dispossessed or their intellectual representatives. He had come to reject both Hegelian theory and Young Hegelian revisionism. By the mid-1840s he stood alone socially, politically, and intellectually. This was a situation that he not only recognized but that he embraced; for the outcome of his successive disappointments with the politics and philosophy of the day was the formulation of a theory of withdrawal, a theory that resisted any association with existing society.[102]

In the *Literatur-Zeitung*, Bauer announced the advent of "pure criticism" (*reine Kritik*), criticism without presuppositions or limitations. Where criticism in the *Posaune* was directed only against the tyranny of existing religion, pure criticism was directed against the tyranny of all existing beliefs and institutions. Politics, the masses, other Young Hegelians, and even Hegel himself—these were all attacked by the pure critic. He sought to throw off all connections to the existing reality.[103] As Horst Stuke has noted, Bauer's theory at this point was no longer dialectical—it no longer sought a reconciliation of opposites.[104] Rather, pure criticism was committed to ruthless negation, the unconditional destruction of reality.

Yet despite Bauer's new, relentless negativism, he remained in a crucial sense tied to the world he sought to efface. For although he denounced Hegel and the Young Hegelians, he continued to adhere to an important Hegelian principle. He still believed in the Hegelian notion of freedom. For the pure critic, freedom and the means to freedom remained philosophical, acts of rational cognition. Man's nature was thinking activity:

If one comprehends thought only as a power and indeed as a special power, then it is still a real positive power, a power through which man is what he is, which he cannot lack without ceasing to be a man, without consequently ceasing to be.[105]

But unlike the Hegelian thinker, Bauer's pure critic could have no institutional counterpart in the existing world. Subject was severed from substance.

Bauer acknowledged the solitary place of the philosopher whose principles had ceased to be grounded in reality. In the *Literatur-Zeitung* he argued that free thought was not to be found in the world at large or in the traditions of philosophy. It was real and present in the critic alone, in his cognitive act of criticism. The pure critic relied only on himself:

> Thus the critic renounces all joys of society, but its sorrows too remain distant from him. He knows neither friendship nor love; but for that reason calumny strikes powerlessly against him: nothing can offend him; no hate, no envy affects him; jealousy, vexation, and anger are for him unknown passions. The philistines, who still throw stones at him, misinterpret him, and attribute impure motives to him in order to make him like them, are not ridiculed by him, for it is not worth the effort, but are calmly looked through and sent back to their insignificant significance.[106]

Thus Bauer's final answer to the "verkehrte Welt" was to penetrate its delusion with the pure, knowing gaze of a detached Olympian reason.

5

Bauer did not take part in the events of the 1848 Revolution, but he was an interested spectator. In 1849 he published his observations in *Die bürgerliche Revolution in Deutschland* and in a work on the Frankfurt Parliament, *Der Untergang des Frankfurter Parlaments*.[107] His conclusions about the 1848 Revolution in Germany were an extension of his views about mass society and the psychopathology of German philosophy. The Revolution occurred because the traditional social order had disintegrated.[108] The atomized elements of modern society—state, aristocracy, middle and lower classes—shared a common flaw: they were all weak-willed, empty of psychological and rational substance. Because of this defect German governments easily collapsed in March 1848.[109] Because of the same defect, the German middle class later failed to consolidate its rule. In both the Frankfurt Parliament and the Prussian National Assembly, it showed that it was afraid of allying with the lower classes to challenge the authorities in a radical way.[110]

The German governments managed to take advantage of the weakness of the middle class. In December 1849 the Prussian government suppressed the revolution in Prussia, yet the return of traditional authority did not rejuvenate Germany. On the contrary, German political life continued to waste away.[111]

Bauer's sense of the psychological and philosophical enfeeblement of modern society seemed to intensify in the years after 1849. By 1853 he in fact felt that Germany's spiritual debility had come to characterize all of Europe. In *Russland und Germanenthum* (1853) he argued that European societies had fallen into decadence, a condition manifested in such political degradations as democracy and imperialism.[112] Soon a new power, alien to Western traditions, would sweep away this enervated civilization. Russia would bring about the West's final "catastrophe" and allow a new and better society to emerge in its place.[113] Bauer had become so alienated from his "civilization" that he now invoked a foreign power to destroy it.

As a sign of Western civilization's decay, the Prussian Young Hegelian discussed its present state of learning, focusing on philosophy in Germany. For the past twelve years, he said, German philosophy had been languishing. It had shown itself to be infertile, incapable of producing new ideas. It was justly neglected by the state. Hegelian philosophy, he noted, had become a subject of ridicule. It had long proven its inability to live up to its absolutist claims. With some satisfaction Bauer concluded that "the end of philosophy" was at hand.[114]

Part III

Arnold Ruge and the Crisis in Political Theory

5

The Unity of Idealism and Realism

In 1862, after almost a decade and a half of political exile in England and eighteen years before his death in the same place, Arnold Ruge published the first of four volumes of memoirs.[1] These reflections on his past are the essential documents for understanding the course of his early life. For many historians, they are also useful sources of information about German politics in the Vormärz, providing, among other things, important material on the student political associations, the Burschenschaften. Yet the value of these memoirs has generally been underestimated. Historians tend to treat them naively, forgetting that their author was not just a politician with memories but a Hegelian philosopher with a theoretical system. They assume that his memoirs are an unproblematical empirical record, and consequently they accept Ruge's statements as straightforward descriptions of events. They rarely ask why the author has represented these events as he has.

Ruge's biographer Walter Neher goes beyond this simple empiricist approach by searching out inconsistencies in Ruge's representation of events. Neher shrewdly points out, for example, that Ruge, the political rationalist of 1862, tones down in his memoirs the romantic and emotional features of the 1820s Burschenschaft to which he had belonged.[2] Neher's method reflects a sophisticated empiricism. It compares Ruge's account of events with other accounts and tries to explain discrepancies by showing how Ruge's representation of events was distorted by his state of mind at the time he was writing.

But despite its many excellences, Neher's study does not do justice to Ruge's memoirs as an interpretation of events. It misses several important cases where Ruge's story breaks down into conflicting representations. At one point, for instance, Ruge implies that he was always a democrat, and a critic of the conformist tendencies in Hegelian philosophy.[3] A little later, however, he painfully admits that during the same time he and his friends were fervid believers in Prussia's rationality and in its ethical and religious supremacy. Indeed, they were such enthusiasts that they became strenuous apologists for the Prussian government.[4]

As well as missing such revealing inconsistencies, Neher fails to ask a larger and more important question that given Ruge's Hegelian turn of mind seems wholly reasonable: Does Ruge's manipulation of events in his memoirs extend beyond a few instances to affect the entire work? This is not to imply that Ruge might have made up the events in his memoirs, but to ask why he chose, ordered, and described the events in the manner he did. In other words, do Ruge's memoirs constitute a total interpretation, in which the author invested his story with overarching philosophical significance?

Using Ruge's memoirs, this chapter aims first to present a descriptive account of Ruge's life up to his discovery of Hegel, and to point out the discrepancies and tensions of representation that appear in his memoirs. It then attempts to demonstrate how Ruge's representation of his life is in itself Hegelian. I argue that Ruge's memoirs were shaped as a Hegelian phenomenology, describing an evolution from natural harmony through alienated and contradictory forms of consciousness—what I refer to as "idealism" and "realism"—to the unity-restoring self-consciousness of Hegelian theory. By showing how Ruge gave his memoirs this Hegelian form and meaning I hope to demonstrate that, like Bauer, Ruge conceived of his coming to Hegelian philosophy in the 1830s as part of the cosmic evolution of spirit. Ruge, too, found redemption in his identification with absolute spirit.

1

Arnold Ruge was born on 13 September 1802 on the island of Rügen, located just off the Pomeranian coast of the Baltic Sea. Since the Thirty Years' War, Rügen had been a Swedish possession, and at the time of Ruge's birth his father was the chief administrator of the Rügen estates of the Swedish Count Brahe.[5] In 1804, however, following the tradition of a family of independent peasants and artisans,[6] Ruge's father gave up his office and became a leaseholder on the same island. As Ruge tells us in his memoirs, his was an idyllic childhood on his father's lands.[7] He was a "wild" child of nature,[8] an energetic spirit who was given free rein in a land that could be both pastorally beautiful and awesomely grand in its sea storms and winters.[9] His father was a good-hearted and enlightened family man. While administrator for Count Brahe he had undertaken to reduce the services and dues of the estate's peasants.[10] He was a man of the world, who had seen such far-off places as Stockholm[11] and had given up the superstitions of the time by accepting natural religion.[12] The father's calm, perhaps even meek, spirit was incongruously paired to the fierce but never tyrannical character of the mother. Ruge highlights their contrasting tempers as he describes their involvement in the first major event that disrupted Rügen's long-established pattern of life: the French occupation.

As part of its Russian campaign, the Napoleonic army entered Rügen in 1811 and left in 1812 with the retreat from Moscow. Ruge's 1862 memories of the French in 1811 are oddly ambivalent. He recalls acts of apparent tyranny, then neutralizes the impression of resulting distress, only to show later that the French occupation was indeed terrible. On one occasion Ruge's father, who had been put in charge of fodder and wagon deliveries, was ordered to produce coaches for the French. But the coaches were not to be obtained because, as his father tried to explain to the French, the local landowners were too poor to own coaches. The French commander, however, refused to believe Ruge's father and threatened to have him shot. The family feared for his life. Ruge's mother led her children to the French headquarters, in order, Ruge wrote, "to liberate the father." But by their arrival, the father had successfully appeased the commander and was released unharmed.[13]

On another occasion Ruge's mother displayed a similar fearless impetuosity. A French soldier quartered at their home added extra salt to her soup. Finding then that it was inedible, he became angry and struck her. Outraged, she took her broom and beat the soldier to the floor until he was unconscious.[14]

These and similar acts of French arbitrariness must have filled Ruge's family with anxiety, yet he represents these deeds in such a way that they appear to have had the opposite effect. As a nostalgic exile and an enthusiastic believer in the French Revolution, he tends to dissolve the terrors of the French occupation by conferring on such incidents a humorous tone and a happy ending. The father's run-in with the French he presents as a comedy of errors; the mother not only escaped punishment, but the defeated soldier's amused commanding officer became a friend of the family. Ruge further smooths down the hard edges of events by suggesting that the French were better rulers than the Swedes. The imperial army, Ruge tells us, repaired the roads, introduced humanitarian penal reforms, and on the whole treated the people in a "humane and good-natured" fashion.[15]

Yet the memoirs also provide irrefutable evidence for the suffering of the population. The occupation was not merely capricious, but also took a heavy toll on the local economy, badly damaging the financial state of Ruge's own family.[16] Moreover, regardless of how benevolently the French might have ruled, the people of Rügen were plainly hostile to their conquerors. Ruge recounts how the local population was lifted up in the great swell of German patriotism and Francophobia that buffeted Germany after 1812.[17] Learning of the glorious "German-Slav movement" against Napoleon, Ruge wrote, "We, like the people everywhere, felt . . . only the upsurge of an elevated and ennobled life, of an enthusiasm for freedom and fatherland."[18] A local militia (*Landsturm*) was formed in which Ruge's father became a lieutenant. Ruge's own excitement ran high and continued unabated even two years later when he was thirteen years old and in grade school. At that time, he closely followed current events and despaired when he learned of Napoleon's return from Elba. He was in fact so overcome by worry that while on holiday at home he could not sleep, and in the middle of the night entered the garden to pray for the tyrant's downfall. There the young and overwrought Ruge swore an oath: to slay Napoleon with his own hand if he should ever again subjugate the German people.[19]

With the Vienna settlement, Sweden lost Rügen to Prussia. Thus in 1818, after seven successful years of grade school,[20] Ruge entered the Gymnasium of nearby Stralsund as a Prussian citizen. He found both these changes agreeable. As an ethnic German, he had previously identified Prussia and Germany as the proper objects of his patriotic enthusiasm.[21] And as a Gymnasium student, his progress was swift and rewarding. Ranked at the top of his class, liked by his teachers and peers, and acknowledged as a leader among the students,[22] he felt his abilities and interests flowering at the same time that a reformed Prussian society seemed to be opening itself to talent and ability. Ruge recalls how in 1821 after passing through a final set of Gymnasium examinations, he could rhapsodize to a less ambitious friend about maturity's infinite opportunities in this new land. "'I look forward to the new world . . . in that we now enter into the revelation of all the secrets of which the schoolroom knows nothing!'"[23] He sought to accomplish great deeds—"'I aim at nothing less than to write my name among the stars, . . .'"[24]—and he was contemptuous of settling for a mundane life. "'If I only wanted to earn money,'" Ruge said in 1821 expressing one of his prejudices, "'then I would be like a Jew.'"[25]

Ruge decided to enter the University of Halle, but just before leaving a sobering concern was forced on him. His father surprised him by telling him of the financial problems the family had accrued during the war. Through gifts from his father's friends there was enough to pay for Ruge's first year of university, but thereafter the money for his education would be uncertain. His father then expressed his deep anxiety about the family's condition and his hope that Ruge would one day be able to give assistance. He suggested too that Ruge choose his studies accordingly. Something safely practical such as law, the father said, would be both honorable and provident.[26]

Ruge was deeply touched by this, but he could not surrender to his father's wishes. In his memoirs he quotes his response:

Dear father, that [the law] is only a trade, not a science; they who take it up actually want to learn nothing, but only to hold any stupid office in which they can become provincial [*verbauern*] for the rest of their lives. I find it impossible to resist the impulse to be educated in that which I do not know but hope to learn at the high institution.[27]

In his first year at the University of Halle, Ruge suffered from a "burning hunger" to learn.[28] He juggled ten colloquia at once. He tried theology, but rapidly lost interest, finding its concern for biblical and dogmatic details completely alien to the religion of nature in which he and his parents believed.[29] Philosophy and philology were of greater interest, but he soon discovered that his true love was for the classics.[30]

Through an old friend, Ruge met some members of the local Burschenschaft. Though at first reluctant to meet these notorious "enthusiasts," he soon found himself captivated by their political earnestness and idealism.[31] Unlike the unreformed student associations, the Corps, which continued a long tradition of drinking and brawling, the Halle Burschenschaft impressed Ruge with its selfless devotion to a noble cause. "It was clear," Ruge writes in 1862, that "they were not only enthusiastic about, but lived and acted for the future of the fatherland in that they cultivated and strengthened a new, noble spirit in the youth."[32]

As historians have noted, the Burschenschaften of the 1820s were of a different ideological cast from their predecessors of the preceding decade. Where they had once received public recognition, they were now constituted illegally, having been banned throughout Germany by the Carlsbad Decrees of 1819. Their commitment to national rejuvenation was consequently all the more dangerous, determined, and political. The tendency toward Christian medievalism was now muted by modern demands for a popular constitution and for greater individual freedom, demands that in some cases issued in republicanism and a susceptibility to notions of violent revolution.[33]

In the resurrected Halle Burschenschaft, Ruge found a vehicle for his own driving idealism. He soon stopped seeing his old friends from Rügen, many of whom had joined the rival Corps.[34] After entering the Halle Burschenschaft, he rose rapidly in its ranks. He made a national tour of other Burschenschaften and then, back in Halle, became a branch leader and spokesman.[35]

Although Prussia under the Carlsbad Decrees was especially unpropitious for the fulfillment of the new Burschenschaften's political longing, Ruge recalls in 1862 how the defeats of the early 1820s—political repression and Frederick William III's refusal to live up to his constitutional promise—failed to dampen their spirits. In these years, Ruge was sure that his innermost idealism would ultimately prove irresistible: "In the years of developing manhood one did not despair, and with the obstacles the courage only grew; the spirit of 1813 and 1815 was not to be banned again, the victory of the old abuses was only superficial."[36] But the new Burschenschaften's efforts to implement their program of national rejuvenation encountered only increasingly firm resistance from the authorities. Conflicts between students and governments occurred with increasing frequency and bad feeling.[37]

Denied a political outlet, some Halle members called for a revolutionary plot, but Ruge rejected these suggestions as foolish: they had, he objected, no support from the people, no army to lead.[38] He did not know, however, that such a conspiracy had already been organized. In 1821, Karl Sprewitz was sent on a mission by Karl Follen, an old Burschenschaft extremist who had fled to Switzerland after the Carlsbad Decrees. Sprewitz was to organize in the universities a secret League of Youth (*Jünglingsbund*), which would coordinate its activities with a League of Men (*Männerbund*), together working with foreign revolutionaries to foment a popular uprising.[39] The League of Men never got off the ground,[40] but Sprewitz managed to recruit for the League of Youth about a hundred members of the Burschenschaften in a handful of universities.[41] One reason these few joined was that they believed in an unlikely but comforting rumor: that several senior members of the Prussian army—men such as the reform-minded General Neithardt von Gneisenau—were part of the conspiracy. With these secret allies, victory did not seem impossible, and thus, when convinced that they were not alone, Ruge too fell into the conspiracy.[42] Although soon disabused of this outrageous rumor, for the moment, as he later wrote,

we lived in the happy deception and every day expected the great news of the rising of the army for the true realization of the aim of the impulses of freedom, the recovery of Germany.[43]

At the same time that Ruge had utterly committed himself to the Burschenschaften, his financial situation took a turn for the worse. Like a "thunderblow," he received a letter from his father telling him that the family had lost its leasehold and had moved to a nearby town. The father seriously worried about maintaining the family, but hoped at least that Ruge could support himself and later help them. Ruge wrote in 1862 that he felt "an abyss of unhappiness" opening before him. His beloved family was in a helpless situation, while he had just entered into a war with the state. He was torn between obligations: to aid his family or to struggle for freedom?

Should I immediately hasten home? But what could I accomplish there? Should I break off the connection with my friends and pull myself completely back into my studies? But how was that possible? My entire soul depended on my friends and on our great purpose.[44]

Ruge did not return home. Instead, he continued with the Burschenschaft at Halle and rapidly exhausted the remainder of his savings.[45] And as his resources dwindled, he finally learned that no conspiracy existed in the Prussian army. Yet he and others decided that there was no turning back. They had already gone too far: they had committed themselves to high treason.[46]

Though resolute in their commitment, neither Ruge nor other conspirators performed any truly revolutionary activities. The League of Youth was, in fact, in its death throes, soon dissolving in some places, falling into internal conflicts in others.[47] Having used up his income and refusing to become financially dependent on the Burschenschaft, Ruge decided to quit school and return home. He made a last visit to other Burschenschaften, and while in Jena he had a stroke of luck. A wealthy friend and fellow Burschenschaftler Eduard Simon offered Ruge part of his ample income.[48] Ruge accepted, and even though the Prussian government had previously banned all Prussian citizens from attending this institution, he moved to the University of Jena.[49]

At Jena, he quickly became a leader of its Burschenschaft and a constant irritant to the local and university authorities.[50] Indeed, he was eventually expelled for initiating disruptive behavior, and with Eduard Simon moved to Heidelberg.[51] Compared to those of Jena and Halle, the Burschenschaft at Heidelberg was less politically conscious, more conciliatory to the authorities, and therefore too conservative for Ruge.[52] Never one to refuse a challenge, he would likely have set out to engineer reforms but for an intervening misfortune. The conspiracy that he had joined, had never actively worked for, and had ceased to believe in, was betrayed. Just before Christmas 1823, Ruge learned that his friends were being arrested for participating in the subversive League of Youth, and having declined to flee, he too was taken into custody.[53]

2

As a Prussian citizen, Ruge was handed over to the Prussian authorities and sent to Berlin.[54] His investigation at Köpnick fortress lasted a full year. During that time, he felt cruelly abandoned by the German people, for not a single voice in Germany, he said, protested against the arrest of its heroic youth. "The Germans," Ruge later wrote, "were and wanted to be slaves."[55]

He acknowledged his helplessness, but he remained proud and defiant. When counseled by the chief Prussian interrogator Karl von Kamptz to speak the truth, Ruge angrily retorted:

Why are you concerned for the truth? Have you ever sought it or ever done anything to promote it? Or am I speaking with a great philosopher? That is not likely, for the truth liberates man, it does not throw him into prison.[56]

In December 1824, Ruge was sentenced to fifteen years imprisonment, though an act of royal clemency would later remit nine of those years.

Between December 1824 and New Year's 1830, he was incarcerated in a Prussian fortress.[57]

In their imprisonment some of his friends experienced a psychological and physical collapse. But Ruge did not allow imprisonment to defeat him. Indeed, he bolstered the decaying morale of his cell mate, another Burschenschaft conspirator,[58] and he sought to make the most of his isolation. His state-assigned legal advisor provided him with books and writing materials. Using these resources, Ruge set himself a tough regimen of study that concentrated on classical texts. He read Greek dramas and made a translation of Sophocles's *Oedipus at Colonus*. He read Greek historians, and from Thucydides's *History of the Peloponnesian War* he translated the famous speech of Pericles. That speech, in which Pericles called on the citizens of democratic Athens to sacrifice themselves for the city's defense, embodied Ruge's ideal of a free and noble political consciousness, the consciousness that he now thought was so sorely lacking in modern Germany. As he bitterly commented in his memoirs, what was not possible in his everyday life, he studied in theory and history.[59]

The same growing cynicism about modern political life manifested itself in another literary venture. He composed, in prison, an epic poem about the Prussian Major Ferdinand von Schill, who in 1809 attempted to launch a rebellion, unsuccessfully, against Napoleon in Stralsund. Ruge attributed Schill's failure not only to Napoleon's stronger forces but also to the resistance of the Pomeranian population. Schill met his doom, Ruge believed, because the Germans preferred tyranny to liberation.[60]

In other writings of his prison period, Ruge further reflected on Germany's political backwardness and on the limitations of the human will. He acknowledged in two unpublished essays the futility of isolated individuals trying to establish the unity of the people against the untimeliness of historical forces and the external power of the state. His recognition of the German people's political inertia was thus coupled with a realistic appreciation of the power of the state.[61]

Besides attempting to elucidate his present situation in these writings and reflections, he sought to find solace for his frustrated idealism in other studies. He read more classical writers, Jean-Paul's *Vorschule der Aesthetik*, and then the works of Plato, in which he found a deliverance from prison. This philosopher, he rejoiced, showed the way to a metaphysical world of free spirit. Through Plato's writings, he and his cell mate were able to change prison into a "temple of freedom."[62]

Released in 1830, Ruge returned home and then set out for Halle. En route he stopped in Berlin where he tried to get his translation of Sophocles and his poem on Schill published. Thinking he might return to a Prussian university, he also wrote an appeal to the king in which he asked for a restoration of the rights he had lost for attending the banned University of Jena.[63]

In Halle Ruge obtained employment in a Gymnasium as a teacher of classical languages.[64] He made new friends, including the pro-Prussian and Christian Hegelians Karl Rosenkranz and Theodor Echtermeyer, and the former Hegelian and now Pietist historian Heinrich Leo. With these and others Ruge formed the "Friday Society," a club of scholarly discussion for young intellectuals.[65] Eventually dissatisfied with his position in the Gymnasium, he resigned[66] and reentered the University of Halle, where he wrote a *Habilitationsschrift* in philology on Plato's aesthetics and became a Privatdozent in philosophy.[67]

Shortly afterwards, Ruge's landlady introduced him to Louise Düffer, the daughter of a deceased Halle professor. Ruge soon fell in love with this attractive young woman, who had already rejected eleven suitors.[68] She reciprocated his love and they were married in 1832. Louise had received a considerable inheritance from her father, so that with this marriage Ruge's chronic financial problems came to an end.[69] Propertied and established, he soon became a citizen of the city.[70]

Since his release from prison, Ruge had steadily advanced into Prussian middle-class society, acquiring as he went a profession, a wife, social connections, money, and local responsibilities. His earlier disaffection and detachment now seemed entirely superseded, his earlier revolutionary enthusiasm converted into the virtues of a good Bürgher. He displayed little interest in either the July Revolution or the resulting agitation in Germany.

Ruge had become conformist, but not in a crude, calculating fashion. His state of mind was more complex. Throughout his incarceration he had continued to assert the justice of the Burschenschaft cause, but he had also come to acknowledge the impossibility of realizing that cause under Germany's present political conditions. Consequently, he began to relegate the fulfillment of his idealism to the lost world of democratic Athens or to a dimly perceived future. His new realism displaced his idealism from its former central position, pushing it into the limbo of what was and will be. With his idealism banished, his realism by default determined his actions, drew him into the institutions of his society, made him, in effect, a conformist.[71]

While on the way to Italy in 1832 with his recent bride, he met an old friend from the Burschenschaft, Gustav Bunsen, who was still as idealistic as Ruge had once been. Bunsen told Ruge of the Hambach festival and invited him to a similar assembly of patriots at Hanau. But Ruge declined, justifying himself with the pessimism of a disillusioned radical:

It is too late. The spirits have cooled off and the authorities have established themselves again. Hambach and Hanau are not Vienna and Berlin. I share the aim [of your struggle], but it is not to be attained at present.[72]

The political movement, Ruge added, had reached its high tide in 1830 and since then had steadily receded.[73] Later, as he related this accidental meeting to his wife, he predicted the crowding of Prussian prisons if the movement should try to continue now that its force was spent.[74]

Ruge had become cynical about his own ideals: they existed abstractly but were impossible to realize. In the void of a life emptied of its highest meaning, he had placed the homelier values of academic recognition, Bürgher respectability, and familial contentment. His cynical realism, while freeing him from the practical demands of his moral and political aims, also worked to integrate him into the middle-class world of the German Vormärz.

Yet Ruge's demystified bourgeois realism proved to be no more enduring than his earlier unworldly idealism. In Italy Ruge and his wife contracted cholera, struck by the same epidemic that killed Hegel in 1831. Ruge recovered, but his wife's condition worsened until, in October 1833, she died.[75]

To console him, Ruge's family came to Halle from Rügen, but consolation became a second tragedy: early in 1834, Ruge's father also died.[76] In a state of shock, Ruge removed himself to his house in the country. There, he later recalled, buried and forgotten under a mass of packages, were the works of Hegel.[77] On this dramatic note, with which Ruge concluded the third book of his memoirs, he prepared us for his transfiguration.

3

As a Burschenschaftler Ruge had never read Hegel, yet he had held strong opinions about Hegelian philosophy. He had automatically drawn from the common stock of Burschenschaft ideology, which maintained a dark image of the philosopher: Hegel as a lackey of the Prussian government, a pseudophilosopher who justified Prussia's worst vices and attacked its righteous opponents.[78] Out of prison and back in Halle, Ruge befriended some Hegelians and started to read Hegelian philosophy, but he was only vaguely interested and never penetrated Hegel's dense volumes.[79]

In the fourth book of his memoirs, Ruge describes his true conversion to Hegel in 1834. He calls this volume's first section, which is exclusively concerned with the discovery of Hegel, "Studies in the Prolonged Absence" (*Verschollenheit*), by which he ostensibly refers to his retreat from society into seclusion and study. Yet in this same section there is another sense in which Ruge removes himself or disappears; that is, the subject of the memoirs, the persona Arnold Ruge, vanishes. His memoirs now are transformed from a description of his life into an extensive exposition of Hegelian philosophy, a study so long—400 pages—and detailed that it can easily count as a philosophical treatise in its own right.

Ruge's exposition attempts to present a comprehensive survey of Hegelian philosophy first by outlining Hegel's history of philosophy—from Pythagoras to Hegel himself—and then by showing the internal unfolding of philosophical categories, from the simplest—pure being—through the different forms of nature and the subjective spirit, to the objective embodiment of reason in the state. This two-way genetic and systematic approach is itself eminently Hegelian. It is meant to show how Hegel had demonstrated the historical necessity of the appearance of his own philosophy, and then to explain precisely what that philosophy logically entailed, its nature qua philosophy.

As a critical study of Hegel, this long philosophical interlude deserves praise for its simple and rigorous working of ideas.[80] But as part of a memoir it is unsuitable, a long digression that in its exacting detail is of no apparent aid in understanding Ruge and his time. An autobiography will naturally describe those theories and ideas that have influenced its author. Throughout his *Autobiography*, John Stuart Mill, for example, provides inventories of what he was reading or of the ideas that appeared important to him during certain periods in his life. On occasion, he summarizes a book or even a philosophy and tells us its significance for him at that point in his intellectual development. But in contrast to Ruge's exhaustive treatment of Hegel, Mill's presentation of an idea or a philosophy is always brief and explicitly relates that idea or philosophy to his life.[81]

This is not true of Ruge's exposition of Hegel. He draws no explicit

correspondences between the ideas he is expounding and the developments of his life. Nor are there any obvious implicit connections that tie
them together. To know, for instance, how Hegel related Stoicism to
Epicureanism or explained the transformation of magnetic into electrical
energy does not help us to make out the shape of Ruge's life. Yet he felt
a need to break off his story and to work such details into a comprehensive
discussion of a philosophy that in 1867 he no longer entirely believed.
What, then, as a writer describing his life, did he hope to accomplish
with this interruption, this description of the life of philosophy?

By way of justification, he suggests that his exposition of Hegel is
related to what he had been writing about before:

What I now . . . have to impart is of a different type. It is indeed the same spirit
of the time in its development, but pressed back into its highest and final point,
into the movement of creative thought, into the area of the science of philosophy,
which rules all.[82]

This section of his memoirs is, in other words, not a digression but a
recapitulation. It describes, he says, the same subject, the spirit of the
time, but where earlier this was done prosaically, in terms of Ruge's life
and times, it is now done philosophically, as the evolution of concepts
and states of being. These are not divergent descriptions of life and
philosophy but identical movements, variations on a single theme. In a
letter to Ludwig Bamberger written just after the completion of this
volume of his memoirs, Ruge makes this relation of identity explicit:

I have pursued [in this fourth volume] a new type of Platonism in which I let
the everyday development and the development of thought course beside and
through each other, but with a strong reference to their identity.[83]

To understand fully this strategic shift and identification, we should
recall the Hegelian method employed by Bauer in his biblical studies.
Bauer regarded his philosophical interpretation of the Bible as both an
exposition of the evolution of spirit in the Bible and the final outcome
of that same evolution. To write about the Bible was circuitously to write
about himself: the philosopher, the text, and the object studied formed
a single internally related whole.

Writing in 1867 of his 1834 discovery of Hegel, Ruge seems to be
trying to convey a sense of an experience similar to Bauer's. His section

on Hegelian philosophy recapitulates in a different form, he says, the spirit that determined his life. It demonstrates synchronically the emergence of philosophy culminating in Hegel, and diachronically the movement of concepts ending in their manifestation in the social and political reality. In the earlier volumes of his memoirs, Ruge presents his biography from his life as a child of nature to his discovery of Hegel. The trajectories of these two movements, philosophy and Ruge's life, converge at the same point: Hegelian philosophy in the world. By insisting on this equivalence and conjuncture, on the identity of these two movements, Ruge could thus see his life as a philosophical unfolding with the structure and significance of Hegelian philosophy. His life too was a necessary genetic and conceptual progression, a development of states of consciousness, culminating in the concrete self-awareness of this same process, in Hegelian philosophy, in the redemption of oneself and the world.

To demonstrate exactly how Ruge invested his life with philosophical meaning, we must go over his history again, this time from the vantage point of his conversion to Hegelian philosophy. If we survey his life from a Hegelian point of view, we can extract a buried dialectic of consciousness. Ruge represents his life in his 1862–1867 memoirs as a Hegelian dialectic of idealism[84] and realism.

4

From 1834 until his death in 1880 Ruge regarded Hegelian philosophy as the focal point of his life. Its concepts and procedures organized his way of thinking about himself and the world. Thus in his memoirs he gives his life the "plot" of a Hegelian phenomenology: Ruge as spirit ascends from a rudimentary condition of nature to a pure state of spirit. He pictures his life as a progression from a condition of natural wholeness through alienated states of detached idealism and crass realism to a restored higher unity of the two in the philosophical self-awareness of Hegelian philosophy.

In the first volume of his memoirs, Ruge describes his early childhood as a pleasing pastoral existence. His first memory is of being left alone by his nurse in a field of grazing cattle. Among these "giants" he felt perfectly at ease, absorbed in observing them and pained when he was forced to leave.[85] Nature was Ruge's element, his home.

But this direct relationship with nature on his father's land was soon disturbed by the French occupation. The primary unity was broken by external forces. And with this disruption of natural wholeness came a differentiation—Ruge's separation from the natural, untroubled world of his youth. Ruge the schoolboy gradually ceased to relate to his environment in terms of immediate perceptions. Instead he began to apply high abstractions to the world. Justice, honor, freedom—all these came into play in Ruge's mind as his family suffered under French occupation. With liberation, this differentiation from his natural childhood became more extreme, the abstractions more intense. He became the crudest kind of idealist: a patriot.

There was now no turning back to the unproblematical days of his childhood. He had acquired the critical apparatus that allowed him to distinguish himself from nature, to determine by abstract standards what he ought to be. His enthusiasms were not socially alienating; on the contrary, they allowed the schoolboy to feel at one with the passion that animated Prussian society in the first years after 1812. Gymnasium deepened his character, giving it more intellectual content and the burning desire for knowledge. But it also marked the beginning of his separation from society. He was so consumed by his burgeoning powers and the world's infinite possibilities that he failed to notice the declining economic state of his family. And when his father suggested that Ruge choose a practical career in order to help his family, he refused, preferring instead the nobler unworldly life of the mind. Thus the abstract thinking that had brought the child Ruge out of nature into society had developed a power of its own. It had acquired a measure of independence from its surroundings. It could make demands of Ruge that could fall into conflict with the constraints of his immediate society.

At the University of Halle, Ruge's participation in the Burschenschaft reinforced his idealism at the same time that it strained his connection with the world. The Burschenschaft set him at odds with the various levels of social authority—family, university, city, and state. His idealism was strongest and his tie to society weakest when he joined the League of Youth, a secret subversive conspiracy. His idealism was now an engine out of control, carrying him beyond the possible—or even probable, as Ruge's belief in a military coup showed. Idealism or the world—these were no longer related parts of a whole, but separate entities, one to be chosen over the other. The agonized Ruge had to decide between returning home to support his now more destitute family or staying with the

Burschenschaften to participate in an unlikely conspiracy. He opted for his high moral and political aims, even after he had recognized the impossibility of their fulfillment in the world; for having learned that the conspiracy had no allies in the army, he acknowledged its total isolation and therefore his idealism's alienation from the world.

In the *Phenomenology* and elsewhere Hegel repeatedly showed that "spirit" (*Geist*) or human consciousness matured beyond a certain form or stage of its development when it had exhausted that form's ability to enhance its content. To continue in an unsuitable form would subject spirit to alienating conditions. Consequently, spirit would acknowledge the inadequacy of that form and then, reacting against it, would assume a new and opposing form. Ruge's youthful idealism had raised him from nature to society, imbuing him with spiritual content. But it had soon exhausted that positive function and, in continuing, produced only negative, alienated results; namely, Ruge's separation from the world. Thus, following the rules of phenomenological change, Ruge shows in his memoirs how his idealistic life had to pass into an opposing, remedial form of consciousness.

The confirmation of his idealism's untenable situation was the uncovering of the conspiracy of the League of Youth and the subsequent imprisonment of its members. The forsaken world thus recognized and revenged itself on an overweening idealism. Prison led Ruge inward. Through a self-imposed, strenuous course of study, he pacified and strengthened his will. A new Ruge was released. Sensitive to the limits of individual striving and realistic about the power of the state, he reconciled himself to the unfulfillment of his ideals. This period of his life witnessed an inversion of his earlier condition. An opposite relation between his idealism and reality obtained: he turned away from his ideals and steadily worked his way into society. Becoming a Gymnasium teacher, then a Privatdozent, marrying and ending his financial problems—Ruge's progress since Colberg prison resembled an exemplary bourgeois life. He lived for professional integrity, civil respectability, and family happiness. His wife, after Ruge told her of his meeting with an old Burschenschaftler, aptly summed up Ruge's new situation when she said: "If we cannot live for them [the political idealists], then we can still live for each other."[86]

Ruge now embraced the world, but only by setting aside his most profound beliefs, by suspending his deepest values. Yet this realistic reaction to his earlier alienated idealism was, in truth, an overreaction.

Cynical realism by Hegelian standards of wholeness was also imperfect. By renouncing idealism so thoroughly Ruge rendered his world shallow, drained it of its spiritual meaning. Like his former detached idealism, Ruge's cynical realism was one-dimensional, far removed from Hegel's symmetrical unity of reason and reality. And consequently, as an inadequate form of spirit this alienated realistic consciousness also had to pass. Ruge describes the collapse of his realistic world by recounting the death of its central defining figure, his wife, and, as if to confirm that her death was not pure happenstance but a necessary judgment of the high court of Hegelian reason, he also tells us how his father died soon after.

Ruge now entered a second phase of isolated study and contemplation, deepening his spirit. But where his earlier reading was haphazard, accidental, his present reading was a concerted investigation of a systematic philosopher, Hegel. In his retreat, Ruge lost himself in the study of Hegel and lived the life of philosophy.

Ruge calls this period of "disappearance" into philosophy a spiritual "recovery,"[87] and this, I might add, was in the senses both of a return of strength and of a reappropriation of values. He came back from his retreat refreshed, ready to carry on in the world, and enlightened, full of a new truth. As he shows in his comprehensive description of Hegelian philosophy, Hegel had taught him a new form of knowing. What he had formerly perceived through isolated, unordered intuitions he said he now understood conceptually and systematically, as philosophically integrated into a continuous pattern. In Hegel's dialectic, he writes, "lay the entire world of nature and spirit stretched out before me in one great development."[88] All the contradictions of logic, collisions of nature, and tensions of history were absorbed into a single coherent scheme of reason. All these different antagonisms worked for no other aim than to bring one to an awareness of their interconnectedness, to the self-consciousness of Hegelian philosophy.

Ruge thus found in Hegelian philosophy an all-embracing model of redemption, and by extension, an existential justification for the struggles and defeats of his life. Hegelian philosophy proved that like the dialectical flow of logic, nature, and history, the equivalent movement of his life had a magnificent unifying purpose: to render him a spiritual being, to carry him to the highest level of self-consciousness, to create, in other words, the conditions for his reception of Hegelian philosophy. That Ruge presents the full plan of Hegelian philosophy at this point in his memoirs makes perfect sense: he is demonstrating his assumption of self-consciousness. For on Hegel's theory, the first act and experience of complete self-consciousness is to review philosophically spirit's development to self-consciousness. The philosopher displays and proves his spiritual self-awareness by rationally comprehending spirit's development to self-consciousness. This coming to Hegelian self-consciousness is precisely what Ruge is trying to demonstrate, genetically and systematically, in the philosophical section of his memoirs. That section is the documentation of his self-consciousness, the first defining act of which was to reinterpret philosophically the development of his life as the development of philosophy issuing in self-consciousness.

Thus through an acquired self-consciousness—the system of Hegelian thought—Ruge was able to understand the course of his life as a necessary development that aimed at producing his present self, a Hegelian philosopher. Hegelian theory was the means of restoring harmony to his life, of redeeming his banished idealism and his discredited realism, for the point of Hegelian philosophy was precisely to show how one could be an idealist in the world.

Ruge returned from his seclusion to his lecturing position at the University of Halle. He took up again and increased his social contacts. He performed once more the civil duties of a citizen and eventually became a deputy to the city council,[89] and he soon happily remarried. In short, he ostensibly resumed the social forms of his previous life. But there was now an important difference: he felt inspired by a great ideal that he recognized as present in his existing world, the self-consciousness of spirit. He was one with his world, part of the great unity of reason.

Ruge's representation of his life in his memoirs possesses all the features of a Hegelian phenomenology: a simply original unity shattered into differentiated entities; successive attempts to restore a wholeness to the world and to oneself; crises that proved the inadequacy of each attempt; a necessary and cumulative progression of forms of consciousness and relations to the world; a constant deepening of spirit; and finally an ultimate crisis issuing in a resolution—the restored unity of a philosophical self-consciousness in the world. He came back from his retreat a realist who had regained high values, an idealist who had made his peace with society. And this transfigured Ruge, an idealist in the world, a Hegelian, soon elucidated and confirmed philosophy's affinity with the existing world in the founding of the *Hallische Jahrbücher* and in its first major controversy, the Cologne episcopal dispute.

5

Throughout his life Ruge had displayed an ability to adjust quickly and adeptly to a new environment. He now showed a similar skill in dealing with the new situations created by his conversion to Hegel. Since his conversion he closely followed developments in Hegelian philosophy, and given his earlier rationalist faith and attenuated piety, he naturally gravitated in the middle of the decade toward the emerging Straussian camp. Ruge and others in this younger left-wing minority felt cramped by the arrogant, "Brahman-like" hegemony exercised by the older Hegelians in the leading Hegelian journal, the Berliner *Jahrbücher für wissenschaftliche Kritik*. In an 1837 article, "Unsere gelehrte kritische Journalistik," he attacked the current state of journalism in Germany and made a plea for a renewal of philosophical criticism.[90]

Ruge's friend Theodor Echtermeyer was greatly impressed by this article. As Echtermeyer also suffered from the same frustrations with traditional academic journalism, he approached Ruge about establishing a new journal based on Ruge's reformist principles. Ruge agreed, and together they found a sympathetic publisher, Otto Wigand in Leipzig, and then searched for talented contributors. The first issue of their new periodical, the *Hallische Jahrbücher für deutsche Wissenschaft und Kunst*, appeared on the first of January 1838.

For Ruge this new journal was more than just a medium for enlightened opinion. It was nothing less than spirit incarnate: "Such a journal," Ruge wrote in 1867, "does not merely accompany, but is directly itself the development of the philosophical and general spirit of the age."[91] It was the appropriate form for a self-conscious philosophy to take in the existing world, the organ of a rational philosophy that corresponded to a rational world.

Although the *Hallische Jahrbücher* were based, Ruge tells us in 1867, on the principles of Straussian criticism, he never thought that this position was hostile to either Protestantism or Prussia. On the contrary, he regarded the *Jahrbücher*'s philosophical criticism as their most intimate friend and ally. Philosophy, Protestantism, and Prussia—this was an equation of identity that summed up the inner and outer rationality of the existing world. Thus, far from attacking the Prussian state and its religion, Ruge rushed to defend them when he saw their authority challenged by a Catholic opposition in 1838. In the Cologne episcopal dispute Ruge emerged as a champion of Protestantism and Prussia.

At the Congress of Vienna, Prussia acquired new territories in its northeast and southwest. With these new territories came new problems. To integrate into Protestant Prussia the large Catholic population of the new lands proved to be a vexing task throughout the nineteenth century.

The government's first attempts to win over its Catholic citizens failed. In its administrative, economic, and constitutional policy it acted like a foreign power enforcing an arbitrary will on a subject people.[92] Since the middle of the 1820s, Prussia had been negotiating with the Vatican over the issue of mixed marriages. Frederick William III sought to institute a ceremony that was amenable to both Protestant and Catholic, but this turned out to be immensely difficult to attain. Before the Pope would sanction mixed marriages, he demanded that the Catholic bride be warned she was committing a mortal sin and demanded that any children of mixed marriages be raised in the Catholic Church.[93] Such demands were anathema to the Protestant dignity of Frederick William, and following the advice of the Prussian representative at the Vatican, Christian von Bunsen, he sought to circumvent them by working out a private agreement with the bishops of western Prussia.[94] An understanding was in fact reached in June 1834 with Archbishop Spiegel of Cologne, but about a year later Spiegel died and was replaced by the injudicious and ultramontane Clemens August von Droste-Vischering.[95] The new archbishop immediately set out to stir up the already agitated religious atmosphere in western Prussia. His first objective was to eject the rationalists from the theological faculty of the University of Bonn.[96]

In early 1836, the secret arrangement between the Prussian government and Archbishop Spiegel was brought into the open.[97] Droste, in September 1836, pledged himself to forbid the consecration of mixed marriages unless the Vatican's requirements were fulfilled.[98] After unsuccessfully trying to win over Droste or convince him to resign, the Prussian government arrested him in November 1837 for disobeying state orders.

With this act of power, Prussia exposed itself to widespread criticism in the press. To many observers, Prussia appeared as an untrustworthy power, a furtive, shady dealer who once exposed reacted with tyrannical vengeance.[99] A great literary war began with the Catholic writer Joseph Görres excoriating Protestant Prussia in his book *Athanasius*.[100] Protestant intellectuals were encouraged to reply, and Heinrich Leo, one-time Hegelian and now a Pietist historian at Halle, especially distinguished himself as a defender of Protestantism. His effectiveness could in fact be measured by the intense hostility he evoked in Catholic writers.

As other parties joined the conflict, the clashes became more heated and the lines of battle more confused. Some liberals, such as the Baden political theorist Karl Rotteck, were not allies of the Catholic Church but still condemned what they regarded as Prussian despotism. Ruge and the *Hallische Jahrbücher* blurred loyalties even further by rushing to Prussia's defense—but only to strike down its apologists. Ruge raised the dispute to another order of conflict: he sought to purge the Prussian camp of its false friends.

In one article of the *Jahrbücher*, he criticized Görres,[101] but his preferred objects of abuse were Heinrich Leo and Prussia's Pietists. In a series of pieces[102] he sought to expose their duplicity. Görres, Ruge wrote in the first of these articles, was a benighted Catholic, a mortal enemy of Protestant Prussia, but he was at least honest in his hate. Leo wrote against Görres in defense of Prussia, but in truth, Leo too was its enemy. In fact, as a Pietist, Leo was essentially the same as Görres, for like Görres, he was dissatisfied with the present, seeing it as a nightmarish distortion of what should have been.[103] Leo too despised the existing state, church, and science, and for precisely the same reasons: pagan and mechanistic, they constituted an abstract *Beamtenstaat* (state of bureaucrats).[104]

From this same hateful point of view, Leo spurned the modern era's great defining movements—the Reformation, the Enlightenment, rationalism, and the French Revolution—as unnatural deformations.[105] He was an antimodernist who longed for a romanticized past, a "hypochondriac"[106] who believed the present to be blighted, never recognizing that not the world but his own spirit was diseased. Leo, the great opponent of Görres, Ruge ironically concluded, was himself an "unconscious" Catholic.[107]

Yet, Ruge allowed, Leo might sincerely protest that he was a good Protestant. But he could only do so, Ruge added, because he had an incorrect understanding of Protestantism. Leo subscribed to an "unfree" idea of the meaning of the Reformation, for he did not recognize it as the "self-knowledge of spirit," but as a set of positive dogmas.[108] He mistook historical appearance for spiritual essence. Not surprisingly, then, such an impaired historical vision was incapable of understanding the significance of the Reformation, of seeing how it issued forth a continuous stream of reason that flowed through the Enlightenment to empty into contemporary Prussia.[109] Leo was out of phase with his time, a man who had no sense of spirit's historical development and who therefore could not feel at ease in the present.

Ruge's assault on Leo immediately diverted some attention from Görres and the Catholics, opening a second front in the religious conflict. Pietists and Prussian conservatives now heaped abuse on their newly declared enemy, prompting Ruge and the *Jahrbücher* to reply in kind. Throughout the rest of 1838, Ruge struck at an increasing number of enemies—Leo, the *Berliner Wochenblatt*, and Ernst Hengstenberg and the *Evangelische Kirchenzeitung*—and he protested his loyalty to the state.

Ruge's strategy of operations remained the same. He accused the Pietists of deceiving themselves about history and the world. They were de facto Catholics, suffering from a sickness of spirit, incapable of accepting the glorious present. Against their denunciation of the Young Hegelians as godless, rabble-rousing subversives,[110] Ruge referred to Pietism's willful blindness to history; the revolution of reason that it feared, Ruge announced, had already taken place in Prussia. The *Landrecht* (legal code), the Beamtenstaat, centralization, Protestantism, free science, and free discussion: all these proved that a change of revolutionary proportions had occurred, but one that was for Prussia, not against it.[111] Moreover, Ruge added, as 1830 had clearly shown, there was no need to fear a violent uprising in Prussia. Such an event was patently impossible in a country governed by the rational principles of the modern era.[112] In "the principle of voluntary development, the principle of the Reformation," Ruge wrote, "Prussia possessed the guarantee against forceful advance."[113]

Ruge's conversion to Hegelian theory, to an idealism in the world, had made him into a Prussian apologist. The Prussian state and its Protestant religion were the objective realizations of the same free self-consciousness that determined his thought, the external equivalents to Hegelian philosophy.[114] This was a relation of identity which Ruge believed to be solidly established in the political reality of 1838, which he thought was resistant to threats from either the Pietist right or the revolutionary left. With a smug confidence, he proclaimed his own invincibility:

I am a free citizen of a free land; I am a Prussian who knows his rights and his obligations; I hold them from my city and from my state. Thus there is no man on earth who can punish me with favor or disfavor, before which I am protected by majesty of the King and by the law and the constitution of the country.[115]

Yet in the following years, the balance of political and social forces would shift in favor of Ruge's enemies. The rational equation of philosophy, Prussia, and Protestantism would cease to obtain in a world that by Hegelian standards was disturbingly irrational.

6

The Antagonism Between
Politics and Philosophy

1

The Prussian state in the Vormärz displayed a remarkably contradictory nature. While politically oppressive in many ways, it could also be tolerant and merciful. Arnold Ruge had witnessed both sides of its character. As a Burschenschaftler he had suffered from the wrath of a vindictive and paranoid state, but after prison the prodigal was welcomed back by the state into respectable society.

Released from prison in 1830, he petitioned the Prussian government to restore the rights that he had lost for attending the banned University of Jena, so that he might resume his education.[1] As evidence of his academic seriousness and rehabilitation, he sent his poem on Schill and his translation of Sophocles to Johannes Schulze, the Prussian official in charge of higher education.[2] The state granted his request and thus gave its official blessing to his reentry into society. In the following years, the former radical transformed himself into a responsible citizen, a loyal Hegelian, and a Privatdozent at the University of Halle.

Throughout this period of social reintegration he did not forget how important the patronage of the state was to the constitution of his new identity. He kept it posted on significant developments in his academic career. In accordance with convention, he sent Schulze and Altenstein his Habilitationsschrift on Plato's aesthetics.[3] For almost a decade after 1830 he carried on an unambiguously amiable relationship with the authorities. In 1837 the government promoted a colleague to the post of associate professor. Ruge had hoped the position would go to him and he also felt that the person selected was less qualified, but he was not troubled with doubts of the state's benevolence.[4] His accomplishments, he thought, would ultimately speak for themselves. Reason's work would inevitably be rewarded by reason's state.

Shortly after this incident, Ruge in fact produced his most considerable achievement to date and one that he believed would greatly impress the authorities. With Theodor Echtermeyer, he established the *Hallische Jahrbücher*, the first issues of which he sent to Altenstein and Schulze for official viewing.[5] The two officials replied in May and June of 1838 with praise for the new magazine's high philosophical and literary quality.[6]

Later in June, Ruge wrote the first of his articles on Heinrich Leo and the Cologne episcopal dispute. This crucially altered Ruge's association with the state: their clear unity of interests and beliefs now became clouded with controversy. While Ruge thought that in attacking Pietism he was acting in defense of the state, the government preferred to avoid what it regarded as an unnecessary conflict. Altenstein tried to tread a path between the two camps, turning down Pietist calls to suppress the *Jahrbücher*, but also denying the magazine public support.

What encouragement Ruge did receive for his academic labors was communicated privately, including, apparently, a reassurance that his eventual promotion had not been forgotten. But he disliked the disparity between the state's private approbation and its public silence. Self-consciously older than most Privatdozenten, passed over for those he thought were lesser men, and locked in an escalating dispute with the Pietists, he craved public recognition, a promotion that would at once confirm his academic legitimacy and show his enemies that the state stood by him. Although he found it humiliating to do so, he appealed directly to Schulze in 1838 for an upgrading of his academic status. While never outrightly accusatory, he implied in his petition that the state had ill-used him and ignored his achievements.[7] But he remained confident that the state would correct its oversight.

The state proved to be less attentive to his interests than he had hoped. Two months later Ruge was stunned to learn that his friend and fellow Privatdozent at the University of Halle, the Young Hegelian Julius Schaller, had been promoted to the position that Ruge had been so long and anxiously awaiting. While pleased for Schaller, he again felt that he had been badly treated by the government. In a letter to Schulze, he reproached the government for its insensitivity. It knew of his situation, he wrote, and, at the very least, it should have arranged for his promotion along with Schaller's. Instead Schaller's advancement seemed an implicit "condemnation" of Ruge; from the point of view of his ongoing conflict with the Pietists, the government's slight amounted to a great defeat for the Jahrbücher.[8]

Ruge was deeply hurt by what he considered the government's lack of tact, but he still sought its goodwill. In November, Altenstein granted him a private audience, during which the Minister reassured him of the state's continued belief in free discussion and free thought, of its support for the *Jahrbücher,* and of its genuine intention to promote Ruge. Altenstein hoped, however, that the Young Hegelian would in the future avoid turning theoretical disputes into personal attacks, a suggestion that Ruge agreed to follow.[9] Altenstein's admonition must have seemed particularly ironic to Ruge when he returned from Berlin in November. For he then learned that his enemies had brazenly done what he had just forsworn: twenty-three German professors denounced him in the *Leipziger Zeitung* as a "disturber of the peace." This was the signal for some contributors and subscribers to abandon the *Jahrbücher* as the magazine approached the end of its first year.

The year 1839 began with a major defeat for the Young Hegelian movement. David Friedrich Strauss had accepted a professorship at the University of Zurich, but public outrage at the hiring of this notorious "atheist" forced the University to retire the newly appointed professor shortly after he arrived. Ruge was surprised by the hostility of the Swiss to Young Hegelian theory, and he showered abuse upon them in the *Jahrbücher.*[10] Although he attributed the conservatism of the Swiss to their low level of spiritual development—a level far inferior to that of Germany[11]—his faith in the unity of reason and reality was nonetheless shaken: contrary to what he had always assumed, the general public might actually be opposed to Hegelian philosophy.

Despite Altenstein's admonishment not to confuse personalities with theoretical issues, Ruge continued to single out Leo and Hengestenberg for criticism.[12] Altenstein apparently reprimanded Ruge for violating their agreement and privately called on the Young Hegelian to stop his attacks on the Pietists. In a letter to Altenstein in May 1839 Ruge acquiesced, but he also complained of the state's ingratitude: the Minister must be aware, he wrote, of Ruge's service to the state and of his literary successes, yet the government had been unable to alter his status, to end his "humiliating and insecure situation."[13]

Ruge now apparently ceased to restrain his doubts about his ties with the state. He seemed to cultivate his injured pride, his sense of the state's infidelity, as if to prepare himself for a decisive break. Not surprisingly, his relations with the state deteriorated throughout the summer at an accelerated rate. In August, four professors at the University of Halle, including Leo and the right Hegelian Johannes Eduard Erdmann, sent an unsolicited report to Altenstein denouncing Ruge as an enemy of the university. Ruge attempted to defend himself against what he considered unjust accusations, but Altenstein apparently accepted the report and privately censured the Young Hegelian.[14]

Altenstein's support of his opponents consumed what remained of Ruge's loyalty to the existing order. He now openly despaired of it, seeing its docile surrender to his enemies. "Are there no more Steins and Hardenbergs?" he lamented to his friend, the Hegelian philosopher Karl Rosenkranz. Had Prussian statesmen given up the rational principle that has hitherto determined their history? The answer, he wrote, was yes: they did not want a "principle," but the "indeterminateness" of Romanticism.[15]

His clarified sense of betrayal, the humiliation of his lowly university position, and the attack of his enemies finally led Ruge to disentangle himself from his constricting ties with the state. In November 1839, he resigned from his position at the University of Halle. Henceforth, he wrote to Rosenkranz, philosophy would no longer be susceptible to the caprice of a fickle government and to the malice of the "mercenary" and "spiritless" movements to which it had fallen prey.[16] He would no longer have to compromise himself. The free spirit could now "take up the sword" against all its enemies.[17]

The first public declaration of Ruge's new militancy appeared in his November 1839 article "Karl Streckfuss und das Preussenthum." This critical review of a book by the Prussian bureaucrat Streckfuss gave formal expression to Ruge's frustrations and to his long-suppressed doubts about the rationality of the existing order. The Prussian state, he bluntly announced, was "hostile to reason." It was opposed to a constitution and to a free press.[18] It had followed the lead of reactionary Austria and sided with religious and political obscurantists.[19] It had abandoned philosophy.[20] By forsaking its own rational development and Protestant essence, the state had become retrograde: it had developed into the political equivalent of Catholicism.[21] Like the Roman Church, modern Prussia was organized as a hierarchy that gave only a few access to the "absolute," to political power. The rest of the population were reduced to lesser priests and laity; they were forced into subservience. Modern Prussia was thus a fractured vessel, divided into the common domain of civil society and the privileged domain of politics.[22] Such a state necessarily forfeited its world-historical significance, and cut itself off from the mainstream of history.[23]

Yet despite their unabashed tone, Ruge's criticisms were not meant to separate him irrevocably from the state. Although he was sufficiently disillusioned with the state to abuse it publicly, he could not bring himself to accept responsibility for his deed. He published the article under the pseudonym "the Württemberger" and even reinforced in a note from the editor the pseudonym's implication that the author was someone from outside both the *Jahrbücher* and Prussia.²⁴ Moreover, rather than present the article as an outright declaration of defiance—as he claimed to have done in a letter to Rosenkranz²⁵—he blandly suggested that it was intended to begin a "theoretical discussion"²⁶ of political matters, implying thereby that his quarrel with the state was largely hypothetical, a way of opening an academic debate.

These mitigating measures were not intended simply to mislead the Prussian censor, but also to serve a positive purpose: Ruge did not want to preclude a reconciliation with the state. Despite all his disappointments, he still clung to the Hegelian notion of the ideal rational state,²⁷ and even if modern Prussia was not that state now, its historical mission was still to become it.²⁸ Ruge, in short, condemned the existing state, but hoped for its reformation. He remained a Hegelian who believed that spirit would manifest itself as substance, that reality would assume a rational and harmonious form. Thus the effect of Ruge's new-found clarity about the existing state's fall from spirit was to intensify his anxiety: he had come to recognize how antagonistically irrational the state had become, but he nonetheless expected its imminent return to reason.

In the course of the following year Ruge's intense ambivalence about the Prussian state was made all the more harrowing by the fact that Prussia's political situation had become extremely uncertain. Altenstein and Frederick William III were dying. The crown prince was preparing to assume power. And while the Young Hegelians wanted to believe that the new king would serve as a patron of philosophy in the tradition of Frederick the Great,²⁹ they were also extremely suspicious of his close association with Pietists and conservatives, the enemies of philosophy.

In his correspondence Ruge gloomily reflected on the Romantics' takeover of the state:

In Prussia, the *Hegelei* [i.e., the Young Hegelians] fulfill their destiny. . . . From day to day, from moment to moment, we sink only more and more; and the turn to dumb Christianity and to the support of the aristocracy, to the dreadful, lying theology, instead of to philosophy and to the Protestant accomplishment, proceeds with giddy quickness.[30]

But in his public writings, Ruge remained careful not to exclude a possible rapprochement. He continued to follow the ambivalent stick-and-carrot policy that he had used in his Streckfuss article, vigorously criticizing the state and then downplaying his criticisms with conciliatory gestures.[31]

But regardless of his repeated efforts to publicize his complicated policy of criticism and appeasement, the new king disregarded the Young Hegelian's double message. For Frederick William IV, the voice of the *Hallische Jahrbücher* was clear: it was the voice of the enemy. Although the new king at the beginning of his reign experimented with a relaxed censorship, he singled out the *Jahrbücher* for exceptional treatment.[32] The magazine was commanded to move its press from Leipzig to Prussia in order to submit to the total control of the Prussian censor. Recognizing that such an order meant the emasculation of the *Jahrbücher* in Prussia, Ruge decided to move the magazine to Saxony, where he had received a sympathetic response to his inquiries from an important member of the Saxon government, Bernhard August von Lindenau.[33] Ruge and the *Jahrbücher* transplanted themselves in the summer of 1841 to Dresden, where the editors rechristened the paper the *Deutsche Jahrbücher für Wissenschaft und Kunst.*

Ruge identified the persecution of the *Jahrbücher* in Prussia as an important defeat for the Young Hegelian movement, but at the same time he believed that he had made an important advance in political consciousness: all his ambivalence about Prussia was at last overcome. His expectation of Prussia's imminent return to philosophy had perished under the new regime.

2

A defining element of Hegelian philosophy was its belief in the existing unity of reason with the world, in the reconciliation of all logical and historical oppositions. Emblematic of this unity was the affinity between the existing philosophy and the existing state: together they defined reason's universal presence, the unity of spirit as subject and substance.

As we have seen, when Ruge had first accepted Hegelian philosophy, he had also accepted its "present-mindedness." He believed that Hegelian theory was the necessary companion of the reformed Prussian state. But once the existing government proved that it was not the rational state but in fact the enemy of philosophy, the entire Hegelian notion of an existing rational unity was cast into doubt. Consequently, when Ruge began to criticize the Prussian state he was also naturally led to question its subjective counterpart, Hegelian philosophy. The discrediting of the existing state's claim to be the fulfillment of reason necessarily implied that the prevailing philosophy's equivalent claim was also discredited. Thus Ruge came to criticize Hegelian philosophy after 1840, although, as we shall see, his criticisms were tempered by an essential loyalty to the same philosophy.

Unlike Bruno Bauer's *Posaune*,[34] Ruge's critique of Hegel never denied the present-mindedness of Hegelian philosophy: but Ruge's changed understanding of the existing state assigned a different value to Hegel's notion of an existing rational unity. He had once regarded that notion as the great strength of Hegelian philosophy, but now he considered it to be the system's great defect, the aspect that deformed the rest of the philosophy. Hegel, Ruge asserted, distorted philosophy into a justification of the status quo. He altered logical categories to fit the shape of the existing world.[35]

Because the present had turned out to be irrational, Ruge was forced to revise Hegel's timetable. He placed reason's fulfillment in the future, and he criticized Hegel for preferring the conformist category of "is" to the critical category of a future-oriented "shall," a category that asserts that nothing is eternal, but that all must be further developed.[36] As Ruge wrote in 1840,

For Hegel the final objective is always present, the rational always actual, the immanent purpose of the absolute always attained; with his philosophy there is no objective at the end of the course, but it grasps actuality as it is, not an actuality that shall be. The philosophical or Hegelian idea is therefore, according to numerous statements and according to the entire disposition of his philosophy, "the conceived actuality," or "the actuality of the concept"; in no way, as the critic would have it, an ideal of the future, but a reality of the past or present.[37]

In an article of 1842,[38] Ruge identified the source of Hegel's fixation on the present. He considered Hegel in the context of his time. This philosopher, Ruge wrote, produced his theory in an age unfavorable to public or political life.[39] The state kept its subjects from participating in

politics. Precluded from expressing himself politically and strongly influenced by Protestant inwardness, Hegel came to the conclusion that one
could be free theoretically without being free politically. He chose to
avoid conflicts with the state so that he might carry philosophy to its
highest theoretical level.[40] But to be content with a merely theoretical
freedom required that he deny the importance of political freedom; deny,
that is, the real dissonance between philosophy and the existing world.
He therefore masked philosophy's conflict with politics by turning politics into philosophy. Through a philosophical sleight of hand he redefined
the existing irrational world as rational; he defined it as the world that
created his philosophy. The inadequacies and contradictions of history
and society were necessary, he argued, for the production of his theory.
Powerless in the world, he came to imagine himself all-powerful in
thought. He inverted in his mind the real condition of alienation, transformed it into a harmonious abstract unity.[41]

Under Ruge's critical scrutiny, Hegelian philosophy shed its privileged
status as pure and authoritative truth. It was exposed as a mental compensation for the deficiencies of Germany's political development. In com-
pensating for those inadequacies it ended up legitimizing them, conferring
on them an aspect of logical necessity. Hegelian philosophy was ideology.

Ruge's 1842 criticisms of Hegelian theory as ideology bear a striking
similarity to those of Marx in 1843 and 1844, but unlike Marx in those
years Ruge was one with Bauer in retaining a residual faith in the power
of philosophical reasoning. Even though Ruge now regarded Hegelian
philosophy's claim to autonomy and worldly authority as mere delusion
and, for the philosopher, self-delusion, he continued to want to believe
that the exercise of philosophical thought could master reality. Indeed,
like Bauer again, he asserted that the debunking of philosophy was part
of a necessary evolution. According to Ruge, Hegelian theory should
itself be treated dialectically as constantly developing. He pointed out
that despite Hegel's fantasy of reconciliation, the real world's existing
situation of division persisted. The dissonance between theory and reality
continued, and indeed intensified as the state became increasingly irrational. Hegel could only look upon the world with calm assurance of its
rationality so long as he directed his gaze at its rational features—at his
own philosophy. But the moment the world's growing irrationality broke
through this narcissistic preoccupation Hegelian philosophy became troubled, dissatisfied with its limited point of view. It thus began to struggle
against its self-enforced narrowness—it became critical of its world.[42]

Ruge believed, in other words, that Hegel's quietistic ideology inevitably fell into self-contradiction, out of which issued a purified critical theory. He attributed to Hegelian philosophy an inherent critical power: latent in Hegelian theory, he wrote, was the "Götterdämmerung of absolutism." Moreover, the development of Hegelian philosophy into critical theory was well under way. The dawning of a new era was prefigured by the establishment of radical Hegelian journals, including Ruge's own *Deutsche Jahrbücher*.[43]

Bauer, too, had insisted on Hegelian philosophy's critical potential, but his notion of the constitution or application of that potential was very different from Ruge's. Bauer found in the recesses of Hegelian theory a purified critical theory that renounced politics and society. Ruge, however, sought to show how a purified critical philosophy led to a practical political program.

At first glance, one might think that Ruge's desire to render Hegelian philosophy politically practical entailed a true overturning of Hegel's political principles. But ultimately, like his treatment of Hegel's conception of philosophy, his criticism of Hegelian political theory was ambivalent: he remained committed to idealist principles in politics. He had canceled out as ideology and then reaffirmed as critical theory his loyalty to Hegel's notion of the worldly authority of philosophy. He now attempted to cancel out his loyalty to Hegel's notion of the rational state, but then reaffirm it by showing how the notion of the rational state could be brought into phase with the radical demands of the time.

As we have seen, in the *Philosophy of Right* Hegel acknowledged the existence of free and equal egoistic individuals. Yet his acknowledgement was ambivalent: the subjective freedom of the "abstract will" was one of reason's great and necessary achievements, but it was a freedom that was rational in only the most rudimentary fashion. A creature of contingent sensuousness, of natural need and desire, the abstract will often displayed a profound hostility to the necessary and universal ways of reason. Against the social contract theories of liberals and democrats, Hegel argued that the simple bringing together of egoistic individuals did not automatically convert their capricious irrationality into reasoned and ethical behavior. On the contrary, merely thrown together, these individuals constituted a "formless mass whose commotion and activity could . . . only be elementary, irrational, barbarous, and frightful."[44]

For Hegel, the great challenge of a modern political system was to incorporate the free subject into institutions that would preserve its private interests yet counteract its irrationality and educate it in the ways of universal reason. In the *Philosophy of Right* Hegel pictured a society in which the original egoism of the individual in civil society was progressively mediated by rehabilitated traditional social and political forms (i.e., the police, corporations, and Estates) until it was transformed into an ethical and responsible will. Yet even mediated, the egoistic subject remained for Hegel extremely suspect, and he seemed to do all he could to create restraints for its potential irrationality. He granted the people's deputies no more than vaguely defined legislative powers that they shared with the monarch and a separate executive authority, while actual sovereignty was absolutely invested in the person of the hereditary monarch.

Beginning with the same general principles, Ruge inverted Hegel's reasoning. He agreed with Hegel that the state was the objective embodiment of reason, a universal political form that also incorporated the free subjective interests of individuals. But he could not understand why Hegel had so strictly circumscribed the political power of the people. To confer sovereignty solely on a hereditary monarch was an act of "pure arbitrariness." It invested in a contingent, empirical being—a product of an accident of history—all the value of a logical-metaphysical necessity; and such contrived thinking forced Hegel to produce further monstrosities of reason, such as his philosophical justification of primogeniture.[45]

For Ruge, the Hegelian principle of the rational and ethical supremacy of the self-determining self-consciousness necessarily led to the notion of the sovereignty of the people and to its corollary, popular representation.[46] If the individual self-consciousness is rational, as Hegel supposed, then an assembly of self-conscious individuals must of necessity also be rational. And because reason can never disagree with itself, one need not worry that such an assembly could be dominated by particular egoistic interests. The voice of the majority of self-conscious individuals must be the voice of truth: "In the long run, those who have knowledge (*die Wissenden*) are . . . never abandoned by the majority." "Egoism" and "malevolent capriciousness" are always possessions of the "minority."[47]

The stark opposition between Hegel's profound suspicion of the popular will and Ruge's attempt to rehabilitate the same in Hegelian terms was evident as well in their different conceptions of public opinion. For Hegel, public opinion was such a confused mixture of truth and prejudice that it was impossible to distinguish between the two. He therefore believed that the first step to achieving a rational politics was to protect it from the influence of public opinion. As the servant of this false knowledge, the press was especially deserving of scorn. While philosophy presented itself in a detached and carefully defined manner, the press reproduced subjective opinion in an immoderate and ambiguous language. The essence of the press was to distort the truth, and consequently it was at most to be suffered, controlled by the state.[48]

As a champion of the rational public, Ruge offered the converse view of public opinion. For him, the press was self-consciousness incarnate. It was the "speech of the universal spirit with itself," and consequently any external control of the press was unconscionable.[49] Indeed, as the public voice of spirit, the free press should be cultivated. It, rather than a reconstruction of traditional institutions, was the means of restoring the estranged members of civil society to the political domain.[50] Ruge thus attempted to render the Hegelian state more liberal and democratic, more susceptible to the direct participation of its citizens. Spirit would still ultimately manifest itself in a rational state, but that state would be based on the will of the general public.

Ruge's criticism of Hegel's conception of philosophy's relation to the existing world and his conception of the rational state was an attack on the overarching notion of an existing unity of spirit as subject and substance. But it is clear that the attack was an ambivalent one. His criticism of Hegelian philosophy as ideology and of the Hegelian state as insufficiently democratic betrayed, in the final analysis, a continued reliance on idealist principles. Rational spirit, Ruge believed, would triumph in the end, on the one side as critical theory, and on the other as a popular state.[51]

Commentators have noted that radical Young Hegelians, including Bauer and Ruge, sought to "fulfill" Hegelian theory, to render it more critical and practical. The result, we are told, was the overcoming of Hegelian idealism.[52] Our examination of Bauer and Ruge, however, indicates that the aim of "fulfilling" Hegel was much less straightforward than this standard view allows. Bauer and Ruge were both profoundly ambivalent about rejecting Hegelian theory. They criticized it with an eye to redeeming it. They did not so much reject Hegelian principles as give them a new valence: purified of its conformist delusion, Hegelian philosophy would release its essential negative power; it would become critical theory. The notion of a powerful critical theory continued to have at its center a Hegelian premise: that philosophical thought could raise itself above and master a contrary reality. We have already seen how

Bauer's faith in this belief, embodied in his theory of "pure criticism," left him isolated and estranged, suffering from delusions of Olympian grandeur. Ruge's more political version of critical theory did not save him from a similar fate. As we can see in his ongoing attempts to cope with political reality, he continued to experience dislocation and disorientation. Even a critical idealism remained out of phase with a changing world.

3

Ruge's writings in 1841 and 1842 on the Prussian state ostensibly recapitulated the themes of 1840—namely, Prussia's rejection of its own philosophical essence, its consequent loss of historical significance, and the separation of state from society.[53] But along with these apparent similarities, there was also an important difference in emphasis. Now that he had come to accept Prussia's deviation from spirit as something that would not immediately be overcome, he paid more attention to understanding the nature of that deviation, its origin, duration, and future. Where he had once treated Prussia's conservatism as a momentary lapse of faith, incidental to the state's true spiritual nature, he now sought to understand it as a deeply rooted historical movement, as a constitutive part of Prussian history. This shift in point of view is especially apparent in Ruge's first major article of the Deutsche Jahrbücher, "Der protestantische Absolutismus."[54]

In 1839 Ruge had conceived of Prussian history as the continuous and cumulative advance of reason, a progressive development that found its exemplary manifestation in Frederick II.[55] Two years later in "Der protestantische Absolutismus," Ruge had come to revise this view. Prussian history was now one of troubled progress and regress: a fitful advance to Frederick II, then a fitful decline to the present.

Ruge begins "Der protestantische Absolutismus" by reiterating his older view. He shows how the Prussian state since the end of the Middle Ages had evolved through more or less increasingly rational forms, culminating in the monarchy of Frederick II.[56] Frederick marked the state's highest development; he surrendered his personal egoistic existence to the rational universality of the state.[57] At this point in the article, however, Ruge abandons his former view of Prussian development and strikes new ground. He tells us that Frederick's successors failed to understand his great achievement. Instead of taking his work one step farther by formally renouncing their egoistic authority in a liberal constitution, they returned to the patrimonial notion of the state.[58] Prussia thus fell back into a lower stage of its evolution. The reforms introduced after 1806 were unable to halt the state's decline. While they had the sanguine effect of partially liberating and politicizing the Prussian people, of turning, that is, a *Spiessbürgerthum* into a potential *Staatsbürgerthum*, the reforms were prematurely choked off by the reaction that gained control after 1818. The constitution promised in 1815 went unfulfilled.[59]

Ruge further observes that the result of the struggle for hegemony between the two powerful antithetical forces of Prussian history—reason and the irrational, modernity and tradition—was the extremely fragmented political situation of present-day Prussia. Because of the rational, progressive aspects in its history, existing Prussian society, Ruge writes, "is now according to its essence fully republicanized."[60] Its members had at last reached political maturity; they were prepared to hold positions of responsibility. Yet at this same moment when the people had attained a high level of political self-awareness, the Prussian state underwent a "self-loss."[61] It turned against its own rational impulses, hardened itself against constitutionalism, and continued to treat its potential citizens as benighted subjects.[62] Though Prussian society was politically advanced, it was still governed by backward rules.[63]

The outcome of this monstrous "contradiction"[64] was to demoralize the politically alert Prussian. The would-be citizen felt himself utterly subservient to an alien authority:

The political person sees himself excluded from the state. . . . Everywhere, even where he offers his life to the universal, is he now the subject of an alien determination, on which he is not entitled to exert the slightest influence.[65]

This estrangement from the state induced apathy and brought about a return to the "egoistic and limited standpoint of the Spiessbürger."[66] The people came to accept their own inability, their own "self-contempt and cowardice," while the once liberal, reforming bureaucracy became increasingly reconciled to its servility. The political struggle was consequently sublimated into conflicts within areas that lay beyond and below politics: the abstract realm of philosophical idealism and the crass underworld of economic materialism.[67]

Ruge's analysis of the tensions and paradoxes of Prussia's history and its social and political structure in the Vormärz at first seems remarkably cogent and bears striking resemblances to some of the more sophisticated views of recent historians.[68] It discusses the historic separation of state and society, the latter's demand in the eighteenth century for reentry into the public domain, and the collapse of its hopes for popular political participation in the early nineteenth century. Moreover, Ruge suggests that the failure to bring about a reunification of politics and society was linked to the subsequent generation of a rarefied philosophy and the intensified economic activity of civil society.

But as one investigates Ruge's analysis more closely, one finds that its perceptive views of Prussian conditions is accompanied by many confusions. In particular, he seems to have difficulty coherently discussing the forces of tradition. He refers on one occasion to the "antiquated form of state" as "historically overcome," indicating its enfeeblement.[69] But he then proceeds to speak of its vigorous success at thwarting the realization of a constitution in Prussia, implying tradition's continued vitality.[70] Earlier in the article, he expresses the same kind of confusion about the vigor and persistence of the old when he tells us that the revolution of reason has already been spiritually accomplished yet has also been externally suppressed.[71] Such a statement indicates that the modern spirit has triumphed in one sphere but, inexplicably, has been defeated in another.

Both the astute perceptiveness and the disorienting inconsistencies of Ruge's article stem from his continued adherence to Hegelian principles. As we have seen, Hegelian philosophy asserts the steady, cumulative rise of spirit to the present. Although this rise is propelled by conflicts and contradictions, those oppositions are always productive, issuing in the existence of spirit as subject and substance.

But in Ruge's time, although spirit had indeed found its highest subjective form—at first in Hegelian philosophy and then, mutatis mutandis, in a modified, critical Hegelianism—it had failed to evolve a suitable objective counterpart. Far from steadily advancing to higher forms of rationality, the Prussian state had become increasingly retrograde, and it had allowed itself to be taken over by irrational Romanticism.

Ruge in 1841 still wanted to believe in an essentially Hegelian idealism, in spirit's ineluctable advance through history and logic to its fulfillment in his own time, but he was realistic enough to recognize that such a fulfillment had occurred only in philosophy, in himself and not in the world. His philosophy rendered him in this sense superbly realistic; the ideal of the general rational unity of the present made him sensitive to how perversely irrational the existing external world had actually become. He thus came to characterize so perceptively modern Prussia's paradoxes and tensions. Yet at the same time that his continued adherence to Hegel's belief in an existing rational unity enhanced his awareness of the dissonances in Prussia's past and present, it also prevented him from attaining a complete understanding of the enduring and in some ways resurgent power of Prussia's traditional and irrational tendencies. Because he still believed in spirit's necessary and imminent triumph in theory and practice, he could not quite bring himself to admit explicitly to the tenacity of regressive elements in Prussian history. To say that they were at present intractable and not about to be superseded would be to acknowledge the successful suppression of spirit by morally and rationally inferior forces. Ruge was able to recognize the presence of the old, but unable to acknowledge that it was still a vital, integral part of modern Prussia. For him, tradition and the irrational could not ultimately belong to the present. Their existence was strictly anomalous, incidental, and, he hoped, transitory.

Because he could see the powerful presence of traditional forces in modern Prussia while being blind to exactly how powerful and enduring they truly were, he had to settle for a partial understanding of modern Prussia: a recognition of its existing dissonances, but not an understanding of how they came about. His conception of history in 1841 was oddly schizophrenic, almost incoherent in its inability to follow consistent analytic principles. He considered Prussian history up to Frederick II to be determined by the necessary internal unfolding of spirit. But after Frederick, Prussia inexplicably lost its inner drive toward the fulfillment of reason. Instead, its history was now conditioned by accidental, external, and particular events (e.g., Prussia's defeat by Napoleon) or by the egoistic caprice of its rulers (Frederick William II's policy of religious intolerance; Frederick William III's failure to fulfill his constitutional promise).[72]

One can sense that Ruge felt considerable tension in trying to hold together the incompatible elements of a residual Hegelian idealism and a realistic view of existing politics that contradicted that philosophy. The only way he could live with these contrary states of mind was to insist on their imminent resolution, on the soon-to-be reconciliation of philosophy and political reality. In "Der protestantische Absolutismus," he points to signs of an escalation in reason's struggle against the reaction and the consequent greater likelihood of revolution.[73] To support this prognosis, he mentions the radicalization of philosophy and the renewal of political discussion and public life in Germany.[74] But even Ruge's expectation of an imminent reconciliation of existing conflicts proves to be unstable. These optimistic portents of a political resurgence in Germany are forgotten only a few pages later when he gives us a fresh assessment of the vitality of the Spiessbürger consciousness, of the unabating fear of change which brought the Romantics to power.[75]

In 1841, Ruge experienced a rebirth of his youthful opposition between idealism and realism, although it now appeared in the more sophisticated form of a conflict between radical Hegelian theory and political reality. As the latter continued to be resistant to theory, Ruge began to suffer from a troubling uncertainty about spirit's imminent fulfillment. Beneath his hope for an emerging revolution in the cause of reason arose the dark fear that the state was forever lost to spirit.

Throughout his stay in Saxony, Ruge faced problems within the *Jahrbücher* and without. He could not maintain discipline in the Young Hegelian ranks. Not all these philosophers cared for the increasingly politically radical tone of the *Jahrbücher* and after the magazine declared itself openly against God, country, and Hegel (or at least aspects of Hegelian theory), some contributors left. The most notable loss was David Friedrich Strauss, who with his followers established a nonpolitical organ of Young Hegelian philosophy in Tübingen.[76]

Soon after these desertions, Ruge began to encounter difficulties with his new patron, the Saxon state. In December 1841, the *Jahrbücher's* Leipzig censor Professor W. Wachsmuth, who was sympathetic to much of the magazine's rationalistic liberalism, cautioned Ruge about arousing the ill-will of the government.[77] But this friendly warning went unheeded. Early the following year, Wachsmuth's superiors ordered Ruge to tone down the magazine's religious and political criticism and reprimanded Wachsmuth for not being strict enough in his censorship.[78] The rest of 1842 witnessed a steady deterioration of relations. Both Ruge and the government stiffened in their opposing positions, with the unfortunate Wachsmuth caught in between.[79]

Saxony's new policy of more severely censoring the *Jahrbücher* disabused Ruge of his belief in the Saxon state's benevolent rationality. He now recognized that it was as benighted as Prussia. The same inverted relation between philosophy and the state obtained: a rational philosophy was governed by an arbitrary, irrational power. "No law," Ruge wrote in an angry letter to the Dresden censorship college, "but the pure arbitrariness and the subjective standard of the censor of the college strikes out the most important and worthwhile discussions."[80]

Ruge's disenchantment with the Saxon state intensified his radicalism in two ways. First, he now shed his good opinion of Protestantism and assumed instead Bruno Bauer's iconoclastic view of religion as absolute, unredeemable alienation, although, just as with Feuerbach's humanism, Ruge gave Bauer's atheism a political meaning. At the end of 1843 in "Der christliche Staat," Ruge announced his complete abandonment of pro-Protestant radicalism and his ascension to a higher state of religious cynicism. In this article he renounced outright his earlier view: the Württemberger of the 1839 Streckfuss article, he said, was wrong to think of Protestantism as the realization of freedom. It was in fact no better than Catholicism. Both were instruments of oppression and mystification. They turned human attributes into divine entities, rendered the concrete abstract, and diverted human beings from the real political world.[81] If one were to distinguish between these two types of Christianity one would have to say that Protestantism, far from being superior to Catholicism, was even more perniciously depoliticizing, for Protestantism glorified the inner self and in so doing made the self accepting of the external world as it was.[82]

The second way Ruge's radicalism deepened during his years in Saxony was his eventual open acceptance of democratic and republican principles. As we have seen, in contrast to Hegel, Ruge had identified reason with the popular will. His belief in popular sovereignty and representation clearly expressed a shift toward democratic and republican politics, but from the beginning of 1840 to the end of 1842, he did not fully or openly embrace those principles. In early 1840, after his first criticisms of the Prussian state and Hegelian conformism, he still hoped for a reconciliation with the Prussian state. He continued to believe in the possibility of a reformed constitutional monarchy, even if he never specified in detail how such a state could be organized in accordance with the principles of popular sovereignty.[83] With the suppression of the *Hallische Jahrbücher* in 1841, he still did not lose faith in the ideal of a constitutional monarchy, but transferred his hopes for its fulfillment from Prussia to Saxony.

Thus, although his criticism of Hegelian political theory after 1840 implied a position that was compatible only with a republican and democratic constitution, he continued to seek in practice the patronage of the German monarchies. For this reason, his radical political tendencies never found full expression in calls for a democratic republic, but were instead dispersed into demands concerning secondary institutions (more press freedom, trial by jury).[84] Only when he fell into conflict with Saxony as well as with Prussia did he at last give his radicalism free rein. After announcing his absolute rejection of all Christianity at the end of 1842, he also proclaimed in the beginning of 1843 his absolute rejection of monarchical government.[85] For the first time, he separated himself from the moderate, conciliatory liberalism of most German reformers and identified himself as a democrat and a republican. He called for the "dissolution of liberalism into democracy."[86]

The response of Prussia and Saxony to philosophy's new radicalism was to rid itself of philosophy altogether. In early 1843 the Prussian government suppressed Marx's *Rheinische Zeitung*, the other principal organ of politically radical Young Hegelianism.[87] At the same time, Ruge's conflicts with the Saxon state came to a head. In 1838 the government had allowed the *Jahrbücher* to publish in Saxony without a concession. In 1842 it had forced a concession on the magazine. In early January 1843, accusing the magazine of being irreligious and subversive, it revoked the concession, and the police confiscated some of the *Jahrbücher's* January issues.[88]

Hoping to circumvent the government, Ruge appealed to the Saxon Landtag for a reprieve, but to his great disappointment, the Landtag not only denied his request but praised the government for condemning the organ of radical Young Hegelianism. Soon afterwards, the magazine was permanently closed, its property confiscated, and its editor forbidden to establish another periodical in Saxony for five years.[89]

Ruge had expected to suffer injustice at the hands of the government, but he was surprised by the utter lack of support of the Saxon people, either in the Landtag or at large. He was now completely disillusioned with the political spirit of the German people. "They [the Germans]," Ruge wrote bitterly to Marx, "have . . . perished historically." "The German spirit, as far as it has appeared, is base."[90]

His bitterness blended with a sense of shame and despair. To have believed so long in the spirit of Germany was to have deceived himself over and over again:

It is cowardly enough, that no man in Germany protests and that all wait timidly for the future. I loathe this development—that . . . the old, rigid despotism always has the last laugh [*das Ende vom Liede*]. One acts therein like an ass, which another rides; but one is even stupider than it, for it suffers from no illusions that it will be again rescued.

The experiences of the previous five years left him with one damning conclusion about his people: "We are a nation of dogs."[91]
    Politically blocked in Prussia and Saxony and devoid of all hope for German politics, Ruge prepared to leave the country. As an alternative to Germany he naturally looked to Paris, the birthplace of the Great Revolution. There he hoped to find a truly public society, one receptive to political and philosophical discussion. With Marx, whom he planned to meet in Paris, Ruge thus took radical Hegelian philosophy into exile.

4

Ruge's arrival in Paris during the late summer of 1843 restored his political hopes. Like many other exiled German radicals, he saw in Paris the active political life that was so sorely lacking in Germany. For Ruge, France was the fountainhead of revolutionary impulses, the political nation par excellence. While Germany failed to give political significance to its philosophy, the French, he wrote soon after arriving in Paris, turned their theories into practical politics.[92] He thought that he had found in this political people the solution to Germany's political backwardness and philosophy's isolation. A collaboration with the French would reconnect Young Hegelian theory to political reality, provide it with a practical power that it hitherto lacked. German "philosophy," Rugè wrote, "will not become a power, until it steps forth into Paris and with the French spirit."[93]
    With these hopes and aims in mind, Ruge immediately plunged himself into the whirl of French politics. He attended a variety of political meetings. He met many of Paris's political luminaries—Alphonse de Lamartine, Flora Tristan, Victor Considèrant, Etienne Cabet, and Theodore Dézamy.[94] He read the works of Proudhon and wrote an introduction for the German translation of Louis Blanc's *The History of Ten Years, 1830–1840.*[95]
    During these first months of hectic activity, Ruge continued to be immensely pleased by the enormous difference between French energy and German apathy in politics; but he was not so dazzled as to become blind to all criticism of the French. On the contrary, two doubts about

them began to intrude on his mind. First, he began to suspect that the French might be *too* political, too enthusiastic for political organization and debate. Their diverse political parties seemed to Ruge to be so willfully sectarian that a unified political movement was almost impossible to achieve.[96] Second, Ruge became aware of the religious beliefs of the French radicals. When he had first arrived in Paris he had thought that as the children of the Enlightenment its radicals were equally adept in theory and politics. But after meeting them, he revised his opinion of French philosophy. He learned that even the most extreme of the French radicals, the communists, had not yet begun to question the superstitions that German radicals had already abandoned. The French were, in a word, still religious.[97]

Upon closer scrutiny of conditions in Paris, Ruge found that the relation between theory and politics in France was the opposite of that in Germany. The Germans were philosophically advanced but politically backward. The French were politically advanced but philosophically backward. The discovery of this asymmetry on the French left did not at this time trouble Ruge. On the contrary, it reinforced his belief in the necessity of a union between the two nations. Where he had earlier envisioned a unidirectional relationship in which the French would teach politics to the Germans, he now conceived of a reciprocal relationship in which the Germans would teach the French philosophy in return for learning about politics.[98]

Ruge's faith in the French as the answer to German inadequacies thus emerged intact from his initial critical reassessment of French politics. He believed more than ever that the Germans and the French were destined to be partners in spirit's realization. But both the French and the Germans proved recalcitrant. The French disliked the philosophical atheism of the Germans, and the German exiles in Paris succumbed to the French vice of sectarian fragmentation. They remained disorganized, politically isolated from each other.[99]

These circumstances predetermined the failure of Ruge's and Marx's collaborative project, the *Deutsch-Französische Jahrbücher*. This magazine was to be the keystone of a general French-German alliance, but the sole issue of the magazine, which appeared in 1844, was in tone and substance exclusively German. Moreover, to Ruge's disappointment, it even failed to be comprehensively German, to represent the entire community of German exiles in Paris. Although its contributors included some of the most illustrious German radicals, such as Marx, Heinrich

Heine, and Moses Hess, they were predominantly of one political persua-
sion—communism.

The failure of the magazine to create an alliance of French and German
radicals was brought home to Ruge with jarring force by the French
reception of the new publication. Intended to be the first link joining the
two nations, the magazine had instead the paradoxical effect of alienating
the French from the Germans. The first issue of the *Jahrbücher* elicited
only hostility from French radicals. In newspaper reviews, the prominent
radicals Lamennais and Louis Blanc—men who Ruge had hoped would
have become his allies—blasted the magazine for its godless philosophy.[100]
Ruge became in consequence annoyed with the stubborn superstitions of
France's political avant garde. Their religiosity proved, he wrote, that the
French had made a great leap backward in the history of spirit; they had
abandoned the heritage of the Enlightenment for the "muddy emotion"
of Romanticism.[101]

This falling-out with the French did not have, as one might have
expected, the compensatory effect of drawing Ruge closer to the Germans. On the contrary, the publication of the *Jahrbücher* had the further
paradoxical result of estranging Ruge from other German exiles. Against
his wishes, the magazine had been commandeered by the philosophical
communists grouped around Marx. Their takeover of the *Jahrbücher*
reinforced Ruge's negative opinion of the communists and mass society.

Before he had come to Paris, Ruge had displayed his unease in dealing
with the emerging mass of socially dispossessed. In an article of 1842, he
acknowledged the tendency to identify as part of that group outcast
intellectual journalists such as himself. The disinherited philosophers also
appeared to be troublemakers at the fringe of society. But after recognizing this apparent affinity between the uprooted intellectual and the uprooted poor, Ruge then did his best to separate the former from the latter.
Philosophical journalists, he said, were essentially concerned with the
"ideal interests of politics," and once their quarrel with the existing unfree
state reached a head, once political life was rejuvenated by their exertions,
they would be recognized for what they truly were: agents of human and
political liberation. They would then cease to be seen as "bourgeois
proletarians."[102] The implication of Ruge's strenuous maneuver to separate outcast intellectuals from dispossessed "proletarians" was that the
latter were unpolitical and unfree; they had no conception of the "ideal
interests of politics." Proletarians, Ruge seems to be telling us, are incapable of rational political thought and behavior. Ruge thus continued to

adhere to an essential principle of Hegelian politics: only those removed from the brutalizing sensuousness of civil society are suited to political participation. While still in Germany, he therefore showed little interest in or sympathy for the political movements associated with the new dispossessed.[103]

But after he left Germany for France he was forced to reassess the emerging socialist and communist movements. Variants of those movements were strongly influential in the Parisian radical groups that he sought as allies. Thus once in Paris he summoned up a sympathetic if occasionally condescending interest in socialist ideas, especially those of the Fourierists.[104] He was pleasantly amused by their exuberant style and theatrical rhetoric.[105] But as he came to know the socialists better and tried to collaborate with the German communists, he returned to his negative estimation of them; he found both difficult to work with. He felt uneasy with their working-class supporters, who he thought were lacking in cultivation, and he disagreed with the communists about political tactics and aims. Communists were preoccupied with the social question and sought a social solution, the establishment of a communal society. Ruge, however, believed that sensuous mass society could not solve its problems on its own. Lasting social reform, he thought, required prior political reform. Social inequality would be mitigated by a political constitution guaranteeing equal rights. Against the importance that communists ascribed to social matters, Ruge asserted the primacy of extrasocial political concerns. Human fulfillment was not to be found in a community of material goods, but in a rational state of equal individuals.[106]

By the time of the publication of the *Deutsch-Französische Jahrbücher* Ruge had worked up considerable hostility against the communists. With the collapse of the magazine he gave vent to his feelings. Those features that he had once regarded as amusing and innocent quirks of personalities he now considered the intellectual and psychological vices that defined the essence of communism. He scorned the communists for their simpleminded belief that a single blow would change the world.[107] Even more, he feared and condemned their fanaticism. With its proselytizing zeal, its mystical formulas, and its militant chiliasm, communism resembled a religion, and therefore Ruge damned it with the worst epithet he could muster: it was like Christianity.[108]

The German exiles' turn to communism ultimately appeared to Ruge to be yet another manifestation of the characteristic vice of the German spirit: its weakness for abstract thinking, its tendency to create theoretical systems hopelessly divorced from political reality.[109] German communists placed their faith in mass society, and then to justify that faith generated false images of that society's future realization.

Politics was Ruge's measure of a healthy private and public spirit. He had condemned first Prussia then all of Germany for being deaf to the call of politics. Shortly before arriving in Paris, he had broken with Bauer and his Berlin coterie because of their turn to the bohemian, isolationist, and above all antipolitical theory of pure criticism.[110] Now, after the unsatisfactory publication of the *Deutsch-Französische Jahrbücher*, Ruge separated himself from Marx and his friends because of their communism, their elevation of social over political questions.[111] Along with financial difficulties, this separation led to the demise in March 1844 of the short-lived magazine. Ruge, estranged from both French radicals and German exiles, then gave up public life, devoting himself instead to reflecting and writing on German philosophy and his Paris experiences.[112] His belief in the primacy of the political had the ironic effect of driving him from political activity into a contemplative existence, although he soon found himself drawn back into politics because of new troubles with the authorities.

The strident criticism of *Vorwärts!*, a predominantly German communist newspaper published by German exiles in Paris, had bothered the Prussian authorities enough for them to pressure the Guizot government to purge Paris of its German radicals. In January 1845 the French government ordered the ejection of some prominent German exiles from Paris, including Marx and Ruge. As well as protesting the government's lumping of him with the communists, Ruge tried to convince the authorities that he was not a political troublemaker. Pointing to his voluntary inactivity of the previous few months, he appealed for permission to stay, and with the eventual support of some French newspapers he received a reprieve from the Prefect of Police.[113]

During and after this brief flurry of reinvolvement in politics, Ruge composed a lengthy essay on the last ten years of German philosophy, "Unsre letzten zehn Jahre."[114] This is the most sustained and complex piece of philosophical analysis to come out of his otherwise unproductive stay in Paris. It is also notable for its intensely self-reflective point of view. Ruge attempts in this essay to evaluate the origin, progress, and future of Young Hegelian theory. He undertakes a kind of self-assessment.

As we have seen, Ruge had come in 1843 to regard Protestantism as a worse spiritual evil than Catholicism. Both were conditions of alienation but the former in particular directed the human spirit inward, away from external political reality. It enhanced man's private self, but only by diminishing his public self, by depriving him of a political existence.[115]

In "Unsre letzten zehn Jahre," Ruge gives German Protestantism all the significance of original sin: its occurrence had resulted in man's loss of wholeness. "German [Protestantism]," Ruge writes, "has given to the princes and others of eminence the entire visible world to secularize and satisfied itself with the invisible church; it has surrendered public life for all eternity, and reconciled itself to private life and to the eternal duration of its wretchedness."[116]

This inward drive of German Protestantism determined the nature and evolution of German philosophy. With the exception of the ultimately unsuccessful Enlightenment, German philosophy had forsworn politics, contenting itself instead with pure theory. This detachment from reality had in one respect the paradoxical result of binding philosophy to reality. By becoming unconcerned with politics, philosophy implicitly accepted whatever the politics of the day had to offer.

The high point of the evolution of Protestant inwardness was Hegelian philosophy. Hegel systematized all spiritual development up to himself. He codified all forms of inwardness before him, working them into a single all-embracing synthesis.[117] By asserting that the working out of this synthesis in one's mind was the highest form of freedom, Hegel reconciled himself to the existing world. He was satisfied with a purely "philosophical freedom,"[118] and left matters of state in the hands of the authorities.[119]

Because Hegel had developed inwardness into its most complete form—Ruge calls his philosophy the "close of Protestantism"—his immediate successors, the orthodox Hegelians, could do no more than broaden and repeat his views. At this juncture, then, the development of Protestant inwardness reached a crisis. The essence of Protestantism was to press ever more inward to assume increasingly abstract and introspective forms, yet with Hegel the most complete form of inwardness had been reached. Consequently, the ongoing Protestant drive toward its own interior was blocked, deflected on itself. Henceforth Protestant inwardness had to turn against itself. Abstract theory, unable to expand further into greater and greater syntheses, reacted on itself, became critical of itself:

Every finished system speaks out its own judgement of death. It is always the end of its world. As Aristotle concluded the Greek, so concludes Hegel the Christian world. What now follows can only be dissolution—criticism.[120]

Thus within Hegelian philosophy's most conservative domain, theology, there arose Hegelian critics of Hegelian philosophy.[121] These heretics within the movement, the Young Hegelians, found in Hegel's philosophy a set of critical principles that they used against the abstract theorizing and the implicit political quietism of the same philosophy.[122] From its initial emergence, the Young Hegelian movement passed quickly through increasingly radical phases: from Strauss to Bauer and from Bauer to Feuerbach, philosophy was steadily demystified; its religious, alienated nature relentlessly unmasked. But this movement was not merely negative or critical; it was also productive: it directed philosophy back to the real world. Feuerbach in particular marked a turning point in philosophy's development; he showed the way out of abstract thinking to the world of man. He transformed the abstractions of religion and philosophy into the activities of concrete humanity and therefore made humanity, rather than God or spirit, the source and standard of all values.[123] This new philosophy of humanism signaled the beginning of a political revolution, the end of the disjuncture between private and public life:

The necessary consequence of a criticism that makes humanity the principle of the intellectual and ethical world is the overcoming [*Aufhebung*] of this duality between the life of the state and human life; the politicization of all humanity . . . and the humanization of the state—each is the purpose of the state.[124]

The agent of this new politicized philosophy was the *Hallische and Deutsche Jahrbücher*. That magazine had originated as a forum for Protestantism and Prussia, but once it fell into conflict with the Romanticism that had taken over the state it assumed the higher consciousness of political humanism. Yet even though the magazine was now imbued with this new philosophy, it did not at first give up hope for the Prussian state's return to reason. It tried to win the state back from the Romantics, but in this it failed, and indeed, acknowledged that it had to fail, for it could not restore to Prussia something it never had. The Prussian state, it recognized, was Protestant and therefore by nature inaccessible to reason, averse to losing its monopoly on politics.[125] Thus philosophy's defeat at the hands of Protestant Prussia gave the *Jahrbücher* a new clarity: philosophy abandoned its illusions; it renounced the false idols of Protestantism and monarchism. Consequently the *Jahrbücher*, now in Saxony, finally came to embrace reason's proper political ethos: democracy. But philosophy's demand for the return of man's public or political being brought upon it the wrath of the old powers. Radical Young Hegelianism was driven out of Saxony, forced to emigrate.[126]

In Paris, Young Hegelian philosophy sought to realize its new political clarity by allying itself with the politically active French. But its attempt at collaboration, the *Deutsch-Französische Jahrbücher*, was a complete failure. Nonetheless, Ruge adds, the assimilation of French elements into German philosophy through the founding of a foreign press remained a "logical and historical necessity."[127]

While Young Hegelian theory in France worked to establish a union with the French, philosophy in Germany continued to develop—but now even more convulsively than before. It progressed, Ruge writes, as a succession of "pronunciamentos"[128] in which each new Hegelian philosopher denounced all those who came before him. The latest of these philosophical coups was Max Stirner's *Der Einzige und sein Eigentum* (The Unique One and His Property, 1844). In this book, Stirner presented a philosophy of sensuous egoism. The individual sensuous ego, he asserted, was the true reality, and all abstract notions of human essence—be it spirit or species—were illusions that were meant to conceal from the ego its sensuous uniqueness.[129] Stirner thus criticized the recent abstract theories of German philosophy that postulated a human essence. Hegel, Bauer, Feuerbach, and the socialists were all condemned for robbing the sensuous egoist of freedom.[130]

As a firm upholder of philosophical essences, Ruge did not of course agree with Stirner's radical nominalism. Yet he granted Stirner's philosophy a momentous historical significance. It represented, he believed, the absolute decadence of German philosophy, its last and most depraved form.[131] Ruge recognized that Stirner's book used distinctively Hegelian and Young Hegelian methods. It had for instance a dialectical argument and its key principle was the notion of alienation. But Stirner used Hegelian techniques in order to subvert Hegelian philosophy. He denied any validity to rational and universal—that is, to all philosophical—categories. He elevated in their place the utter capriciousness of the individual's sensuous needs and desires. Willfulness, inconstancy, and selfishness—these were the ruling principles of his philosophy or, more accurately, of his antiphilosophy.[132]

Despite Stirner's slaughter of all previous forms of Hegelian theory and his claim to have transcended them, Ruge believed that Stirner's philosophy was itself another product of the same German tendency it had sought to deny—the tendency to supplant concrete reality with abstract thought. Stirner attacked pure philosophy, but on its own ground. He hated theory, but in theoretical terms. His creed of irrational selfish egoism was, in the last analysis, just another exercise in abstract thinking. Absolute egoism was itself divorced from reality, impossible to realize in the actual world of historical and physical constraints.

But for precisely this reason Stirner's book was of the greatest importance. By annihilating all abstract forms of philosophy, yet failing to connect itself to the real world, Stirner's *Einzige* announced the end of pure theory. Stirner was the last instance of abstract thinking. Philosophy would henceforth have no other choice than to proceed outward. Without other alternatives, it would have to follow the path of those Young Hegelians in France, the path to political practice.[133]

"Unsre letzten zehn Jahre," Ruge's recapitulation of the crisis of Hegelian theory, contains the themes of his earlier writings. Religion and philosophy were forms of ideology: they were systems of abstract thought that compensated for and justified a miserable world. Hegelian theory was the most accomplished, systematic form of ideology, but as such it signaled the end of one condition and the beginning of a new one. As Ruge had argued before, philosophy necessarily transformed itself into critical theory, and emblematic of that transformation was the emergence of radical Young Hegelianism.

Earlier Ruge had marked this turning of Hegelian theory to reality by pointing to the Young Hegelians' conflicts with the Prussian state and the establishment of radical journals such as the *Hallische* and *Deutsche Jahrbücher*. Ruge's analysis in "Unsre letzten zehn Jahre" incorporated as well his recent experiences in France and the conflicts between Young Hegelians. Like Bauer and Marx, he was deeply affected by the internecine warfare in the Young Hegelian movement. With these others, he interpreted it as a sign of the decadence of German Idealism, of philosophy's rapid, fitful decline. But he gave his interpretation a unique twist: he conferred on this negative, fratricidal conflict among Young Hegelians a positive value. That conflict was necessary, he argued, to purge philosophy of its residual abstractness, to cure it of its aversion to reality. Ruge thus turned the debilitating disputes among Young Hegelians into a necessary and productive philosophical progress.

Yet if we view this essay from the larger context of Ruge's immediate political situation, this same message sounds remarkably hollow. He composed this essay when his experiences in Parisian politics had proved the converse of the essay's sanguine theme; philosophy had just shown itself once more to be unsuitable for politics. Ruge's attempt to turn theory into practice in the founding of the *Deutsche-Französische Jahrbücher* had failed miserably, earning from the French nothing but scorn for the magazine's atheistic German philosophy. Moreover, Ruge had become alienated from the most politically active of the Germans in Paris, the communists, and he also knew that Germany itself remained hostile to Young Hegelian theory. He feared he would be arrested if the French government forced him to return there.

An honest appraisal of these circumstances is notably missing in Ruge's essay. The only mention of them is an admission of the fiasco of the *Deutsche-Französische Jahrbücher,* and even in that reference, he pays the event scant attention, hurrying instead to other matters.[134] As an attempt to demonstrate the end of abstraction in philosophy and its inevitable turn to political practice, Ruge's essay is itself surprisingly abstract. It is guilty of the same German vice that it condemns: it compensates in theory for a bad reality. It converts his own political failures and the disarray of radical Hegelianism into prefigurations of impending victory.

The loss of spirit's unity with the present had left the Prussian Young Hegelians with a sense of dislocation from their world and their history. In their views of modern Prussia, paradox and contradiction came to prevail where formerly there had been coherence and uniformity. These philosophers struggled to regain a wholeness with their time. In their efforts to reunite themselves with the world, they also sought to distance themselves from the abstract philosophy that was so detached from it. This sensitive aversion to excessively abstract philosophy produced a chain reaction of Young Hegelian writings. Each Young Hegelian sought to condemn all idealist philosophy before him and to pronounce at the same time his own return to reality. This syndrome of combining intense criticism of one's own philosophical tradition and immediate milieu with an equally intense longing for reality assumed the aspects of an obsession. Over and over again and with ever-increasing ferocity each accused the others of being excessively abstract and protested his own innocence of the same vice. But what made this syndrome appear almost pathological was that each new polemic only seemed to recapitulate the same philosophical error it was trying to overcome—extravagant abstractness. Each philosopher's supposed cure turned out in almost all cases to be yet another symptom of the same disease.

To complicate still further this analysis of Ruge's particular state of mind, one can also say that he was not altogether unaware of his own self-defeating abstract attempt to go beyond abstraction. Even though he claimed to have superseded abstract philosophy, he seemed to suffer at the same time from the nagging fear that reality remained implacably hostile. Thus rather than simply living in the illusion of spirit's imminent return to the world, he would instead oscillate violently between an unreasonable expectation of spirit's triumph and an absolute despair in its defeat. During 1845 in Paris and then throughout 1846 when he had moved to Switzerland, Ruge displayed this kind of schizophrenia. His expectation of a happy turn of events manifested itself in such writings as "Unsre letzten zehn Jahre," while in his gloomier moments he could proclaim with finality that "a direct political effectiveness is not possible in Germany. . . . Prussia has already perished . . . and it is not to be misunderstood that the people have neither the intelligence nor the courage to tear themselves out of this desperate situation of [being] an absolute nullity."[135]

Ruge suffered from an extreme, nerve-wracking ambivalence. The events of 1847 and 1848 would free him from his oscillations and buoy up his hopes; but the ultimate results of the 1848 Revolution would confirm his darkest fears.

5

In early 1847, Ruge moved back to Leipzig where he finished editing his collected works. The quiet of his academic labors lasted until April 1847, when the opening of the United Landtag in Berlin rekindled his hopes for political change. "It is a revolution," he wrote to the philosopher Kuno Fischer. "It is the rebirth of the most progressive epoch and the most glorious victory over the reaction."[136] Less than a year later, this initial impression was reassuringly confirmed by the events of spring 1848. The revolutions in Paris and Berlin left Ruge ecstatic: his expectation of philosophy's fulfillment was at last vindicated. History has decreed, Ruge said in a speech in July 1848, that the Germans have the unique honor of being the people "which has consistently furthered philosophy and brought forth the blossoming of pure, free, accomplished, liberated philosophy."[137]

For the first time in several years Ruge felt at one with his time. The Revolution restored a sense of wholeness with society and history, inspiring him to engage once again in political activity. He traveled throughout Germany and established a network of connections with other democrats. In Leipzig and Berlin he started *Die Reform*, an organ of democratic politics.[138] In April 1848, with the support of some of the extreme left in Leipzig, he tried to run for a seat in the Frankfurt Parliament, but he was outmaneuvered by the more tactful, if no less radical, Robert Blum.[139] But Ruge was not destined to be excluded from the center of political action. With the aid of Bakunin, he was elected by the Breslau constituency to Germany's new National Assembly.

While not a major leader of the left wing at Frankfurt, he was nonetheless one of that faction's more prominent members. According to his biographer, Ruge composed its manifesto of 26 May 1848, a tract that called for popular sovereignty, a republican constitution, and a centralized state.[140] Such a program was naturally at odds with the objectives of the political moderates who dominated the Assembly. These less radical members of the Assembly wanted to preserve some continuity with Germany's dynastic and particularist traditions, advocating therefore a federalist constitutional monarchy for a united Germany.

The first major clash in the National Assembly between radicals and moderates concerned the issue of establishing a provisional central authority. Both sides agreed on the need to have one, but then disagreed on what kind to have. "The Left," writes the historian Frank Eyck, "wanted an authority exclusively elected by and subservient to the assembly, the moderates a power nominated—at least in the first instance—by the governments, accountable to the assembly, but not its slave."[141] In other words, the dispute between the two groups was over the nature of the central authority's responsibility. The radicals sought what would amount to a republican president who was directly responsible to parliament. The moderates hoped to establish an "irresponsible" authority with responsible ministers, an authority that would allow for a monarchical head of state.[142]

On 24 June 1848 Ruge argued passionately, if turgidly, in the Assembly for a republican president, a head of state who would make manifest the new spirit of the time, who would embody the Revolution's principle of popular sovereignty. He called the alternative of the moderates—to invest executive and legislative power in a hereditary monarch—"high treason." Such an institution, Ruge said, "would be a blow against the very sensitive thoughts and feelings of the German nation, it would be a blow against the idea of the time, against the impulse of the century, against the principle in whose name we are here assembled."[143]

Ruge's words did not find a receptive audience. The majority of the Assembly voted to establish a *Reichsverweser* (regent of the empire) who would not be responsible to parliament.[144] Just as Ruge feared, this new position was given to a dynastic figure, the Archduke John of Austria.

This defeat of German democracy disabused Ruge of his belief in the Assembly's revolutionary potential. In 1849, reflecting on the appointment of a Reichsverweser and the later monarchical constitution that it foreshadowed, he remarked on the confused and self-defeating mentality that prevailed in the Assembly, a state of mind that wanted "a freedom and a unity" that was "at the same time neither freedom nor unity."[145]

Ruge's estrangement from the Assembly deepened in the following month when he became entangled in the dispute over the status of Germany's Polish territories. The Polish population of Prussian Posen sought to reunite that territory with other Polish lands in a reconstituted and independent Poland. The radicals supported Polish aspirations and called on the Assembly to allow Posen to secede from Prussia and Germany. But the moderates, more affected by German nationalism yet not entirely callous to Polish ambitions, preferred to break up Posen and incorporate into a united Germany those areas that were predominantly German in population.[146]

As a radical and a representative of Breslau, which contained a large Polish population, Ruge felt himself doubly involved in this controversy. In the debates of late July he tried to convert the nationalist Assembly to a modern cosmopolitanism. Germany's revolutionary claim to freedom and unity was derived, he said, from the larger principle of the free self-determination of all peoples. This was a principle that provided not only for Germany's independence but also for that of other nationalities. Thus once Germans had embraced this principle, consistency demanded that they work both to realize their own national freedom and to aid other nationalities in the fulfillment of theirs. Germany should therefore seek to establish a free Poland and then a "Congress of Peoples," an international parliament of free nationalities which would guarantee an enduring international peace.[147]

But like his proposal for a provisional republican president, Ruge's vision of an association of independent nations remained a dream. The majority of the Assembly committed what he called a "shameful injustice": it voted for the incorporation of parts of Posen into Germany.[148] Ruge now abandoned all hope in the Assembly's ability to carry through the Revolution. With this "fourth partition," he wrote, it had returned to the politics of the traditional reactionary powers. Henceforth Ruge looked to Berlin as the source of revolutionary change.[149] After shifting his attention to the northern capital, he resigned from the National Assembly in early October 1848.[150]

In Berlin Ruge immediately joined the radicals in their agitation for parliamentary control of the military.[151] He also tried to work up popular sympathy for the recent Vienna uprising. With others he organized in October a public demonstration in support of revolutionary Vienna, but the demonstration got out of their control and nearly turned into a mob uprising against the Prussian National Assembly.[152] This mismanaged affair marked the high tide of Ruge's revolutionary activity. In the following month came a series of crucial defeats that pulverized the revolutionary movement in Prussia. On the first of November Berlin learned of the fall of revolutionary Vienna. On the next day, Frederick William IV appointed Count Frederick William Brandenburg prime minister. During the rest of November and the first part of December, the new government acted quickly and decisively: it removed the Prussian National Assembly from Berlin; it ordered the military suppression of rebellion in Silesia and the Rhineland; it dissolved the Assembly; and it forced a constitution on the country.

Ruge was stunned by this rapid turn of events. His paper *Die Reform* had been closed on November 5th, leaving him politically stranded, without an effective public forum. On 2 May 1849 the government ejected him from Prussia and formally confiscated *Die Reform* along with the rest of his property in Prussia.[153]

Ruge returned to Leipzig just in time to learn of the uprisings that followed Frederick William IV's rejection of the Frankfurt constitution. Ruge attempted to rally support in Leipzig for the revolution in Dresden, but none was forthcoming. The Leipzig citizenry, he lamented, had deserted the Revolution for the reaction.[154]

Once Prussian and Saxon troops quashed the Dresden Revolution, which Ruge had vociferously supported, he was forced to flee the country. He soon reached Paris where he witnessed the defeat of the radical uprising of June 13th. The ruthless suppression of the radicals left Ruge embittered and disgusted with the French. It confirmed the fear that had come into his mind after the recent presidential and parliamentary elections in France—the fear that the French had forsaken their own political principles. They, like the Germans, had now proved that they were afraid of their own freedom. They had repudiated it for slavery and crushed those who had tried to save it. "The election of the pretender Louis Napoleon and this shameless, traitorous assembly," Ruge wrote to his wife on June 13th, "is the French nation's betrayal of itself."[155]

The outbreak of the 1848 Revolution released Ruge from his tortured ambivalence about Germany's political future, his oscillation between unrealistic hope and absolute despair. He felt liberated, both from the tyranny of the existing governments and from his own doubts about the possibility of overcoming tyranny. In the Revolution he found a new unity with the world, and actively took part in it by founding a democratic newspaper, by participating in the Frankfurt Parliament, by working side by side with the people in Berlin and Leipzig. But each experience turned out to be a defeat, leading up to the triumph of the reaction and the humiliation of the revolutionaries. The 1848 Revolution began by raising his hope for philosophy's political fulfillment but ended by confirming his worst fear—that the Germans were deeply, intractably unpolitical. Like Bauer, Ruge ultimately came to regard the 1848 Revolution as a sham, a lot of sound and fury meant to conceal Germany's crucial defect, its lack of political will. Ruge's pessimism about the fate of philosophy and democracy deepened further when he fled to Paris, where he found that the French, the political people par excellence, had displayed the same suicidal political tendency that characterized the Germans. In the end the French also abandoned their revolution. They shamefully voted for its destruction and welcomed its suppression. In June 1849 Ruge felt profoundly disappointed with his world. His political faith tottered beneath the weight of political defeat, the betrayal of the German and French peoples, and philosophy's repeated failure to link up with the present. In his last letter to his wife on the eve of his departure from Paris for exile in England, he wrote,

The destruction of all the invaluable accomplishments of 1848 by the people themselves is a much sadder degradation of humanity than the old oppressive relations that we believe we have outgrown and whose falling away appears to be only a question of time. . . . The dissonances in world history persist so long that many people have lost the patience to wait for their dissolution into harmony.[156]

In this passage, Ruge declares almost out of habit spirit's inevitable triumph over the old order ("the falling away" of the "old, oppressive relations"). But as we have noticed before, this sentiment is incongruously, ambivalently paired with a testimony to the vigorous persistence of the "old, oppressive relations" and to spirit's manifest weakness in the present, its inability to assume an enduring form in reality. Moreover, we find in Ruge's admission of a growing impatience with the delayed resolution of existing conflicts another recurring theme of Prussian Young Hegelian experience—namely, the longing for a lost unity and the partly concealed fear that it was lost forever.

Part IV
Karl Marx and the Crisis in Social Theory

7

The Serenity of Philosophy

1

Like the cases of Bauer and Ruge, the young Marx's conversion to Hegelian philosophy can be seen as a Hegelian phenomenology. He too passed through contradiction and alienation to the redemption of Hegelian theory. Moreover, his unity-restoring conversion was also conducted in an eminently Hegelian fashion: he became a devoted Hegelian when he philosophically demonstrated that the course of his life had the structure and significance of a Hegelian phenomenology. Finally, with Bauer and Ruge again, Marx conceived of his adoption of Hegelian theory as a return to his community. As a Hegelian, he felt united to the existing rational state, to reformed Prussia.

Before demonstrating how the young Marx's development had the form and function of a phenomenology, it is first necessary to defend this approach against previous interpretations. Biographers conventionally have pictured the young Marx's evolution not as culminating in a sense of rational harmony but as defined by continuous social alienation and escalating political opposition. As the son of a Jew who had been forced by the Prussian government to convert to Christianity in 1816, Marx had, according to one biographer, developed a profound resentment against the state that had "grasped and bent" his father's "personal identity."[1] We are frequently told that as a boy growing up in the Rhineland city of Trier in the 1820s and 1830s, Marx had absorbed that liberal city's hostility to the Prussian state.[2] As a Gymnasium student in the mid-1830s, he had apparently flouted the school's conservative authorities and had dedicated himself to the service of humanity.[3] In the late 1830s he became a leader of the radical wing of the Prussian Hegelian movement, a group that had fallen into conflict with the country's religious and political conservatives.[4] And as the editor of a liberal newspaper, the *Rheinische Zeitung*, in the early 1840s, he had collided with the censors of the Prussian state.[5] The major experiences of Marx's youth and early manhood thus seem to constitute an education in political discontent.

Given the mature Marx's career as a socialist revolutionary, it is not surprising that interpreters have searched for causes and foreshadowings of radicalism in the experiences of the young Marx. But the tendency of interpreters has been to convert what should be merely a hypothesis into a foregone conclusion, a generalization that is imposed on the historical record. A close scrutiny of the surviving documentary evidence does not support a pattern of political radicalization in the young Marx's development. There is a lack of explicit substantiating testimony. Until his conflicts with the Prussian censors in the early 1840s, there are no explicit criticisms of Prussian politics. Nor can one find any explicit assertions of resentment against the state made by the person who is supposed to have led Marx to rebellion, his father Heinrich Marx. On the contrary, the father's political statements are the direct converse of what one would expect from a malcontent: they all praise the Prussian state.[6]

The lack of outright hostility to the existing order on the part of the young Marx has forced some of his biographers to argue that such a sentiment is implicit or latent in his unpolitical statements.[7] And Heinrich Marx's expressions of political loyalty, we are often told, are meant ironically and hence also contain veiled political criticism.[8] But the problem with these attempts to find hidden messages in the documents is that there is no unconcealed or explicit contemporaneous testimony to corroborate them. Biographers are in the awkward position of telling us that what Marx and his father said was not what they had meant to say.

To make up for the absence of explicit supporting documentation, biographers have tried to show how in his youth Marx was exposed to powerful radical influences, but this "contextual" argument for the young Marx's political disaffection is also suspect. Recent work on the politics of the Rhineland had challenged the assumption that the region was irreconcilably opposed to the Prussian state that had incorporated it in 1815.[9] And, as I shall argue below, Marx's initial encounter with Hegelian philosophy was not an encounter with an agent of radicalism. Further, the usual connections that have been made between possible radical influences and the young Marx's concrete experiences have been extremely tenuous.[10]

The biographer's preoccupation with incipient radicalism in the young

Marx has also resulted in the neglect of much of what was considered important by the young man himself. For several years he had been deeply committed to a passionate Romanticism; yet because it had no ostensible political effect on him, it has generally not been taken seriously, and has sometimes even gone unmentioned.[11] During the time that he was a Romantic, Marx was also seriously at odds with his father and his fiancée Jenny von Westphalen. Because those conflicts seemed to lack political consequence they also have been little interpreted.[12]

Recent psychological studies of Marx have offered more perceptive and complex insights than one finds in conventional biographies, but they too have attempted to force Marx's development into an a priori scheme that conflicts with explicit testimony. The result had been the production of psychological variations of the characteristic distortions of conventional biographies—certain events are given an arbitrary psychological meaning,[13] while other events to which Marx himself attached great psychological significance are altogether ignored.[14]

In writing the phenomenology of the young Marx, I have attempted to adhere strictly to the explicit empirical record and to the young man's actual concerns. The conclusion of my "empirical phenomenology" is that the evolution of the young Marx was not a straightforward process of radicalization but the opposite: it was a dialectical process of social and intellectual reintegration. As the young Marx himself acknowledged, this dialectic of reunification issued in his conversion to Hegelian theory. That philosophy allowed him to overcome alienation and opposition, to attain a wholeness of self and a unity with society.[15]

2

In 1777 Heinrich Marx was born into a prominent Jewish family in the Rhineland city of Trier.[16] Like many of his ancestors, Heinrich's father was a Trier rabbi, a position that Heinrich's older brother Samuel later assumed.[17] It was thus likely that Heinrich Marx was raised in a strong Jewish tradition. Yet as a young man he left home to study in French and German schools, where he was introduced to Enlightenment thought. In his later letters to his son Karl, he would refer to the views of Newton, Locke, Leibniz, and Kant as the source of his own moral beliefs.[18] After receiving a credential in law in the spring of 1815,[19] he became an attorney for the appeals court in Trier. His career was apparently successful. He was highly esteemed by his colleagues and by the community in general.[20]

Although Marx's father had become a convert to the Enlightenment and an active member of Trier's secular and political life, he was not at first entirely assimilated. He retained his membership in the Jewish community, and in November 1814 he married the Dutch-born Henriette Presburg, who, like himself, was descended from a long line of rabbis.[21]

Heinrich Marx tried to strike a compromise between the traditional religion of his father, the ethos of the Enlightenment, and the practical demands of his office. We do not know the psychological effects of his compromise.[22] On the surface, he seems to have had no trouble subsuming opposing world views. He could justify the Jewish religion and its profound differences from the rationalistic deism and secular way of life of the Enlightenment by appealing to the Enlightenment principles of religious tolerance.[23] But regardless of how personally tenable his reconciliation of traditional religiosity and modern rationalism might have been, external circumstances ultimately forced him to choose between them.

Historians are generally agreed that France's absorption of the Rhineland in 1794 was welcomed by the region's population.[24] The citizens of Trier gladly received French revolutionary law, which brought the end of traditional privileges and divisions. Heinrich Marx and the Jews of the Rhineland had an additional reason for approving of French rule. In 1791 the French National Assembly had granted French Jews full rights of citizenship, and these were now extended to the Jews in the newly absorbed areas.

With the coming of Napoleon, however, some of the Rhineland's inhabitants became dissatisfied with their French status, because Napoleon not only drained the region's economy but retracted some of the Revolution's liberal laws. In 1808, for example, he reinstated limitations on Jewish mobility, trade, and marriage.[25] Also, many members of the local population had been drawn into the surge of German nationalism that arose after 1812. When Prussian troops entered Trier in January 1814, they were greeted by a large number of people, including Heinrich Marx, as liberators.[26]

After the Rhineland was incorporated into Prussia in 1815 some Rhenish groups became disenchanted with the Prussian state. The government estranged the Rhineland's Catholics with changes in marital laws and in the regional system of universities.[27] The new Jewish members of the expanded Prussian state were also upset by enforced disruptions of their lives. In 1815 Heinrich Marx petitioned the Governor-General of the area to overturn Napoleon's 1808 decrees. Instead of liberating the Jews from

Napoleon's restrictions, the Prussian government left the decrees in force, and in 1816 applied to the Rhineland its even more onerous 1812 decree that forbade unconverted Jews from entering the state civil service.

Heinrich Marx's position in Trier's judicial administration was endangered, and consequently, like many other Prussian Jews, he converted to the Evangelical church in 1816. Karl Marx, who was born in 1818, was baptised with his siblings in 1824, and his mother followed in 1826.[28]

Heinrich Marx's first experiences with the Rhineland's new ruler proved that it could be as intolerant as Napoleon. But he did not turn against the Prussian state as he had against the French emperor. He did not react with hostility to his required conversion. On the contrary, he was a Prussian patriot until he died in 1838. In January 1834, Trier's liberal political club, the Casino Society, held a dinner in honor of the deputies for the provincial Landtag. During this dinner Heinrich Marx, who was one of the club's leaders, gave a speech that concluded with the highest praise for the King of Prussia Frederick William III:

There . . . where justice reigns, there must the truth also find entry. For that reason let us look forward with the deepest trust toward a bright future, for it rests in the hands of a good father, a just king. His noble heart will always remain gracious and open to the just and rational wishes of his people.[29]

Three years later in a letter to his son Karl, he reiterated his patriotic sentiment when he suggested that the latter write something for the anniversary of the Battle of Waterloo, something that would "redound to the honour of the King and afford the opportunity of allotting a role to the genius of the monarchy."[30] And in the same year, while extremely ill, the father recommended that Marx compose a polemic on the Cologne episcopal dispute (a dispute between the Prussian state and the Catholic Church) that would justify the actions of king and state.[31]

Heinrich Marx's political convictions were those of a moderate liberal bureaucrat in the Prussian administration. Like many other liberal bureaucrats schooled in the Enlightenment, including Marx's future father-in-law, Ludwig von Westphalen, he tried to reconcile constitutionalism with loyalty to the state. He assumed that Prussia's present failure to implement the promised constitution would be corrected by the state itself.[32]

This faith in Prussia's ultimate benevolence was reinforced by a desire to secure the prosperity of his family in the newly expanded state. As we have seen, the Prussian reform movement led first by Karl vom Stein and then by Karl August von Hardenberg failed to turn the Prussian state into a constitutional monarchy, but the reformers did manage to create a less restricted society. The government eliminated many remnants of serfdom and guild restrictions, and it opened the army and bureaucracy to individual talent. Economic innovation and enterprise were systematically encouraged. Although the reformers failed to create a consistent set of conditions for a liberal state, they succeeded in fostering many of the essential conditions for a liberal civil society.[33]

Heinrich Marx conceived of reformed Prussia as a land of increased social and economic opportunity. The state, he thought, would now welcome individual initiative and ability.[34] And thus he encouraged his son to be ever alert to ways of enhancing his place in society. In 1837 the father suggested, for example, that Marx, who was then lost in Romantic daydreaming, put his literary talents to more practical use. He should produce a work, the father said, that would glorify the monarchy and thereby earn him the esteem of the government.[35] On another occasion, the son was urged not to neglect any opportunity to cultivate government contacts.[36]

Heinrich Marx dispensed practical wisdom in such letters to his son, which often seemed to advise Marx to play the sycophant to the Prussian authorities. But the father's concern for social and material success in Prussian society was not a crude mercenary opportunism. On the contrary, he believed that the methodical pursuit of self-interest and social advancement was necessarily connected to the cultivation of virtue.

This linking of calculating self-interest and virtuous selflessness stemmed from the Enlightenment belief that the rational unfolding of an individual's personality and moral character naturally harmonized with the well-being of society. An implication of this belief was that an accomplished moral development was reflected in a harmonious and successful social life. A rational, moral person was a socially successful person, one who was honored by the community; or as Diderot wrote in his play *Le Fils naturel:* "I appeal to your heart: ask it, and it will tell you that the good man lives in society, and only the bad man lives alone."[37]

In a letter to his son, Heinrich Marx made explicit his identification of moral self-cultivation and sociability:

They [one's natural character and talents] should be used for one's ennoblement. But how? One is a human being, a spiritual being, and a member of society, a citizen of the state. Hence physical, moral, intellectual and political ennoblement. Only if unison and harmony are introduced into the efforts to attain this great goal can a beautiful, attractive whole make its appearance, one which is well-pleasing to God, to one's parents and to the girl one loves.[38]

Personal realization yields harmony with society, and that, in turn, is mirrored in social approbation. Self-development is thus implicitly equated with social success.

Heinrich Marx handed down his Enlightenment view of his world to his son Karl, whose absorption of the Enlightenment ethos must also have been expedited by his friendly association with Ludwig von Westphalen. Certainly, by the time Marx had completed his Gymnasium education—an education designed as a program of practical and moral learning by the Gymnasium director Johann Hugo Wyttenbach[39]—his "indoctrination" was complete. In an essay that he wrote in 1835 as part of his final Gymnasium examination, Marx expressed his commitment to the Enlightenment principles of his father's world. One finds in "Reflections of a Young Man on the Choice of a Profession" the combination of moral commitment and the desire for social advancement that Enlightenment thinking entailed. Early in the essay Marx states that the improvement of oneself and of society was compatible with the assumption of any social position:

To man . . . the Deity gave a general aim, that of ennobling mankind and himself, but . . . he left it to him to choose the position in society most suited to him, from which he can best uplift himself and society.[40]

Selflessness and selfishness could be joined together. At times this pairing could assume a dynamic dialectical form, such as one finds at the conclusion of Marx's essay. Here Marx first appears to renounce his self-interest for the sake of humanity. But as we read on, we discover that this virtuous self-sacrifice fulfills a higher, transcendent form of self-interest: it brings immortality, the adoration of a noble posterity:

If we have chosen the position in life in which we can most of all work for mankind, no burdens can bow us down, because they are sacrifices for the benefit of all; then shall we experience no petty, limited, selfish joy, but our happiness will belong to millions, our deeds will live quietly but perpetually at work, and over our ashes will be shed the hot tears of noble people.[41]

After Marx had completed his Gymnasium education, he entered the University of Bonn where he began to study law, the usual prerequisite for a future in the Prussian state service. The elder Marx acknowledged his son as his proper heir who would become everything that the father had hoped to be himself: "I should like to see in you," he wrote to Marx in November 1835, "what perhaps I could have become, if I had come into the world with equally favorable prospects."[42] In the following years, Heinrich Marx would be disappointed and dumbfounded by his son's behavior. The *Aufklärer*, who had tried to impart to his son his own commitment to moral idealism and social harmony, would soon lose him to the shattered consciousness of Romanticism.

3

Marx began his first year at the University of Bonn with great enthusiasm. He plunged into his studies, working night and day to support an unusually heavy load of courses, until he became ill. The letters from his parents display constant worry about their son's tendency to overtax himself. They repeatedly advised him to get enough sleep and exercise, to look after his diet, and to curb his intellectual passions.[43]

Marx also gave his parents cause for anxiety in his new social life. After his arrival at Bonn he joined a club of students from Trier, which principally occupied itself with drinking and carousing. Marx soon became a prominent member of the club and a leader in its delinquent activities. He spent one night in university detention "for disturbing the peace by rowdiness and drunkenness."[44] On another occasion, he became involved in a duel with a Prussian aristocrat from a rival student organization.[45] In his first year at the university he also cultivated a taste for Romanticism. He tried his hand at composing poetry and joined a club of poets.[46]

Marx's father was generally disappointed with his son's conduct at Bonn. Rather than leading an ordered and rational life, dedicated to practical and moral pursuits, his son had surrendered himself to excess, to a life of self-indulgence. It was therefore decided that Marx should be placed in another, calmer environment, and arrangements were made for him to attend the University of Berlin in the next academic year.

Before Marx left for the University of Berlin, he further increased his father's worries. While at home for the summer, Marx fell in love with his childhood friend Jenny von Westphalen, the daughter of Ludwig von Westphalen. She reciprocated his feelings; nevertheless, their relationship was far from unproblematical. There was a serious complication: Jenny was not only a gentile but a member of the German nobility. It was likely that her family would object to her romance with an eighteen-year-old of Jewish descent who did not yet have a secure place in the world. But regardless of their fear of opposition, Karl and Jenny became engaged. At first Marx's parents opposed the engagement, but they eventually gave their consent; the von Westphalens were not informed.[47]

Some historians have acknowledged the anxiety that attended Marx's engagement to Jenny and have tried to explain its origin by referring to the social and familial problems that the couple encountered. According to these commentators, Marx's love for Jenny was intrinsically straight-forward, complicated only by external problems.[48] This interpretation does not do justice to the complexity of their relationship. Although the social complications were distressing, they were not the sole or even perhaps the prime cause of the couple's anxiety. Long after Jenny's father gave his consent in March 1837 to the engagement, Marx and Jenny continued to be extremely anguished over their relationship.

A study of their correspondence before 1840 and of Marx's Romantic poetry suggests that more was at issue in their relationship than the fear of alienating Jenny's relatives. From these sources it appears that external social concerns intensified Marx's already unsettled state of mind. Even before he met Jenny, he suffered from a disturbing anxiety. In the Romantic poetry that he had begun to write in Bonn and that he continued to write in Berlin, he revealed an uneasy attempt to define the social and psychological contours of his emerging adult identity. To understand his state of mind in the late 1830s and his relationship with Jenny we must first examine the nature of his Romanticism.[49]

Like other movements that have been collected under the label of German Idealism,[50] German Romanticism sought to join two not easily reconciled principles.[51] In opposition to the Enlightenment's rendering of nature as a soulless external object, the Romantics wanted to restore to it a spirituality. In this way they, as spiritual beings, hoped to recover a sense of wholeness or unity with a spiritual world. At the same time, they were at one with the Enlightenment in their belief in the absolute autonomy of the self, in the subject's unlimited ability to express its inner powers, even against external obstacles.

Sometimes these two principles could merge harmoniously in the Romantic notion of a cosmic Promethean subject who, infused with spiritual energy, creates a spiritual universe. Such a theme is found in Marx's poem "Creation":

> Creator Spirit uncreated
>   Sails in fleet waves far away
> Worlds heave, Lives are generated
>   His Eye spans Eternity.
> All inspiring reigns his Countenance.
> In its burning magic, Forms condense.[52]

Here the Romantic self regards the universe as its own product, fashioned out of its own energy. The Romantics also considered spiritual energy to be uncontrollable. It could not be limited by a fixed form, but strove for ever more novel expressions. Hence the Romantic self, driven by its passionate energy, was never satisfied with any of its creations. It sought its own unending self-transcendence:

> I am caught in endless strife,
> Endless ferment, endless dream;
> I cannot conform to Life
> Will not travel with the stream.[53]

To be in a state of constant self-transcendence was to deny the permanence of all existing forms of self, society, and nature. For unchanging forms were limits to the impassioned self; they were determinations that secured it to a fixed point. An unchanging world resisted the romantic subject. In "The Song of Stars" Marx converts what are conventionally objects of rapturous appreciation into objects of hate and despair:

> You [the stars] are false images,
>   Faces of radiant flame,
> Hearts warmth and tenderness
>   And Soul you cannot claim.
>
> A mockery is your shining
>   Of Action, Pain, Desire.
> On you is dashed all Yearning
>   And the heart's song of fire.
>
> Grieving, we must turn grey
>   End in despair and pain
> Then see the mockery
>   That Earth and Heaven remain.[54]

The two principles of Romanticism were in essential disagreement with each other. The Romantic self longed for a spiritual unity with the world; to accomplish that it had to assume a stable coherent form. Yet to assume such a form was to deny the integrity of the Romantic self, to frustrate the self's unrelenting desire for self-transcendence.

Caught in the pull of these two opposing principles, many Romantics ultimately decided to renounce the self's claim to an absolute and restless freedom for an established form of spiritual integration, usually a type of orthodox Christianity.[55] Suffering from the dilemma of Romanticism, Marx also contemplated the exchange of the self's disquieting passion for an accessible form of spiritual unity, but he was never interested in the religious alternatives. For him, unity was to be found in a more secular shape—in earthly love.

In "Transformation" Marx dons the persona of the Romantic hero who sets out on an ocean voyage. Once at sea, the hero feels the need to soar beyond the ocean's dominion:

> I clung to Thought high-soaring
> On its two wings did ride,
> And though storm winds were roaring,
> All danger I defied.

Spurning earthly temptations for "journeys limitless," he takes flight, aspiring to reach the heavens. But he is unable to escape the waves, and tumbles out of the sky. Rising again he finds himself emptied of vitality. "My powers all were gone / And all the heart's glow lost." For the hero, "Void was the Bosom's Land."

The world had defeated his strivings. But the hero is not yet condemned to a shallow life of natural limitations; he now turns from both the world and his own ambitions to find succor in his beloved, who sustains peacefully within herself "the purest light of soul." The Romantic self is redeemed by love:

> I left the waves that rush,
> The floods that change and flow,
> On the high cliff to crash
> But saved the inner glow.[56]

Earthly love, Marx hoped, was the medium that would first quell the restlessness of the Romantic self without extinguishing its soul, its "inner glow"; and then restore to the self a spiritual wholeness with the external world, embodied in the loved one. But for both practical and theoretical reasons, this solution to the Romantic dilemma was illusory.

Marx wrote "Transformation" as part of a collection of love poetry which he dedicated and sent to Jenny after he had arrived in Berlin. But Marx's problematical and at least partially secret engagement to Jenny was far removed from the serene love of "Transformation." His love for Jenny involved as much fear of frustrated or unrequited love as it did hope for a happy union. Several of Marx's poems reflected his worry about the uncertainty of their arrangement. In these love does not appear as redemption but as a torment; foiled or unrequited, it leads to suicide.[57]

Even if Marx's love for Jenny had been in itself unproblematical, there remained another crucial reason why his turn to earthly love was not a viable solution to the Romantic dilemma. There is no reason why love should not be considered a constraint to the Romantic need for self-transcendence. To be in love is to be tied to one's lover, to be fixed to the external world. Thus although Marx on occasion represented fulfilled love as a form of redemption, he more often conceived of it in negative terms: as enslavement, a denial of self. And such a condition is one that the self-transcending subject cannot help but strive to overcome.

In "Siren Song" Marx relates the story of a "youth" who, seduced by the ocean's sirens, is kept from "seeking the All. . . . " He is "held captive in Love's sway / To burning passion lost." But then, out of inner necessity, "deep Thoughts stir in his soul." He struggles to regain his autonomy, to cast off earthly love for unceasing self-transcendence—and he succeeds:

> The Gods in my breast rule,
> And I obey them all;
> I mean no treachery.
>
> You shall not captivate
> Me, nor my love, nor hate
> Nor yet my yearning's glow.[58]

The Romantic self was defined by its insatiable need for ever newer ways of expressing itself, for unending self-transcendence. The self continually strove to be other than what it was at any moment. It always sought the negation of the existing. Such a will to negate whatever existed could assume the form of simple annihilation, the destruction of self, society, and nature. Romanticism had a weakness for apocalypse. But the same desire for negation could also manifest itself in a more ethereal way, in the form of longing. Longing entails a dissatisfaction with one's existing condition. To long for something is to wish for change, to negate, at least in one's mind, the conditions of one's existence.

The objective of Marx's longing was spiritual unity, first with the cosmos and then in earthly love. Once those possibilities proved antithetical to the self-transcending subject, he renounced them. With those objects of his longing removed, the Romantic self was left with nothing to long for but longing itself, for the self's nonbeing: the youth repudiated love for "yearning's glow."

Not surprisingly, the conflicting tendencies of Marx's state of mind, embodied in his Romanticism, had unsettling effects on Jenny von Westphalen. From the time of their engagement in 1836 to at least the end of 1839, she was deeply troubled. Confused by and confusing further Marx's ambivalent passion, her stable sense of self gave way to discordant feelings. Her unhappy distraction is apparent in a letter that she wrote to Marx sometime in 1839 or 1840. Here Marx's love summons up both exultation and despair:

Oh Karl, what makes me miserable is that what would fill any other girl with inexpressible delight—your beautiful, touching, passionate love, the indescribably beautiful things you say about it, the inspiring creations of your imagination—all this only causes me anxiety and reduces me to despair.[59]

She feared his love and therefore could not, she said, give herself entirely to it; but at the same time, she admitted that she could not resist it. It had irrevocably affected her, captured her heart and mind: her "whole life and being," she said, were "but one thought" of him.[60]

Like Marx again, she resisted her own feelings because she distrusted her lover. She suspected that he was incapable of enduring love.[61] For Jenny the only conceivable situation in which their love might become permanent was one in which her love for Marx was equated with mastery over him. On learning that he had become involved in a duel, she had at first become frightened but her alarm then turned into elation:

Day and night I saw you wounded, bleeding and ill, and, Karl, to tell you the whole truth, I was not altogether unhappy in this thought: for I vividly imagined that you had lost your right hand, and, Karl, I was in a state of rapture, of bliss because of that. You see, sweetheart, I thought that in that case I could really become quite indispensable to you, you would then always keep me with you and love me.[62]

The relationship between Marx and Jenny was in a state of constant turbulence. Each seemed to delight in expressing and then withdrawing love, in tormenting the other with doubts. The message of Marx's poetry is rarely happy. It more often asserts that love, whether successful or not, ultimately issues in the death of one's passionate soul. For Jenny love is also unstable, untrustworthy. Enduring love is control of the loved one. Marx and Jenny were caught in lines of force that simultaneously drew them together and wrenched them apart. Entangled in this web was the sharer of the secret of their engagement, Heinrich Marx.

4

When his son's taste for Romantic poetry first developed while he was at the University of Bonn, Heinrich Marx tried to show a sympathetic interest. He did his best to understand, but his son's troubled state of mind ultimately left him puzzled. In one amusing attempt to comprehend Marx's poetry, he even tried to translate the poet's passionate longing into terms that were more accessible to the Aufklärer:

I have read your poem word by word. I quite frankly confess, dear Karl, that I do not understand it, neither its true meaning nor its tendency. In ordinary life it is an undisputed proposition that with the fulfillment of one's most ardent wishes the value of what one wished is very much diminished and often disappears altogether. That is surely not what you wanted to say.[63]

One suspects that the father was humoring his son, hoping that he would soon grow out of his Romantic tendencies. Heinrich suggested to Marx that the latter should not publish his poems until his talents had further matured and meanwhile should circulate them only within the family. At the same time, the father encouraged his son to pursue something more practical and less self-indulgent, such as legal studies. Both parents also tried to wean Marx from his Bohemian style of manic activity, sleepless nights, and alcoholic dissipation.[64] The father did not become seriously concerned about Marx's Romanticism until it proved to be more than a passing fancy. It alarmed Heinrich Marx when it entered into a more intense phase and affected not only his own family but also that of his friend Ludwig von Westphalen.

After Marx had become engaged and had left for the University of Berlin, his father sent him reports about Jenny's troubled mind, in the hope that he would write her a soothing letter.[65] But as Heinrich Marx recognized, for his son to calm Jenny he first had to be drawn out of his Romantic ponderings and back to the reasonableness of the Enlightenment. In life, the father wrote to Marx shortly after the latter had arrived at Berlin,

you have undertaken great duties and, dear Karl, at the risk of irritating your sensitivity, I express my opinion somewhat prosaically after my fashion: with all the exaggerations and exaltations of love in a poetic mind you cannot restore the tranquility of a being to whom you have wholly devoted yourself; on the contrary, you run the risk of destroying it. Only by the most exemplary behaviour, by manly, firm efforts which, however, win people's goodwill and favour, can you ensure that the situation is straightened out and that she is exalted in her own eyes and the eyes of the world, and comforted.[66]

He tried to convince his son that true love was characterized by self-control and the performance of one's duties and that its natural results were mental calmness and the approbation of the community.

But the ideal of controlled and sociable passion could not have been further removed from the self-abandonment represented in Marx's Romanticism. He ignored his father's admonishments. As his Romantic effusions continued and as Jenny became more troubled, Heinrich Marx began to wonder if his son had lost his senses. Was he, the father asked rhetorically, possessed by a "demon," which rendered him incapable of "truly human, domestic happiness" and of "imparting happiness" to others?[67] Throughout the autumn of 1836 and the spring of 1837, Heinrich Marx attempted to offset his son's Romanticism with sensible advice. The rational clarity and existential stability of the Enlightenment were pitted against the psychological dissolution of Romanticism. But as Marx's problems with Jenny continued unchanged throughout the summer of

1837, the father also began to lose his bearings: "all this [trouble] has deeply affected me and at times depressed me so much that I no longer recognised myself." This drift into a psychological disorientation was accompanied, as it was for Marx and Jenny, by a drift into physical illness.[68]

In a letter of August 1837, the father finally let loose his rage against his son's behavior. Here he did not equivocate in his condemnation of Marx's destructive self-indulgence:

To abandon oneself to grief at the slightest storm, to lay bare a shattered heart and break the heart of our beloved ones at every suffering, do you call that poetry? God protect us from the most beautiful of all nature's gifts if that is its immediate effect. No, it is only weakness, over-indulgence, self-love and conceit which reduce everything to their own measure in this way and force even those we love most into the background![69]

The father had at last come to recognize that the Romantic sensibility was fatal to the preservation of his world.[70]

I have argued above that the elder Marx's Enlightenment beliefs implied a certain psychology and social behavior. To be guided by personal and moral standards was to conduct oneself and one's relations with others in a controlled and harmonious fashion, in a way that linked self-expression and social approbation. This style of being has been described by Lionel Trilling as "sincerity." The sincere self, Trilling writes, "consists in his wholeness of self, in the directness and consistency of his relations to things, and in his submission to a traditional morality." This kind of self pursues one main objective: a coherent life "of order, peace, honor, and beauty." The realization of that objective requires the successful satisfaction of material needs.[71]

Although raised in the ways of "sincerity," Marx had come to reject his cultural inheritance. Sincerity's combination of existential stability, self-righteousness, and calculating self-interest lacked what he and many other young Germans craved: spirituality, an intensity of soul.[72] Marx spurned the harmonious life of sincerity for the impassioned life of Romanticism. He ignored social conventions, familial advice, his own health. He entered into an injudicious engagement, and then, as if to show his utter moral irresponsibility, proceeded to torment his fiancée, his father, and not least himself. Marx initially looked upon his Romantic exertions as an expression of his self's uncontainable power, of its ability to transcend objective limitations. He thought that as the Romantic self he could transform himself and the world into a spiritual unity. But the more he persisted in his Romanticism, the sicklier his spirituality became, for both in his real life and in his poetry, the world proved to be hostile to Romantic striving. The Romantic self was then left with nothing to glorify but its own self-transcendence, its own nonbeing.

The unhappy fate of the Romanticism of the young Marx and the troubled identity that it represented had been foretold less than a decade earlier by a prominent German philosopher. In his analysis of Friedrich Schlegel's notion of irony, Hegel had located beneath the Promethean pretensions of Romanticism an impulse for self-destruction, a need to negate all existing forms until it had even negated its own substance. "If the I," Hegel wrote, "remains at this point of view [of uncompromising negation], all appears to it as worth nothing and as vain, excepting its own subjectivity, which thereby becomes hollow and empty, and itself mere conceit."[73] But Hegel did not think that the self was thereby hopelessly lost to oblivion. The Romantic sensibility, he believed, could be no more than a way station to a higher form of consciousness. It ultimately led to the self's reunion with the world in a spiritual whole, to the attainment of his own philosophy. In the autumn of 1837 Marx would make Hegel's belief his own.

5

Marx must have been upset by his father's disapprobation, for despite their disagreements, he had always remained devoted to him. Even after the latter's hostility to Romanticism had become apparent, Marx continued to show his literary creations to his father in the hope of ultimately winning approval. On the occasion of his father's birthday in the spring of 1837, he dedicated and sent to him a book of poetry.[74] Thus when Marx had at last accepted the fact that his father had become an intractable enemy of his Romanticism, he might very likely have begun to reexamine his beliefs.

The father in turn did his best to encourage such a turn of events, for although his denial of Romanticism had become absolute, he did not renounce his son. In his mind, he distinguished between his son and the "demon" that possessed him. He was always careful to let Marx know that if he should come to his senses, he would be welcomed back into the father's good graces.[75]

In the single surviving document of Marx's turn away from Romanticism—his extraordinary letter of November 1837—there are signs of
Marx's desire to appease his father. But Marx does not consider such a
desire to be due to external pressure; rather he sees a reconciliation with
his family as emerging out of an internal process, a process of intellectual
and psychological clarification. In his letter to his father Marx recounts
his mind's passage from the unworldly idealism of Romanticism to the
realistic idealism of Hegelian philosophy. By becoming a Hegelian, he
believed that he had found a way of reuniting himself with the world of
his father.

Marx begins the story of his spiritual journey by recalling how in the
summer of 1836 when he had just left Trier for Berlin he was possessed
by an intoxicating passion, by his love for Jenny. His ardor was so
overwhelming that it dulled his perception of the external world. He lost
himself in the appreciation of his own passion:

Even the journey to Berlin, which otherwise would have delighted me in the
highest degree, would have inspired me to contemplate nature and fired my zest
for life, left me cold. Indeed, it put me strikingly out of humour, for the rocks
which I saw were not more rugged, more indomitable, than the emotions of my
soul, the big towns not more lively than my blood, the inn meals not more
extravagant . . . than the store of fantasies I carried with me, and, finally, no
work of art was as beautiful as Jenny.[76]

Compared with his internal states, the outside world paled into insig-
nificance. This preoccupation with his inner life consequently led him to
break off "all hitherto existing connections," to make social visits "rarely
and unwillingly," and instead, to "immerse" himself in "'science and
art'."[77] Yet at the same time that he was interested only in the cultivation
of his inner states, he found that activity to be unsatisfying; he recognized
that his love for Jenny was insubstantial. It was defined by unfulfilled
longing, hence he called it "a passionately yearning and hopeless love."[78]
In short, he recognized that his love at once excited his soul and frustrated
it. His passion pressed him away from the prosaic world, deeper into his
subjective states, at the same time that it emptied those states of content.
This insubstantiality of self manifested itself in his poetry:

But owing to my attitude and whole previous development, it [his poetry] was
purely idealistic. My heaven, my art, became a world beyond, as remote as my

love. Everything real became hazy and what is hazy has no definite outlines. All the poems of the first three volumes I sent to Jenny are marked by attacks on our times, diffuse and inchoate expressions of feeling, nothing natural, everything built out of moonshine, complete opposition between what is and what ought to be, rhetorical reflections instead of poetic thought.[79]

The dynamic of Romantic longing, he recognized, resulted in the Romantic poet's own dissolution: "The whole extent of a longing that has no bounds finds expression there in many different forms and makes all poetic 'composition' into 'diffusion'."[80] The obsessive cultivation of passion extinguished passion, left his poetry strained and inert, "a mere formal art, mostly without objects that inspire it and without any impassioned train of thought."[81]

During his first term at the University of Berlin, Marx's inner activity also took on a more academic form. Despite his devotion to poetry he managed to keep up an interest in his legal studies, and he took courses on civil and criminal law.[82] But the more he read, the more he found himself drawn from the investigation of positive law to an inquiry into the theoretical foundations of law. He felt "the urge to wrestle with philosophy," and after further reading he committed himself to an enormous project: "to elaborate a philosophy of law covering the whole field of law."[83]

Marx began to compose this study—as he did all his studies—with great energy. He very quickly wrote about three hundred pages. Yet he found in these pages little that satisfied him, and he consequently stopped writing. But at least he had no trouble identifying the problem with this "unhappy opus." It was the same flaw that he had found in his poetry: a lack of reality. "Here, above all," writes Marx, "the same opposition between what is and what ought to be . . . stood out as a serious defect."[84] After rallying his intellectual energy, he enthusiastically started his project again, but he was eventually "once more compelled to recognise that it was wrong."[85]

Thus at the end of his first academic term he felt doubly frustrated in his spiritual pursuits. His poetry and his philosophy were both defective, insubstantial. By renouncing the external world to pursue his spirituality, he had committed himself to an ethereal life of unfulfillment. But the real world revenged itself for his neglect: he became sick. A doctor ordered him to the country for a rest, and in the village of Stralow, outside of Berlin, this rest became a transformation. "I had no inkling," Marx wrote to his father, "that I would mature there from an anaemic weakling into a man of robust bodily strength."[86] Marx was speaking metaphorically: at Stralow he had become a Hegelian.

Marx admits in his letter to his father that he had earlier read "fragments of Hegel's philosophy," but he had not cared for their "grotesque, craggy melody."[87] Indeed, as a Romantic Marx once had nothing but scorn for Hegel. To the perpetually self-transcending Romantic ego, Hegel's reconciliation of the ideal and the real seemed a homely affair, far inferior to the more exalted visions of that philosopher's predecessors. In one of his poems Marx had Hegel say:

> Kant and Fichte soar to heavens blue
> Seeking for some distant land,
> I but seek to grasp profound and true
> That which—in the street I find.[88]

As Marx became increasingly skeptical of the psychological and intellectual legitimacy of Romanticism, he began to cast about for another intellectual orientation. He read widely in different philosophies, including those of Kant and Fichte. Although they offered him little satisfaction, at least they showed him, in what he regarded as their deficiencies, the proper philosophical orientation; or, as he put it in his letter, he had "arrived at the point of seeking the idea in reality itself."[89]

Marx's Romantic standpoint had come to invert itself. No longer did he seek to fill his spiritual needs by overcoming the existing world; he now sought spirituality in the world itself. Marx wrote: "If previously the gods had dwelt above the earth, now they became its centre."[90] He was now predisposed to accept Hegelian philosophy.

Just as for Bauer and Ruge, Marx's intellectual clarification occurred in the course of writing a piece of philosophy. At Stralow he composed a twenty-four-page philosophical dialogue entitled "Cleanthes, or the Starting Point and Necessary Continuation of Philosophy." This work has not survived, but from Marx's description of it in his letter to his father, we can piece together the ways in which, like Bauer and Ruge again, he conceived of his coming to Hegelian philosophy as having the form and function of a Hegelian phenomenology.

First, Marx said that the dialogue dealt with a logical, ontological, and historical evolution. "Cleanthes," he wrote, was a "philosophical-dialectical account of divinity, as it manifests itself as the idea-in-itself, as religion, as nature, and as history."[91] Second, this evolution likely had a rational character, was powered by its internal contradictions, and issued in a condition of restored unity. For these elements are part of what Marx elsewhere in his letter described as the correct philosophical method, a method that could be comfortably called "philosophical-dialectical":

in the concrete expression of a living world of ideas as exemplified by law, the state, nature, and philosophy as a whole, the object itself must be studied in its development; arbitrary divisions must not be introduced, the rational character of the object itself must develop as something imbued with contradictions in itself and find its unity in itself.[92]

If we put these elements together we have the following: like Hegel's *Phenomenology*, "Cleanthes" is concerned with how spirit—here as "divinity"—evolved from a condition of simple, abstract self-unity ("the idea-in-itself"), through increasingly articulated, concrete, and rational but always alienated or contradictory forms (nature, religion, history), to a higher restored unity in reason. As in the *Phenomenology*, the final accomplished state of unity in "Cleanthes" was Hegelian philosophy itself: "My last proposition," Marx writes, "was the beginning of the Hegelian system."[93]

In chapter 1 we have seen that in the *Phenomenology* spirit attains its fulfillment as rational self-consciousness when it recapitulates its development in purely conceptual and logical terms. That recapitulation is the *Phenomenology* itself. This act of philosophical recapitulation, moreover, directly identifies spirit with the individual philosopher. By writing a phenomenology of spirit, he proves himself to be absolute spirit incarnate. We have also seen how Bauer and Ruge extended the process of philosophical recapitulation and the resulting identification of fulfilled spirit with the individual philosopher to give significance to their personal lives. In their writings, the recapitulation of spirit's development is so constructed that the necessary evolution of spirit to Hegelian philosophy is identified with the necessary evolution of the author-philosopher to his acceptance of that philosophy. In this sense, the moment of recapitulation becomes a moment not only of cosmic but also of personal redemption. The individual philosopher can comprehend his troubled development as necessary and meaningful, invested with spiritual purpose.

Although there is no explicit mention in Marx's letter about such an occurrence taking place in "Cleanthes," one can still find in the letter distinct traces of an experience of recapitulation and redemption. Marx begins his letter by announcing that he had recently passed through an important transition: "There are moments in one's life which are like frontier posts marking the completion of a period but at the same time clearly indicating a new direction."[94] He then goes on to say that the defining aspect of such a transition is not only a rational evaluation of one's present condition but also of one's past. "At such a moment of transition," he writes, "we feel compelled to view the past and the present with the eagle eye of thought in order to become conscious of our real position."[95] His personal recollection of the past is then identified with a larger, cosmic process, with the recollection of spirit:

Indeed, world history itself likes to look back in this way and take stock, which often gives it the appearance of retrogression or stagnation, whereas it is merely, as it were, sitting back in an armchair in order to understand itself and mentally grasp its own activity, that of spirit.[96]

Marx then proceeds to recapitulate his development from the alienated idealism of Romanticism to his recovery of the world in Hegelian philosophy. This recollection of his transformation is meant to have a redemptive function, to justify his past and reunite him in the most immediate way with his world: by telling his father of his painful but necessary spiritual development, he hopes to obtain his father's absolution. The purpose of his letter to his father, Marx says, is

to erect a memorial to what we have once lived through in order that this experience may regain in our emotions the place it has lost in our actions. And where could a more sacred dwelling place be found for it than in the heart of a parent, the most merciful judge, the most intimate sympathiser, the sun of love whose warming fire is felt at the innermost centre of our endeavours: What better amends and forgiveness could there be for much that is objectionable and blameworthy than to be seen as a manifestation of an essentially necessary state of things.[97]

Marx saw in Hegelian philosophy the way of satisfying both himself and his father, of mediating between his spiritual needs and his father's Enlightenment ideals. Hegel's philosophy was at one with his father's view of the world in its glorification of rational clarity and social harmony, of coherent self-expression and social integration. But at the same time, Hegel rejected both the facile smugness of the Enlightenment's conception of the self and the despiritualized character of its conception of nature. He recognized that the self's rational coherence was gained only after an arduous struggle, and only because the self acknowledged its unity with the larger spiritual world. For Marx, Hegelian philosophy had succeeded in reconciling the Enlightenment with Romanticism, in fusing their virtues without accepting their vices.

But Marx was hasty in believing that his new state of mind would also clarify the state of his life. Heinrich Marx did not believe that there was an affinity between Hegelian philosophy and his own Enlightenment point of view; he considered Hegelian philosophy to be no better than Romanticism. Both mystified him; they seemed to him unpractical and self-indulgent. He continued to reproach his son for squandering his natural talents on "senseless and inexpedient erudition."[98] Whether the father and the son were ever reconciled is unclear. Heinrich Marx died in May 1838, and there is no indication that he saw his son before his death.[99]

Hegelian philosophy failed to reconnect Marx to his world in another crucial respect. Just as he was still estranged from his father, so he had not been able to improve his relationship with Jenny von Westphalen, who continued to be as troubled as before.[100]

Besides discovering that Hegelian philosophy did not immediately solve his familial and romantic problems, Marx also found the social life of a Hegelian in the late 1830s to be uncongenial. After he returned to Berlin, he began to associate with other Hegelians in the Doktorklub, where he betrayed a strange mixture of feelings about Hegelianism—the more convinced he became of the truth of Hegelian philosophy, the more removed he felt from other Hegelians. "In the controversy here [at the Doktorklub]," Marx wrote, "many conflicting views were expressed, and I became ever more firmly bound to the modern world philosophy from which I had thought to escape, but all rich cords were silenced and I was seized with a fury of irony, as could easily happen after so much had been negated."[101]

Becoming a Hegelian near the end of 1837, Marx joined the Hegelian school when it had fallen into disarray. In the two years after Strauss's *Life in Jesus*, the followers of Hegel had come to quarrel over the meaning of Hegelian philosophy. Marx had accepted Hegelian philosophy's claim to be a unified system of knowledge, a philosophy of reconciliation, when the dissension among Hegel's followers seemed to make a mockery of that claim. Marx had become a Hegelian, but in 1837 that could no longer be the final philosophical standpoint. One more choice remained to be made: what kind of Hegelian one should be. That was the issue that Marx attempted to resolve in his dissertation.

6

From the beginning of 1839 to early 1840, Marx read widely in Greek philosophy. He then began to write his dissertation on Democritean and Epicurean atomism, completing it in March 1841. Although he had written it as a student at the University of Berlin, he submitted it to the faculty of philosophy at the University of Jena, from which he received a doctorate in April 1841.

The dissertation and Marx's notebooks for the dissertation together provided a general outline of Greek philosophy. This outline is organized according to Hegelian principles. Marx places the development of Greek philosophy in the larger framework of the Bildungs-progress of spirit. The history of Greek philosophy is the story of spirit's struggle to raise itself out of nature, to win through to a recognition of its own spirituality. Rather than make a detailed analysis of Marx's outline of spirit's evolution, I shall focus on its general principles and on those aspects that relate to the clarification of Marx's philosophical identity.

Some historians have seen in parts of Marx's study of Greek philosophy the attempt to define a philosophical condition that was analogous to the recent developments of Hegelian philosophy,[102] but they have generally underestimated the complexity of Marx's "analogy." His views are far from clear. At times he notes that there is a justifiable comparison between the two types of philosophy; on other occasions, he seems to consider the analogy to be a bad one.

Marx at least clearly dissociates the fate of Hegelian philosophy from the tragedy of Socrates, which represents for Marx a turning point in the development of spirit. But to understand the significance of Socrates, we must first consider the general principles that determined the evolution of Greek philosophy.

In the Hegelian scheme of things, spirit at its lowest stage of development is submerged in nature. Existing in a primordial unity with nature, it does not recognize itself as existing apart from nature. Nor is it recognized by ancient man as something independent of nature; on the contrary, he instinctively feels that nature is the creative power that rules his life. Marx calls this rudimentary form of spirit "substance."[103] Substance manifests itself in a religion of nature and in a communal order based on a natural authority. Substance also defines the form and content of early Greek philosophy.

According to Marx, the first Greek philosophers appear as wise men especially well possessed of natural wisdom. They are the vessels, Marx writes, "from which the substance resounds in general, simple precepts; their language is as yet only that of substance become vocal, the simple forces of moral life which are revealed."[104] In other words, they are not philosophers who analyze ideas, but honored men who give voice to the established customs of the natural community. Hence they exist in a perfect natural unity with the community, for they merely articulate its unarticulated assumptions.

As philosophy develops it becomes increasingly abstract, ever more removed from the natural sensuous world. The wise man changes with this development. He comes to admire abstractions in themselves, as something different from the prosaic world; he generates the notion of an independent world of spirit. At first this increasing separation of the ideal from the real existing world does not result in conflict. Spirit and substance peacefully coexist.[105]

But as spirit becomes progressively conscious of its ideal character, its sense of being something superior to the unreflective natural community also grows. The wise man eventually confronts unthinking substance with critical and rational standards. That confrontation appears in Greek philosophy as the tragedy of Socrates.

In Marx's account, Socrates manifests an untenable contradiction. As a member of the traditional natural community, he must live under the rule of substance. But as a philosopher, as pure spirit embodied in an individual, he is governed by ideal and hence antinatural principles. Consequently, when he judges and condemns the world he also judges and condemns himself. He thus wills his own death.[106]

Immediately following his analysis of the contradiction of Socrates, Marx digresses to take issue with some critics of Hegelian philosophy who had argued that its present situation resembled that of Socrates. Hegelian philosophy, they said, was a set of abstractions that were hostile to the practical demands of the prosaic world. Against this view, Marx asserted the pervasiveness of spirit:

It is self-evident how stupid was the comparison drawn in recent times between the relation of Hegelian philosophy to life and the case of Socrates, from which the justification for condemning Hegelian philosophy was deduced. The specific failing of Greek philosophy is precisely that it stands related only to the substantial spirit; in our time both sides are spirit and both want to be acknowledged as such.[107]

Here Marx emphatically believes that Hegelian theory is spiritually joined with the existing world, but elsewhere in his notebooks, he offers a more confusing opinion.

After following the further evolution of spirit into still purer forms in the totalistic philosophies of Plato and Aristotle, Marx tells us that those systems collapsed into the simpler competing theories of the Epicureans, Stoics, and Skeptics. He then tries to explain why such an apparent disintegration of totalistic philosophy occurred. This in turn leads him to compare that situation with the modern condition of philosophy after Hegel.

Some recent commentators have argued that in this comparison Marx displays his belief in Hegelian philosophy's opposition to the existing world.[108] One of Marx's statements would seem to support this view:

As Prometheus, having stolen fire from heaven, begins to build houses and to settle upon the earth, so philosophy, expanded to be the whole world, turns against the world of appearance. The same now with the philosophy of Hegel.[109]

Philosophy is here considered to be in conflict with the "world of appearance." It seems to be hostile to existing society, but such a reading ignores the statement's complexity. Although Marx does say that philosophy is opposed to the world of appearance, he has previously said that philosophy has "expanded to be the whole world." This part of the statement would indicate that Marx believed that philosophy had permeated the world, that philosophy also forms the world of appearance.[110] In the next line he reiterates this opinion: "philosophy has sealed itself off to form a consummate, total world."[111]

This confusion and seeming contradiction can be dispelled if we pay closer attention to the detail of Marx's complicated reasoning. After saying that philosophy has formed a "consummate, total world," he immediately adds:

The determination of this totality is conditioned by the general development of philosophy, just as that development is the condition of the form in which philosophy turns into a practical relationship towards reality; thus the totality of the world in general is divided within itself, and this division is carried to the extreme, for spiritual existence has been freed, has been enriched to universality, the heart-beat has become in itself the differentiation in the concrete form which is the whole organism. The division of the world is total only when its aspects are totalities.[112]

These two convoluted sentences entail several explicit propositions and some implicit ones. The first explicit propositions of the first sentence are: 1) the nature of philosophy's penetration of reality is determined by the nature of philosophy's evolution, and 2) philosophy's penetration of the world appears as self-division ("the totality of the world is divided within itself"). The implicit proposition that joins these two is that the development of philosophy entails self-division or contradiction. These three propositions taken together could thus read: Like the development of philosophy, which is characterized and powered by contradictions, so the present actualization of philosophy is characterized and powered by contradictions.

The next part of the first sentence refines this meaning, asserting that the contradictions of spirit's penetration into the world are extreme ones. But the remainder of the first statement goes against this affirmation of spirit's contradictory relationship with reality: it fuses the contradictions of spirit's entry into the world back into a unity. Released into the world, "spiritual existence," like a "heart-beat," might manifest itself in diverse places, but in each place, it remains the same. Spirit is the "whole organism." It is one and united even if it appears in differentiated forms. The second sentence repeats this theme of unity in diversity in conventionally obscure idealist language. Decoded it might read: each of the diverse individualities that constitute the divisions of the world actually reflects in itself the unified whole. Like monads, each determination is both a particular individual and a reflection of the totality.

Marx's tortuous account of philosophy's entry into the world as a unity that appears as a diversity is more than a laborious exercise in philosophy. He seeks to show how unity can include fragmented individuality in order to explain and justify the reality of Hegelian philosophy. This is implied in the discussion that follows his establishment of the principle of unity in diversity. The encounter between society and a total philosophy results, he writes, in the appearance of a "world torn apart."[113] This transparently corresponds to the religious and political controversies that surrounded Hegelian philosophy. Marx then says that this conflict

with the world affects philosophy itself and issues in the apparent degeneration of philosophy into conflicting subjective forms, so that it too
"appears torn apart and contradictory."[114] This corresponds to the divisions within the Hegelian school. Together, the external conflicts of the
world (Hegelians against Pietists and conservatives) and the internal conflicts in modern philosophy (Hegelian against Hegelian) appear to under-
mine Hegel's philosophy of reconciliation. But for Marx this seemingly
antagonistic diversity actually conceals a unity. It is required to produce
a higher harmony:

> But one must not let oneself be misled by this storm which follows a great
> philosophy, a world philosophy. Ordinary harps play under any fingers, Aeolian
> harps only when struck by the storm.[115]

And a little later Marx writes, "titanic are the times which follow in the
wake of a philosophy total in itself and of its subjective developmental
forms, for gigantic is the discord that forms their unity."[116]

Division does not necessarily mean dissolution. On the contrary, it is
the attribute of a superior spiritual unity. To hold the view of some
Hegelians—"who," Marx writes, "understand our master wrongly"—
that spirit's entry into the world results in a featureless unity, is to
"assert . . . that *mediocrity* is the normal manifestation of absolute
spirit."[117] In other words, the apparent disunity of subjective forms of
philosophy is needed to assure spirit's vitality. Without the appearance
of conflicting manifestations, without a diversity in its unity, spirit would
become complacent. In this way Marx not only seeks to justify the
dissension within Hegelian ranks as something that is only apparent, that
actually reflects a complicated unity; he also wishes to say that that
apparent dissension is indispensable to spirit, the form spirit must assume
if it is not to atrophy.

Marx thus elected to side with the Young Hegelians. Against the
orthodox Hegelians, he believed that the criticism of a complacent reconciliation with the existing world keeps spirit alive, energetic. Yet paradoxically criticism does not render spirit disunited with its world, for
its apparent antagonism masks a deeper unity. This paradox becomes
comprehensible if we consider the kind of criticism of the existing world
Marx accepted at this time and how he linked it to Hegel's notion of
philosophy's reconciliation with the world. These themes are systemati-

cally developed and connected in Marx's dissertation, "The Difference Between the Democritean and Epicurean Philosophy of Nature."

Marx organizes his dissertation around an apparent paradox: both Epicurean and Democritean philosophy begin from the same rational principles—the concepts of the atom and the void—yet they reach diametrically opposed conclusions. Democritus believes that reason is the sole means of acquiring truth. For him, knowledge that is given by the senses is unreliable. Sense perception and reason are therefore irreconcilable, for uncertainty cannot consort with certainty. The problem that arises for Democritus begins in his belief that all knowledge of the real, external world is derived from sense perception and is hence untrustworthy, merely "subjective semblance."[118] The "real" world is thus removed from the "true" world of philosophical reason. But as something real, the empirical world still retains a power or quality that philosophy lacks and that demands to be appropriated by reason. Thus Democritus falls into a contradiction: he seeks to understand the sensuous world, which is resistant to understanding. He seeks for a truth that cannot exist. Marx describes the contradiction of Democritus by uniting the different anecdotes about his life:

Democritus is supposed to have blinded himself so that the *sensuous light of the eye* would not darken the *sharpness of the intellect.* This is the same man who, according to Cicero, wandered through half the world [in search of empirical knowledge].[119]

Epicurus is the opposite of Democritus. He is convinced that the real sensuous world corresponds to the true rational one. He scorns the search after positive empirical knowledge because he is satisfied with rational philosophy, comfortable with its place in the world. Democritus devotes himself to the restless search for the impossible; Epicurus takes as his principle the *ataraxy* (serenity) of philosophy, "the serenity of thought satisfied in itself, the self-sufficiency that draws its knowledge *ex principio interno.*"[120]

Democritus should remind us of Marx the Romantic, who, like the Greek philosopher, suffered from the inability to reconcile the real and the ideal. Epicurus, however, resembles Marx the Hegelian who believed that reason dwelt in harmony with its world. But while Marx admires

Epicurus for his serenity, he does not believe that serenity is incompatible with criticism and subjective freedom. In his view, serenity is enhanced by them.

The Democritean philosophy of nature considers the motion of atoms to be governed by blind necessity. An external compulsion forces the atom to behave in two ways: to fall in a straight line and to be repelled from other atoms. Epicurus accepts these two notions, but adds a third of his own. Although atoms fall in a straight line, they can also "swerve" or decline from that line, and by declining they repel and are repelled from other atoms. The atom's tendency to swerve arises from an internal urge to resist the external force that seeks to govern it. Marx writes: "the declination is that something in its [the atom's] breast that can fight back and resist."[121] In contrast to the passive atom of Democritus, the atom of Epicurus can call upon an inner ideal will to oppose the external compulsion of nature. It is not entirely dominated by natural forces; because it is partly ideal in character, it is partly free.[122]

For Marx, Epicurus is a better philosopher than Democritus because Epicurean philosophy has more spiritual content.[123] It conceives of the atom as more than nature's pawn. It also avoids the crippling contradiction of Democritean epistemology. Yet when Marx investigates Epicurus's attempt to extend his abstract idea of the free atom to a general explanation of how real heavenly bodies behave, he finds that Epicurean philosophy also falls into a serious contradiction.

The Democritean view of the heavens shares the traditional Greek belief that the heavenly bodies are one, eternal, and unchanging. But Epicurus believes "that in the meteors everything occurs in a multiple and unregulated way, that everything in them is to be explained by a manifold of indefinitely many causes."[124] Such a view does not logically flow out of Epicurus's notion of the atom. It contradicts the conception of the atom as a free agent, as an individual that acts according to its internal will, because this conception of the self-determining atom ought to lead to the conception of the eternal heavens:

The heavenly bodies are eternal and unchangeable; they have their centre of gravity in, not outside, themselves. Their only action is motion, and, separated by empty space, they swerve from the straight line and form a system of repulsion and attraction while at the same time preserving their own independence. . . . *The heavenly bodies are therefore the atoms become real.*[125]

Instead of accepting this logical conclusion, Epicurus arbitrarily insists on the changeable and unpredictable nature of heavenly bodies. His philosophy is in a state of self-contradiction.[126] But where Marx believes that the contradiction of Democritean philosophy renders that philosophy untenable, he considers the contradiction of Epicurean philosophy to be productive. It completes the spiritual development of Greek philosophy. It allows that philosophy to sever its remaining connection to the natural world and to emerge as an entirely independent self-consciousness.[127] Epicurus refuses to extend his notion of the free abstract atom to the concrete reality of the heavens because to do so would lead to the worship of the heavens. A conception of unique, unchanging heavenly bodies would yield, he thought, a mythological belief in their divinity. That in turn would disturb the ataraxy, the serenity of philosophy:

Yes, in wrath and passionate violence he . . . declares that . . . those who accept something Unique, hence Eternal and Divine in the meteors, fall victim to idle explanation–making and to the slavish artifices of the astrologers; they overstep the bounds of the study of nature and throw themselves into the arms of myth; they try to achieve the impossible, and exert themselves over absurdities; they do not even realise where ataraxy itself becomes endangered.[128]

Philosophy's serenity would be threatened by the worship of the heavens because philosophy would become dependent on them. It would sacrifice its own freedom to acknowledge the freedom of heavenly bodies. This is another way of saying that philosophy would become alienated from itself if it was forced to obey the gods, to be servile to a religion.

Epicurus is to be admired, Marx thought, because he refused to submit philosophy to the rule of the gods. His ideals of ataraxy and spiritual freedom were uncompromising. In Epicurean thought, Marx writes, "Philosophy makes no secret of it. The confession of Prometheus: 'In simple words, I hate the pack of gods,' is its own confession, its own aphorism against all heavenly and earthly gods who do not acknowledge human self-consciousness as the highest divinity. It will have none other beside."[129]

Marx's dissertation is thus a Young Hegelian tract, reflecting the mixed strategy of that group of philosophers. For Marx and other Young Hegelians, religion and philosophy are mutually exclusive forms of consciousness, and he consequently criticizes those who seek to reconcile them. But while he allows philosophy to be critical of religion, he seeks to preserve philosophy's ataraxy, its unity with the world. By arguing in his notebooks that there is an existing spiritual unity despite the apparent fragmentation of Hegelian philosophy, he tries to keep alive the redemptive significance of Hegelianism. In his dissertation, Marx reinforces this argument by linking the idea of unity and the possibility of criticism, Hegel's philosophy of reconciliation and the denial of religion.

Although Marx left no explicit testimony of his state of mind as he was finishing his dissertation, there is some evidence to suggest that with its completion he had achieved a serenity that he had lacked in 1837. First, one finds in the dissertation a sure, confident voice. His dissertation shows that his doubts about Hegelianism had been resolved: he had committed himself to the radical atheism of the Young Hegelians, without, he thought, sacrificing the serenity that came with Hegel's theory of redemption. In his public life this new self-assurance was reflected in his association with other Young Hegelians. By 1839 he had become not only a devoted radical but a leader of the radicals. He had formed close friendships with such Young Hegelian luminaries as Bruno Bauer and Carl Friedrich Köppen.[130] In 1840 he contemplated writing other pieces of religious criticism, which would have included attacks on prominent orthodox Hegelians,[131] and he later planned to collaborate with Bruno Bauer on further works in religious and aesthetic theory. Marx seemed to have at last secured his philosophical identity.

Second, the stability of his philosophical self was reinforced by a new stability in his relationship with Jenny von Westphalen. In 1839 and 1840, she had remained confused and agonized by her love, but by August 1841, that emotional muddiness had passed into the certainty that their love was unassailable from within and without. Her letters to Marx after 1840 reflect this new sense of sureness. Ambivalent passion was no longer present. She could tease her fiancé, engage in amused domestic banter, and express her affection with a charmed simplicity:

My little wild boar,

How glad I am that you are happy, and that my letter made you cheerful, and that you are longing for me, and that you are living in wallpapered rooms, and that you drank champagne in Cologne, and that there are Hegel clubs there, and that you have been dreaming, and that, in short, you are mine, my own sweetheart, my dear wild boar.[132]

From this new emotional stability arose the marriage that endured for their lifetimes.

Marx's apparent serenity was finally strengthened by his belief that he could now fulfill the ideals of his father. He planned to live a life of reason and clarity in the service of the Prussian state. He expected his dissertation to bring him an appointment at a university, ideally at the University of Bonn where his friend Bauer was teaching.[133] But like the similar convictions of Bauer and Ruge, Marx's belief in the affinity between Hegelian theory and the Prussian state would soon be fatally tested. While Hegelian serenity might incorporate religious criticism and dissension within the Hegelian school, it would soon succumb to the adverse social and political changes that were already taking place.

8

The Hegemony of Sensuousness

1

By the spring of 1841 Marx had clarified his personal and philosophical relations.[1] He had committed himself to the radical Young Hegelian belief in the irreconcilable antagonism between religion and philosophy. But although he had become an opponent of the existing religious order, he did not think that this antagonism was politically subversive; on the contrary, with Bauer and Ruge he believed that to purge the world of superstition was to strengthen the power of the Prussian state. For Marx, the state remained philosophy's objective counterpart—"the great organism," he wrote, "in which legal, moral, and political freedom must be realised."[2] The existing state was still philosophy's natural ally.

But in the course of the same year, the Prussian Young Hegelians began to wonder if Hegel had not miscast Prussia. Under the new regime of Frederick William IV the state seemed to reject its own rationality. Far from being the institutional embodiment of rational spirit, it was becoming increasingly hostile to reason. In the summer of 1841, the government drove the *Hallische Jahrbücher* out of Prussia, and at the end of the same year it enacted a more rigid censorship law. In the spring of 1842, Bruno Bauer lost his lectureship at the University of Bonn. Bauer's dismissal also affected Marx, for he had hoped that with Bauer's help he might obtain an academic position. He now recognized that that was impossible: a conservative and Pietist opposition to atheistic Young Hegelianism dominated the state's universities.

In the following year, after Marx had turned to journalism as an alternative career,[3] he became a direct victim of the state's increasing antagonism to Young Hegelian philosophy. His sole contribution to the

Deutsche Jahrbücher—an article on the December 1841 censorship law—was suppressed by the government.[4]

By 1842 Marx was thus undoubtedly aware of official hostility, yet he did not forsake his belief in the essential rationality of the existing state. In contrast to some of the political opposition in Prussia, he continued to seek reason's fulfillment in the present, in the reality of the existing order.[5] This ambivalent attitude toward the Prussian state—his awareness of its hostility and his faith in its benevolence—manifested itself in the appearance of two opposing tendencies in his journalism of 1842 and 1843.[6] First, like other Young Hegelians, he sought to preserve the Hegelian notion of philosophy's unity with the present by adapting that notion to the new political conditions. To accomplish this he would now have to do in his political journalism what he had earlier done in his dissertation: he would have to explain the unity of apparently disunited entities. But at the same time that he sought to maintain philosophy's affinity with the present state, he also found himself pursuing an opposite train of thought. While searching out the hidden unity of the present, he discovered more and more evidence that all unity was lost. In his journalism he showed that divisive particular interests had triumphed over universal reason.

The first tendency of Marx's journalism, his desire to adapt Hegelian philosophy to the changed political conditions, is especially apparent in an article that he wrote in July 1842 against the *Kölnische Zeitung*. Here he emphatically asserted philosophy's harmony with the present:

Philosophers do not spring up like mushrooms from the ground, they are products of their time, of their nation, whose most subtle, valuable and invisible juices flow in the ideas of philosophy. The same spirit that constructs railways with the hands of workers, constructs philosophical systems in the brains of philosophers. Philosophy does not exist outside the world any more than the brain exists outside man.[7]

Although this simple assertion of unity might once have seemed self-evident, it was no longer, as Marx recognized, very convincing. To preserve the credibility of this principle of an existing unity, he now had to show how it accounted for the apparent separation of philosophy from the world. Marx first asserted that the presence of apparent division within true unity was not unusual: "But philosophy . . . exists in the world through the brain before it stands with its feet on the ground, whereas many other spheres of human activity have long had their feet rooted in the ground and pluck with their hands the fruits of the world before they have any inkling that the 'head' also belongs to the world, or that this world is the world of the 'head.'"[8]

To explain how philosophy could be at once divided from and united with the world Marx had recourse to a conventional Hegelian distinction. The spiritual content of a period, he asserted, might initially manifest itself in an inappropriate form. Rational spirit might constitute the essential nature of the existing world, without the world recognizing spirit; but such a dissonance between form and content was merely temporary. It was the necessary transition to a harmonious unity of spirit, to the world's recognition of its spiritual content:

Since every true philosophy is the intellectual quintessence of its time, the time must come when philosophy, not only internally by its content, but also externally by its form, comes into contact and interaction with the real world of its day. Philosophy then ceases to be a particular system in relation to other particular systems, it becomes philosophy in general in relation to the world, it becomes the philosophy of the contemporary world.[9]

This alignment of form and content was even now being realized. Philosophy was ineluctably pressing its way into the salon, into the priest's study, and most important, into the editorial office.[10] The fact that philosophy had left its traditional academic isolation for the public domain of journalism was for Marx an unmistakable sign of the imminent fulfillment of spirit's unity with the world. Once it was firmly embodied in the press, there would be an identity of form and content, of philosophy and society:

The free press is the ubiquitous vigilant eye of a people's soul, the embodiment of a people's faith in itself, the eloquent link that connects the individual with the state and the world, the embodied culture that transforms material struggles into intellectual struggles and idealises their crude material form. It is a people's frank confession to itself, and the redeeming power of confession is well known. It is the spiritual mirror in which a people can see itself, and self-examination is the first condition of wisdom. It is the spirit of the state, which can be delivered into every cottage. . . . It is all-sided, ubiquitous, omniscient. It is the ideal world which wells up out of the real world and flows back into it with ever greater spiritual riches and renews its soul.[11]

That Marx made the philosophical press the instrument of philosophy's return to the world is especially striking because such a proposition went against the grain of Hegelian philosophy. As we have seen, the notion of a philosophical press was for Hegel a contradiction in terms. In his view, the press was the embodiment of capricious public opinion and hence an inappropriate medium for rational philosophy. But for Marx the press was the only means of returning to philosophy the power that he thought it once had.

Marx's elevation of the press reflected the harassed position of Young Hegelian philosophy in Prussia. Expelled from the universities, radical Hegelian philosophy was forced to rely solely on its journalistic organs. Marx sought to make the most of this situation. To preserve the Hegelian notion of philosophy's unity with the world, he glorified the press. In his view, the apparent diversion of philosophy to newspapers and journals was in truth an advance—it was the unquestionable sign of philosophy's impending fulfillment as a public power.

In light of the state's successful persecution of the philosophical press, Marx's belief in the increasing power of the press clearly involved an element of self-deception, although he did not altogether avoid the fact that philosophy was in retreat. The same articles that carried the message of reason's imminent unity with the world also documented a pattern of its increasing separation from the world.

Marx's first article on the censorship law of December 1841 admitted that Pietists and conservatives had successfully taken over the state. The new press law, he wrote, showed that the "confusion of the political with the Christian-religious principle has indeed become *official doctrine.*"[12] This "confusion" of the rational with irrational religion entailed a twofold inversion of the proper order of things. First, reason was now dominated by superstition. The rational state had become subject to the arbitrary whims of Pietists and Romantic conservatives.[13] Second, the universality of reason was now dominated by a particular interest: the narrow selfishness of the religious clique.[14] This double inversion resulted in an apparent exchange of identities: the limited and irrational Christian point of view gained the appearance of universality, while reason seemed to represent a particular opinion. "You [the Christian state] assume," Marx wrote, "that the officers [censors] will act quite impersonally, without animosity, passion, narrow-mindedness or human weakness. But what is impersonal, *ideas*, you suspect of being full of personal intrigue and subjective vileness."[15] The usurpation of the rational universal by the irrational particular was the leitmotif of Marx's journalism in the early 1840s. The political success of conservative and Pietist groups led him to reevaluate the Hegelian relation between universal and particular interests. That relation was always supposed to operate in favor of the universal. Universal reason should have converted particular interests to its own purpose. But in his journalism, Marx found that in Prussian society particular or private interests refused to be domesticated by the universality of the rational state. The debates of the Rhineland's Landtag over the freedom of the press revealed, for example, that this supposedly impartial political body was merely the vehicle of the private interests of different estates. The estates' concern for their own privileges rendered them deaf and blind to the interests of the state as a whole.[16]

Marx's most searching investigation of the nature of particular interests was his October 1842 analysis of the Rhenish Landtag's debates on the laws governing the theft of wood. He identified in those deliberations a ruthless and systematic debasement of universal reason by private material interests. The forest owners of the Rhineland called on the Landtag to abolish the Rhenish people's customary right of wood gathering. They also wanted their own forest wardens to be the sole administrators of the new law. Their agents would apprehend the wood thief, determine the value of the stolen wood, and fine the thief. The wood gatherer, Marx noted, would thus fall under the total control of the forest owner.[17]

Marx recognized in the forest owner's demands an absolute selfishness. For the forest owner to gain complete control over the wood gatherers entailed not only the denial of the latter's traditional rights but also the denial of their general humanity. To dominate other human beings, private interest redefined them according to its own narrow terms. Marx writes:

The petty, wooden, mean and selfish soul of interest sees only one point, the point in which it is wounded, like a coarse person who regards a passer-by as the most infamous, vilest creature under the sun because the unfortunate creature has trodden on his corns. . . . Private interest makes the one sphere in which a person comes into conflict with this interest into the person's whole sphere of life.[18]

Moreover, private interest's attempt to reduce universality to its own point of view engendered a paradox: to make the universal particular, it had to pretend that its own particular interests were universal, in the interest of all humanity. "When it is a matter," Marx writes, "of making other people the victim of its tools and giving a favorable appearance to dubious means, selfishness puts on its rose-coloured spectacles, which impart an imaginary glory to these tools and means, and deludes itself and others with the impractical, delightful dreaming of a tender, trusting soul."[19]

In other words, to fulfill its selfish material desire, private interest had to represent itself in a universal form. It had to claim to speak for all humanity. And the inevitable outcome of this drive to universalize itself was for private interest to seek control of the universal in its objective form: it plotted to take over the state.[20] The egoistic individual demanded that his private interest be made into a universal law. Thus the wood gatherer, Marx comments, might have "robbed the forest owner of wood," but, under the new law, "the forest owner has made use of the wood thief to purloin the *state itself.*"[21]

Although Marx had borne witness to the increasing expropriation of the state by private interests and hence to the increasing improbability of realizing Hegelian beliefs, he still hoped throughout 1842 that the state could be drawn back to the ways of philosophy. He especially wanted to believe that philosophy's new embodiment in the press was the beginning of a movement that would turn back private interests—whether of Pietists, conservatives, bureaucrats, or forest owners. He thought that the philosophical press could domesticate their imperialist impulses. "What makes the press," Marx wrote, "the most powerful lever for promoting culture and the intellectual education of the people is precisely the fact that it transforms the material struggle . . . of flesh and blood into a struggle of minds, the struggle of need, desire, empiricism into a struggle of theory, of reason, of form."[22] But this idealist hope in the ability of universal reason to master society's egoistic sensuous interests collapsed in the spring of 1843 when the Prussian state suppressed the *Rheinische Zeitung.*

2

Throughout the winter of 1842 and the spring of 1843, the period of the *Rheinische Zeitung's* most intense conflict with the Prussian censor, Marx did not renounce his loyalty to the state. He still believed that the state contained a reservoir of reason, which could be tapped by the philosophical press; the strategy of Marx's paper was reformist rather than revolutionary. "Far from intending to attack the basis of the Prussian constitution," he wrote in February 1843, " . . . the Rh[einische] Z[eitung], on the contrary, was convinced that it was attacking only deviations from this base."[23]

The suppression of the Young Hegelian paper disabused Marx of his faith in the state. His previous ambivalence now gave way to a clarified and resolute radicalism. The existing state, he believed, had irretrievably fallen into the hands of the enemies of philosophy. The outcome, Marx wrote, of the "unsuccessful attempt to abolish the philistine state on its own basis . . . has been to make it evident to the whole world that for despotism brutality is a necessity and humanity an impossibility."[24]

Marx's disillusionment with Prussia was of such intensity that he found it intolerable to remain in Germany.[25] When Ruge proposed that they emigrate to Paris, where they could organize a new philosophical press, Marx gladly agreed. But before Marx left for Paris in the fall of 1843, he undertook two more "clarifications" of his life. First, after a seven-year engagement, he married Jenny von Westphalen in June 1843. After a brief honeymoon, Marx and Jenny spent the rest of the summer at the Westphalen house at Kreuznach, a spa just east of Trier. There Marx began to work through the consequences of his alienation from the state. This attempt to elucidate his situation not only involved a searching investigation of the nature of German politics but also a reexamination of Hegelian theory. As in the cases of Bauer and Ruge, the discrediting of the Prussian state as the objective agent of reason naturally led Marx to question the philosophy that had first convinced him of that political ideal.

Several commentators have identified in Marx's Kreuznach criticism of Hegel—the so-called "Contribution to the Critique of Hegel's Philosophy of the Right"—the influence of Feuerbach and Bauer. From these other Young Hegelians, Marx accepted what Shlomo Avineri has called the "transformative method"—the critical technique of reversing a proposition's subject and object.[26] According to these interpreters, Marx used the transformative method in the "Contribution" to argue that Hegelian theory had inverted the actual order of things: Hegel had made the concrete human being into an emanation or predicate of an illusory abstract subject, namely, spirit. In truth the opposite obtained: spirit was the creation of real human beings.[27]

This characterization of Marx's reevaluation of Hegel is both accurate and cogent, but it is also incomplete. It does not tell us how Marx tried to explain why Hegel inverted reality. Why, Marx also asked, did Hegel seek to mystify the actual relation between human beings and spirit?

Marx's explanation of Hegelian philosophy's treatment of reality is derived from his characterization of a paradox in Hegel's political philosophy. According to Marx, Hegel appears to be uninterested in the real state. For Hegel, Marx writes,

The essence of the definitions of the state is not that they are definitions of the state, but that in their most abstract form they can be regarded as logical-metaphysical definitions. Not the philosophy of law but logic is the real centre of interest. Philosophical work does not consist in embodying thinking in political definitions, but in evaporating the existing political definitions into abstract thought. . . . The logic does not serve to prove the state, but the state to prove the logic.[28]

Hegel did not deal with the existing world on its own terms, but sought instead to absorb the world into the development of an autonomous logic. He bracketed empirical political facts with abstractions, so that, Marx writes, "the whole of the philosophy of law is only a parenthesis within logic."[29]

But at the same time that Hegel refused to treat the real empirical existent in its own right, investing the object instead with an extraneous abstract meaning, he also completely accepted the empirical existent. Idealism did not criticize the existent, but merely absorbed it as it was into a pattern of logical development. "The inevitable outcome of this [Hegel's method]," Marx wrote, "is that an *empirical existent* is *uncritically* accepted as the actual truth of the idea; for it is not a question of bringing empirical existence to its truth, but of bringing truth to an empirical existent, and so what lies to hand is expounded as a *real* element of the idea."[30] Hegel's project, according to Marx, was to invest an empirical existent with an aura of transcendent rationality. The philosopher was a political conservative who sought to justify existing irrationalities by making them appear to be part of a larger rational development. This confusion of empirical existent with a transcendent logic resulted in many hopeless contradictions in Hegel's political philosophy.[31] For example, the natural and hence contingent person of the monarch was made into a logical necessity.[32] Hegel's conservative idealism twisted things out of shape. It created a "verkehrte" world: "That the rational is actual is proved precisely in the *contradiction* of *irrational actuality,* which everywhere is the contrary of what it asserts, and asserts the contrary of what it is."[33]

But although Marx thus identified the source of the Hegelian mystification of reality in Hegel's conservatism, he did not regard that conservatism as a political attitude that blindly accepted everything. He recognized that it was more complex: as he noted, Hegelian theory both denied and preserved the existing world. Hegel did not accept the empirical world's own justifications, but sought to ground it in a systematic logic, and according to Marx, he attempted to make his own complex justification of the existing order because he was sensitive to that order's present divisions and contradictions. He recognized the tensions and conflicts of the existing world, and therefore, to preserve that world, he tried to overcome its problems in thought.

Marx's identification of the conservatism of Hegelian theory was thus tied to the analysis of German society and politics which he made in the "Contribution." This analysis was an expansion of his earlier journalistic investigations of Prussia's social and political conditions. In those investigations he had sought to understand how private sensuous interests were opposed to the universal, rational state. The "Contribution" was concerned with the background of that opposition. It focused on the origin of the conflict between self-interest and universal interest or, as they appeared historically, civil society and the state.

According to Marx, private and general interests were not always opposed to each other. In the Middle Ages society was made up of "private spheres," each of which had a political character. An estate, for instance, was a social group that also exercised political power, both in regulating itself and in dealing with other social-political groups. As a member of such a corporate body, an individual's private social interest was also a general political interest. His life was socially and politically unified.[34]

But the private political spheres did not coexist harmoniously; on the contrary, some sought to dominate others. Eventually, one of these particular spheres—the monarchy—began to expropriate the other spheres' political power. It began to strip corporate bodies of their self-governing authority, thereby reducing them to social groups held together by nothing more than material self-interest. This development of political power issued in the absolute monarchy, the monopolization of political power by the monarchical state.[35] Under this regime the former corporate unity of private and political interests collapsed: the general interest of the community became the restricted domain of the state, while the private interests of individuals were confined to civil society.

This division between the universal and the particular, the state and civil society, was completed by the French Revolution. All remnants of the old corporate society were now irreparably destroyed. Political power was concentrated into a single body—the monolithic state—which existed in opposition to the many private material interests that comprised civil society.[36]

Further, the disjunction between particular and universal was now more than an external division between the state and civil society. It also manifested itself within each individual as a self-division. As a member of civil society, the individual was motivated solely by private, egoistic interests; yet he was also a citizen of the state and therefore possessed a universal, political character. These two aspects of his character were unbridgeable, and indeed at odds with each other. As a member of civil society, he sought the unfettered pursuit of his own interests. But as a member of the state, he sought to curtail the narrow selfishness of egoistic interests in the general interest of the community.

A person could not attempt to resolve this dualism by simply choosing one aspect of his character over the other. Separated from its complement, each was necessarily unfulfilling. As a member of civil society, the individual was limited to the slavish life of narrow egoistic interests.[37] As a citizen of a detached state, one's political existence was ethereal; it lacked meaningful content. An individual, Marx wrote,

in order to behave as an *actual citizen of the state,* and to attain political significance and effectiveness . . . must step out of his civil reality, disregard it, and
withdraw from this whole organisation into his individuality; for the sole existence which he finds for his citizenship of the state is his sheer, blank *individuality,* since the existence of the state as executive is complete without him, and
his existence in civil society is complete without the state.[38]

According to Marx, Hegel recognized the existing division of the state from civil society; he had made this division the "starting-point" of his philosophy by assuming that civil society, as a category, was logically and historically prior to political categories.[39] But although Hegel accepted the existing separation of social from political forms, he felt uneasy about that division. He liked existing institutions, but disliked their

antagonisms. Hence he tried to show how the separation of civil society from the state ultimately issued in a unity that left existing institutions unchanged. He sought to preserve the existing forms of society and politics in a way that would annul their division or opposition, and thus he attributed to antagonistic empirical existents an extraempirical or logical significance that joined them together. For example, the agent of the state, the bureaucracy, was on Hegel's theory a logically determined mediation between the universal interest of the state and the particular interests of civil society,[40] and the estates of civil society were given a limited legislative or political function that would unite them with the state.[41]

But Hegel, Marx tells us, deceived himself: he did not supersede real existing divisions, but merely shrouded them with abstractions. Far from bridging the gap between the state and civil society, the bureaucracy regarded the state as its private domain.[42] And the civil estates, once given legislative power, did not abandon their narrow egoism in the interests of the body politic but on the contrary, as Marx's own experience had demonstrated, used their political position to manipulate the general interest in favor of their private interests.[43]

Hegel's shortcoming, according to Marx, was that he could not bring himself to acknowledge the fact that the division between existing social and political forms was a necessary attribute of those forms. Hegel was an intensely ambivalent conservative. He wanted to preserve the existing order, yet he could not be comfortable with the divisions of that order. To overcome society's divisions without altering society, he produced an idealistic bracketing of existing institutions. But this philosophical approach was ineffectual: it did not resolve existing divisions, it merely concealed them.

For Marx, the overcoming of the division between man's private and public characters involved the overcoming of both the existing society and the existing state. They could not be arbitrarily joined together by abstractions as Hegel had tried to do, nor could one be chosen over the other, for that would mean accepting a one-sided and alienated existence.

In the "Contribution," Marx linked his critique of Hegelian philosophy with his analysis of long-term problems in German politics and society (an analysis similar to Ruge's in "Der protestantische Absolutismus"). Hegelian theory, Marx argued, was an attempt to preserve the existing reality while banishing its problems in thought; it was both a justification of and compensation for the ills of the existing world.

Shortly after Marx used his newly developed social and political analysis to elucidate Hegelian philosophy, he further applied it to challenge the views of a fellow Young Hegelian. In his quarrel with his friend Bruno Bauer on the so-called Jewish Question, Marx first indicated that his discontent with Hegel was also affecting his relations with his fellow Prussian Young Hegelians. The product of his disagreement with Bauer, his essay, "On the Jewish Question," showed how his ideological criticism of Hegel could be widened to include his own comrades in arms.

As we have seen, Bauer opposed the political emancipation of the Jews for two reasons. First, to give Jews political equality was to perpetuate an alienated religious consciousness that for Bauer was even more degraded than the defective consciousness of Christianity. Membership in a servile religious sect was incompatible with membership in a universal political community. Second, emancipation would encourage the release of sensuous interests, the consolidation of "mass" society, for the Jews were the representatives par excellence of the egoistic domain of brutalized natural need and desire.

In his essay "On the Jewish Question," Marx took issue with both of Bauer's arguments. Marx dealt with Bauer's first argument by reversing its procedure. Where Bauer explained a person's political limitations in terms of his religious limitations, Marx sought to explain a person's religious limitations in terms of his political ones. To do this, he brought to bear the social and political analysis formulated in the "Contribution." As Marx had noted in that work, the characteristic relation between the modern state and modern society was one of division. This division occurred in the period after the Middle Ages as princes collected for themselves the diffuse political power of various social groups; or, as Marx put it in "On the Jewish Question," the modern state emerged by extricating itself from the conditions and restrictions of various groups in society. But this process of distilling political authority from those social groups and concentrating it in the monarchical state did not mean that the state destroyed the social conditions and restrictions of these groups. On the contrary, the modern state required their perpetuation, for it was defined in opposition to them: it had a monopoly of universal, political authority only so long as it stood over against a sphere of particular interests and distinctions.[44]

The modern state had emerged through a process of abstraction: political authority was abstracted from particular social groups. The state thus gained the appearance of a universal entity opposed to particular social distinctions and conditions. One of the particular conditions that the emerging state had detached itself from and had relegated to civil society was religious belief. Religious affiliation had once been a condition of public, political authority, but in its desire to monopolize political power, the modern state could not allow itself to be subject to another agency in society, namely, the Church. Religion was thus rendered a matter of private conscience, consigned to the domain of atomized individual interests and restrictions. It was banished to civil society. It became one of the necessary particular conditions of society against which the universal state defined itself. Political emancipation—the rise of the modern state and with it the modern citizen—thus came about not, as Bauer believed, through the elimination of one's particular religious affiliation, but through the creation of a tension between that affiliation and one's membership in a universal political community. "The *decomposition*," Marx writes, "of man into Jew and citizen, Protestant and citizen, religious man and citizen . . . is *political emancipation itself.*"[45]

Bauer's opposition to the political emancipation of the Jews was not only wrongheaded; it was also, Marx implied, ineffectual. It ignored the existing social and political reality.[46] Bauer failed to recognize that Jewish emancipation was an inevitable development of history, a necessary consequence of the separation of state and society. For Bauer, consciousness determined the limits of political participation; for Marx, social and political processes defined the horizons of consciousness. Marx, in short, was pressing toward a materialist explanation of ideas and a materialist critique of the ideas of his fellow Young Hegelians.

Bauer's second reason for opposing Jewish emancipation—that it further released the disturbing sensuousness of civil society—was also challenged by Marx's analysis of the separation of state and civil society. In the second part of "On the Jewish Question" Marx disarmingly agreed with Bauer's characterization of Jewish secular life. The Jew, Marx wrote, was motivated primarily by self-interest; his world was "huckstering"; his "God" was "money."[47] But unlike Bauer, Marx did not find this Jewish social character to be unusual or alarming. On the contrary, for Marx it was exemplary of the general character of the existing order of things. The Jew was a representative of depoliticized civil society, a society powered by egoistic need and desire. He was merely a "particular manifestation of the Judaism of civil society."[48]

Bauer's second argument against the Jewish emancipation was thus also founded on a lack of realism. He was right, according to Marx, to identify the Jew as a manifestation of emerging "mass society," but he ignored the real extent of that society: it had become the general condition of modern social life. Marx seemed to imply that Bauer's fear of the Jew was ultimately a fear of reality, an attempt to cancel out the general consolidation of brutalizing civil society by denying political rights to one of its members. The sensuous egoism of the Jew would not be abolished by imposing political restrictions on him, but by doing away with civil society, and, with it, its severed political counterpart, the state.[49]

In both the "Contribution" and "On the Jewish Question," Marx connected Hegelian and Young Hegelian theory to existing social and political forms, and recognized the necessity of going beyond those forms. But it is unclear what he hoped for the future. Some commentators have argued that in 1843 Marx was a communist, because in the "Contribution" he specifically attacked primogeniture as a pernicious form of private property and generally called for the abolition of civil society and the existing state.[50] But this argument is unpersuasive. Although he identified primogeniture and traditional privilege in general as forms of alienated private property, he defended modern business, arguing that it was a true expression of humanity.[51] Marx was scarcely an opponent of capitalism. Moreover, also at about this time, he had been reading contemporary communist theories and he was not convinced that they offered either an adequate critique of the present or a viable plan for the future. On the contrary, he suspected that they might share the vice of German philosophy: in a letter to Arnold Ruge he called communism a "dogmatic abstraction."[52]

Finally, Marx clearly did not believe in a total "withering away of the state." He was opposed to the existing state, which was severed from social life, but he still believed in the possibility of a harmonious and rational future state.[53] In the "Contribution" he called this ideal unified state "true democracy," but beyond the obvious fact that it would be based on a democratic suffrage, he gave no further details about what it would be like.[54]

In 1843, on the eve of his departure for Paris, Marx seemed to share the general political beliefs of his friend and soon-to-be collaborator

Arnold Ruge. Like Ruge, Marx continued to adhere to the Hegelian principle of a political solution to the existing divisions and problems of society.[55] A revolution that would establish a democratic state would restore rational harmony to politics and society. But unlike Ruge's strong commitment to Hegel's rationalist politics, there were suggestions that Marx felt uneasy about his political program. In a letter of September 1843 to Arnold Ruge, Marx told his ally, "Not only has a state of general anarchy set in among the reformers, but everyone will have to admit to himself that he has no exact idea what the future ought to be."[56] The sweep of Marx's statement would suggest that he counted himself among those who had "no exact idea what the future ought to be." That uncertainty about the new world might explain the lack of detail in his picture of "true democracy." It also suggests that his commitment to such a state was very insecure indeed.

3

In the autumn of 1843 Marx arrived in Paris, where he collaborated with Arnold Ruge in the establishment of the *Deutsch-Französische Jahrbücher*. His association with the democrat Ruge did not, however, strengthen his commitment to a political revolution that would lead to a democratic state. On the contrary, once in Paris he began to move away from his belief in the importance of politics. He made a more rigorous and appreciative study of French and German communist writings, including those of Friedrich Engels.[57] Further, he had become extremely impressed with the active social and political life of French and immigrant German workers.[58] The solidarity and enthusiasm of their associations contrasted starkly with the disarray and isolation of German philosophy. Where German theory had increasingly come to seem ethereal, detached from concrete existence, the social life of the workers seemed immediately and palpably real. In a letter to Feuerbach, Marx wrote, "You would have to attend one of the meetings of the French workers to appreciate the pure freshness, the nobility which bursts forth from these toil-worn men."[59]

Marx's favorable reevaluation of communist theory and his enhanced appreciation of the working class profoundly affected his thinking. First, they provided him with the elements that his previous criticism lacked—namely, a means of transcending the existing order and a more concrete notion of an ideal future order. Workers' associations offered both the revolutionary cadres of the present and the nuclei of the communities of the future. Second, communist theory's emphasis on class conflict gave Marx a way of organizing his observations about civil society and the state and his discontent with Hegelian and Young Hegelian theory into a more systematic view of social, political, and philosophical change. And indeed, the first theoretical piece that he wrote in Paris, the so-called "Introduction to the Critique of Hegel's Philosophy of Law," can be regarded as a prototype of historical materialism.

This article, which Marx published in the first and only issue of the *Deutsch-Französische Jahrbücher* and which he intended to be the introduction to his critique of Hegelian politics, is also interesting for another reason. Like Ruge's major Paris essay "Unsre letzten zehn Jahre," Marx's piece was an interpretation of recent developments in German history and philosophy. In other words, the "Introduction" was a kind of self-examination: in this recapitulation of his recent experiences, Marx sought to comprehend the significance of his own political and philosophical dislocations. His alienation from Germany was transparent in the "Introduction"; like Bauer and Ruge he identified Germany as a historical anomaly. In the "Introduction" his homeland appeared as a nation that was out of step with the modern age.

Marx begins the "Introduction" by announcing the end of an important stage in Germany philosophy. "For Germany," he writes, "*the criticism of religion* is in the main complete. . . . "[60] Marx plainly refers to philosophical criticism's recent success in unmasking the alienated nature of religion. Religion's true function has been revealed: "It is the *fantastic realisation* of the human essence because the *human essence* has no reality."[61] It is, in other words, merely an epiphenomenon of social and political processes, a mental compensation for an inadequate reality. Religion, Marx goes on to say in what has become one of his famous lines, "is the opium of the people."[62]

Now that religion has been demystified and the criticism of religion thereby completed, one must proceed to investigate the social and political processes that generated religion. "The immediate *task of philosophy* . . . " Marx concludes, "once the *holy form* of human self-estrangement has been unmasked, is to unmask self-estrangement in its *unholy forms.*" The "*criticism of religion* should now turn into the *criticism of law* and the *criticism of theology* into the *criticism of politics.*"[63]

But immediately after announcing that philosophy's new imperative is to criticize existing conditions rather than abstractions from those conditions, Marx does an about-face: he tells us that he does not intend to deal with law and politics in this work, but with Hegel's philosophy of law and politics. He intends to deal with abstractions. Marx justifies this turnabout, this rejection of the criticism that he had just prescribed, by saying that he must deal with an extraordinary subject. The standard methods of social and political analysis must be suspended when one considers a historical anomaly—namely, Germany.[64]

According to Marx, Germany is out of phase with the modern age because, unlike other European countries, it did not pass through a political revolution. Where other countries destroyed their old political orders, Germany's "ancien regime" has become stronger. Or, as Marx put it, "we shared the restorations of the modern nations although we had not shared their revolutions."[65]

In contrast to the dynamic middle-class regimes of other European countries, Germany has remained parochial, clinging to a dead past. Where other nations, for example, have instituted free trade, Germany has begun a movement toward economic protectionism. "Like a clumsy recruit," Marx writes, Germany "still has to do extra drill in matters that are old and hackneyed in history."[66]

Germany has perversely resisted the modern trend in politics, but in one way it has managed to keep up with modern developments. It has accomplished in thought what other nations have accomplished in politics. Marx writes, "We are the *philosophical* contemporaries of the present without being its *historical* contemporaries."[67]

The condition of German thought and politics is thus disjointed: Germany's politics are backward, but its philosophy is advanced. The reason for this disjunction is that philosophy functions like religion: it is an abstract compensation for an inadequate reality. It attempts to achieve in theory what other nations have achieved in fact. "German philosophy," Marx writes, "is the *ideal prolongation* of Germany history."[68]

The disjunction between an advanced theory and a backward reality issues in further dislocations. German philosophy eventually becomes even more estranged from reality: it generates a radical form of criticism that criticizes, not Germany's backward reality, but the theoretical abstraction from that reality: namely, German philosophy. "What in advanced nations is a *practical* break with modern political conditions,"

Marx writes, "is in Germany, where even those conditions do not yet exist, at first a *critical* break with the philosophical reflection of those conditions."[69] In short, the critical theory of the Young Hegelians is twice removed from German reality. It struggles against an illusion of reality.

The true overcoming of German reality has to take into account both Germany's backward politics and its advanced philosophy. To negate only the philosophy—as Bruno Bauer and his Berlin coterie tried to do—would leave the reality untouched.[70] And to negate only the existing politics would merely raise Germany to the level of other countries, the level of the "partial" political revolution of the middle class. Such a level would still be a step away from a fully integrated human existence.[71]

Moreover, even if Germany wanted a political revolution, it would not be able to attain it. A political revolution takes place only when "*part of civil society* emancipates itself and attains *general* domination."[72] Such a social group—a class—is active and powerful, and can appear to transcend itself by mobilizing the entire nation. It can arouse, Marx writes, "a moment of enthusiasm in itself and in the masses, a moment in which it fraternises and merges with society in general, becomes confused with it and is perceived and acknowledged as its general representative."[73]

In Germany, however, no such "estate"[74] has the "breadth of soul that identifies itself, even for a moment, with the soul of the nation." Instead, the constituent groups of German society are narrow-minded, "philistine." They are characterized by a "*modest egoism*" that "asserts its limitedness and allows it to be asserted against itself."[75]

What is required is an agent that with a single blow would revolutionize Germany, driving the nation beyond both its own traditional limitations and the more modern limitations of other countries, which are reflected in German philosophy.[76] Such an agent of uncompromising revolution would thus have to be a member of the present society which had no interest in preserving either traditional or modern society. It would in other words have to be utterly exploited, denied any possibility of fulfillment in either traditional or bourgeois society. It would have to be, in Marx's words, "a class with *radical chains,* a class of civil society which is not a class of civil society, an estate which is the dissolution of all estates, a sphere which has a universal character by its universal suffering and claims no *particular right* because no *particular wrong* but *wrong* generally is perpetrated against it." This agent of absolute change is, of course, the proletariat.[77]

Marx's "Introduction" was his third attempt since 1841 to comprehend the disjointed nature of German life. In his first attempt, his journalism of 1842, he had located the source of Germany's problems in the usurpation of the universal state by particular social or civil interests. But while he had recognized that the existing state was no longer rational, he still believed that it could become so. He continued to think that the state was in essence if not in existence philosophy's objective counterpart. He was still a follower of Hegel's political idealism.

At Kreuznach, however, Marx subjected Hegelian philosophy to a thorough reexamination. He now developed, in his second attempt to understand Prussian conditions, the "Contribution" of 1843, a historical account that was the converse of Hegel's: where the latter had conceived of the rise of the modern state as the integration of social groups into a unified whole, Marx saw in the rise of the state the distintegration of a social and political whole into irreconcilable parts. The unified corporate society of the Middle Ages had given way, he argued, to a radical opposition between the state and civil society. In the modern world, human beings were fractured: their private, social being was entirely detached from their public, political being.

Although the "Contribution" was a continuation of the social and political concerns of Marx's journalism, it also marked a departure from his journalistic views. The "Contribution" postulated an unbridgeable gulf between the existing civil society and the existing state, where his journalism had implied a unity. In the *Rheinische Zeitung*, Marx had argued that particular interests were not separated from the state but, on the contrary, that they sought the most intimate connection with it. They sought to make it the instrument of their egoistic desires.

The "Introduction" offered a third view of social and political development, a view that in one respect marked a return to the ideas expressed in his journalism. In the "Introduction" Marx again postulated between the existing civil society and the existing state the same intimate connection that was absent in the "Contribution." He once again argued that particular interests controlled or sought to control the state. But the "Introduction" also differed from his journalistic thought in a crucial respect. It abandoned the Hegelian conception of the state as an institution that was essentially rational and universal. Marx no longer believed that the state ever was or ever could be as Hegel had imagined it. According to the "Introduction," the state was utterly bereft of independent substance; it was nothing more than the representative of the interests of a particular class of civil society. Marx now considered the state to be merely the political appearance of social interests.

Thus the evolution of Marx's social and political thought from his journalism of 1841 to the "Introduction" of early 1844 did not follow a single or consistent line. Marx proceeded from the idea of an intimate, if undesirable, connection between civil society and the state, to the idea of their unbridgeable gulf, and then back to the idea of an unfortunate connection.[78] Yet throughout this apparent fluctuation one theme remained constant. In all of Marx's writings of 1842–1844, one can make out a steady derogation of politics in general and of the state in particular.

In his articles of 1842, Marx believed that the state, though at present misguided, offered the only possibility of a harmonious and rational life. It would ultimately rationalize and unify the particular interests that sought to overrun it. By 1843, Marx had ceased to believe that the existing state had even potentially any such universal significance. He now asserted that it was and would always be a mere shadow of man's former corporate universality. A year later, he did not even grant the state the dubious distinction of being an alienated, unfulfilling universal. In the "Introduction" of 1843 it appeared as an illusion of human universality, an illusion generated by social interests. The idea of the state as a superior rational entity that domesticated the chaotic sensuous interests of civil society altogether vanished. In the "Contribution" Marx thus fully renounced the Hegelian conception of the state. Politics was now in principle nothing more than an epiphenomenon of society's sensuous interests.

This final derogation of politics in the "Introduction" was accompanied by a similar derogation of philosophy. We have already seen that in the "Contribution" Marx explained Hegelian political theory in terms of existing social and political concerns. Hegelian theory was a justification of and a compensation for the separation of state and society. In "On the Jewish Question" Marx further showed how Bauer's analysis was also tied to that existing reality. Out of his fear of sensuous civil society, Bauer had generated a false conception of the Jew's social and political role, which, Bauer then argued, should be restricted. Bauer sought, in other words, to compensate for his fear of reality by condensing that general reality into an illusory particular enemy that could be overcome. In the "Contribution" and "On the Jewish Question" Hegel and his follower were thus shown to be engaging in ideology. In the "Introduction" Marx went beyond demonstrating these specific cases of philosophy as ideology to stating as a general principle that all German philosophy operated as ideology. Hegelian and Young Hegelian theories were manifestations of a broad attempt to compensate for an inadequate reality.

Like Bauer's and Ruge's turning against Hegelian philosophy, Marx's hostility to that philosophy was tied to his sense of having been betrayed by it. From originally regarding Hegelian theory as the systematic expression of an absolute truth, he had, like the other Prussian Young Hegelians, come to see it as a deception that distorted the true nature of reality. Hegel had promised his followers a glorious truth that had turned out to be only a grandiose lie. This feeling of having been deceived by Hegelian theory left Marx with a deep suspicion of all abstraction. And this suspicion predisposed him to find a solution to Germany's problems in an entity that seemed eminently unabstract: the proletariat. As we have seen, Marx was extremely impressed by the working men's associations that he had visited in Paris. In the course of 1844 his admiration of the proletariat was reinforced by the heroic revolt of the Silesian weavers. For Marx, the suffering and solidarity of workers contrasted sharply with philosophy's illusions of grandeur. Where abstract thought had proved itself deceitful, proletarian sensuousness was compellingly honest and real.[79]

Thus as well as considering Hegelian philosophy to be derivative of its social and political environment, Marx's "Introduction" further diminished the status of philosophy in another way. In the "Introduction," he made present critical philosophy into the servant of the proletariat.

This interpretation of the relation between critical philosophy and the proletariat in the "Introduction" is apparently contradicted by a famous remark that Marx makes at the end of the "Introduction." Here he writes, "The *head* of this [human] emancipation is *philosophy*, its *heart* is the *proletariat*."[80] Some commentators have interpreted this remark as a call for an alliance between philosophers and workers,[81] implying that Marx gives a status to philosophy that is equal to, if not greater than, that of the proletariat. But this interpretation is simplistic. While Marx does conceive of an alliance between philosophy and the proletariat, he does so in a way that entirely denies the conventional meaning of philosophy. Philosophy's alliance with the proletariat amounts to philosophy's self-destruction.

Marx argues that for philosophy to appeal to workers, it must address their immediate sensuous needs. "Theory can be realised in a people," he writes, "only insofar as it is the realisation of the needs of that people."[82] But to address the proletariat's sensuous needs requires that philosophy do more than talk about the content of those needs or what the proletariat lacks. To address sensuous needs philosophy must converse in a way that can be sensuously apprehended. In other words, it can make itself intelligible to the proletariat's sensuous nature only if it presents itself in a sensuous form; but a sensuous form is not a rational form. Philosophy cannot influence the proletariat with austere logical argument. It must instead sway the workers' senses. It must become affective in approach. To work with the proletariat it must appeal emotionally to the proletariat's beliefs and inclinations. Marx writes: "Theory is capable of gripping the masses as soon as it demonstrates *ad hominem*."[83]

But to have to appear in an affective form, to be allowed only arguments ad hominem, is to reject the traditional ideal of philosophy as a purely rational or logical discourse. If philosophy is to serve the sensuous needs of the proletariat, it must cease to be philosophy in the conventional sense. The alliance of philosophy with the proletariat is thus the abolition of philosophy.

4

In the course of 1844, Marx continued to criticize Hegelian theory. The so-called *Paris* or *1844 Manuscripts* contain a hostile analysis of Hegel's dialectical method, and Marx's subsequent works, *The Holy Family* (1844) and *The German Ideology* (1845–1846)—both composed with Friedrich Engels—are extended attacks on Young Hegelians. These critiques of Hegel and his radical followers are essentially of a piece, elaborations of the ideological analysis of philosophy begun in the "Contribution" and the "Introduction."

At the same time that Marx continued his criticism of philosophy, he also further developed his understanding of social and political processes. For although his discovery of the proletariat in the "Introduction" provided him with an important theoretical element that he had earlier lacked—namely, a new agent of historical change—his understanding of the proletariat was still undeveloped, confined to little more than the intuition of its potentially revolutionary character. He still needed a more extensive theoretical and historical comprehension of it. Where did it come from? Why should it necessarily be revolutionary? Was the proletariat the agent of revolution only in Germany or in all of Europe? These were questions that the "Introduction" either left unanswered or answered ambiguously.[84]

Soon after the appearance of the "Introduction," Marx in fact expressed his dissatisfaction with the present state of his social theory. In 1844, when the *Deutsch-Französische Jahrbücher* had collapsed and when Marx had become estranged from Arnold Ruge, he stated that he thought that the "Introduction" was "utterly unsuitable,"[85] and he began an intensive study of the nature of labor and capital, of the historical evolution of human sensuousness. This investigation led to the writing of the sections on labor, capital, and economic alienation in the *1844 Manuscripts* and culminated in the first systematic formulation of historical materialism in *The German Ideology*.

On the surface these two projects—his continued critique of Hegelian theory and his articulation of historical materialism—supported each other. The more critical he became of Hegelian theory, the more he sought an alternative materialist theory of history, and vice versa. In this sense, the two projects were compatible and conjugated: one entailed the other. But Marx's state of mind was more complex. There was by 1844 an essential tension between his two projects, and that tension reflected a lingering ambivalence about the sovereignty of philosophical thinking. This ambivalence was only completely overcome when his project of formulating a theory of historical materialism won over his preoccupation with philosophical criticism. Such a resolution was made in *The German Ideology* of 1845. There he ruthlessly rejected philosophical criticism for common-sensical empirical experience, for the hegemony of sensuousness. In the rest of this chapter, I first consider Marx's final criticism of Hegelian and Young Hegelian theory, the ambivalence about philosophical thinking that was embodied in that criticism, and the supersession of that ambivalence in his formulation of historical materialism in *The German Ideology*.

In the "Contribution," Marx criticized aspects of Hegel's political philosophy; in the *1844 Manuscripts*, he closely examined Hegel's dialectical method, particularly as it was used in the *Phenomenology*. His investigation in the *Manuscripts* applied the general analytic principles that he had established in the "Contribution." He once again asserted that Hegel had bracketed the events of the real world in a transcendental development of ideas;[86] the philosopher had made them into emanations of an illusory supermundane subject, spirit. Hegelian philosophy, Marx argued, transformed real human activity into acts of spirit's cosmic consciousness: it turned human history into the history of thought.[87] This procedure was, paradoxically, an attempt on Hegel's part to solve real problems: once converted into ideas, the problems of history were made apparently amenable to resolution in thought. Subsumed in the logic of spirit's unfolding, the alienation and exploitation of humanity ceased to be seen as mundane problems but appeared to be stages in spirit's development. They seemed to be mere way stations on spirit's course to the restored wholeness of philosophical self-consciousness. For Hegel, alienation could thus be resolved in contemplation, in the ultimate self-consciousness of the philosopher.[88]

Hegel's idealist method was, in Marx's view, ideological in two respects. First, it only pretended to overcome human alienation. It banished alienation in thought, yet alienation continued to exist in reality.[89] In this sense, Hegelian philosophy did not actually resolve the inadequacies of reality but compensated for them by deluding the philosopher into thinking that he had attained freedom and wholeness in consciousness. Second, after the philosopher had come to think that he had overcome alienation, he looked back on it as his "true mode of being"[90]—as a necessary and ultimately beneficial stage in the evolution of consciousness. In conferring on the defects of reality a transcendent meaning, a logical, moral, and historical necessity, the philosopher sanctioned them. Spirit's "supersession" of alienation, Marx writes, was actually a "confirmation" of alienation.[91] Hegelian theory ended up justifying the same bad reality it sought to overcome in thought.[92]

Marx's 1844 analysis of Hegel's method was the prelude to and paradigm for further and even more detailed criticisms of Young Hegelian theory. In 1844 and 1845, he once again entered into conflict with his former allies—in particular, with Bruno Bauer, Ludwig Feuerbach, and Max Stirner.[93]

Marx's previous criticism of the Young Hegelians in the "Introduction" of 1843 showed that he was sensitive to the intense fratricidal quarrel among radical Hegelians—a quarrel in which each philosopher claimed to have superseded not only his master but also each other. Marx, moreover, considered those defiant declarations to be false. Each Hegelian, he believed, had not overcome his past, but had recapitulated it.

Each continued to avoid facing up to reality, seeking instead a solution to his problems in philosophical criticism. The rest of the "Introduction" provided a general sociological explanation of the cause of this tendency in German philosophy.

After 1843, as Young Hegelian denunciations continued to pour forth, Marx again felt compelled to show his former friends that they were repeating the sins of the past. For Marx in 1844 and 1845 the theories of the Young Hegelians had become mere "caricatures" of Hegel's philosophical vision, manifestations of the "putrescence of absolute spirit."[94]

We have seen how, in his criticism of Bauer's opposition to Jewish emancipation, Marx implicitly showed that Bauer was engaged in ideological thinking: Bauer sought to defeat mass society by condensing it into an imaginary enemy—the Jew—who was then restrained by philosophical argument. After 1843, when Marx had raised his criticism of ideology from case studies to general principles, he examined the general theory of pure criticism enunciated by Bauer and the Freien. Bauer's pure critic, Marx asserted in *The Holy Family*, subscribed to Hegel's dialectical method. The theory of "*Absolute Criticism*," Marx wrote, "has learnt from Hegel's *Phänomenologie* . . . the art of converting *real objective* chains that exist *outside me* into *merely ideal*, merely *subjective* chains existing merely *in me* and thus of converting all *external* sensuously perceptible struggles into pure struggles of thought."[95]

Having turned the constraints of reality into constraints of thought, the pure critic could then break them philosophically. But that victory was illusory: reality was in fact untouched.[96] Nonetheless, Marx goes on, now that the pure critic believed he could not be affected by the mundane world, he became infatuated with himself, with his own illusory power. The consequence of this blindness to reality and this self-absorption was isolation from society: the pure critic felt content to dwell in a delusion of freedom and grandeur. Bauer's theory of pure criticism sealed him off from reality.[97]

Given his quarrel with Bauer in "On the Jewish Question" and in his correspondence with Ruge, it was not surprising that Marx would again attack Bauer using the broad principles of criticism in the *Manuscripts*. What was more surprising was that in the mid-1840s he would also turn against Ludwig Feuerbach. As late as 1844 Marx had seen in Feuerbach an ally and even mentor. He had adopted Feuerbach's definition of humanity as a sensuous yet universal or social being—what Feuerbach referred to as the "species." Marx's writings in 1843 and 1844 were laced with Feuerbachian concepts and expressions, but by 1845, he had come to reevaluate his adherence to Feuerbach's humanism. It now seemed to him to be much less materialist than he had imagined. It was still contaminated with Hegelian idealism. It too was ideological.

Marx began his criticism of Feuerbach by noting that Feuerbach failed to allow historical development into his picture of human sensuousness.[98] That philosopher, Marx wrote, regarded "the sensuous world around him" as a "thing given direct from all eternity, remaining ever the same."[99] Feuerbach's procedure was to cancel out the concrete and changing particularity of sensuous activity by absorbing it into unchanging philosophical categories. Empirical human activity was thereby transformed into an emanation of a universal, abstract "essence":[100] human beings, working, creating, and suffering in history, appeared to be variations of an all-embracing "species." For Feuerbach, Marx concluded, sensuous human practice was nothing more than an object of contemplation: Feuerbach recognized it as the efflux of the ideal species. Active sensuousness was thereby turned into passive contemplation.[101]

Feuerbach's "*contemplative* materialism"[102] was idealist and hence ideological in two respects. First, it attempted to avoid reality. In contemplating the real sensuous world, Marx explained, Feuerbach "necessarily lights on things which contradict his consciousness and feeling, which disturb the harmony he presupposes, the harmony of all parts of the sensuous world and especially of man and nature." Encountering a bad reality, he then takes flight into philosophical abstractions: "To remove this disturbance, he must take refuge in a double perception, a profane one which perceives 'only the flatly obvious' and a higher, philosophical one which perceives the 'true essence' of things."[103] Feuerbach, in other words, restored his consciousness to equanimity by regarding the ideal essence of things while ignoring its supposedly unimportant appearance—namely, defective reality.

The philosopher compensated for real inadequacies by generating a false image of the world, and to compensate ideologically was moreover to justify. In downgrading actual material conditions in favor of a false glorified image, Feuerbach allowed those conditions to continue, and, indeed, conferred on them the mystique of being manifestations of an ideal essence. Marx illustrated this point nicely in his discussion of Feuerbach's occasional claim to be a social reformer, a friend of the poor. In reality, according to Marx, Feuerbach's revulsion against material poverty led him to accept it: when Feuerbach, Marx writes, "sees instead of

healthy men a crowd of scrofulous, overworked and consumptive starve-
lings, he is compelled to take refuge in the 'higher perception' and in the
ideal 'compensation of the species,' and thus to relapse into idealism at
the very point where the communist materialist sees the necessity, and
at the same time the condition, of a transformation both of industry and
of the social structure."[104] Like Hegel and Bauer, Feuerbach's relation to
the world was one of anxiety—an anxiety that was self-reinforcing, that
paradoxically ended up sanctioning the world that generated it.

The longest and most venomous of Marx's attacks on Hegelians was
his criticism of Max Stirner. Stirner had been associated with the Freien,
Bauer's circle in Berlin, but in 1844, in his book *Der Einzige und sein
Eigentum*, Stirner turned against Bauer's critical humanism. In *Der Einzige*, Stirner attempted to fuse together elements of the philosophies of
Feuerbach and Bauer. He combined Feuerbach's emphasis on sensuousness with Bauer's emphasis on the sovereignty of the critical subject.
Linking those ideas together in his notion of the unique sensuous egoist,
Stirner then engaged in a characteristic Young Hegelian practice: he
denounced as mystification all philosophy before him, including the
theories of Feuerbach and Bauer. For Stirner, the unique sensuous ego
could not be adequately defined by philosophical abstractions.

Stirner's theory of sensuous egoism caused a brief sensation among
radical Hegelians. Before it and its author disappeared into obscurity after
1845, his book provoked indignant reviews from Bauer, Ruge, and Marx,
among others. As we have seen, for Ruge, Stirner's theory represented
the culmination of philosophy's deliquescence: it was the most degraded
expression of Hegelian theory up to that time. Marx shared Ruge's view.
For Marx, Stirner introduced nothing new to criticism but merely blended
together the stale old ingredients of Hegelian and Young Hegelian ideology. According to Marx, Stirner operated like other philosophers: he too
converted real sensuous activity into forms of consciousness and then
philosophically overcame those forms to attain a unity in consciousness.[105]
He too invented nonexistent ideal subjects—the "Unique One," the
Egoist in history—that overshadowed the actions of actual human beings.[106] For Stirner, Marx writes, "the speculative idea, the abstract conception, is made the driving force of history, and history is thereby
turned into the mere history of philosophy."[107] And finally, like other
Hegelians, Stirner's idealist stratagems, in that they did not deal with
reality but only obscured it, served "to canonise the existing world." "It

is obvious," Marx observed, "that Stirner has to remain wholly conservative in practice." [108]

Marx's criticism of Stirner was yet another application of the general analytic principles he had employed against Hegel, Feuerbach, and Bauer. What makes the analysis of Stirner of unique interest, however, is how tightly Marx connects it to the immediate social and political conditions of Germany, especially of Prussia. We have considered Marx's repeated demonstrations of how Hegelian and Young Hegelian theory ideologically compensated for and justified an inadequate reality,[109] but we have not yet asked what Marx considered that inadequate reality to be. What specific social and political conditions led Hegelian philosophers to construct apologetic illusions?

In the "Introduction," Marx spoke very broadly of the social and political conditions in Germany that determined the nature of its philosophy. Hegelian philosophy appeared to be the philosophical reaction of the "nation" in general and, so Marx vaguely implied, of the middle class in particular. In the preface to *The German Ideology*, where Marx briefly discussed Hegelian theorists in general, he again connected Hegelian theorizing to the general inadequacies of the nation: "the boasting of these philosophical commentators," he wrote, "only mirrors the wretchedness of the real conditions in Germany." But he now also explicitly identified the Hegelian as the representative of a specific class: his theory "merely imitates in philosophic form the conceptions of the German middle class." [110] In the preface to *The German Ideology*, Marx thus sought to link philosophy more securely than before to a specific social group, not just to the amorphous nation-at-large. He attempted to attain a greater concreteness in his case studies of Hegelian ideologists than could be found in what he considered to be his less than satisfactory "Introduction." This aim was most thoroughly realized in his analysis of Stirner, who was shown to be a spokesman of the German petty bourgeoisie. But to understand how Marx linked Stirner to this social group, we must first examine what he thought of the German middle class.

In criticizing Stirner's analysis of political liberalism, Marx gave an extended account of the development of the bourgeoisie in Germany. He compared it unfavorably to the bourgeoisie of other countries. The French middle class, Marx wrote, established its place in the world through great acts of revolution and conquest, the English through its revolutionizing of industry, its subjugation of India, and its domination of world trade. The German middle class achieved little in the social and political world: it had only produced notable philosophers.[111]

Since the Reformation, "German development," Marx wrote, "has borne a completely petty-bourgeois character." The "old, feudal aristocracy" was destroyed in the peasant wars. Those who were left were confined to minor estates and local, or at most provincial, economic and political interests. The German bourgeoisie was meanwhile overwhelmed by its much more aggressive Dutch counterpart, and consequently it too was forced to eke out a petty local existence. This "fragmentation of economic interests" rendered national unification or governance impossible.[112] Rather, in place of politically organized national classes, there emerged an especially active and seemingly extrasocial state organization. The state developed to fill the gaps between local social interests and thereby "built itself up into an apparently independent force."[113] For this reason, middle-class members of the bureaucracy seemed superior to the narrow local interests of the middle class in society. And correspondingly, middle-class academic theoreticians, as members of the bureaucracy, ostensibly did not give voice to those particular interests but spoke with apparent autonomy for the universal concerns of all humanity. In truth, however, these theoreticians, like the state itself, were prisoners of their social conditions.[114]

The paradox of apparent autonomy and real servility in German theory was evident, according to Marx, in Stirner. He appeared to be a disinterested, unworldly critic, but he actually expressed the petty-bourgeois character of the German middle class. This character made itself manifest in Stirner's most important notion—in how he conceived of the sensuous egoist. For he argued that his notion of absolute sensuous egoism logically issued in the egoist's absolute right to own property. The egoist, according to Stirner, could exist only if he freely and selfishly possessed property. In this argument of Stirner's Marx saw a typical bourgeois ploy: namely, to equate individuality with the ownership of property. The bourgeois, Marx wrote, "believes himself to be an individual only insofar as he is bourgeois."[115]

The social character of Stirner's world also appeared in his narrow conceptualization of social forms such as future communism, which he thought amounted to no more than equal wages for all, and competition, which he believed should be constrained in a manner reminiscent of traditional guilds.[116] Finally, Stirner reflected his petty-bourgeois nature precisely in those statements in which the egoist glorified himself as an unrestrained and irrepressible power. In these "self-embellishments," Marx explained, "the German petty-bourgeois consoles himself for his own impotence."[117] The "petty, shy and timid behavior" of Germany's petty bourgeoisie found, for Marx, its logical "counterpart" in the "noisy, blustering and impertinent public boasting" of Stirner's sensuous egoist. In that self-glorification, the petty bourgeois forgot his own inferior condition and imagined himself to be the heroic bourgeois individual found in other countries.[118]

In *The German Ideology* and especially in the section on Stirner, Marx displayed, in his criticism of philosophy as ideology, a striving to be more concrete, to attain a greater sociological specificity. Stirner's theoretical posturings were linked to the material and psychological inadequacies of the German bourgeoisie. But if we consider Marx's critique of the Young Hegelians in 1844 and 1845 from another point of view, this project must seem profoundly lacking in concreteness and worldly significance. Since 1843 Marx's ideological criticism of Hegelian philosophy had led him to conclude that the philosophical analysis of philosophical theories had little impact on the real world. A preoccupation with philosophy, he believed, accomplished nothing in society or politics. He wrote in 1844: "*Ideas* can never lead beyond an old world order but only beyond the ideas of the old world order. Ideas *cannot carry out anything at all.*"[119] But if the criticism of philosophy was incapable of affecting reality, why did he then devote so much attention to criticizing the Young Hegelians in 1844 and 1845, especially when there were other pressing theoretical and practical concerns? Indeed, if one applies to Marx his criticism of the Young Hegelians in the "Introduction," one can argue that he was now three times removed from reality: he criticized the criticism of an abstraction from reality.

Marx's passionate concern with eradicating a powerless and defunct form of consciousness recalls the similar concerns of Ruge and Bauer. Like Marx, they had ceased to believe in the efficacy of idealism, but could not stop treating it as a threat. After having been so badly misled by idealist theory, they now seemed to be obsessed by it. Marx's repeated attempts to bury Hegelian theory betrayed a fear of its continued vitality. Despite the results of his own analysis, he continued to act as if abstractions were indeed powerful and had to be reckoned with. But as we have already noted, as well as this preoccupation with abstraction *The German Ideology* contained, in its analysis of Hegelians and especially of Stirner, an attempt to be more concrete in analysis. That book embodied two opposing impulses: on the one side, a continued commitment to philosophical criticism; on the other, a desire to overcome philosophy by grounding oneself in the particularities of the sensuous world. In the end, this conflict was resolved in favor of the second impulse. As Marx later noted, in *The German Ideology* he "settled" his "accounts" with his "erstwhile philosophical conscience." [120] This overcoming of his lingering adherence to the Hegelian preoccupation with abstract thinking was not just a matter of making an exhaustive negative refutation. On the contrary, as also seen in the cases of Bauer and Ruge, each such refutation only called forth another even more extensive one. What was still required to lay Hegelian idealism to rest was a positive alternative: a fully worked out understanding of the evolution of human sensuousness. Such a demonstration needed to be antiphilosophical in two senses: it had to renounce the use of ideal philosophical categories and arguments, and it had to show how and why ideal processes were in principle necessarily derived from sensuous or material processes. Marx had to explain in an unphilosophical manner why philosophy should be seen as the efflux of human sensuousness.

A thoroughgoing positive demonstration was not easily achieved. In the *1844 Manuscripts*, Marx attempted to produce a view of history that rested on an analysis of economic alienation. But as Marx himself noted in 1845, there were in the *Manuscripts* residues of idealism that compromised his materialist message.[121] Indeed, in the *Manuscripts* he recapitulated the same Hegelian procedure that he criticized—namely, the bracketing of material reality in an extramundane logic of development. Human history in the *Manuscripts* appeared to be predetermined by a metahistorical plan, by the necessary unfolding of an ideal human essence, which Marx, following Feuerbach, called "species-being." To develop all its latent potentialities, the human essence, Marx argued in 1844, necessarily fell from initial self-unity into alienation and then returned to a higher unity of self-consciousness. The concrete social and political conditions that Marx found in history were subsumed into this cosmic plan. Thus, contrary to empirical appearance, private property was considered not the cause but the product of workers' alienation: the analysis of alienated labor, Marx wrote, "shows that though private property appears to be the reason, the cause of alienated labor, it is rather its consequence, just as the gods are *originally* not the cause but the effect of man's intellectual confusion. Later this relationship becomes reciprocal." [122] And

at the other end of the evolution of the human essence, the realization
of humanity's overcoming of alienation, its return to unity, was the
establishment of full communism, but the defining moment of that was
self-consciousness: "The entire movement of history, just as its [com-
munism's] *actual* act of genesis—the birth act of its empirical existence—
is . . . also for its thinking consciousness the *comprehended* and *known*
process of its *becoming*."[123]

Marx's attempt to purge his thinking of idealist conceptualization was
thus still incomplete in 1844. His ongoing preoccupation with philosophy
not only determined his obsessive negative investigations of Hegelian and
Young Hegelian theory but also affected his positive explication of an
alternative materialist theory of history. Yet Marx was, as already noted,
aware of this contradiction. He recognized the inadequacy of the theory
of history in the *Manuscripts* and he subsequently worked hard to purge
his thinking of lingering Hegelian formulations. He came to reject
explicitly the idea of the autonomous development of "species-being," of
an ideal human essence,[124] concerning himself instead with finding a
rigorously unphilosophical view of "living human individuals."[125] The
culmination of this contest between his residual loyalty to Hegelian
idealism and his urge to articulate an unphilosophical theory of history
was *The German Ideology* of 1845. In that work, Marx gave his
philosophical preoccupations their most extravagant expression. In
exhausting, belabored detail, he condemned Young Hegelian theories.
But in that same book he also produced the first systematic description
of historical materialism, and with that achievement he then put aside his
Hegelian obsessions. The book that contained his first systematic description of historical materialism also contained the last expression of his
preoccupation with Hegelian idealism.

To say that *The German Ideology* was the first systematic expression
of historical materialism is perhaps misleading. The book does not contain
one formulation of historical materialism, but several.[126] Each formulation
begins with what Marx in one place calls "real premises,"[127] that is,
indisputable assumptions about reality. The most elementary of these are:

1) living human beings exist,
2) these beings have irreducible needs (To live they must eat, drink,
   and so on),
3) they must produce the means of fulfilling their needs (for example,
   gather food, hunt, and so on),

4) the satisfaction of basic human needs leads to human reproduction, which in turn results in the expansion of human needs.[128]

From these premises Marx derives the rise and fall of economic structures, the generation of the state and philosophy, and the emergence of communism.

One especially striking aspect of Marx's formulations is their combination of theoretical ambitiousness and apparent simplicity of presentation. They are ambitious because they seek to account for all of human history, but they are also remarkably simple and prosaic in the concepts and arguments that they employ. Reading the various formulations of historical materialism, one feels that one is being given not theoretical arguments, but simple, empirical descriptions. There is no speculation about the eternal essence of the species which predetermines the empirical activities of human beings. Marx's analysis remains entirely on the level of immediate empirical appearance. Economic exploitation stems from how individuals, driven by sensuous needs, interact with the natural environment and with one another. In this sense, Marx embraces the definition of a human being that Hegel had tried to supersede: namely, the individual as a being motivated solely by sensuous need and desire, the individual as an "abstract will." The theory of history in *The German Ideology*, to use Helmut Fleischer's rather unfelicitous term, is "pragmatological." History no longer appears, as it did in the 1844 *Manuscripts*, to be the unfolding of humanity according to a predetermined metahistorical plan. It is now the contingent product of humanity's concrete practice, "the outcome, more blind than the result of any tendency to a specific goal, of the actions of individuals and groups impelled by their needs in the situations in which they find themselves."[129]

The historical formulations in *The German Ideology* are empirical in the most straightforward way. Marx in fact seems to shun any association with philosophical abstraction. For although he allows the possibility of making general statements that sum up the results of empirical observation, he emphasizes that these, "in themselves, divorced from real history, have no value whatsoever." They might help to arrange historical material, "to indicate the sequence of its separate strata." "But," he insists, "they by no means afford a recipe or a schema, as does philosophy, for neatly trimming the epochs of history."[130]

Marx thus adamantly refuses to have anything to do with abstract theorizing. For him, the only valid knowledge of the world is "empirical study, a straightforward looking-at, which presupposes . . . no independent abstractions, categories, or theoretical structures." [131] The proper historical method is a simple empirical method. [132]

But one might well ask: If Marx abjures philosophical thinking and argument, how does he know that his simple empiricism is valid and how can he convince us of its validity? Given his intellectual training, he was certainly cognizant of the epistemological objections that could be and had been raised against simple empiricism. For example, one philosopher that Marx had read—David Hume—strenuously argued that knowledge gained from sense perception was essentially untrustworthy. Yet Marx felt no need to deal with such objections. As he said in the second thesis on Feuerbach, such questions were for him strictly "scholastic." [133] Nonetheless, he asserts that his materialist assumptions are self-evident and hence irrefutable. But in what sense are they so? What is his non-philosophical standard of knowledge or belief?

The ultimate foundation of his antiphilosophical empiricism is suggested in his attacks on the Young Hegelians in *The Holy Family* and *The German Ideology*. There he expends considerable energy ridiculing philosophers who believe in the primacy of philosophical abstraction. Marx's procedure here is to show that the convoluted arguments of these philosophers violate what everyone knows to be true: they go against common sense. Marx tells us, for example, that the ordinary, over-worked, and ill-educated worker has a better grounding in reality than the pompous philosopher. Mocking Bauer's belief in the liberating power of pure criticism, he writes:

These *mass-minded* communist workers, employed, for instance, in Manchester or Lyons workshops, do not believe that by *"pure thinking"* they will be able to argue away their industrial masters and their own political debasement. They are most painfully aware of the *difference* between *being* and *thinking*, between *consciousness* and *life*. They know that property, capital, money, wage-labor and the like are no ideal figments of the brain but very practical, very objective products of their self-estrangement and that therefore they must be abolished in a practical, objective way for man to become man not only in *thinking*, in *consciousness*, but in mass *being*, in life. [134]

In his formulations of the empirical evolution of human sensuousness, Marx also ultimately appeals to an antiphilosophical common sense. Where philosophical reason seeks to question our ordinary assumptions about the world, Marx in these formulations stays on the surface of our everyday experience—he relies on our common sense. "One has to 'leave philosophy aside,'" he writes, "one has to leap out of it and devote oneself *like an ordinary man* to the study of actuality."[135]

In calling the first premises of historical materialism self-evident, Marx means that they are premises of our everyday experience, what our common, mundane experience must believe to be true: common sense tells us that living human beings exist, and that to do so they must eat, drink, find shelter, and so on. That Marx rejects philosophical argument for common sense shows his loyalty to the mandate for a new "philosophy" that he outlined in the "Introduction." His empirical descriptions in *The German Ideology* are arguments ad hominem. Rejecting out of hand the philosophical questioning of everyday or common-sensical belief, they enshrine the everyday consciousness as the arbiter of truth.

The common-sensical, antiphilosophical empiricism of *The German Ideology* is the culmination of the intellectual development that we have followed in the young Marx. In that work he combines into a new, rigorous synthesis the elements that he had earlier developed but had left tinged with idealism. *The German Ideology* contains his most systematic argument so far for the hegemony of sensuousness; here he demonstrates the primacy of sensuous activity by absorbing into his empirical, materialist scheme of history Hegel's idealist scheme of the evolution of spirit.

In his second formulation of historical materialism, Marx explains the origin and evolution of human consciousness. After stating in his fourth premise that human reproduction results in the creation of new needs, he adds in a fifth premise that men have consciousness.[136] This original consciousness is inseparable from human needs and human society. Like language, it "arises from the need, the necessity, of intercourse with other men."[137] At first, human consciousness is rudimentary. It is the "consciousness of one's immediate sensuous environment." It is, in other words, a consciousness of nature, a nature that overawes human beings, for it confronts them "as a completely alien, all-powerful and unassailable force."[138]

But as society grows, as its population and hence its needs increase, people cease to be cowed by nature. They become detached from it. They develop away from an immediate relationship with their environment as they become caught up in increasingly complex social arrangements, and as society becomes ever more complicated, the possibility of each member of society performing all or many social functions ceases. Specific social activities come to be identified with specific persons. In short, there arises a general division of labor.

One aspect of this differentiation of activities is a "division of material and mental labour." With this social development, consciousness obtains the appearance of being detached from nature and society:

From this moment onwards consciousness *can* really flatter itself that it is something other than consciousness of existing practice, that it *really* represents something without representing something real; from now on consciousness is in a position to emancipate itself from the world and to proceed to the formation of "pure" theory, theology, philosophy, morality, etc.[139]

The separation of consciousness from reality is of course only apparent: it is actually a reflection of the existing social relations, of the nature of the division of labor.

Just as consciousness obtains the appearance of autonomy from the social organization, so too the state obtains the appearance of an independent entity. Society's division of labor paradoxically yields 1) private individuals with distinct roles and interests and 2) the interdependence of all private individuals and interests. In other words, a division of labor issues both in individuals with narrow private interests and in interdependent individuals with a common interest. The conflict of these two forms of interest results in the formation of the common interest into a body that is seemingly independent of private interests—namely, the state.[140]

But although the common interest now appears as the state, which seems to be above private interests, the state is only "an illusory community." In the relentless pursuit of its narrow aims, private interest refuses to acknowledge the legitimacy of the common interest. Instead, organized into classes, private interest makes use of its interdependence with other social interests to dominate that interdependence. It takes over the state, rendering the general interest its servant.[141] While the state might appear to represent the general interest—the interdependence of all private interests—it is actually nothing more than the instrument of a single class of private interests.[142]

What for Hegel were the expressions of an autonomous spirit are thus for Marx merely illusions of autonomy. All political and intellectual constructs are emanations of the organization of human sensuousness. On the basis of present and past empirical trends in the evolution of sensuousness, Marx goes on to anticipate further developments in humanity's social organization. He argues that the division of labor continues to evolve until it eventually subverts itself. It develops to a point where a divided social, political, and intellectual existence is no longer necessary or possible. It then issues forth a communal organization that operates without a rigid differentiation of functions. In communism, the last stage of social development, Marx writes, "nobody has one exclusive sphere of activity but each can become accomplished in any branch he wishes, society regulates the general production and thus makes it possible for me to do one thing today and another tomorrow." Human sensuousness ceases to be broken apart in a division of labor. In communism, each person affirms his sensuous character in all his activities.[143]

Although many details remained to be worked out, Marx had produced in *The German Ideology* a coherent and comprehensive view of the historical development of human sensuousness. This achievement was largely due to his creative use of the idea of the division of labor. It allowed him to clarify and harmoniously integrate his earlier concerns without using idealist conceptualization or argument. It provided a strictly materialist explanation of the origin of economic exploitation: alienation was the result of the differentiation of labor and economic interests. It refined his notion of the takeover of the state by private interests, showing how and why both private interests and an apparent general interest where necessarily generated and how the former could take over the latter. Moreover, the idea of the division of labor accounted for the rise of the idealist conceptions of philosophy and the state. It explained in strictly materialist terms both the evolution of consciousness from a natural to an abstract and apparently autonomous condition and the appearance of a universal and apparently independent state. Here Marx had brought about a reversal of what he had identified as the method of Hegelian idealism. Where Hegel had bracketed sensuous reality by placing it in a logical development of ideas, Marx bracketed idealistic formations—philosophy and the universal state—by placing them in the empirical development of human sensuousness.

Finally, the idea of the division of a labor did more than explain the dislocations of the present. It also promised that the future contained the real possibility of overcoming humanity's fractured condition. The division of labor, Marx argued, issued in its own abolition, in humanity's elevation to a free and harmonious life.

In *The German Ideology*, Marx produced his first generally satisfactory materialist account of human development. It was the foundation for his later writings. And even though, with the failure of the 1848 Revolution, he rehabilitated the use of theoretical abstraction, he never again felt compelled to wrestle with Hegelian philosophers.[144] In *The German Ideology* he laid to rest his long and obsessive struggle with idealist philosophy. A unified theory of the evolution of human sensuousness effectively silenced the haunting voice of Hegel. In this sense, *The German Ideology* also marked the end of the crisis of the Prussian Young Hegelians. This systematic materialist view of history was the uncompromising completion of what Bauer and Ruge had unsystematically and ambivalently started: the discrediting of the sovereignty of philosophy, the search for a new relation to reality, the creation of a formal theory of ideology.

Conclusion

The End of Philosophy

1

The first formulation of the theory of ideology emerged as the intellectual response of the Prussian Young Hegelians to a social, political, and intellectual trauma. It was their answer to social and political dislocation and the resulting collapse of Hegelian philosophy.

That philosophy had promised its followers a twofold harmony. Invested with Hegelian self-consciousness, the philosopher could identify himself as spirit incarnate. He was spirit made into a subject. As such, he conferred rational order and spiritual meaning to his life, for if he was spirit's embodiment, then his life was part of its providential plan. His personal trials and conflicts were spiritually necessary and productive. In conceiving of their personal lives as variations of spirit's phenomenology, Bauer, Ruge, and Marx were able to restore a sense of wholeness to their troubled lives.

As well as the promise of existential coherence, of spirit as subject, Hegel offered a political harmony. He sought in his political philosophy a reconciliation of the conflicting political developments of the age. To produce a rational social and political order, liberalism's social atomism and popular politics should be mediated by refurbished traditional corporate institutions. Moreover, this plan for a rational policy, so Hegel believed, was not a transcendent ideal but a forming reality. He thought that the Prussian state was evolving into a constitutional monarchy with an enlightened bureaucracy that encouraged the pursuit of philosophy. To be a Hegelian in Prussia was thus to attain not only spiritual unity but also political community. For the Prussian Hegelian, spirit was real both as subject and substance. Bauer, Ruge, and Marx thus felt that as Hegelian philosophers they could make academic careers in the Prussian state, that reason's substance would heed and honor reason's subject.

Hegel's delicate theoretical balance of tradition and modernity came to a bad end in the late 1830s and early 1840s. It proved to be inadequate to the changing and paradoxical reality in Prussia. On the one side, Hegel underestimated the vigor of traditionalist, conservative politics. Prussia's conservative aristocracy refused to be modernized and aligned with liberal political institutions; after the 1820s it became increasingly hostile to liberal reform. On the other side, Hegel overestimated the ability of the state to control the centrifugal forces of modern civil society. At the same time that political modernization was stagnating, social and economic liberalization advanced. The emancipation of the peasantry and the dissolution of guilds, combined with unprecedented population growth, produced a new concentration of poor which by the 1840s posed a threat to the social order. Hegel died when there were already signs of the growing disjuncture between his theory and reality, although the experience of the complete collapse of Hegelian hopes and expectations was a legacy he left to his followers.

2

The discrediting of Hegelian philosophy did not occur as an autonomous intellectual reexamination of the philosopher's premises and arguments but was bound up with the immediate social and political experience of Hegel's followers. In the late 1830s and early 1840s, the increasing dominance of conservatives in the universities and in the government thwarted the academic careers of the Prussian Young Hegelians and led to the suppression of their newspapers. The leaders of the Hegelian movement in Prussia were pushed from the center of the state to the periphery, from a unity of public and personal existence to an opposition between the two. This social and political dislocation was followed for Ruge and Marx with a physical dislocation: they felt compelled to go into exile. The encounter with an increasingly hostile Prussian state presented the Prussian Young Hegelians with what was by Hegelian standards an impossible contradiction: spirit as subject was fulfilled in the mind of the philosopher, but spirit as substance embodied in the existing Prussian state was retrograde. The Hegelian unity of spirit seemed to be coming apart.

The social crisis of the 1840s intensified the Prussian Young Hegelians' sense of dislocation in two ways. First, it meant another serious challenge to Hegelian theory. The surging forth of sensuous natural need and desire

in their most degraded form—in the form of mass and unruly poverty—
contradicted the Hegelian belief in the existence of a rationally regulated
social order. Second, the growing presence of a mass of dispossessed
intensified the Prussian Young Hegelians' anxiety about their social
status. The new poor were defined by their adversarial relation to existing
society. Uprooted, mobile, unaided by traditional groups or by the state,
and with little hope for an improvement of circumstances, they were cast
in the role of society's negation. Deprived of social position and ejected
from the state, the Prussian Young Hegelians appeared to be in a similar
position. Indeed, they conceived of themselves in the 1840s as having a
distinctly negative function: they were ruthless critics of existing society.
They thus had a sociological affinity with the new mass of dispossessed.
Both groups were in the same social (or antisocial) situation; both groups
were outsiders. Yet all their philosophical training had taught the Young
Hegelians that rational philosophy was incompatible with the particular
sensuous interests of civil society. They were, in other words, forced to
consort with those they had been taught to scorn.

The social and political experiences of the Young Hegelians thus falsified the philosophy that had transfigured their lives. Hegelian theory
had succumbed to the paradoxical evolution of Prussian politics and
society—to its resurgent political conservatism and its simultaneous social
modernization. That something was awry in Prussian development was
registered in Young Hegelian writings. Bauer's *Die gute Sache*, Ruge's
"Der protestantische Absolutismus," Marx's articles in the *Rheinische
Zeitung* and his "Introduction to the Critique of Hegel's Philosophy of
Right"—in these and other writings, the Prussian Young Hegelians recognized that Prussia had failed to progress uniformly. It had dropped
out of what they thought was the mainstream of history. And the result
of Prussia's contradictory, deviant development was to make into outsiders those who were committed to a unified progressive evolution in
politics. One who subscribes to a philosophy of the coherent unfolding
of spirit, they acknowledged, is necessarily rendered deviant in an incoherent state. Initially, all the Prussian Young Hegelians tried to ride out
the crisis, asserting that the reality would soon match the theory. But
time and again, their hopes were disappointed. Defeated by the turn of
social and political events, they finally accepted the bad reality as given,
and with that, they were then confronted with the question of what to
do with the theory.

The critical reexamination of Hegelian theory by Hegel's Prussian followers proceeded in two ways. First, there were piecemeal critiques of different aspects of Hegelian theory: Bauer, for example, attacked Hegel's religious theory; Ruge condemned his aversion to democracy; Marx criticized his dialectic. Second, there were systematic, genetic examinations. Each thinker produced critical histories of the rise and fall of Hegelian theory, histories that included accounts of their own experiences. Bauer's *Vollständige Geschichte*, Ruge's *Unsre letzten zehn Jahre*, Marx's "Introduction to the Critique of Hegel's Philosophy of Right"—these and other writings attempted to retell the history of Hegelian philosophy in a way that would coherently account for the Young Hegelians' experience of its collapse.

In these efforts to mold their difficult experiences with Hegelian philosophy into a comprehensible narrative of its development, we can see a standard Hegelian strategy: to redeem the past through a self-conscious recapitulation. But unlike the serene self-consciousness attained at the completion of a Hegelian phenomenology, the self-consciousness of the Prussian Young Hegelians was profoundly troubled. Their recapitulation of the development of Hegelian theory ended up not as a glorification of an autonomous philosophical self-consciousness that exercised mastery over history but as the opposite: they asserted that systematic abstract thought was weak and deceptive, both blind to and dependent on a mundane reality.

Their recapitulations were further troubled in that they seemed unsatisfactory: each Young Hegelian's recapitulation did not resolve his anxiety about theory's relation to reality but compulsively generated more recapitulations. Young Hegelian writings seemed to be mired in an obsessive, self-lacerating self-consciousness. In both aspects of this anxious self-consciousness—in its antiphilosophical sociology and its dissatisfaction with its own explanatory power—we can see emerge, with all its problems, the modern theory of ideology.

3

In their self-conscious recapitulations of the development of Hegelian theory, the Prussian Young Hegelians posed three questions: first, why should that theory make grandiose claims about philosophy's sovereignty over the world when the opposite was clearly true; second, how could people such as themselves have been so taken in by Hegelian theory's false claims; and third, what should be the proper relationship between the thinker and mundane reality? All three Prussian Young Hegelians answered the first two questions in the same way, in a manner we now identify as the characteristic approach of the theory of ideology: Hegelian abstractions emerged as both a compensation for and justification of a deficient social and political reality. The philosopher, these critics agreed, was at the mercy of a hostile state and society. To make the best of a bad situation, he inverted it in his mind: he believed that the existing state was derived from the principles of his philosophy. The servant appeared to be master, but in actuality, he only strengthened his servitude: he gave intellectual legitimacy to existing conditions. Bauer in *Vollständige Geschichte* described the pathological dependency of the philosopher on a state that hated him; Ruge in *Unsre letzten zehn Jahre* and other writings argued that Hegelian theory's retreat to inner life was both a symptom and a reinforcement of the existing polity; and Marx in his "Introduction to the Critique of Hegel's Philosophy of Right" and elsewhere asserted that Germany's underdeveloped political life had resulted in an over-developed—that is, overly abstract—intellectual life.

To explain the emergence of Hegel's extravagant abstractions in a socially and politically deficient state, the Prussian Young Hegelians generated prototypes of the theory of ideology. That Hegel attracted followers was explained in the same fashion: an anemic public life had led them to seek relief in philosophical abstraction, which only justified the same inadequate condition.

Bauer and to an extent Ruge incorporated not only their political experiences but also their experiences with the social crisis of the 1840s into their formulations of what counted as ideological thinking. In *Vollständige Geschichte*, Bauer argued that philosophers' theorizing about the "masses" was a continuation of their earlier psychopathology. Feeling abandoned by the state but still lacking independent content of their own, they now glorified another aspect of a deficient reality—namely, the brutalized masses. Ruge asserted in *Unsre letzten zehn Jahre* and other writings that socialism's fascination with the plight of workers functioned like religion. It was another way of avoiding political thought and action. Marx also responded to the social crisis of the 1840s and incorporated his experience of it into his theory of ideology, but his approach was the direct opposite of Bauer's and Ruge's. He embraced the new declassé and in doing so resolved in his mind one of the crucial problems that was at the center of the new theory of ideology.

4

Later theorists of ideology, such as Karl Mannheim, have argued that the theory is extremely problematical because of its implicit relativism. According to these commentators the theory asserts that all ideas are determined by their particular social and political context and hence lack objective, universal validity. But if that assertion is correct, then it must apply to the theory itself, which therefore must also lack objective validity. In short, the theory of ideology breaks down into hopeless self-negation.

This was the notion of ideology formulated by Mannheim and many others since him, and they suggested that it was an "unpacking"[1] of Marx's theory of ideology. But this version of the theory was not that held by Marx and other Prussian Young Hegelians. They believed that while other theories were ideological, theirs were not. Their criticisms of philosophy and society were undistorted by their particular interests.

What is important to note is that they arrived at this conclusion not because they simply ignored the potential problems in the theory of ideology. On the contrary, they continually wrestled with the issue of extending the theory to include their own ideas. It was in fact this concern with the implications of their new conception of the relation between thinking and being that accounted for the anxiety so characteristic of their writings and that ultimately determined their answer to the third question found in those writings: what should be the critical thinker's proper relationship with society? How to theorize about ideology without being an ideologist was the underlying and nerve-wracking leitmotif of Young Hegelian development.

On the surface, the Young Hegelians' belief that they could be exempt from ideology is founded on simple logic. To argue that some ideas are conditioned by their social and political context does not necessarily entail that all ideas are. One might logically contend that others think ideologically but that one's own ideas are unaffected by one's social and political interests.[2] This claim can be supported by showing that one has an "objective" point of view, a focus free of social distortion. The claim can be proved illegitimate by showing that these ideas are in fact crucially affected by a social and political situation.

Each Prussian Young Hegelian attempted to demonstrate that Hegel and his followers thought ideologically. He described how philosophical abstraction was warped by a specific social and political situation. To make his analysis convincing he had to assume that he was unaffected by social and political biases. He needed to believe that his own point of view was accurate, in some essential sense different from the point of view of philosophy. But this assumption was profoundly untenable, for he came from a social and intellectual milieu similar to that of the philosophers he criticized for being ideological. In other words, there was every reason to believe that the critic's theory was also distorted since he too was a product of the conditions that had rendered his fellow philosophers ideologists. The Prussian Young Hegelians were thus directly confronted with the problematical nature of the theory of ideology. If their fellow thinkers were guilty of thinking ideologically, could not they be guilty as well?

This anxiety about their possible complicity in the ideology of the age showed itself in two ways. First it manifested itself in a "repetition compulsion," in the Prussian Young Hegelians' obsessive repudiations of Hegelian theory in particular and of philosophy in general. They strained to convince themselves and others by repeated assertion that they no longer subscribed to ideologically tainted thinking.

Their anxiety about being trapped in the "German ideology" also manifested itself in the pressing urge to attain a new point of view, one uncorrupted by the ideological inadequacies of philosophy and hence capable of apprehending the true order of things. In other words, to feel at home with the theory of ideology, they recognized that it needed some kind of "post-philosophical" grounding. Bauer's attempt to become the "pure critic" who renounced all social, political, and philosophical assumptions was an attempt to remove himself from the distorting influence of philosophy and the world it justified. Ruge hoped that political practice would vindicate his political rationalism. He subscribed, that is, to a type of political pragmatism: he believed that his beliefs about the rational nature of politics would be proved true if they "worked," if they changed the world to conform to them. But judged by their own standards Bauer's and Ruge's efforts to attain an ideologically uncontaminated point of view ultimately failed. For they could not fully repudiate the philosophical assumptions that they regarded as ideological: they remained in the end loyal to the supremacy of philosophical reason, and this loyalty continued to render them incapable of addressing the changing social reality.

This is most clearly seen in how they reacted to the social crisis of the 1840s. Both thinkers recognized a problem in the formation of a new group of socially dispossessed and even saw that they bore a sociological affinity to that group, but they were unable to deal with the social problem except in inadequate Hegelian terms. For them, the new poor represented the welling up of brutalized sensuous need and desire and hence by Hegelian definition was chaotic, impervious to rational development. The masses for Bauer were to be spurned by the pure critic; for Ruge, they were to defer to the rational politician. Neither could allow the new poor to be governed by their own principles of development. Confronted with what Hegel had taught them to regard as a dangerous and uncontrollable disruption of society, Bauer and Ruge fled back to Hegelian abstraction. Thus as outcasts from conventional social and political institutions, but averse to aligning themselves with the great mass of social outcasts, they consigned themselves to social and theoretical isolation. The pure critic was increasingly ignored; Ruge died an unheeded and lonely exile in England.

Marx's search for a new nonphilosophical—and hence nonideological—point of view was no less agonized but ultimately more successful than those of his fellow Prussian Young Hegelians. Unlike Bauer and Ruge, he repudiated their remaining philosophical assumption that abstract reason could master sensuous reality. He surrendered himself to sensuous society. This was accomplished in two ways. First, in his writings, especially in his most antiphilosophical piece, *The German Ideology*, he rejected philosophical abstraction. His method was to stay on the surface of empirical experience. His reasoning was based on a common-sensical experience of material needs and interests, thus his reconstruction of human history abjured the use of the a priori philosophical categories found in his earlier writings. History for Marx in 1845 was an arrangement of contingent mundane events, of the actions of ordinary human beings impelled by sensuous needs and interests.

The second way in which Marx repudiated philosophy and embraced sensuous society was to formulate a pragmatism more thoroughgoing than Ruge's. Marx agreed with Ruge that one could verify the validity of one's views by carrying them out in practice. If they recreated the world in their own form, then they were "true." But where Ruge believed that his rational political plan would be fulfilled by rational political actors, Marx believed that his antiphilosophical understanding of the world would be vindicated by those who were profoundly antiphilosophical, by those who were moved by nothing but sensuous necessity. In short, Marx's new antiphilosophical point of view would be proved true if it contributed to proletarian revolution; in the years immediately after 1845, he ceased to quarrel with Hegelian philosophers and focused his writings on influencing the proletariat. Philosophical analysis gave way to political polemic. His critical and historical analysis was now reshaped into a body of political doctrine that would spur the working class to action. The praxis-oriented *Communist Manifesto*, in which Marx does not so much argue as assert his views, is the fitting successor to *The German Ideology*.[3]

For Marx in 1845 the quandary that so bothered the Prussian Young Hegelians—namely, how to indict others of ideology without being one-self an ideologist—was thus resolved, on the one side, by his first systematic version of historical materialism, and on the other, by his commitment to proletarian revolution. The crisis of the Young Hegelians drove them all toward the formulation of the theory of ideology, the theory of how abstract thought can justify or compensate for an adverse social and political reality. And although all confronted the theory's inherent problem of relativism in that all worried about their entanglement in ideology, only Marx resolved the problem with any thoroughness. He alone superseded the philosophical point of view that the Prussian Young Hegelians regarded as ideological and reached what he considered to be an objective perspective, a focus synchronized with reality. He was unique in presenting a formal theory of ideology systematically grounded in an unphilosophical view of the world.

5

With his anxiety about his complicity in the "German ideology" laid to rest, there was after 1845 a shift in emphasis in Marx's theory of ideology, a shift that determined how the theory was used for the subsequent hundred years. The theory formulated by Marx and the other Prussian Young Hegelians in the early 1840s contained two elements: philosophical ideas, they argued, functioned as a compensation for and a justification of a deficient reality. In writing about Hegelian and Young Hegelian philosophy, Marx, Bauer, and Ruge emphasized the first element, which directly incorporated their own experiences with the Prussian state and sensuous society. They argued that Hegelian philosophers theoretically inverted their subservience to a bad reality in order to conceal from themselves and others their own powerlessness. And although Marx and the other Prussian critics of philosophy considered how this compensation then justified certain bad aspects of existing society, their concern was primarily with the philosopher's deceptions and self-deceptions.

But after the mid-1840s, as some commentators have noted, Marx shifted the emphasis in his theory of ideology. The notion of ideology as social justification now appeared in the foreground of the theory and almost blotted out the notion of psychological compensation.[4] This shift reflects in another way the watershed that Marx passed through in 1845. The point of view of *The German Ideology* had allowed him finally to come to terms with his failed Hegelian expectations and his anxiety about being caught in ideology. With that accomplished, the question of how philosophers dealt with the world became less pressing. The aspect of ideological compensation lost its psychological and intellectual significance now that Marx had attained what he believed to be a post-philosophical, extra-ideological perspective.

Moreover, the nature of Marx's new point of view logically emphasized the theory's sociological aspect of justification. He was now committed to proletarian revolution and concerned with the ability of the existing order to resist revolution. He became more interested in the ability of the dominant classes to legitimize their rule and therefore prevent revolutionary challenges. This issue of how the existing order perpetuated itself gained even more importance when after the failure of the 1848 revolutions Marx realized that revolutionary change would not occur as easily or automatically as he had thought in the mid-1840s.[5]

After Marx, social theorists who employed the theory of ideology continued to emphasize its notion of justification, but their elaboration of this notion led to further significant alterations in the theory. From arguing that ideology was a set of beliefs that justified a particular set of social conditions, theorists in the last half of the nineteenth century came to define ideology as a body of thought that one generated in order to give coherence to one's world. It was a means of exerting control over chaos or a hostile external condition.[6] This extension of the idea of justification tended to strip the theory of the pejorative or politically critical meaning that Marx and other Prussian Young Hegelians had given to it. In redefining ideology to mean *Weltanschauung*, social theorists used the term in a seemingly neutral and even positive fashion. This made possible its adoption by unpolitical academics as a respectable tool of the social sciences. Since the end of the nineteenth century, the neutral sense of ideology has coexisted beside the pejorative sense. The neutral meaning of ideology has become so conventional in social thought that even some twentieth-century Marxists—most notably Lenin—have accepted it, speaking, as Marx never did, of the "ideology" of the proletariat.[7]

More recently, as Clifford Geertz has pointed out, social scientists inspired by Freud, Durkheim, and others have resurrected the notion of ideology as compensation. For these commentators ideology has again come to mean an intellectual response to a "chronic malintegration of society."[8] In this revival of a central element of the Young Hegelian theory of ideology, social theory has in effect returned to its beginnings, to the original dual meaning of the theory of ideology. In modern social theory, ideology functions as a justification of or compensation for an adverse reality. For some commentators as for the Young Hegelians, this theory of ideology is a critical analytic method; for others, it is simply a neutral tool of the social sciences.[9]

The theory of ideology formulated by the Young Hegelians has become entrenched in modern social theory. It has become so complete with its dualistic model of explanation, its critical import, and, in Mannheim's and others' extension of Marx, its problem of relativism. Mannheim's continued theorizing about ideology and its inherent problems highlights a final element of the Young Hegelian theory of ideology that has also persisted: the relation between the formulation of the theory and social and political dislocation.

I have argued that the advent of the theory was the response to the falsification of Hegelian principles by social and political problems related to Prussia's uneven modernization. Hegel's ideas about the nature of philosophical thought, including the general idea of the sovereignty of philosophy, appeared to the Prussian Young Hegelians to be rendered nonsensical in a rapidly changing and paradoxical world. Those ideas made sense only if they were considered to be that world's ideological efflux. The formulation of the theory of ideology emerged out of the collapse of traditional social and intellectual expectations brought on by dramatic social and political change.

After the Young Hegelians, ongoing social and political modernization continued to create anxieties for intellectuals, and with those anxieties came further formulations of the theory of ideology. In Germany the increasing importance of market relations and popular politics brought about the increasing marginalization of pure intellectual activity. The primacy of instrumental rationality in industrial society and the threat of being swamped by the seemingly irrational masses led many intellectuals to a profound doubt about the efficacy of a pure and autonomous rationality. They came to question what was in effect the principle of the sovereignty of philosophical reasoning.[10]

Karl Mannheim, the greatest theorist of ideology since Marx, was one of these troubled Wilhelmian intellectuals. As he himself acknowledged, the problems that he had with his identity as a German "mandarin" issued in his attempt to clarify the theory of ideology, to produce what he called the "sociology of knowledge."[11] Like that of the Prussian Young Hegelians, Mannheim's theorizing was the work of an anxious self-consciousness. At the same time that he questioned the power of abstract thought by showing how it was limited by the mundane world, he recognized that for his analysis to be coherent he had to show how it was not subject to such limitations. He too felt a logical and psychological compulsion to find an objective, independent point of view from which he could escape the ideology of the age. Mannheim, in fact, was the first theorist to conceptualize explicitly what the Young Hegelians had tried to deal with implicitly: the problem of relativism in the theory of ideology. But Mannheim's answer—that a place for epistemological certainty could be found in a class of "free-floating" (*freischwebende*) intellectuals, intellectuals without particular social interests—satisfied no one, not even Mannheim himself.[12] Like Bauer's and Ruge's theories of ideology, Mannheim's remained without an adequate conclusion. He never found his way out of the conditions he judged to be ideological.

The formulation of the theory of ideology in the twentieth as in the nineteenth century remains tied to social dislocation. It both registers an intellectual's traumatic experience of dislocation and seeks to overcome it. On the one side, it asserts that the traditional concept of the sovereignty of systematic abstract thought is a delusion, a notion that is far removed from reality. The theory of ideology, to quote Mannheim, is the "systematization of doubt"[13]—the doubt of an intellectual about his relation to reality. But on the other side, the theory tries to establish itself as the definitive theory of how thought operates in the concrete world. In this way, the intellectual seeks to reconnect theory to reality, even if at the expense of a derogation of the former. The theory of ideology strives to remedy the intellectual's sense of being severed from the real world. Its formulation is his attempt to come to terms with a world that has forsaken him.

Notes

Introduction: Philosophy and Ideology

1. David Hume, *A Treatise of Human Nature,* quoted in Karl Marx, "Difference Between the Democritean and Epicurean Philosophy of Nature," in Karl Marx and Friedrich Engels, *Collected Works* (New York, 1975), 1:30. Marx's emphasis.

2. Marx and Engels, "The German Ideology," in *Collected Works* 5:59.

3. In his well-known essay on the theory of ideology, Clifford Geertz summarizes contemporary research on the theory and singles out these two elements—justification and compensation—as the functions usually ascribed to an ideology. Clifford Geertz, "Ideology as a Cultural System," in *The Interpretation of Cultures* (New York, 1973), 201 ff.

4. Commentators disagree about the extent and kind of abstraction that is ideological. Some include the empirical sciences, but most exclude them. See Jorge Larrain, *The Concept of Ideology* (London, 1979), 18–24. Most commentators who have recognized the danger of the theory's self-negating relativism attempt to exempt their own views from the charge of ideology. In other words, there is no consensus among theorists of ideology about the *necessity* of ideology in all abstract thinking. This important issue, the theory's relativistic implications, is discussed more extensively below in the conclusion, "The End of Philosophy."

5. Some commentators have also observed that the theory of ideology significantly changes after the mid-1840s. I discuss these changes and their relation to Young Hegelian theory in the conclusion. For now I might note that the later changes in the theory do not vitiate the crucial role of the Prussian Young Hegelians in the theory's formulation. As we shall see, those later developments in the theory were elaborations of certain aspects of the theory of the early 1840s. They were extrapolations and variations of the principles assumed by all the Prussian Young Hegelians and given their most formal expression by Marx.

6. Hans Barth, *Wahrheit und Ideologie* (Zurich, 1945), 37–53.

7. Karl Mannheim, *Ideology and Utopia* (New York, n.d.; first published in English in 1935), 63; Larrain, *Concept,* 18–24.

8. Barth, *Wahrheit,* 54–73; Larrain, *Concept,* 24–32; Mannheim, *Ideology,* 63.

9. Barth, *Wahrheit,* 16; Emmett Kennedy, "'Ideology' from Destutt de Tracy to Marx," *Journal of the History of Ideas* 40 (1979), 354; George Lichtheim, "The Concept of Ideology," *History and Theory* 4 (1965), 165–170.

10. Barth, *Wahrheit,* 21, 24. These figures' partial skepticism about ideas is an example of what Mannheim calls the "particular" conception of ideology, in which only certain ideas are singled out as ideological. Mannheim, *Ideology,* 55–70.

11. Barth, *Wahrheit,* 38; Kennedy, "'Ideology',” 364. For political motives behind Napoleon's attack see Kennedy, "'Ideology',” 364; Hans-Christoph Rauh, "Zur Herkunft, Vorgeschichte, und ersten Verwendungsweise des Ideologiebegriffs bei Marx und Engels bis 1844," *Deutsche Zeitschrift für Philosophie* 18 (1970), 703; Ulrich Dierse, "Ideologie," in *Geschichtliche Grundbegriffe* 3 (Stuttgart, 1982), 131, 137 ff.

12. Larrain, *Concept,* 18–32; and see Lichtheim, "Concept," 173–174.

13. Ludwig Feuerbach, "Vorläufige Thesen zur Reformation der Philosophie," in Arnold Ruge, ed., *Anekdota zur neuesten deutschen Philosophie und Publicistik* 2 (Zurich, 1843), 80. An excellent treatment of the development of Feuerbach's anti-Hegelianism is Marx Wartofsky, *Feuerbach* (Cambridge, 1977).

14. Both Strauss and Feuerbach explained the source of religious alienation in a distinctly Hegelian manner: it is derived from humanity's urge to overcome nature and attain a condition of free spiritual self-unity. See David Friedrich Strauss, *The Life of Jesus Critically Examined,* trans. from the fourth edition by George Eliot (Philadelphia, 1972), 780; Ludwig Feuerbach, *The Essence of Christianity,* trans. George Eliot (New York, 1957), 177–178, 184. This central notion in Hegelian theory is extensively discussed below in Part I.

15. Karl Löwith, *From Hegel to Nietzsche* (Garden City, N.Y., 1967), 308.

16. Two other figures associated with Young Hegelian philosophy in Prussia, Moses Hess and Max Stirner, have proved to be of historical and intellectual interest, but neither is an appropriate subject for this study. Neither was in the mainstream of academic Hegelianism, and neither had an enduring influence on the development of Young Hegelian theory. Hess was an amateur philosopher who at most dabbled in Hegelian theory and freely combined it with other philosophical and religious ideas. Stirner's claim to fame lies in his work *Der Einzige und sein Eigentum,* which did cause a stir among Young Hegelians when it appeared in 1844. But Stirner's importance was transitory. He ceased to write philosophy after 1845, and he never gained a following among Hegelians. Stirner and Hess did not share the sociological background of Bauer, Ruge, and Marx— the former were not academic thinkers committed to the linking of Hegelian philosophy with the Prussian state. They consequently did not engage in the agonized reappraisal of the relation between philosophy and social and political

reality when that connection was severed. Rather their importance lies in being, as it were, products of the crisis of the academic Prussian Hegelians, for Hess and Stirner assimilated in their own ways the uprooted Young Hegelians' attempts to turn Hegelian philosophy into critical theory. Both were deeply influenced by Bauer, and later Hess fell under the sway of Marx. Hess and Stirner would be, in other words, important subjects for a study of the general intellectual influences of the dislocation of academic Hegelian philosophers: they were social outsiders who rallied to the banner theories of the newly outcast philosophers. But they do not figure significantly in an analysis of the formation and development of that dislocation or in how it issued in the theory of ideology. On Hess see Horst Stuke, *Philosophie der Tat: Studien zur "Verwirklichung der Philosophie" bei den Junghegelianern und wahren Socialisten* (Stuttgart, 1963), and Auguste Cornu, *Moses Hess et al gauche Hégélienne* (Paris, 1934). On Stirner see John Henry Mackay, *Max Stirner: Sein Leben und sein Werk* (Berlin, 1914), R. W. K. Paterson, *The Nihilistic Egoist: Max Stirner* (London, 1971), and Lawrence S. Stepelevich, "Max Stirner as Hegelian," *Journal of the History of Ideas* 46 (1985), 597–614.

1. Spirit as Subject

1. Charles Taylor, *Hegel* (Cambridge, 1975), 51–64; Panajotis Kondylis, *Die Entstehung der Dialektik: Eine Analyse der geistigen Entwicklung von Hölderlin, Schelling und Hegel bis 1802* (Stuttgart, 1979); John Toews, *Hegelianism: The Path Toward Dialectical Humanism, 1805–1841* (Cambridge, 1980), 30–48; Mark C. Taylor, *Journeys to Selfhood: Hegel and Kierkegaard* (Berkeley, 1980), 25–51; Franz Nauen, *Revolution, Idealism, and Human Freedom: Schelling, Hölderlin, and Hegel and the Crisis of Early German Idealism* (The Hague, 1971); Raymond Plant, *Hegel* (Bloomington, Ind., 1973), 15–55; Franz Rosenzweig, *Hegel und der Staat* 1, (Berlin, 1920), 17–62; H. S. Harris, *Hegel's Development Toward the Sunlight, 1770–1801* (Oxford, 1972), 154 ff. and passim.
2. G. W. F. Hegel, "The Positivity of Christianity," in *Early Theological Writings*, trans. T. M. Knox (Philadelphia, 1971), 67–181.
3. Ibid., 158.
4. Kondylis, *Die Entstehung der Dialektik*, 194. And see H. S. Harris, "Hegel and the French Revolution," *Clio* 7 (1977), 5–18.
5. See G. W. F. Hegel, "Aus den 'Vertrauliche Briefe über das vormalige staatsrechtliche Verhältnis des Wadtlands (Pays de Vaud) zur Stadt Bern,'" in J. Hoffmeister, ed., *Dokumente zur Hegels Entwicklung* (Stuttgart, 1974), 247–257. An English translation of some of Hegel's notes to the piece is Z. A. Pelczynski, trans., "Commentary on the Bern Aristocracy" in *Clio* 8 (1979), 405–416.
6. Hegel to Friedrich Schelling, 16 April 1795, in G. W. F. Hegel, *Briefe*

von und an Hegel, ed. J. Hoffmeister, 4 vols. (Hamburg, 1952–1960), 1:24. See Jürgen Habermas, "On Hegel's Political Writings," in *Theory and Practice* (Boston, 1973), 181; Rosenzweig, *Hegel und der Staat* 1:31.

7. Rosenzweig, *Hegel und der Staat* 1:63–107; Taylor, *Hegel,* 64–75; Toews, *Hegelianism,* 41–47; Plant, *Hegel,* 79 ff.; Kondylis, *Die Entstehung der Dialektik*; Shlomo Avineri, *Hegel's Theory of the Modern State* (Cambridge, 1972), 69–70.

8. See, for example, his cogent analysis of Germany's political problems at the beginning of the nineteenth century. G. W. F. Hegel, "The German Constitution," in *Hegel's Political Writings,* trans. T. M. Knox (Oxford, 1964), 143–148, 202.

9. Ibid., 145.

10. Ibid.

11. Taylor, *Hegel,* 72.

12. See, for example, G. W. F. Hegel, *The Philosophy of History,* trans. J. Sibree (New York, 1956), 20.

13. Taylor, *Hegel,* 76–124; Plant, *Hegel,* 198; Emil Fackenheim, *The Religious Dimension in Hegel's Thought* (Bloomington, Ind., 1967), 31–73; Quentin Lauer, *Hegel's Concept of God* (Albany, N.Y., 1982), 133–161.

14. Taylor, *Hegel,* 114.

15. G. W. F. Hegel, *Phenomenology of Spirit,* trans. A. V. Miller (Oxford, 1979), 10; *Philosophy of Right,* trans. T. M. Knox (Oxford, 1973), pars. 26–27, 142–144; *Philosophy of History,* 43, 104, 447, 456. See Rudolf Haym, *Hegel und seine Zeit* (Berlin, 1857), 357; Herbert Marcuse, *Reason and Revolution* (Boston, 1969), 151–155; Rosenzweig, *Hegel und der Staat* 2:178–179.

16. There is no consensus on how to translate this expression. Sibree uses "self-contained existence" in his version of the *Philosophy of History,* 17 and passim, while M. H. Abrams uses the more literary "being-at-home-with-oneself" in *Natural Supernaturalism: Tradition and Revolution in Romantic Literature* (New York, 1971), 234.

17. This is a modified version of Sibree's rather loose translation in the *Philosophy of History,* 17. The original German reads:

der Geist ist das *Bei-sich-selbst-sein.* Dies eben ist die Freiheit, denn wenn ich abhängig bin, so beziehe mich auf ein Andres das ich nicht bin, ich kann nicht sein ohne ein Äusseres; frei bin ich, wenn ich bei mir selbst bin.

Hegel, *Sämtliche Werke,* ed. Hermann Glockner (Stuttgart, 1949: Jubiläumsausgabe), 11:44. Hegel's emphasis.

18. Hegel, *Philosophy of History,* 57, 103, 424, 456; *Philosophy of Right,* pars. 352–353 and addition to par. 151, p. 260; Manfred Riedel, "Nature and Freedom in Hegel's *Philosophy of Right,*" in Z. A. Pelczynski, ed., *Hegel's Political Philosophy* (Cambridge, 1971), 137, 142; George A. Kelly, *Idealism, Politics, and History: Sources of Hegelian Thought* (Cambridge, 1969), 290 f.

19. Hegel, *The Phenomenology of Spirit*, 120, Hegel's emphasis. And see *Philosophy of Right*, par. 21, and *Philosophy of History*, 439.

20. Hegel, *Philosophy of Right*, par. 22, and see J. N. Findlay, *Hegel: A Re-Examination* (Oxford, 1976), 42. I find Findlay's interpretation more agreeable than that of Marcuse, who says that by *infinity* Hegel means endless change. See Marcuse, *Reason and Revolution*, 138.

21. Hegel, *Philosophy of History*, 17.

22. This is the section " 'Sense-Certainty' or 'This' and 'Meaning'," in Hegel's *Phenomenology of Spirit*, 58 ff.

23. Ibid., 485 f., 490 f.

24. Hegel, *The Philosophy of Right*, addition to par. 4, p. 226. Judith Shklar has a very clear analysis of the "topology" of the *Phenomenology* in her *Freedom and Independence* (Cambridge, 1976).

25. Hegel, *The Phenomenology of Spirit*, 492, and see 17, 28.

26. See Hegel's address to his philosophy class at the University of Jena in the summer of 1806, reprinted in Karl Rosenkranz, *Georg Wilhelm Friedrich Hegels Leben* (Darmstadt, 1969), 214–215.

27. G. W. F. Hegel, "Rede zum Antritt des philosophischen Lehramtes an der Universität Berlin," in J. Hoffmeister, ed., *Berliner Schriften, 1818–1831* (Hamburg, 1956), 10–11.

28. Ibid., 11–12.

29. See Hegel, *The Phenomenology of Spirit*, 16; Manfred Riedel, *Theorie und Praxis im Denken Hegels* (Stuttgart, 1965), 209–211; Rosenzweig gives a Hegelian interpretation of Hegel's own adoption of his mature philosophical point of view. See Rosenzweig, *Hegel und der Staat* 1:63–107.

2. Spirit as Substance

1. Like most interpreters of Hegelian theory, I have treated as representative of Hegel's mature political theory the *Philosophy of Right* of 1820. Karl-Heinz Ilting has recently argued that there is no single representative text insofar as Hegel in the 1820s fluctuated between liberalism and conservativism. [See K.-H. Ilting, "Einleitung," to *Vorlesungen über Rechtsphilosophie, 1818–1831* 1 (Stuttgart, 1973), 23–126; and "The Structure of Hegel's *Philosophy of Right*," in Pelczynski, ed., *Hegel's Political Philosophy*, 90–110.] Ilting's thesis has been severely criticized. See Rolf P. Horstmann, "Ist Hegels Rechtsphilosophie das Produkt der politischen Anpassung eines Liberalen?" *Hegel-Studien* 9 (1974), 241–252; Henning Ottmann, "Hegels Rechtsphilosophie und das Problem der Akkomodation," *Zeitschrift für philosophische Forschung* 33 (1979), 227–243. In any event, the specific developments that Ilting discusses are not central to our general consideration of Hegel's mature political theory.

2. See Manfred Riedel, "Hegels Begriff der bürgerlichen Gesellschaft und das Problem seines geschichtlichen Ursprungs," in *Materialien zu Hegels Rechtsphilosophie* (Frankfurt am Main, 1975), 247–275; and his "Gesellschaft, bürgerliche," in Otto Brunner et al., ed., *Geschichtliche Grundbegriffe* 2 (Stuttgart, 1975), 719–800; James Schmidt, "A *Paideia* for the 'Bürger als Bourgeois': The Concept of 'Civil Society' in Hegel's Political Thought," *History of Political Thought* 2 (1981), 472–474. Also see Otto Brunner, *Land und Herrschaft* (Vienna, 1959), 14–15; and his *Neue Wege der Verfassungs- und Sozialgeschichte* (Göttingen, 1968), 137–138, 188; Werner Conze, "Das Spannungsfeld von Staat und Gesellschaft im Vormärz," in Conze, ed., *Staat und Gesellschaft im deutschen Vormärz, 1815–1848* (Stuttgart, 1962), 208 ff.

3. Brunner, *Neue Wege*, 164–165; and his *Land und Herrschaft*, 140–142, 390; G. W. F. Hegel, "Proceedings of the Estates Assembly in the Kingdom of Wurtemburg, 1815–1816," *Hegel's Political Writings*, 263.

4. Leonard Krieger, *The German Idea of Freedom* (Chicago, 1972), 10–11.

5. Brunner, *Neue Wege*, 164–165, 188; Werner Näf, "Fruhformen des 'modernen Staates' im Spätmittelalter," *Historische Zeitschrift* 171 (1951), 237; Jürgen Habermas, *Strukturwandel der Öffentlichkeit* (Darmstadt, 1982), 17 ff.

6. Näf, "Fruhformen"; Brunner, *Neue Wege*, 133, 154, 192.

7. Brunner, *Land und Herrschaft*, 423 ff.; *Neue Wege*, 164–165, 192–194.

8. Brunner, *Land und Herrschaft*, 388 f., 429.

9. Brunner, *Neue Wege*, 171–178, 194–196; Krieger, *German Idea of Freedom*, 12–13; Gerhard Schulz, "Die Entstehung der bürgerlichen Gesellschaft," in Gerhard A. Ritter, ed., *Entstehung und Wandel der modernen Gesellschaft* (Berlin, 1970), 13–19; Hegel, "Wurtemberg," 263.

10. Brunner, *Land und Herrschaft*, 438–439; *Neue Wege*, 178, 195–197; Habermas, *Öffentlichkeit*, 24–25; Krieger, *German Idea of Freedom*, 12; Nannerl Keohane, *Philosophy and the State in France* (Princeton, 1980), 454–457 and passim; and especially Alexis de Tocqueville, *The Old Regime and the French Revolution* (Garden City, N.Y., 1955), 6–136.

11. Krieger, *German Idea of Freedom*, 28–31; Reinhart Koselleck, *Preussen zwischen Reform und Revolution* (Stuttgart, 1975), 83–85; Alfred Cobban, *The Social History of the French Revolution* (Cambridge, 1964), 44–52.

12. Krieger, *German Idea of Freedom*, 27 f.; Klaus Epstein, *The Genesis of German Conservatism* (Princeton, 1966), 179–183; Wilhelm Treue, "Adam Smith in Deutschland: Zum Problem des 'politischen Professors' zwischen 1776 und 1810," in *Rothfels Festschrift: Deutschland und Europa* (Düsseldorf, 1957), 101–153.

13. Conze, "Spannungsfeld," 246; Hans Gerth, *Bürgerliche Intelligenz um 1800* (Göttingen, 1982), 42 ff.; Otto Hintze, "Prussian Reform Movements Before 1806," in *The Historical Essays of Otto Hintze* (Oxford, 1975), 64–87; Walter Simon, *The Failure of the Prussian Reform Movement* (Ithaca, N.Y., 1955), 16 ff.

14. This intensified opposition between the state and society was reflected in a change in political conceptualization. Since antiquity, the term "civil society" ("*societas civilis,*" "*bürgerliche Gesellschaft*") had referred to a political community. Civil society was equivalent to the state. But in the late eighteenth century the term acquired a new meaning; it now referred to the set of interrelated individual economic interests that preceded the state. Civil society was anchored in the market; it was a realm outside of politics. See Riedel, "Gesellschaft, bürgerliche"; Brunner, *Neue Wege,* 138, 171; Ernst Rudolf Huber, *Deutsche Verfassungsgeschichte seit 1789* 1 (Stuttgart, 1957), 97–98.

15. See William H. Sewell, Jr. "Property, Labor, and the Emergence of Socialism in France, 1789–1848," in John M. Merriman, ed., *Consciousness and Class Experience in Nineteenth-Century Europe* (London, 1979), 45–64; and Sewell, *Work and Revolution in France: The Language of Labor from the Old Regime to 1848* (Cambridge, 1980), 114–142 and passim.

16. Koselleck, *Preussen,* 487; Simon, *Failure,* 6–29, 88–103; and Friedrich Meinecke, *The Age of German Liberation* (Berkeley, 1977), 69–102.

17. Koselleck, *Preussen,* 487–556; Simon, *Failure,* 99–103.

18. See Koselleck, *Preussen*; Conze, "Spannungsfeld"; Werner Conze, "Vom 'Pöbel' zum 'Proletariat': Sozialgeschichtliche Voraussetzungen für den Sozialismus in Deutschland," in Hans-Ulrich Wehler, ed., *Moderne deutsche Sozialgeschichte* (Köln, 1966), 112; Dirk Blasius, *Bürgerliche Gesellschaft und Kriminalität* (Göttingen, 1976), 51.

19. See Keohane, *Philosophy and the State,* 457–463; R. R. Palmer, *The Age of Democratic Revolutions,* 2 vols. (Princeton, 1959–1964); Habermas, *Öffentlichkeit,* 76–94; Rudolf Vierhaus, "Ständewesen und Staatsverwaltung in Deutschland im späteren 18. Jahrhundert," in R. Vierhaus and M. Botznehart, eds., *Dauer und Wandel der Geschichte: Aspekte Europäischer Vergangenheit* (Münster, 1966), 344 f.

20. See Koselleck, *Preussen,* 159 ff.; Hintze, "Reform Movements Before 1806."

21. Simon, *Failure,* 68–83, 111–113.

22. Ibid., 11 ff., 52 ff., 205; Koselleck, *Preussen,* 159 ff.; Conze, "Spannungsfeld," 245 ff.

23. Simon, *Failure,* 238.

24. Koselleck, *Preussen,* 317 ff.; and see Simon, *Failure,* 30, 35 f., 52–57.

25. Koselleck, *Preussen,* 318 ff.; Simon, *Failure,* 59–61, 118–139, 209–222.

26. Conze, "Spannungsfeld," 245 ff. Koselleck argues that the bureaucracy now conceived of itself as an "*Ersatzconstitution,*" the medium that would tie together the state and the mixed society. See Koselleck, *Preussen,* 219–237, 239 ff., 259–263.

27. Hegel, *Philosophy of Right,* pars. 149, 260, 352–353; *Philosophy of History,* 41, 57, 103, 140, 424, 456; Kelly, *Idealism,* 290.

238 NOTES TO PAGES 25-29

28. Hegel, *Philosophy of Right*, pars. 257, 272 ff.; *Philosophy of History*, 38 f.

29. See Epstein, *Genesis*, 237–241 and passim; Keohane, *Philosophy and the State*, 312–350; Jacques Godechot, *The Counter-Revolution: Doctrine and Action, 1789–1804* (Princeton, 1981), 3–16.

30. Hegel, "German Constitution," 164; and see Rosenzweig, *Hegel und der Staat* 1:22, and 2:62.

31. Hegel, "Wurtemberg," 257, 267; "The English Reform Bill," in *Hegel's Political Writings*, 300 ff.

32. Hegel, "Wurtemberg," 271–272; and see *Philosophy of Right*, pars. 277 f.; and Rosenkranz, *Hegels Leben*, 333.

33. Hegel, "Wurtemberg," 282.

34. Hegel, *Philosophy of History*, 447. See Joachim Ritter, *Hegel und die französische Revolution* (Frankfurt am Main, 1967), 24 f.; Jürgen Habermas, "Hegel's Critique of the French Revolution," in *Theory and Practice*, 126.

35. Hegel, *Phenomenology of Spirit*, 355–364; *Philosophy of Right*, addition to par. 5, p. 22. See Kondylis, *Die Entstehung der Dialektik*, 187 ff.

36. This is as much true for a powerful as for a minimal state.

37. Hegel, "Wurtemberg," 257–258, 263; *Philosophy of Right*, pars. 303, 315; "Rede," 5; "English Reform Bill," 315; *Philosophy of Mind*, trans. William Wallace (Oxford, 1971), 273 ff. See Habermas, "On Hegel's Political Writings," 189; Rolf P. Horstmann, "Über die Rolle der bürgerlichen Gesellschaft in Hegels politischer Philosophie," *Hegel-Studien* 9 (1974), 232.

38. Hegel, "Wurtemberg," 262; "English Reform Bill," 311; Habermas, "On Hegel's Political Writings," 189.

39. Hegel, *Philosophy of Right*, par. 303.

40. Hegel, *Philosophy of Right*, pars. 301, 308; *Philosophy of Mind*, 273–274; "English Reform Bill," 318–319; "German Constitution," 160. Hegel also attacks one of the major corollaries of liberal political theory—namely, the idea of public opinion. See Hegel, *Philosophy of Right*, pars. 317–320; "English Reform Bill," 295. On the emergence of the idea of public opinion, see Habermas, *Öffentlichkeit*.

41. Hegel, *Philosophy of Right*, par. 11.

42. Ibid., pars. 14–17.

43. Ibid., par. 35.

44. See Habermas, "On Hegel's Political Writings," 186; Ritter, *Revolution*, 41 ff. On the relation of the abstract ego to the French Revolution, see Habermas, "Hegel's Critique of the French Revolution," 121–126; and Ritter, *Revolution*, 30.

45. Hegel, *Philosophy of Right*, pars. 238, 159.

46. Ibid., pars. 19–21.

47. Ibid., pars. 183, 189–198.

48. Ibid., par. 189.

49. Hegel makes no distinction between employers and workers.
50. Hegel, *Philosophy of Right*, par. 203.
51. Ibid., par. 204.
52. Ibid., par. 207.
53. Ibid., par. 185.
54. Ibid., pars. 241–247.
55. Ibid., pars. 241, 252.
56. Ibid., pars. 235–237.
57. Ibid., par. 245.
58. Ibid., pars. 251–252.
59. Ibid., par. 289.
60. Ibid., par. 281.
61. Ibid., par. 287.
62. Ibid., pars. 288–289.
63. Ibid., par. 303.
64. Ibid., pars. 305–307.
65. Ibid., par. 308.
66. Ibid., par. 302.
67. Ibid.
68. See Habermas, "On Hegel's Political Writings," 191; Rosenzweig, *Hegel und der Staat* 1:165, and 2:189; F. R. Cristi, "The *Hegelsche Mitte* and Hegel's Monarch," *Political Theory* 11 (1983), 601–610, 618.
69. Hegel, "Wurtemberg," 263.
70. Hegel to Hardenberg, mid-October 1820, in *Briefe* 2:241–242.
71. On Hegel and the Prussian bureaucracy see Koselleck, *Preussen*, 263. The older controversy concerning Hegel's relation to an authoritarian "Prussianism" has been superseded by more sophisticated analyses of both Hegelian political philosophy and the Prussian state. On the older controversy, see the essays collected in Walter Kaufman, ed., *Hegel's Political Philosophy* (New York, 1970). Also see Eric Weil, *Hegel et l'état* (Paris, 1950). More searching analyses are Rolf Hocěvar, *Hegel und der preussische Staat* (Munich, 1973); Ilting, "Structure" and "Einleitung"; Michael Haller, *System und Gesellschaft* (Stuttgart, 1981); Rosenzweig, *Hegel und der Staat* 2:122 ff., 161–165; Gertrude Lübbe-Wolff, "Hegels Staatsrecht als Stellungnahme im ersten preussischen Verfassungskampf," *Zeitschrift für philosophische Forschung* 35 (1982):476–501. There is no agreement about which of the two reform leaders Hegel was closest to in thinking. Hocěvar (122) asserts that Hegel's ideas resembled Stein's; Toews (*Hegelianism*, 60 f.) asserts that Hegel and Hardenberg were of one mind. On the historiography of interpretations of Hegel's political philosophy see Henning Ottmann, *Individuum und Gesellschaft bei Hegel: Hegel im Spiegel der Interpretationen* (Berlin, 1977).
72. Hegel, "Rede," 4.

73. Steven R. Turner, "The Growth of Professorial Research in Prussia, 1818 to 1848—Causes and Context," *Historical Studies in the Physical Sciences* 3 (1972), 137–182, and his "University Reformers and Professorial Scholarship," in Lawrence Stone, ed., *The University in Society* (Princeton, 1974), 495–531. On the social background of university reform see Wilhelm Roessler, *Die Entstehung des modernen Erziehungswesens in Deutschlands* (Stuttgart, 1961); and Charles E. McClelland, *State, Society, and University in Germany, 1700–1914* (Cambridge, 1980), 106–151.

74. Walter Jaeschke and Kurt Rainer Meist, "Von Humboldt zu Altenstein," in Otto Pöggeler, ed., *Hegel in Berlin* (Berlin, 1981), 31–33. Hermann Lübbe, "Deutscher Idealismus als Philosophie preussischer Kulturpolitik," in O. Pöggeler and A. Gethmann-Siefert, eds., *Kunsterfahrung und Kulturpolitik im Berlin Hegels,* Beiheft 22 of *Hegel-Studien* (Bonn, 1983), 12 ff. And see Friedrich Paulsen, *Geschichte des gelehrten Unterrichts auf dem deutschen Schulen und Universitäten vom Ausgang des Mittelalters bis zur Gegenwart* 2 (Berlin, 1921), 191–382.

75. Hegel, "Rede," 4.

76. Schulze was a close friend and follower of the philosopher. He audited Hegel's lectures, collaborated in the founding of the major organ of Hegelian philosophy—the *Jahrbücher für wissenschaftliche Kritik*—attended Hegel on his deathbed in 1831, and helped to edit the *Phenomenology* for the posthumous edition of Hegel's collected works. See C. Varrentrapp, *Johannes Schulze und das höhere preussische Unterrichtswesen in seiner Zeit* (Leipzig, 1889). Jaeschke and Meist, "Von Humboldt zu Altenstein," 31–37.

77. Max Lenz, *Geschichte der königlichen Friedrich-Wilhelms-Universität zu Berin* 2 (Halle, 1910), passim. Toews, *Hegelianism,* 71 ff.

78. Hegel, *Philosophy of History,* 419–422, 437.

79. Hegel, "English Reform Bill," 300, 324–325.

80. They unsuccessfully attempted to prevent the Pietist theologian Ernst von Hengstenberg from getting into the theological faculty at the University of Berlin. As we shall see, Hengstenberg became in the 1830s a leader of the opposition to Hegelian theory. Lenz, *Geschichte*; and see Robert M. Bigler, *The Politics of German Protestantism: The Rise of the Protestant Church Elite in Prussia, 1815–1848* (Berkeley, 1972), 76–155.

81. Hegel, *Philosophy of History,* 452; Rosenzweig, *Hegel und der Staat* 2:220 ff.; Rosenkranz, *Hegels Leben,* 414 ff.

82. Ironically, part of Hegel's essay was suppressed at the command of King Frederick William, who did not want to antagonize Britain.

83. Hegel, "The English Reform Bill," 15 ff.

84. Ibid., 324–325, 330; and see Marcuse, *Reason and Revolution,* 246–247.

85. Rosenzweig, *Hegel und der Staat* 2:236–237; Habermas, "On Hegel's Political Writings," 192; Marcuse, *Reason and Revolution,* 246–247.

86. Lenz, *Geschichte* 2:390–393; Kurt Reiner Meist, "Altenstein und Gans: Eine frühe politische Option für Hegels Rechtsphilosophie," *Hegel-Studien* 14 (1979), 59 ff.

87. Lenz, *Geschichte* 2:394. Hegel's victory was not total—he was never admitted to the Prussian Academy of Sciences.

88. See Rosenkranz, *Hegels Leben*, 380–381; Heinrich von Treitschke, *History of Germany in the Nineteenth Century* 4 (London, 1918), 568–569.

89. See Walter Jaeschke, "Urmenschheit und Monarchie: Eine politische Christologie der Hegelschen Rechten," in *Hegel-Studien* 14 (1979), 73–108.

90. See Toews, *Hegelianism*, 220–235; Hermann Lübbe, "Die politische Theorie der Hegelschen Rechte," in his *Politische Philosophie in Deutschland* (Basel and Stuttgart, 1963), 175–228; Peter Cornehl, *Die Zukunft der Versöhnung: Eschatologie und Emanzipation in der Aufklärung, bei Hegel und in der Hegelschen Schule* (Göttingen, 1971), 206 ff.

91. See Cornehl, *Zukunft*, 163 ff.; Joachim Mehlhausen, "Dialektik, Selbstbewusstsein, und Offenbarung," (Ph.D. dissertation, University of Bonn, 1965), 92–153; Jürgen Gebhardt, *Politik und Eschatologie: Studien zur der Geschichte der Hegelschen Schule in den Jahren 1830–1840* (Munich, 1963), 49 ff.

92. Toews, *Hegelianism*, 242.

93. See David F. Strauss, *Streitschriften zur Verteidigung meiner Schrift über das Leben Jesu und zur Charakteristik der gegenwärtigen Theologie* 3 (Tübingen, 1837), 95 ff. The term "Young Hegelian" was used by Marx in *The German Ideology* of 1845. Although they had a definite sense of being an established group within the Hegelian movement, the radicals did not refer to themselves with any one name. They called themselves "left Hegelians," "*Hegelei*," "*Hegelingen*," and so on. I have used "Young Hegelians" because that is what they are most commonly called.

Interpreters have conventionally analyzed the development of Young Hegelian theory as a development toward humanism. See William Brazil, *The Young Hegelians* (New Haven, 1970), 265; Udo Köster, *Literarischer Radikalismus: Zeitbewusstsein und Geschichtsphilosophie in der Entwicklung vom jungen Deutschland zur Hegelschen Linke* (Frankfurt am Main, 1972), 79; Jürgen Gebhardt, *Politik und Eschatologie*, 127; and especially Toews, *Hegelianism*, 1, 206.

94. Friedrich Engels, *Ludwig Feuerbach and the Outcome of Classical German Philosophy* (New York, 1974), 16–19; Brazil, *Young Hegelians*, 7–8; Ingrid Pepperle, *Junghegelianische Geschichtsphilosophie und Kunsttheorie* (Berlin, 1978), 30; Marilyn Massey, *Christ Unmasked: The Meaning of "The Life of Jesus" in German Politics* (Chapel Hill, 1983); Werner Schuffenhauer, *Feuerbach und der junge Marx* (Berlin, 1965), 16.

95. On Strauss, see below, the third section of chapter 6. Ruge and Marx called on Feuerbach to join the establishment of a politically radical magazine in

Paris, but Feuerbach declined; Karl Marx to Ludwig Feuerbach, 3 October 1843, in Marx and Engels, *Collected Works* 3:349. And see Simon Rawidowicz, *Ludwig Feuerbachs Philosophie* (Berlin, 1964), 307–320; Brazil, *Young Hegelians,* 120–122, 152–153; Löwith, *From Hegel to Nietzsche,* 308 ff.; Cornehl, *Zukunft,* 258–259. On the inadequacies of Feuerbach's views of communism, see Schuffenhauer, *Feuerbach und der junge Marx,* 129 ff.

96. John Toews, in his synthetic and generally excellent study, *Hegelianism,* has a third view of the origin of the radical Young Hegelian movement. Toews takes issue with interpreters who have focused on the religious criticism of the 1830s as the source of radical Hegelianism (Toews, 220). For Toews, that religious radicalism should be viewed in the context of the political reformism of the 1830s. He thus implies that the social and political radicalism of the Young Hegelians in the 1840s was an extension of *both* the religious and the political criticism of the 1830s (Toews, 220–242). I think this view is problematical in several respects. First, the political reformism of the 1830s is only vaguely related by Toews to the religious radicalism of the Young Hegelians. It serves as a general "background," but it is not specifically shown to be crucial to the intellectual formation of the religious radicals. In fact, they did not appear to have been affected directly by the political reformism of the 1830s. As already noted, Strauss and Feuerbach had little interest in politics. They, Marx, and Bauer were moreover entirely unaffected by the revolutions of the 1830s, the galvanizing force, according to Toews, of the political reformism of the 1830s. And as we shall see below, Ruge was thoroughly disillusioned with political activism when the 1830 revolutions occurred. Second, Toews himself notes that the religious criticism of the Young Hegelians marked a sharp break with the earlier religious criticism of the early 1830s: the former rejected all possibility of reconciliation with Christianity (Toews, 242). This would seem to imply that there was a qualitative change in the Hegelian movement and hence would contradict his suggestion of continuity. Finally, the same would hold true for the political radicalism of the Prussian Young Hegelians in the 1840s. It too marked a qualitative break with earlier Hegelian political criticism. As Toews himself notes, the political critics of the 1830s were reformist: they wished to change the Prussian state, but they still believed that it would be the fulfillment of rational spirit. The political critics of the 1840s, however, were radical: they rejected altogether the possibility of a reconciliation with the Prussian state, and indeed, in Marx's case, the Hegelian idea of the state was abandoned. As I hope to show, the older view of Young Hegelian development still has much to recommend it: Young Hegelian religious criticism was the product of an internal theoretical dispute occasioned by tensions and ambiguities in Hegel's religious theory. But my interpretation of the social and political criticism of the 1840s differs from both the older view and Toews's view: Young Hegelian social and political criticism was precipitated by external social and political pressures.

97. Varrentrapp, *Johannes Schulze*, 439–442.

98. Bigler, *Politics of German Protestantism*, 76–155, and his "The Social Status and Political Role of the Protestant Clergy in Pre-March Prussia," in Hans-Ulrich Wehler, *Sozialgeschichte Heute* (Göttingen, 1974), 175–191; Toews, *Hegelianism*, 243–253.

99. John Gillis, *The Prussian Bureaucracy in Crisis, 1841–1860* (Stanford, 1971), 18–19.

100. Lenz, *Geschichte* 2:514.

101. Jaeschke and Meist, "Von Humboldt zu Altenstein," 36.

102. Koselleck, *Preussen*, 487–501, 508–556.

103. Ibid., 506, 557.

104. Ibid., 589–601, and see Theodore Hamerow, *Restoration, Revolution, Reaction: Economics and Politics in Germany, 1815–1871* (Princeton, 1958).

105. Koselleck, *Preussen*, 606 ff.; Mack Walker, *German Home Towns: Community, State and General Estate, 1648–1871* (Ithaca, N.Y., 1971), 332–336.

106. Werner Conze, "'Pöbel'," 120; Blasius, *Kriminalität*, 14.

107. Blasius, *Kriminalität*, 20.

108. Koselleck, *Preussen*, 620.

109. Koselleck, in *Preussen*, 620 ff., argues that the bureaucracy failed to deal with the social problem.

110. Conze, "'Pöbel'," 117.

111. Ibid., 112, 123; Frederick D. Marquardt, "A Working Class in Berlin in the 1840s?" in *Sozialgeschichte Heute*, 201.

112. Koselleck, *Preussen*, 637.

113. Hegel first suggests that the police provide work projects for the poor, but he then dismisses this proposal by telling us that that would only yield overproduction and hence exacerbate the problem of poverty (*Philosophy of Right*, par. 245). Hegel then suggests that another agency of civil society might help to mitigate the problem. A function of the Corporations would be to provide welfare for their poor members (ibid., par. 252). But this is at best an extremely limited answer to poverty; not only does Hegel expect too much of corporations, but they also do not include the dispossessed (ibid., par. 253), who would constitute the majority of the poor. As a solution to the problem of poverty, Hegel places his main hope in the possibility of colonization (ibid., par. 246), but this is impractical, as Hegel himself acknowledged in his essay on the English Reform Bill. (Hegel, "English Reform Bill," 309; see Avineri, *Modern State*, 154; Plant, *Hegel*, 112; Richard Teichgraeber, "Hegel on Property and Poverty," *Journal of the History of Ideas* 38 [1977], 47–64.)

Hegel's remarks on poverty in "The English Reform Bill" are also interesting because he identifies for Ireland the situation that was developing in Germany. In Ireland, Hegel wrote, "the moment of transition from feudal times to property has slipped by without giving the agricultural class a chance to own land." The result has been the emergence of a "surplus poor." (Hegel, "English Reform Bill," 308; I have modified the translation, which uses the more modern and sociologically misleading "farmer" instead of "agricultural class." The original German is "der ackerbauenden Klasse." See "Die Englishe Reform Bill," in Georg Lasson, ed., *Hegels Schriften zur Politik und Rechtsphilosophie* [Leipzig, 1913], 301.)

3. Biblical Criticism and the Search for Redemption

1. On the condition of skilled artisans in Prussia, see Frederick D. Marquardt, "Sozialer Aufstieg, sozialer Abstieg und die Entstehung der Berliner Arbeiterklasse, 1806–1848," *Geschichte und Gesellschaft* 1 (1975), 43–77.

2. E. Schläger, "Bruno Bauer und seine Werke," *Internationale Monatsschrift* 1 (1882), 378–379.

3. Schläger, "Bruno Bauer," 380.

4. Little is known of the fourth brother, Egino. See Ernst Barnikol, *Bruno Bauer: Studien und Materialien,* ed. Peter Revmer and Hans-Martin Sass (Assen, 1972), 6.

5. Edgar Bauer to Bruno Bauer, 11 February 1841, in Edgar and Bruno Bauer, *Briefwechsel zwischen Bruno Bauer und Edgar Bauer, 1839–1842* (Charlottenburg, 1844), 131.

6. Bruno Bauer, from his "Lebenslauf" of autumn 1838, included in his "Curriculum vitae" of 1839, quoted in Barnikol, *Bauer,* 17.

7. Quoted by Barnikol, *Bauer,* 8.

8. Bauer, from his "Lebenslauf," quoted in Barnikol, *Bauer,* 17.

9. Hegel's evaluation is reprinted in Barnikol, *Bauer,* 18–19 n. 42.

10. Cornehl, *Zukunft,* 127 ff.

11. D. F. Strauss, *The Life of Jesus Critically Examined,* trans. from the fourth German edition by George Eliot (Philadelphia, 1972, reprint of the 1892 publication), 90–91.

12. Ibid., 780–781.

13. See above, chapter 2, section 5.

14. Bigler, *Politics,* 76–155, and his "Social Status," 175–191; Toews, *Hegelianism,* 243–254.

15. Quoted in Bigler, *Politics,* 108.

16. Bauer's reviews of Strauss's works are "Das Leben Jesu," *Jahrbücher für wissenschaftliche Kritik* 2 (1835), 879 ff.; hereafter cited as *J.W.K.*; "Das Leben Jesu, Band 2," *J.W.K.* 1 (1836) 681 ff.; "Streitschriften zur Vertheidigung meiner Schrift über das Leben Jesu und zur Charakteristik der gegenwärtigen Theologie," *J.W.K.* 1 (1838), 817 ff. These are discussed below in section 4 of this chapter.

17. Bruno Bauer, *Die Religion des Alten Testaments in der geschichtlichen Entwickelung ihrer Principien* (Berlin, 1838), 2 vols.

18. See Bauer's programmatic preface in *Die Religion* 1:xxx, xcvii, and 2:vii; and his "Streitschriften," 837.

19. Bruno Bauer, *Herr Dr. Hengstenberg: Kritische Briefe über den Gegensatz des Gesetzes und das Evangelium* (Berlin, 1839).

20. I will assess the differences between these works below.

21. Bauer, *Die Religion* 1:xx–xxii.

22. Ibid., xxv.

23. Ibid., xxxii–xxxiii.

24. Ibid., xxxiv.

25. Ibid., xxxv–xxxvii.

26. Ibid., xxxviii.

27. Ibid., xxxix–xlv.

28. Ibid., xl–xlvi.

29. Ibid., xxx–xxxi, xlvi.

30. Ibid., xlvi, lxxvi ff.

31. Ibid., 76 ff. Bauer called the latter "understanding" (*Verstand*) in *Herr Dr. Hengstenberg*, 112.

32. Bauer, *Die Religion* 1:33–35.

33. Ibid., 77 ff.

34. Ibid., 114–115, 124 ff.

35. Ibid., 145.

36. Ibid., 262. Also see lv, lxvi–lxvii, 173, 326, 329; and *Herr Dr. Hengstenberg*, 47–48.

37. Bauer, *Herr Dr. Hengstenberg*, 29, 46, 51–52.

38. Ibid., 41–42, 49, 67, 80.

39. Ibid., 124; and Bauer, *Die Religion* 1:lv, 252–253.

40. Bauer, *Die Religion* 2:59 ff.

41. Ibid., 102, 126–127.

42. On the idea of the Messiah, see *Die Religion* 2:38 ff. and on the idea of the union of God and humanity see *Die Religion* 1:lvi.

43. Ibid., 2:451 ff.

44. See letters from Marheinecke to Altenstein, 16 June 1839, and Bauer to Altenstein, 19 July 1839, both reprinted in Barnikol, *Bauer*, 463–464.

45. Bauer, *Die Religion* 1:145, 200.

46. Bauer, *Herr Dr. Hengstenberg*, 42, 49, and especially 124.

47. Dieter Hertz-Eichenrode, "Der Junghegelianer Bruno Bauer im Vormärz," (Ph.D. dissertation, Free University of Berlin, 1959), 30–31.

48. Bauer addresses Marx in the familiar "du" form in letters; Marx and Engels, *Historisch-kritische Gesamtausgabe*, ed., D. Rjazanov (Frankfurt-Berlin, 1927–1932), Part I, vol. 1, section ii, references throughout. Hereafter cited as M.E.G.A.

49. Bruno Bauer to Edgar Bauer, 15 March 1840, *Briefwechsel*, 50.

50. Bigler, *Politics*, 57.

51. Ibid., 76.

52. Letter from Professor Nitzsch to Professor Rehfues, both of the Bonn theological faculty, 21 Sept. 1839, reprinted in Barnikol, *Bauer*, 466–467.

53. Edgar Bauer to Bruno Bauer, 29 Dec. 1839, *Briefwechsel*, 22, and Bruno Bauer to Edgar Bauer, 26 Dec. 1840, ibid., 110.

54. Bruno Bauer to Edgar Bauer, 21 Oct. 1839, ibid., 8.

55. Bauer lumped Strauss and the "supernaturalists" together in his *Kritik der evangelischen Geschichte der Synoptiker* 1 (Leipzig, 1841), v–vii, 69, 80, 123.

56. Bauer, *Kritik der evangelischen Geschichte des Johannes* (Bremen, 1840).

57. Bauer, *Johannes*, v.

58. Ibid., x–xiv, and Bauer, *Synoptiker* 1:v–viii for a defense of this procedure against Strauss's methods.

59. See, for example, Bauer, *Johannes*, ix–x, 60, 174, 178 ff.

60. Ibid., 1–2.

61. Ibid., 3–4.

62. Ibid., 402–404.

63. Ibid., 404–406.

64. Bauer, *Synoptiker* 1:xiv–xv, 338.

65. Ibid., 4.

66. Albert Schweitzer, *The Quest of the Historical Jesus*, trans. W. Montgomery (London, 1948, from the German edition of 1906), 41. For an interesting modern study that takes this "literary" interpretation of the Gospels as its point of departure, see Frank Kermode, *The Genesis of Secrecy* (Cambridge, Mass., 1979).

67. Bauer, *Synoptiker* 1:x–xii.

68. Ibid., 120, 338, and passim.

69. Ibid., 2:308. Bauer is not always consistent. He sometimes calls representation *Anschauung*, see *Synoptiker* 1:51, 158, and 2:xiv.

70. Ibid., 2:15, 108, 157.

71. Ibid., 1:xiv, and see Bauer, *Die Religion* 2:11.

72. Bauer, *Die Religion* 1:xxxviii–xxxix.

73. Bauer, *Synoptiker* 1:25–26; 2:156; 3:309, 312.

74. Bauer, *Die Religion* 1:xlvi.

75. Bauer, *Johannes*, 182–183, and see Bauer, *Synoptiker* 1:viii, xx; 3:312.

76. Bruno Bauer to Edgar Bauer, 4 Nov. 1839, *Briefwechsel*, 12.

77. Bruno Bauer to Edgar Bauer, 20 Jan. 1840, ibid., 32.

78. Bruno Bauer to Edgar Bauer, 29 Feb. 1840, ibid., 42.

79. Bruno Bauer to Edgar Bauer, 12 March 1840, ibid., 50. In a letter to Marx, 5 April 1840, Bauer expresses the same sentiment; *M.E.G.A.*, I/1/ii, 240.

80. Bruno Bauer to Edgar Bauer, 23 Jan. 1840, *Briefwechsel*, 118. Bruno

Bauer to Edgar Bauer, 11 July 1841, ibid., 152. Bruno Bauer to Edgar Bauer, mid-April 1842, ibid., 185.

81. Bruno Bauer to Edgar Bauer, 31 March 1841, ibid., 133.
82. Bauer, "Streitschriften," 827.
83. See Cornehl, *Zukunft*, 196.
84. Bauer, *Die Religion* 1:xx, xxv.
85. Bauer, *Johannes*, 181.
86. Bauer, *Die Religion* 1:1.
87. Ibid., lvi.
88. Bauer, *Synoptiker* 1:xiv.
89. Strauss, *Life of Jesus*, 780.
90. Bauer, *Die Religion* 1:xlii, lii–liv.
91. Ibid., xlvii.
92. Bauer, *Synoptiker* 3:57, 310.
93. Bauer, "Das Leben Jesu," 891–892; and see Bauer, *Die Religion* 2:viii.
94. Bruno Bauer to Edgar Bauer, 31 March 1841, *Briefwechsel*, 133.
95. Bauer, *Synoptiker* 1:xxi, 312.

4. Philosophy in a Perverted World

1. Hertz-Eichenrode, "Junghegelianer," 40.
2. Ibid.
3. See, for example, Bruno Bauer to Edgar Bauer, 29 Dec. 1839, *Briefwechsel*, 22.
4. Bruno Bauer to Edgar Bauer, 31 March 1840, ibid., 59.
5. Bruno Bauer to Karl Marx, 30 March 1840, *M.E.G.A.*, I/1/ii, 239.
6. Bruno Bauer to Karl Marx, 1 March 1840, ibid., 236.
7. Edgar Bauer to Bruno Bauer, 4 May 1840, *Briefwechsel*, 68–69.
8. Bruno Bauer to Edgar Bauer, 9 May 1840, ibid., 76–77; Bruno Bauer to Edgar Bauer, 2 June 1840, ibid., 80; and see Bauer to Marx, 5 April 1840, *M.E.G.A.*, I/1/ii, 240, and his earlier letter to Marx, 1 March 1840, in ibid., 237.
9. Bruno Bauer to Edgar Bauer, 21 June 1840, *Briefwechsel*, 88.
10. Barnikol, *Bauer*, 141–146.
11. Hertz-Eichenrode, "Junghegelianer," 75.
12. Letter from Bauer to Eichhorn, 9 Dec. 1840, quoted in Hertz-Eichenrode, "Junghegelianer," 75; and see Arnold Ruge's report of this incident in the *Hallische Jahrbücher*, no. 91, 16 April 1841, 364.
13. The *Landeskirche* was published in Leipzig in 1840. "Der christliche Staat" appeared in the *Hallische Jahrbücher*, nos. 135–140, 7 June 1841, 537 ff.
14. Bauer, *Landeskirche*, 1, and see 9, 18, 94 f., 104.

15. Ibid., 2–3.
16. Ibid., 16.
17. Bigler, *Politics*, 37–41, 165–167.
18. Bauer, *Landeskirche*, 36–43, 47–48, 64, 104.
19. Bigler, *Politics*, 49, 76–155.
20. Bauer, *Landeskirche*, 5–6.
21. Ibid.
22. Ibid., 18.
23. Bauer, "Der christliche Staat," 537, 546.
24. Ibid., 543.
25. Ibid., 552–553.
26. Ibid., 554.
27. See Gebhardt, *Politik*, 27–49; Cornehl, *Zukunft*, 93 ff.
28. Bauer, "Der christliche Staat," 558.
29. Bruno Bauer to Edgar Bauer, 6 May 1841, *Briefwechsel*, 136.
30. Hertz-Eichenrode, "Junghegelianer," 75.
31. Ibid., 76–77.
32. Ibid., 77; and Barnikol, *Bauer*, 151.
33. Bruno Bauer to Arnold Ruge, 24 Dec. 1841, *M.E.G.A.*, I / 1 / ii, 265; and see Gustav Mayer, "Die Anfänge des politischen Radikalismus im vormärzlichen Preussen," reprinted in his *Radikalismus, Sozialismus und bürgerliche Demokratie* (Frankfurt am Main, 1969), 55 ff.
34. Barnikol, *Bauer*, 154–156.
35. Bruno Bauer to Edgar Bauer, 9 Dec. 1841, *Briefwechsel*, 162–163.
36. Bleek to Bauer, 29 March 1842, reproduced in *Briefwechsel*, 186; and Rehfues to Bauer, 31 March 1842, ibid., 188.
37. Published in Zurich in 1842. Hereafter cited as *Die gute Sache*.
38. Bauer, *Die gute Sache*, 3.
39. Ibid., 208–209, 221.
40. Ibid., 42–43, 224.
41. Bauer to Marx, 31 March 1841, *M.E.G.A.*, I/1/ii, 250, and see ibid., 43.
42. Bauer, *Die gute Sache*, 224.
43. Ibid., 62.
44. Ibid., 14–17, 63–77, 193.
45. Bauer, "Bremisches Magazin für Wahrheit gegenüber dem modernen Pietismus," in Arnold Ruge, ed., *Anekdota zur neuesten deutschen Philosophie und Publicistik* 2 (Zurich, 1843), 130–132.
46. For the timing, see Bauer's letter to Ruge, 24 Dec. 1841, *M.E.G.A.*, I/1/ii, 265.
47. Bauer wrote in the same way the sequel to the *Posaune*, *Hegels Lehre von der Religion und Kunst von dem Standpuncte des Glaubens aus beurtheilt*

(Leipzig, 1842). *Hegels Lehre* was originally meant to be the second part of the *Posaune*, not a separate book. Bauer composed the *Posaune* alone, but the authorship of *Hegels Lehre* is controversial. Marx was supposed to contribute a section on Hegel's aesthetics for the originally conceived *Posaune*, that is, the section that came out as *Hegels Lehre* (see letters from Bauer to Ruge, 6 Dec. and 24 Dec. 1841, *M.E.G.A.*, I/1/ii, 264–265). Yet it is almost certain that Marx never finished his share and that Bauer's part went to press alone, appearing as *Hegels Lehre*. On this controversy see Zvi Rosen, *Bruno Bauer and Karl Marx* (The Hague, 1977), 130–131, and Hertz-Eichenrode, "Junghegelianer," 61–62.

48. Bauer, *Posaune*, 69.

49. Ibid., 60 ff.

50. Ibid., 69.

51. Ibid., 150.

52. Ibid., 80, 85.

53. Ibid., 82–83.

54. Ibid., 80.

55. John Toews ("The Innocence of the Self" [Ph.D. dissertation, Harvard University, 1973], 3:911–912) has argued that Bauer was deeply affected by the difficulties he had in being promoted at the University of Berlin, where the opposition of Hengstenberg and others in the theological faculty precluded such a possibility. How much these difficulties preyed on Bauer's loyalty to the state is left open to question, for there is no direct record of Bauer's feelings. If Bauer did harbor ill will, then it was likely dormant until the situation at Bonn aroused it. The state after all had not abandoned Bauer in 1840; it did get him to Bonn. Bauer's unambiguous alienation from the state did not appear until after the *Landeskirche* of 1840.

56. Bauer, *Hegels Lehre*, 49–55.

57. Bauer, "Theologische Schamlosigkeiten," *Deutsche Jahrbücher für Wissenschaft und Kunst*, nos. 117–120, 15 Nov. to 18 Nov. 1841, reprinted in Hans-Martin Sass, ed., *Feldzüge der reinen Kritik* (Frankfurt am Main, 1968), 45–48; *Die gute Sache*, 157, 168, 181; *Das endeckte Christenthum* (Zurich, 1843), reprinted in Ernst Barnikol, ed., *Das endeckte Christenthum im Vormärz: Bruno Bauers Kampf Gegen Religion und Christenthum und Erstausgabe seiner Kampfschrift* (Jena, 1927), 94–95, 109, 118, 129, 131, 141; *Hegels Lehre*, 124; "Leiden und Freuden der theologischen Bewusstseins," in Ruge, ed., *Anekdota* 2:89–113.

58. For Bauer's description of religion as "Verkehrung" see his "Schamlosigkeiten," 49; *Hegels Lehre*, 61–63; *Endeckte Christenthum*, 139 ff.; *Die gute Sache*, 34, 217; "Die Juden-Frage," in the *Deutsche Jahrbücher*, no. 274, 17 Nov. 1842, 113; and "The Capacity of Present Day Jews to Become Free," trans. M. P. Malloy in *The Philosophical Forum* 7 (1978), 146, originally appeared in *Einundzwanzig Bogen aus Schweiz* 1 (1843).

59. A full account of these events is Gustav Mayer, "Die Anfänge," 7–100; and see Fritz Schlawe, "Die junghegelsche Publizistik," *Die Welt als Geschichte* 20 (1960), 30–50.

60. The former was in operation during 1844 and 1845; the latter from Dec. 1843 to Oct. 1844. The *Norddeutsche Blätter* is hereafter cited as *N.D.B.* and the *Allgemeine Literatur-Zeitung* as *A.L.Z.* in the notes.

61. Marx to Ruge, 30 Nov. 1842, *M.E.G.A.*, I/1/ii, 285–286; and Ruge to Marx, 4 Dec. 1842, ibid., 287–289.

62. Marx to Ruge, 9 July 1842, ibid., 278–279.

63. Marx's main criticisms of Bauer and the Freien are found in his article "On the Jewish Question" (1843), and his books, *The Holy Family* (1845) and *The German Ideology* (written in 1845). For the full study behind the break, see Mayer, "Anfänge," 184. Interestingly, Marx was a closer friend of Bauer's than of Ruge's up to the break, for whereas Marx and Bauer addressed each other in the familiar "du" form, Marx and Ruge used the "Sie."

64. Marquardt, "A Working Class in Berlin in the 1840s?" 193; and see Marquardt, "Sozialer Aufstieg."

65. *A.L.Z.*

66. Carl Reichhardt, "Schriften über den Pauperismus," *A.L.Z.*, Heft 1 (Dec. 1843), 21.

67. Ibid., 19–20.

68. Edgar Bauer, "Proudhoun," *A.L.Z.*, Heft 5 (April 1844), 40.

69. Carl Jungnitz, "Biedermanns deutsche Monatsschrift," *A.L.Z.*, Heft 4 (March 1844), 3; and "Englische Tagesfragen," *A.L.Z.*, Heft 9 (Aug. 1844), 30 ff.

70. See *A.L.Z.*, Heft 6:10; Heft 7:7; Heft 11–12:54 ff.

71. G.v. Förster, "De la Republique de Dieu," *A.L.Z.*, Heft 9:16.

72. See *A.L.Z.*, Heft 2:38; Heft 6:1; Heft 10:17.

73. In *A.L.Z.*, Heft 10 (Sept. 1844), 42–48. Hereafter cited as "Gattung."

74. Bauer, "Gattung," 42.

75. Ibid., 43.

76. Ibid.

77. See Bauer's review of "Deutschlands Beruf in der Gegenwart und Zukunft von Theodor Romer," in *Rheinische Zeitung für Politik, Handel und Gewerbe* no. 158, 7 June 1842, Beiblatt. Also see Rosen, *Bruno Bauer*, 119 ff., and for a list of Bauer's articles in the *Rheinische Zeitung*, see Barnikol, *Bauer*, 246.

78. The articles are "Die Juden-Frage," and "The Capacity of Present Day Jews to Become Free," cited above in note 58. The articles were later collected and published as a book, *Die Judenfrage* (Braunschweig, 1843).

79. Bauer, "Capacity," 137.

80. Bauer, "Judenfrage," 1102, 1119.

81. Ibid., 1110; "Capacity," 138 f., 143.

82. Bauer, "Judenfrage," 1096.

83. Ibid.

84. Ibid., 1097 ff.

85. Marx's interpretation of the Jewish Question and how that interpretation fits into his evolution as a Young Hegelian are discussed below in chapter 8.

86. Bauer, "Gattung," 44–45; Bauer, "Characteristik Ludwig Feuerbachs," *Wigands Vierteljahresschrift* 3 (1845), 86–147; and "Ludwig Feuerbach," *N.B.D.*, Heft 4 (Oct. 1844), 1–13.

87. Bauer, *Völlständige Geschichte der Partheikämpfe in Deutschland, 1842–1846* 1 (Charlottenburg, 1847; reprinted 1964), 87–88, 162–163; 2:19–23. Hereafter cited as *Partheikämpfe*.

88. Ibid., 3:32 ff.

89. Published in three volumes in Charlottenburg in 1847, reprinted in 1964 by Scientia Verlag, Darmstadt.

90. Bauer, *Partheikämpfe* 2:5.

91. This is the subject of vol. 1 of *Partheikämpfe*.

92. Ibid. 2:79.

93. Ibid., 76–79.

94. Ibid., 80, 82.

95. Rosen, *Bruno Bauer*, 96 ff. explains the specific variations between Feuerbach's and Bauer's generally similar views of religious alienation.

96. Bauer, "Gattung," 43.

97. Ibid., 46.

98. Ibid.; Bauer, *Partheikämpfe* 3:37–42 on Weitling's utopia.

99. See above, chapter 4, section 3.

100. Bauer, "Ludwig Feuerbach," 5–6, 12; and "Charakteristik," 92, 104, 106, 138–139.

101. Bauer, "Charakteristik," 110, and see 95–96. Bauer displays the same antipathy to Hegel in "Hinrichs politische Vorlesungen," *A.L.Z.*, Heft 5 (April 1844), 23–24; and the Freien follow in train: see *A.L.Z.*, Heft 6:17; Heft 8:27; Heft 9:15; Hefte 11–12:37.

102. See especially the reply to "Correspondenz aus der Provinz," *A.L.Z.*, Heft 6 (May 1844), 31, 34. The editorial replies to these letters to the editor are anonymous, but the contents of the letters and the replies indicate that the author of this reply must be Bauer.

103. Bauer, "Was ist jetzt der Gegenstand der Kritik," *A.L.Z.*, Heft 8 (July 1844), 20–22, 25.

104. Horst Stuke, *Philosophie der Tat*, 140.

105. Bauer, "Charakteristik," 94.

106. Bauer, "Correspondenz aus der Provinz," 32; and see his "Charakteristik," 124 f., 138 f.; *Partheikämpfe* 2:67. Szeliga's article, "Die Kritik," *A.L.Z.*,

Hefte 11–12 (Oct. 1844), 25–46, is a celebration of the aristocratic detachment of cognitive freedom from the practical world. Indeed, Szeliga at one point explicitly scorns "praxis": ibid., 45.

107. The former was published in Berlin by the Gustav Hempel Verlag, 1849; reprinted in 1969 by Scientia Verlag, Darmstadt. Hereafter referred to as *D.B.R.* The latter was published in Berlin by the Gerhard Verlag in 1849. Hereafter referred to as *Frankfurter Parlaments.*

108. Bauer, *D.B.R.*, 155, 294.

109. Ibid., 174, 295.

110. Ibid., 54, 172, 238–239, and Bauer, *Frankfurter Parlaments*, "Vorwort," n.p., and 10, 20.

111. Bauer, *D.B.R.*, 295.

112. Bauer, *Russland und Germanenthum* (1853), excerpted and reprinted in Karl Löwith, ed., *Die Hegelsche Linke* (Stuttgart, 1962), 118–121. Bauer was among the first to anticipate a historical connection between Caesarean imperialism and mass democracy in the modern world, or, as historians call the phenomenon today, Bonapartism.

113. Ibid., 103.

114. Ibid., 99–100, 75–76.

5. The Unity of Idealism and Realism

1. Arnold Ruge, *Aus früherer Zeit*, 4 volumes (Berlin, 1862–1867). Hereafter cited as *Zeit*. The first two volumes, published in 1862, deal with Ruge's childhood, schooling, participation in the Burschenschaften, and resulting imprisonment by the Prussian state. A year later volume three appeared carrying his story from his imprisonment through his release to his discovery of Hegel. A fourth volume came out in 1867. In it Ruge describes the nature of Hegelian philosophy and his career as a Young Hegelian up to the end of 1842. He meant to complete his history with an account of the 1848 Revolution and his exile, but he never managed to resume writing.

2. Walter Neher, *Arnold Ruge als Politiker und politischer Schriftsteller* (Heidelberg, 1933), 1 n. 1. This is the only biography of Ruge. For other analyses of aspects of his life and thought, see Herbert Strauss, "Zur sozial- und ideengeschichtlichen Einordnung Arnold Ruges," in *Schweizer Beiträge zur allgemeinen Geschichte* 12 (1954), 162–173; and Hans Rosenberg, "Arnold Ruge und die 'Hallischen Jahrbücher,'" *Archiv für Kulturgeschichte* (1930); reprinted in his *Politische Denkströmungen im deutschen Vormärz* (Göttingen, 1972), 97–115; Beatrix Mesmer-Strupp, *Arnold Ruges Plan einer Alliance intellectuelle zwischen Deutschen und Franzosen* (Bern, 1963).

3. Ruge, *Zeit* 4:440–441.

4. Ibid., 482–483.
5. Ibid. 1:33.
6. Neher, *Arnold Ruge*, 1.
7. Ruge, *Zeit* 1:33.
8. Ibid., 77.
9. Ibid., 15 ff.
10. Ibid., 65–68.
11. Ibid., 33.
12. Ibid., 257.
13. Ibid., 41.
14. Ibid., 36–37.
15. Ibid., 56–57.
16. This is discussed below.
17. Ruge, *Zeit* 1:53 ff.
18. Ibid., 208.
19. Ibid., 209–210.
20. Ibid., 166, 200, 280 ff.
21. Ibid., 229.
22. Ibid., 338.
23. Ruge quoted in ibid., 367.
24. Ruge quoted in ibid., 368.
25. Ruge quoted in ibid.
26. Ibid., 371–373.
27. Ruge to his father, quoted in ibid., 373–374.
28. Ibid. 2:13.
29. Ibid., 11. For Ruge's earlier rationalism, see also ibid. 1:370.
30. Ibid. 2:12.
31. Ibid., 27.
32. Ibid., 22.
33. Hans Fraenkel, "Politische Gedanken und Strömungen in der Burschenschaft um 1821 bis 1824," in *Quellen und Darstellungen zur Geschichte der Burschenschaft und der deutschen Einheitsbewegung* (Heidelberg, 1966), 3:280–282; and Treitschke, *History* 3:232.
34. Ruge, *Zeit* 2:25–27.
35. Ibid., 60 ff., 163 ff.
36. Ibid., 40.
37. Ibid., 166 ff.
38. Ibid., 172.
39. Fraenkel, "Politische Gedanken," 246–251.
40. Ibid., 251–277.
41. Ibid., 285–288. The most active universities were those in Jena, Halle, Tübingen, and Wurzburg.

42. Ruge, *Zeit* 2:173–175.
43. Ibid., 176.
44. Ibid., 180.
45. Ibid., 181.
46. Ibid., 198–199.
47. Fraenkel, "Politische Gedanken," 292–297.
48. Ruge, *Zeit* 2:224–235.
49. Ibid., 242.
50. Ibid., 252, 340 ff.
51. Ibid., 360.
52. Ibid., 366, 373 ff.
53. Ibid., 384 ff.
54. Ibid. 3:21.
55. Ibid., 28.
56. Ruge to Karl von Kamptz, quoted in ibid., 32.
57. Ibid., 110.
58. Ibid., 117–121.
59. Ibid., 142–165.
60. Ibid., 249–250.
61. Neher, *Arnold Ruge*, 24.
62. Ruge, *Zeit* 3:174; and see 65 and 110.
63. Ibid., 279–280. Ruge's petition is reprinted in his *Briefwechsel und Tagebuchblätter aus den Jahren 1825–80*, ed., Paul Nerrlich (Berlin, 1886), 1:14–15. Also see Ruge's letters to Johannes Schulze, in ibid., 16–19. The appeal was eventually granted.
64. Ruge, *Zeit* 3:329.
65. Ibid., 335.
66. Ibid., 349–350.
67. Ibid., 350–358, and Ruge, *Briefwechsel* 1:18.
68. Ruge, *Zeit* 3:356–359.
69. Neher, *Arnold Ruge*, 29. Neither Ruge nor Neher specifies the exact amount of Louise's inheritance.
70. Ruge, *Zeit* 4:501 ff.
71. Whether Ruge was deceiving himself about continuing to hold his Burschenschaft ideals is open to question. One might suppose that he truly wanted to conform and justified doing so by pretending that his ideals were now unattainable. From this point of view, his cynicism was only an ideological posture. But, although the sources do not allow us to be certain, such an analysis does not seem to fit his situation. Even after he acknowledged the impossibility of achieving his ideals, he risked punishment by angrily defending them against the chief Prussian interrogator Karl von Kamptz.

72. Ruge to Gustav Bunsen, quoted in *Zeit* 3:377.

73. Ibid., 379.

74. Ibid., 380.

75. Ibid., 467–468, and Ruge, *Briefwechsel* 1:40.

76. Ruge, *Zeit* 3 :468. (Ruge does not specify the cause of his father's death.)

77. Ibid.

78. Ibid. 2:251; ibid. 3:97, 171, 223, 285.

79. Ibid. 3:285–288, 341.

80. One admirer is Karl Löwith, who has called this section "an excellent popular history" of Hegelian philosophy. Löwith, *From Hegel to Nietzsche*, 81.

81. See, for example, his treatment of Saint-Simonianism and August Comte in Mill, *Autobiography* (New York, 1957), 105–106.

82. Ruge, *Zeit* 4:4.

83. Ruge to Ludwig Bamberger, 19 May 1867, *Briefwechsel* 2:303.

84. I use the term idealism very loosely here. It includes a range of meanings, from the everyday sense of having political and ethical ideals to the systematic sense of a philosophy that asserts the causal primacy, sufficiency, and exclusiveness of ideas. I believe this loose usage is justified in Ruge's case, where the simpler sense of idealism passes into the philosophical sense. Following Hegel's theory, Ruge shows in his memoirs how simple idealism is contained in and elevated into philosophical idealism, which places and justifies our ideals in the all-encompassing movement of ideas.

85. Ruge, *Zeit* 1:5.

86. Louise Ruge to Arnold Ruge, quoted in ibid. 3:379.

87. Ibid. 4:9.

88. Ibid.

89. Ibid. 4:501 ff.

90. This article is reprinted in ibid. 4:446–464.

91. Ibid., 446.

92. Franz Schnabel, *Deutsche Geschichte im neunzehnten Jahrhundert* (2nd ed., Freiburg, 1951), 4:109–117.

93. Ibid., 128; Treitschke, *History* 4:238.

94. Treitschke, *History* 4:238.

95. Ibid., 240–241; Schnabel, *Deutsche Geschichte* 4:128–135.

96. Schnabel, *Deutsche Geschichte* 4:135–136; Treitschke, *History* 4:245–248.

97. Treitschke, *History* 4:250.

98. Ibid., 251.

99. Ibid., 253; Schnabel, *Deutsche Geschichte* 4:138 ff. And see Frank Eyck, "Liberalismus und Katholizismus in der Zeit des deutschen Vormärz," in Wolfgang Scheider, ed., *Liberalismus in der Gesellschaft des deutschen Vormärz* (Göttingen, 1982), 140–143.

100. Schnabel in *Deutsche Geschichte* 4:142 estimates that ultimately 300 different pamphlets appeared on this controversy, and this number does not include newspaper articles.

101. Ruge, review of "Die Triarier, H. Leo, Dr. P. Marheineke, Dr. K. Bruno von J. Görres," in the *Hallische Jahrbücher für deutsche Wissenschaft und Kunst,* no. 240 (6 October 1838), 1913–1940.

102. Other than the article mentioned above, these include Ruge's review of "Sendschreiben an J. Görres von H. Leo," in ibid., no. 147 (20 June 1838), 1169–1204; his "Die Denunciation der Hallischen Jahrbücher," in ibid., no. 179 (27 July 1838), 1425–1440; and "Leo und die Evangelische Kirchenzeitung gegen die Philosophie," in ibid., no. 236 (2 October 1838), 1881–1896.

103. Ruge, "Sendschreiben," 1180.

104. Ibid., 1181.

105. Ibid., 1181–1183.

106. Ibid., 1180, 1196.

107. Ibid., 1179.

108. Ibid., 1190.

109. Ibid., 1194–1196.

110. Ruge, "Denunciation," 1426–1427.

111. Ibid., 1432.

112. Ibid., 1437.

113. Ruge, "Sendschreiben," 1199. And see Hegel, *Philosophy of History,* 444.

114. Ruge, "Sendschreiben," 1169, 1183.

115. Ruge, "Denunciation," 1430.

6. **The Antagonism Between Politics and Philosophy**

1. Ruge to King Frederick William III, 10 June 1830, *Briefwechsel* 1:14–15.

2. Ruge to Johannes Schulze, 16 September 1831, ibid., 16, and Ruge to Schulze, 26 February 1832, ibid., 18.

3. Ruge to Altenstein, 4 September 1836, ibid., 43–44, and Ruge to Schulze, 4 September 1836, ibid., 45.

4. The promotion was given to the Berlin Hegelian Johannes Eduard Erdmann. On Ruge's promotion hopes, see Ruge to Altenstein, 18 May 1837, *Briefwechsel* 1:63–64. After this incident, Ruge began to shower abuse on Erdmann. See Ruge to Adolf Stahr, 10 August 1837, ibid., 65 and passim.

5. Ruge to Altenstein, 23 February 1838, ibid., 112.

6. Altenstein to Ruge, 29 May 1938, ibid., 130, and Schulze to Ruge, 29 June 1838, ibid., 134–135.

7. Ruge to Schulze, 6 July 1838, ibid., 136–137.

8. Ruge to Schulze, 31 October 1838, ibid., 150–151.

9. Ruge, *Zeit* 4:476 ff. And Ruge to Rosenkranz, 13 November 1838, *Brief-wechsel* 1:153.

10. Ruge to David Friedrich Strauss, 10 March 1839, ibid., 164–165, and Ruge, "Zwei Blätter von Dr. David Friedrich Strauss," in *Hallische Jahrbücher,* no. 124 (20 May 1839), 988 ff.

11. Ibid.

12. Ruge, "Der Pietismus und die Jesuiten," ibid., no. 31 (5 February 1839), 241 ff., and "Das Wesen und Treiben der Berliner Evangelischen Kirchen-zeitung," ibid., no. 175 (23 July 1839), 393 ff.

13. Ruge to Altenstein, 18 March 1839, *Briefwechsel* 1:168.

14. Ruge to Altenstein, 23 August 1839, ibid., 172–175, and Ruge, *Zeit* 4:487.

15. Ruge to Karl Rosenkranz, 2 October 1839, *Briefwechsel* 1:177. At this time, Ruge also wrote a series of articles criticizing Romanticism. Although ostensibly in compliance with Altenstein's order—they do not mention any living persons—they were nonetheless a transparent attack on the Pietists. Pietism, according to Ruge, was a symptom of the larger syndrome of Romanticism, which in turn was a perversion of Protestantism. See Ruge, "Der Protestantismus und die Romantik: Zur Verständigung über die Zeit und ihre Gegensätze," *Hallische Jahrbücher,* nos. 245 and 246 (12 and 14 October 1839), 196 ff.

16. Ruge to Rosenkranz, 17 November 1839, *Briefwechsel* 1:185.

17. Ibid., 186.

18. Württemberger (Arnold Ruge), "Karl Streckfuss und das Preussenthum," *Hallische Jahrbücher,* no. 262 (1 November 1839), 2092.

19. Ibid., 2902, 2097.

20. Ibid., 2089, 2101.

21. Ibid., 2100.

22. Ibid., 2092, 2100.

23. Ibid., 2102.

24. Ibid., 2089.

25. Ruge to Rosenkranz, 17 November 1839, *Briefwechsel* 1:185–186.

26. Ruge, "Streckfuss," 2107.

27. Ibid., 2103.

28. Ibid., 2107.

29. On the Prussian Young Hegelians' glorification of Frederick the Great, see in particular the work by the Berlin Young Hegelian Carl Friedrich Köppen, *Friedrich der Grosse und seine Widersacher* (Leipzig, 1840).

30. Ruge to Rosenkranz, 4 April 1840, *Briefwechsel* 1:201; and see Ruge to Arnold Stahr, 5 May 1840, ibid., 205.

31. His policy of condemnation and appeasement could produce murky and unconvincing rhetoric when its two opposing elements mixed. For example, in Ruge's article, "Europa im Jahre 1840," he argued that the Prussian state had abandoned its world-historical mission (*Hallische Jahrbücher,* no. 85 [8 April

1840], 681). But he then reassured the state that, possessing great reservoirs of spirit and freedom (ibid., 709), it could regain its historical significance; it needed only to readopt the ways of philosophy and Protestantism and reform its constitutions (ibid., 717 f., 721). Ruge further pointed out that liberal constitutional changes would not necessarily be contrary to Prussia's traditional political forms. The divine institution of hereditary monarchy, he wrote, would in fact be enhanced by the political participation of the people (ibid., 715). Yet Ruge never went beyond this vague suggestion to specify exactly how a divinely sanctioned monarch would merge with popular representation in a coherent constitution. Whenever Ruge sought to appease the old order, to get it to adopt voluntarily the new principles of philosophy, he avoided the hard question of where sovereignty and political power would actually lie.

32. See Mayer, "Anfänge," 23.

33. Ruge to Rosenkranz, 2 May 1840, *Briefwechsel* 1:204; Ruge to Rosenkranz, 14 May 1840, ibid., 206; Ruge, *Zeit* 4:523–524.

34. See above, chapter 4, section 4.

35. Ruge, "Die Hegelsche Rechtsphilosophie und die Politik unsrer Zeit," *Deutsche Jahrbücher,* nos. 109 and 111 (10 August and 12 August 1842), 763.

36. Ibid., 757, 759; and *Hallische Jahrbücher,* no. 152 (25 June 1840), 1211; *Deutsche Jahrbücher,* no. 1 (2 July 1841), 2.

37. Ruge, "Politik und Philosophie," *Hallische Jahrbücher,* no. 292 (5 December 1840), 2331, and see Ruge, "Der Protestantismus und die Romantik—Vierter Artikel," ibid., no. 53 (2 March 1840), 417.

38. This article is Ruge's "Rechtsphilosophie," cited above in note 35.

39. Ibid., 756 ff.

40. Ibid., 759–761.

41. Ibid., 760–761.

42. Ibid., 761; and see Ruge to Stahr, 23 February 1843, *Briefwechsel* 1:299.

43. Ruge, "Die Hegelsche Philosophie und der Philosoph in der Augsburger Allgemeine Zeitung," *Deutsche Jahrbücher,* no. 33 (9 August 1841), 138; also see his "Die Zeit und die Zeitschrift," *Deutsche Jahrbücher,* no. 1 (3 Jan. 1842), 3; and "Neue Wendung der deutschen Philosophie," in Ruge, ed., *Anekdota zur neuesten deutschen Philosophie und Publicistik* 2 (Zurich, 1843), 22. The two volumes of *Anekdota,* published in 1843, were made up of articles that were originally intended for publication in the *Deutsche Jahrbücher* but that had been disallowed by the Saxon censor.

44. Hegel, *Philosophy of Right,* par. 303.

45. Ruge, "Zur Kritik gegenwärtigen Staats- und Völkerrechts," *Hallische Jahrbücher,* no. 154 (27 June 1840), 1227–1229; hereafter cited as "Kritik."

46. Ibid., 1225.

47. Ibid., 1235.

48. Hegel, *Philosophy of Right,* pars. 317–319.

49. Ruge, "Die Presse und die Freiheit," in *Anekdota* 1:96 and passim.

50. Ibid., 95. Ruge's notion of the function of public opinion fits nicely with Habermas's analysis in *Öffentlichkeit*, 28 ff.

51. Ruge's ambivalence about the principles—his attempt to preserve them after denying them—conditioned his thinking in yet another important respect in the 1840s: it affected his reception of Feuerbach's writings. In 1841, Ludwig Feuerbach published the most elegant and far-reaching of Young Hegelian criticisms of Christianity, the *Essence of Christianity*, and soon afterwards, he extended his criticism of religion to a criticism of Hegelian philosophy. What Ruge liked about Feuerbach was his attmept to demystify religion and Hegelian philosophy, to return to humanity those attributes that had been given to suprahuman abstractions such as "God" or "spirit." Ruge, in other words, gladly embraced Feuerbach's humanism, and to show his conversion he began after 1841 to use the Feuerbachian expression "species"; yet he did not accept Feuerbach's understanding of that expression. The latter defined the human species in terms of its primary sensuous nature, but Ruge intentionally misunderstood Feuerbach and gave the expression a meaning more amenable to his own idealism. The essence of humanity for Feuerbach, Ruge wrote in an open letter of 1842, was not without physical characteristics, but remained above all "humanity in its understanding, as it is reason and spirit." Ruge thus agreed with Feuerbach's humanism, but rejected his materialism; see Ruge, "An die Schriftsteller der 'literarischen Zeitung' in Januar and Februar 1842," reprinted in his *Sämtliche Werke* (2nd edition; Mannheim, 1848), 9:86–92. (*Sämtliche Werke* is hereafter cited as *S.W.*). In the 1840s Ruge did not yet admit to his disagreement with Feuerbach's materialism. In his memoirs, however, he openly criticizes Feuerbach for his fall from idealism: Ruge, *Zeit* 4:600–602.

52. See Horst Stuke, *Philosophie der Tat*; Toews, Hegelianism, 359–360.

53. Ruge, "Europa im 1840," 673–675; and "Vorwort," *Deutsche Jahrbücher*, no. 1 (2 July 1841), 5.

54. Ruge, "Der protestantische Absolutismus und seine Entwicklung," ibid., no. 121 (19 November 1841), 481 ff. Hereafter cited as "Absolutismus."

55. Ruge, "Streckfuss," 2089.

56. Ruge, "Absolutismus," 486–494.

57. Ibid., 494.

58. Ibid., 495.

59. Ibid., 509.

60. Ibid.

61. Ibid.

62. Ibid., 513.

63. See Ruge, "Europa im 1840," 681.

64. Ruge, "Absolutismus," 513.

65. Ibid.

66. Ibid.

67. Ibid.

68. See for example Conze, "Spannungsfeld"; Koselleck, *Preussen*; and chapter 2, section 1, above.

69. Ruge, "Absolutismus," 517.

70. Ibid.

71. Ibid., 514.

72. Ibid., 495.

73. Ibid., 514.

74. Ibid.

75. Ibid., 519–521.

76. Ruge to Stahr, 8 September 1841, *Briefwechsel* 1:239–240. Ruge noted the altered equilibrium of Hegelian groups that emerged in late 1841. He distinguished between the "old doctrinaires" of orthodox Hegelianism, the Straussian party of politically apathetic religious moderates, and the atheists and political radicals grouped around Bauer, Marx, and himself. The Straussians, he said, made up the "Gironde" of the Hegelian movement, the radicals the "mountain-party."

77. W. Wachsmuth to Arnold Ruge, 15 December 1841, *S.W.* 9:35–36. This letter is part of Ruge's set of published documents, "Actenstücke zur Unterdrückung der deutschen Jahrbücher," first published in *Anekdota* 1 (1843) and then reprinted in his collected works. I have quoted from the latter.

78. Falkenstein from the Königlichen sächsischen Censur-collegium to Ruge, 12 February 1842, *S.W.* 9:37–38; and Wachsmuth to Ruge, 16 February 1842, ibid., 38–39.

79. Wachsmuth's position is exemplary of the paradoxical and at times untenable situation of many liberals in the German bureaucracies. As governments became increasingly conservative, these officials suffered from an intense conflict of loyalties. The result was sometimes bizzarely contradictory behavior. In one instance, Wachsmuth suggested to Ruge that the latter complain about the former's unfair censorship to the government: Wachsmuth to Ruge, 3 June 1842, ibid., 56. On the dilemmas of the liberal civil service in the 1830s and 1840s see Gillis, *The Prussian Bureaucracy in Crisis, 1840–1860*.

80. Ruge to the Saxon Minister of the Interior, 23 June 1842, *S.W.* 9:63.

81. Ruge, "Der christliche Staat," *Deutsche Jahrbücher*, no. 267 (9 November 1842), 1068.

82. Ibid., 1068–1069.

83. See above, note 31.

84. Ruge, "Vorwort," *Hallische Jahrbücher*, no. 1 (January 1841), 2–3, and "Kritik," 1225.

85. Ruge, "Vorwort. Eine Selbstkritik des Liberalismus," *Deutsche Jahrbücher*, no. 1 (2 January 1843), 1–12.

86. Ibid., 12.

87. Arnold Ruge to his brother Ludwig Ruge, 3 January 1843, *Briefwechsel* 1:295.

88. Ruge, *Zeit* 4:610–612.

89. Ibid., 614–621.

90. Ruge to Marx, March 1843, *S.W.* 9:116–120.

91. Ruge to Karl Moritz Fleischer, 1 April 1843, *Briefwechsel* 1:304–305.

92. Ruge, "Über die intellectuelle Allianz der Deutschen und Franzosen" (1843), *S.W.* 2:315 ff.; and "Plan der Deutsch-Französischen Jahrbücher" (1843-1844), *S.W.* 9:155–156.

93. Ruge, "Studien und Erinnerungen aus den Jahren 1843 bis 1845," *S.W.* 5:59.

94. Ibid., 64, 69, 77, 96, 117, 135.

95. Arnold Ruge to his wife Agnes Ruge, 17 August 1843, *Briefwechsel* 1:322; and Ruge, "Allianz," *S.W.* 2:307 ff.

96. Ruge, "Studien," 136.

97. Ibid.; Ruge to Feuerbach, 15 May 1844, *Briefwechsel* 1:347; Ruge to Karl Moritz Fleischer, 20 May 1844, ibid., 353; and Ruge, "Plan," 155–156.

98. Ruge, "Studien," 61.

99. Ruge to Fleischer, 20 May 1844, *Briefwechsel* 1:352; and see Mesmer-Strupp, *Arnold Ruges Plan*, 112 ff.

100. Ruge, "Studien," 147 f., 157.

101. Ibid., 160, 222, 300.

102. Ruge, "Die Presse und die Freiheit," 112.

103. Ruge had a correspondence with Marx in which socialism and communism were criticized. See below, chapter 8, section 3.

104. Ruge, "Studien," 103 ff.

105. See, for example, his encounter with Moses Hess, ibid., 36 ff.

106. Ruge to Ludwig Feuerbach, 15 May 1844, *Briefwechsel* 1:346; *S.W.* 9:375, 377; and see his "Der König von Preussen und die Sozialreform," *Vorwärts*, no. 60 (27 July 1844), 4.

107. Ruge, "Studien," 105.

108. Ibid., 87 and see 321, 340; and *S.W.* 9:374–376.

109. Ruge, "Studien," 344.

110. Ruge to Robert Prutz, 18 November 1842, *Briefwechsel* 1:286–287; and Ruge to Fleischer, 12 December 1842, ibid., 290–291.

111. Ruge to Feuerbach, 15 May 1844, ibid., 343 ff.; Ruge to his mother, 19 May 1844, ibid., 349–350; Ruge to Julius Fröbel, 4 June 1844, ibid., 357; and Ruge to Fleischer, 9 July 1844, ibid., 359.

112. Ruge, *S.W.* 5:397.

113. Ruge, "Studien," 396–406; Ruge to the Prussian Minister of the Interior Ernst von Bodelschwingh, 10 March 1846, *Briefwechsel* 1:414–415. On Ruge's relations to *Vorwärts*, see Mesmer-Strupp, *Arnold Ruges Plan*, 136 ff.

114. The essay is dated February 1845. It appears in volume six of Ruge's *S.W.*
115. See above, chapter 6, section 3, on Ruge's "Der christliche Staat."
116. Ruge, "Unsre letzten zehn Jahre," *S.W.* 6:12. Hereafter cited as "Jahre."
117. Ibid., 27.
118. Ibid., 11.
119. Ibid., 11, 29.
120. Ibid., 17.
121. Ibid., 16.
122. Ibid., 29–31.
123. Ibid., 62.
124. Ibid., 62–63.
125. Ibid., 77–80.
126. Ibid., 83–85.
127. Ibid., 91–95.
128. Ibid., 126.
129. Ibid., 123–127.
130. Ibid.
131. Ibid., 126–127.
132. Ibid., 127.
133. Ibid., 128, and see 133–134. Paterson completely misreads Ruge's views when he attributes to Ruge an uncritical admiration of Stirner (R. W. K. Paterson, *The Nihilistic Ego*, 108). Ruge was scarcely a follower of Stirner.
134. The only hint of an explanation for the magazine's failure is a suggestion that neither side was ready: "Neither a determined core of German writers nor a French tendency, which would have been suitable for the unification with the most recent German philosophy, has found itself" ("Jahre," 91). But he does not elaborate on this and somewhat incongruously says that the founding of a foreign press was still a "logical and historical necessity." Ibid., 94.
135. Arnold Ruge to Ludwig Ruge, 30 April 1846, *Briefwechsel* 1:417.
136. Ruge to Kuno Fischer, 23 June 1847, ibid., 438.
137. Ruge's speech of 24 July 1848 is reported in Franz Wigard, ed., *Steno-graphischer Bericht über die deutschen constituirenden Nationalversammlung zu Frankfurt am Main und Stuttgart* (Frankfurt am Main, 1850), 2:1099.
138. Ruge to Kuno Fischer, 20 March 1848, *Briefwechsel* 2 (1886), 10–11, and see Neher, *Arnold Ruge*, 163.
139. Ruge, *Briefwechsel* 2:42–43. These notes on 1848 and 1849 were written in the early 1870s. See editor's note in ibid., 22; and see Neher, *Arnold Ruge*, 170.
140. Neher, *Arnold Ruge*, 174 ff.; and on the radical left at Frankfurt, see Frank Eyck, *The Frankfurt Parliament, 1848–1849* (New York, 1968), 133–140.
141. Ibid., 188.
142. Ibid.
143. Ruge's speech is reported in Wigard, ed., *Bericht* 1:480.

144. For the voting results see ibid., 606, and Eyck, *The Frankfurt Parliament*, 196.

145. Ruge, *Die Gründung der Demokratie in Deutschland oder der Volksstaat und der sozial-demokratische Freistaat* (Leipzig, 1849), 25 and see Neher, *Arnold Ruge*, 182.

146. Eyck, *The Frankfurt Parliament*, 268–274.

147. Ruge's speech is reported in Wigard, ed., *Bericht* 2:1098–1100. Ruge had earlier attacked nationalism. See, for example, his "Der Patriotismus," in *S.W.* 6:237–242.

148. Wigard, ed., *Bericht* 2:1098–1100, and Eyck, *The Frankfurt Parliament*, 274–282.

149. Arnold Ruge to Agnes Ruge, 22 September 1848, *Briefwechsel* 2:18.

150. Neher, *Arnold Ruge*, 198.

151. Ibid., 199.

152. Ibid., 204–205.

153. Ruge to Julius Fröbel, 8 January 1849, *Briefwechsel* 2:55.

154. Arnold Ruge to Agnes Ruge, 6 May 1849, ibid., 80 and Arnold Ruge to Agnes Ruge, 7 May 1849, ibid., 83.

155. Arnold Ruge to Agnes Ruge, 13 June 1849, ibid., 105.

156. Ibid., 106.

7. The Serenity of Philosophy

1. Jerrold Siegel, *Marx's Fate: The Shape of a Life* (Princeton, 1978), 47.

2. David McLellan, *Karl Marx: His Life and Thought* (New York, 1973), 7–8; Saul Padover, *Karl Marx: An Intimate Biography* (New York, 1978), 33 ff.; Boris Nicolaievsky and Otto Maenchen-Helfen, *Karl Marx: Man and Fighter* (London, 1935), 10–11; Isaiah Berlin, *Karl Marx: His Life and Environment* (Oxford, 1978; first published in 1939), 49–54; Auguste Cornu, *Karl Marx et Friedrich Engels: leur vie et leur oeuvre* (Paris, 1955), 1:58–60. To reduce the monotony of repeating similar titles, biographies of Marx are hereafter cited by the name of the author alone.

3. McLellan, 9–10; Padover, 37–38 and 43–45; Nicolaievsky and Maenchen-Helfen, 13–14; Cornu, 1:61–62; Fritz Raddatz, *Karl Marx: A Political Biography* (London, 1970), 10–13.

4. McLellan, 28–30; Padover, 113–125; Nicolaievsky and Maenchen-Helfen, 31–51; Raddatz, 26–30; Werner Blumenberg, *Karl Marx: An Illustrated Biography* (London, 1972), 38–43; Edward Hallet Carr, *Karl Marx: A Study in Fanaticism* (London, 1934), 15–22; Franz Mehring, *Karl Marx: The Story of His Life* (New York, 1935; first published in German in 1918), 16 ff.; Maximillien Rubel, *Karl Marx: Essai de biographie intellectuelle* (Paris, 1957), 28–31.

5. This is described in all the biographies of Marx.

6. See below, notes 29–31, 34–36.

7. See Siegel's analysis of Marx's Gymnasium essays (Siegel, 46–48). Also see Raddatz, 12–13.

8. Nicolaievsky and Maenchen-Helfen, 10–11; Carr, 7; Cornu, 1:50–52; and especially Heinz Monz, *Karl Marx: Grundlagen der Entwicklung zu Leben und Werk* (Trier, 1973; expanded second edition of *Karl Marx und Trier*), 135, 110–114, 27. Those interpreters who have assumed that Heinrich Marx meant what he said have concluded that he was either a moderate loyalist (see Mehring, 30–33, and Blumenberg, 12) or a sycophant of the Prussian state (see Arnold Künzli, *Karl Marx: Eine Psychobiographie* [Vienna, 1966], 38–39). Raddatz (9) strikes a compromise between the speculative image and what is contained in the documents: he argues that the father vacillated between francophile liberalism and Prussian servility.

9. See Jeffrey Diefendorf, *Businessmen and Politics in the Rhineland, 1789–1834* (Princeton, 1980), 209, 262, 268–269, 326, 334 ff., and 355–356. Diefendorf shows that the discontent of Rhenish businessmen with the Prussian state was that of a "loyal opposition."

10. For example, biographers conventionally point out that the mature Marx mentioned that when he was a youth in Trier he had first heard of Saint-Simonian socialism from one of the city's notables: the Prussian civil servant and Marx's later father-in-law Ludwig von Westphalen. From this passing remark, biographers have implied that the young Marx became, in Trier, seriously interested in socialism (Nicolaievsky and Maenchen-Helfen, 27; Raddatz, 22; Blumenberg, 44; Cornu, 1:63; Hans Pradel, *Wie kam Karl Marx in Trier zum Sozialismus?* [Boppard am Rhein, 1965]). This conclusion is not only unwarranted, given its slight evidence, but it also ignores conflicting evidence: that von Westphalen was a loyal, if not reactionary, servant of the Prussian state (see Monz, 327), and that Marx was uninterested in socialism until 1842 when he explicitly *criticized* it. (See Karl Marx to Arnold Ruge, Sept. 1843, in Karl Marx and Friedrich Engels, *Collected Works* [New York, 1975], 1:143; hereafter cited as *C.W.* Also see Marx to Ruge, 30 November 1842, *C.W.* 1:394; and Marx, "Communism and the Augsburg *Allgemeine Zeitung*," *Rheinische Zeitung für Politik, Handel und Gewerbe*, no. 289 [16 October 1842], reprinted in *C.W.* 1:220–221.) Another example of the same tendency to jump to conclusions is that some interpreters mention that in the 1830s there was a notorious socialist in Trier—namely, Lothar Gall—then assume that Marx knew him or of him, and then imply that Marx was favorably impressed by him (Padover, 35–36; McLellan, 2; and Blumenberg, 44).

11. Mehring (11) describes Marx's work as "youthful poems" that "breathe a spirit of trivial romanticism," and concludes that "very seldom does any true note ring through." Berlin not only ignores the poetry, but asserts that Marx

always "detested romanticism" (Berlin, 7, 22). Very cursory descriptions are found in Carr, 11–12; Nicolaievsky and Maenchen-Helfen, 30; Raddatz, 20–21; Cornu, 1:74 ff., 96 f.

12. Berlin, Nicolaievsky and Maenchen-Helfen, and McLellan do not mention the conflicts. Cursory descriptions are found in Carr, 8; Mehring, 13–14; Cornu, 1:78–80; Raddatz, 18–19. Padover (82–110) and Blumenberg (22–36) provide lengthy descriptions but only superficial analyses. Their treatments are anecdotal. On how the psychobiographies deal with these matters, see below, note 14.

13. Arnold Künzli argues that the young Marx was motivated by Jewish self-hatred (see Künzli, 83 f. and passim). But Künzli employs very tenuous evidence. For example, the author conjectures that while a student in grade school and Gymnasium, Marx was a victim of the anti-Semitism of other students. This experience contributed to the rejection of his Jewish heritage and thus the formation of his self-hatred (68–70). The objection to this interpretation is that there is no direct, explicit evidence that Marx as a schoolboy experienced anti-Semitism. All that Künzli can appeal to—and even this is extremely conjectural—is that the young Marx seemed to have had few close school friends. The infirmity of many of Künzli's arguments is reflected in their form of presentation: they are frequently given as a series of rhetorical questions.

Jerrold Siegel's *Marx's Fate* is a much more cautious and illuminating psychobiography. The book's general theme is that Marx's life was characterized by what Hegel in an early essay had referred to as the "fate" of Christianity—namely, its irreconcilable opposition to the real world (Siegel, 27–31, and passim, and Hegel, "The Spirit of Christianity and Its Fate," in *Early Theological Writings*, trans. T. M. Knox [Philadelphia, 1971]). Siegel's use of Hegel's notion of fate is extremely insightful in his analysis of the mature Marx, but Siegel's search for "fate" in the young Marx sometimes leads him to make questionable conclusions about the young man's relation to society. For example, Siegel asserts that the earliest manifestation of Marx's fate was his youthful resentment against the Prussian state for forcing his father to convert to another religion; but, as mentioned above, there is no explicit evidence that either Marx or his father was bothered by the father's required conversion, nor did they leave any explicit testimony that is hostile to the Prussian state.

14. Siegel mentions but does not give psychological interpretations of Marx's conflicts with his father and with Jenny von Westphalen, or of Marx's Romanticism, or, most significant, of Marx's conversion to Hegelian theory. Künzli has a lengthy analysis of Marx's Romantic poetry, but does not deal with it in relation to Marx's contemporaneous personal conflicts. Rather Künzli speculates on how the poetry manifests Marx's tendency toward self-destruction, which in turn reflects his Jewish self-hatred (Künzli, 148–169).

15. See Karl Marx to Heinrich Marx, 10–11 November 1837, *C.W.* 1:11 ff.

16. Monz, 217. McLellan gives 1782 as the date of Heinrich's birth: McLellan, 3.

17. Monz, 215 ff.

18. Heinrich Marx to Karl Marx, 18 November 1835, in Karl Marx and Friedrich Engels, *C.W.* 1:647. And see McLellan, 7.

19. Whether or not this was a doctorate is uncertain. See Monz, 255–256.

20. Ibid.

21. Ibid., 221 ff.

22. Künzli speculates that Heinrich Marx was tormented by a feeling of being an outsider to all cultures (Künzli, 38–47). There is no evidence to support this speculation. The explicit testimony suggests that Heinrich Marx did not suffer from any psychological complications (see Berlin, 20). Several commentators have asserted that, being an Enlightenment rationalist, Marx's father was uninterested in religion and thus gave it up with an easy conscience (see Mehring, 2–4; Raddatz, 6; Cornu, 1:55).

23. Monz, 245.

24. Ibid., 24–25.

25. Ibid., 30–31.

26. Franz Schnabel, *Deutsche Geschichte im neunzehnten Jahrhundert* (Freiburg, 1951), 4:108; and Cornu, 1:50.

27. Monz, 112–114; and Schnabel, *Deutsche Geschichte* 4:109 ff.

28. Monz, 244–245.

29. Reported in the *Kölnische Zeitung*, no. 24 (23 January 1834), quoted in Monz, 134.

30. Heinrich Marx to Karl Marx, 2 March 1837, *C.W.* 1:672.

31. Heinrich Marx to Karl Marx, March–April 1838, in Marx and Engels, *Historisch-kritische Gesamtausgabe* (Berlin, 1929), I/1/ii, 232. Hereafter cited as *M.E.G.A.*

32. See Monz, 327. This ideology became increasingly untenable in the course of the *Vormärz* and ultimately collapsed in the 1840s. See John Gillis, *The Prussian Bureaucracy in Crisis.*

33. See above, chapter 2.

34. Heinrich Marx to Karl Marx, 18 November 1835, *C.W.* 1:646.

35. Heinrich Marx to Karl Marx, 2 March 1837, *C.W.* 1:672–673.

36. Heinrich Marx to Karl Marx, 16 September 1837, *C.W.* 1:682.

37. Quoted in Arthur Wilson, *Diderot* (New York, 1972), 255. And see Alan C. Kors, *D'Holbach's Coterie: An Enlightenment in Paris* (Princeton, 1976), 317.

38. Heinrich Marx to Karl Marx, 9 December 1837, *C.W.* 1:687.

39. Monz, 160 ff.

40. Karl Marx, "Reflections of a Young Man on the Choice of a Profession" (August 1835), in *C.W.* 1:3.

41. Ibid., 8–9.

42. Heinrich Marx to Karl Marx, 18 November 1835, *C.W.* 1:646.

43. Heinrich Marx to Karl Marx, 18–29 November 1835, *C.W.* 1:647, and postscript to the same letter from Henriette Marx to Karl Marx, *C.W.* 1:649. Heinrich Marx to Karl Marx, beginning of 1836, *C.W.* 1:651. Heinrich Marx to Karl Marx, 28 December 1836, *C.W.* 1:664. Heinrich Marx to Karl Marx, 2 March 1837, *C.W.* 1:673.

44. Certificate of Release from the University of Bonn, 22 August 1836, reprinted in *C.W.* 1:658.

45. McLellan, 17.

46. On this club, see Cornu, 1:70–71.

47. See Heinrich Marx to Karl Marx, 28 December 1836, *C.W.* 1:664–665. Jenny's father gave his consent in 1837, but some members of the family remained hostile to the engagement for years after that (see Monz, 348).

48. See, for example, Cornu, 1:100; McLellan, 24–25.

49. As indicated above in notes 11 and 14, most biographers have not treated Marx's Romanticism seriously. Two notable nonbiographical works that have considered this subject are Günther Hillman's *Marx und Hegel: Von der Spekulation zur Dialektik* (Frankfurt am Main, 1966), and Leonard P. Wessell, Jr., *Karl Marx, Romantic Irony, and the Proletariat: The Mythopoetic Origins of Marxism* (Baton Rouge, 1979). Hillman deals with some of the themes—namely, Romantic subjectivism and longing—that I analyze here, but he does not show how they interact to form an essential conflict in Marx's Romanticism (Hillman, 49–72). Wessel treats Marx's poetry in terms of Romantic irony (see especially 77–81). But after making some interesting points, he overextends his argument to assert that Marx's Romanticism predetermined the nature of his later historical materialism. The book also deteriorates into a conservative diatribe against Marx and socialism in general.

50. See the classic essay by Hajo Holborn, "German Idealism in the Light of Social History," *Germany and Europe* (Garden City, N.Y., 1970), 1–33.

51. This point is brilliantly made by Charles Taylor in the introductory chapter of his *Hegel*, 1–41.

52. Karl Marx, "Creation," in *C.W.* 1:534.

53. Karl Marx, "Feelings," in *C.W.* 1:525.

54. Karl Marx, "Song to the Stars," in *C.W.* 1:608–609; and see his "Human Pride," *C.W.* 1:586.

55. See Taylor, *Hegel*, 46.

56. Karl Marx, "Transformation," in *C.W.* 1:529–530; and see his "My World," *C.W.* 1:524.

57. Karl Marx, "Lucinda," in *C.W.* 1:565–569; and "The Pale Maiden," *C.W.* 1:612–615.

58. Karl Marx, "Siren Song," in *C.W.* 1:544–545.

59. Jenny von Westphalen to Karl Marx, 1839–1840, *C.W.* 1:696.

60. Ibid., 696–697.
61. Ibid., 696.
62. Ibid., 696–697.
63. Heinrich Marx to Karl Marx, 18 November 1835, *C.W.* 1:647–648.
64. See references in note 43.
65. Heinrich Marx to Karl Marx, 3 February 1837, *C.W.* 1:668; and Heinrich Marx to Karl Marx, 3 February 1837, *C.W.* 1:674.
66. Heinrich Marx to Karl Marx, 28 December 1836, *C.W.* 1:664; and Heinrich Marx to Karl Marx, 3 February 1837, *C.W.* 1:668.
67. Heinrich Marx to Karl Marx, 2 March 1837, *C.W.* 1:670.
68. Heinrich Marx, to Karl Marx, 12 August 1837, *C.W.* 1:674; this letter was written from Bad Ems where Heinrich had gone to rest. Also see Heinrich Marx to Karl Marx, 10 February 1838, *C.W.* 1:691, in which Heinrich says that he has been seriously ill for two months.
69. Heinrich Marx to Karl Marx, 12 August 1837, *C.W.* 1:675.
70. Also see Heinrich Marx to Karl Marx, 2 March 1837, *C.W.* 1:671. Here Heinrich senses the imminent collapse of his hopes for his son:

Only if your heart remains pure and beats in a purely human way, and no demonic spirit is capable of estranging your heart from finer feelings—only then would I find the happiness that for many years I have dreamed of finding through you; otherwise I would see the finest aims of my life in ruins.

71. Lionel Trilling, *Sincerity and Authenticity* (Cambridge, Mass., 1978; first published in 1971), 38–39.
72. See in particular Marx's four poems on medical students in *C.W.* 1:547–548. Marx uses the medical student as a representative of the Enlightenment and has him say such things as:

No spirit ever has existed.
Oxen have lived and never missed it.
The Soul is idle fantasy.
 In the stomach it certainly can't be found

73. Hegel, "The Introduction of Hegel's Philosophy of Fine Arts," trans. Bernard Bosanquet, reprinted in J. Glenn Grey, ed., *G. W. F. Hegel on Art, Religion and Philosophy* (New York, 1970), 99–100.
74. Karl Marx, *C.W.* 1:533.
75. Heinrich Marx to Karl Marx, 9 December 1837, *C.W.* 1:691.
76. Karl Marx to Heinrich Marx, 10–11 November 1837, *C.W.* 1:11.
77. Ibid.
78. Ibid.
79. Ibid.

80. Ibid.

81. Ibid., 17.

82. Marx's "Record Sheet" of courses taken at the University of Berlin, reprinted in *C.W.* 1:699.

83. Karl Marx to Heinrich Marx, 10–11 November 1837, *C.W.* 1:11–12.

84. Ibid.

85. Ibid., 17.

86. Ibid., 18.

87. Ibid.

88. Karl Marx, "On Hegel," *C.W.* 1:577.

89. Karl Marx to Heinrich Marx, 10–11 November 1837, *C.W.* 1:18.

90. Ibid.

91. Ibid.

92. Ibid., 12.

93. Ibid., 18.

94. Ibid., 10.

95. Ibid.

96. Ibid. I have modified the translation, which uses the word *mind* instead of *spirit*. The latter corresponds more closely to the German (*"Geist"*). For the original, see Karl Marx and Friedrich Engels, *Werke* (Berlin, 1967), *Ergänzungsband* 2:3.

97. Karl Marx to Heinrich Marx, 10–11 November 1837, *C.W.* 1:10.

98. Heinrich Marx to Karl Marx, 9 December 1837, *C.W.* 1:688.

99. Even if there was no reconciliation, Marx did not cease to revere his father. As Marx's daughter Jenny later recalled, Karl "never tired of talking about him and always carried an old daguerreotype photograph of him," a picture that when Marx died was placed on his coffin by Engels (Jenny Marx, quoted in McLellan, 33–34).

100. Jenny von Westphalen to Karl Marx, 1839–1840, *C.W.* 1:695 ff.

101. Karl Marx to Heinrich Marx, 10–11 November 1837, *C.W.* 1:19.

102. See, for example, McLellan, 36 ff.

103. Karl Marx, "Notebooks on Epicurean Philosophy," *C.W.* 1:435. Hereafter cited as "Notebooks."

104. Ibid.

105. Ibid., 435–436.

106. Ibid., 436 ff.

107. Ibid., 439.

108. See, for example, McLellan, 36; Manfred Friedrich, *Philosophie und Ökonomie beim jungen Marx*, (Berlin, 1960), 35–43; Heinrich Popitz, *Der entfremdte Mensch: Zeitkritik und Geschichtsphilosophie des jungen Marx* (Frankfurt am Main, 1967), 53–59.

109. Karl Marx, "Notebooks," 491.

110. McLellan translates the part of the first sentence which is rendered here as "so philosophy, expanded to be the whole world, turns against the world of appearance," into "so philosophy, which has so evolved as to impinge on the world, turns against the world that it finds" (McLellan, 35–36). The original German reads, "so wendet sich die Philosophie, die zur Welt sich erweitert hat, sich gegen die erscheinende Welt" (Marx and Engels, *M.E.G.A.*, I/1/i, 130).

111. Karl Marx, "Notebooks," 491.

112. Ibid.

113. Ibid.

114. Ibid.

115. Ibid.

116. Ibid., 492.

117. Ibid., 491. Marx's emphasis.

118. Karl Marx, "Difference Between the Democritean and Epicurean Philosophy of Nature," *C.W.* 1:38–40. Hereafter cited as "Difference."

119. Ibid., 41. Marx's emphasis.

120. Ibid., 45. Marx's emphasis.

121. Ibid., 49.

122. Ibid., 52, 64.

123. Siegel offers a different interpretation (Siegel, 71).

124. Karl Marx, "Difference," 69.

125. Ibid., 70. Marx's emphasis.

126. Ibid., 71.

127. Ibid., 72.

128. Ibid., 69, and see 72–73.

129. Ibid., 30.

130. See the correspondence between Bruno Bauer and Karl Marx in *M.E.G.A.*, I/1/ii, passim. The Berlin Young Hegelian Carl F. Köppen dedicated his superb polemic *Friedrich der Grosse und seine Widersacher* (Leipzig, 1840) to Marx.

131. Cornu, 1:178–179.

132. Jenny von Westphalen to Karl Marx, 10 August 1841, *C.W.* 1:707.

133. Cornu, 1:176; and McLellan, 40.

8. The Hegemony of Sensuousness

1. This chapter considers Marx's intellectual development after 1841 in terms of the crisis of Young Hegelian theory in Prussia. Consequently, I have not dealt with his ideas about political economy except as they relate to that crisis. Moreover, because his intellectual career is much better known than the careers of Ruge and Bauer, I have omitted some biographical detail and have ended my treatment in 1845, when, as I argue below, Marx produced a rigorous version of

historical materialism. By that time he was no longer a Young Hegelian but a "Marxist."

2. Karl Marx, "The Leading Article in No. 179 of the *Kölnische Zeitung*," *Rheinische Zeitung für Politik, Handel, und Gewerbe*, no. 191 Supplement (10 July 1842), reprinted in Karl Marx and Friedrich Engels, *C.W.* 1:201–202. The article is hereafter cited as "Kölnische Zeitung," and the *Rheinische Zeitung* as *R.Z.*

3. See McLellan, 42 ff.

4. Marx, "Comments on the latest Prussian Censorship Instruction," in Ruge, ed., *Anekdota zur neuesten deutschen Philosophie und Publicistik* (Zurich, 1843), volume 1, reprinted in *C.W.* 1:109–131. This article was written in the first months of 1842 and was originally destined for the *Deutsche Jahrbücher*, but was prevented from appearing there by censorship restrictions. Hereafter cited as "Comments."

5. Karl Marx, "Debates on the Freedom of the Press and Publication of the Proceedings of the Assembly of Estates," *R.Z.*, no. 125 Supplement (5 May 1842), reprinted in *C.W.* 1:172. Hereafter cited as "Debates."

6. In early 1842 Marx began to write regularly for the *R.Z.* In October 1842, he became the paper's editor.

7. Marx, "Kölnische Zeitung," 195.

8. Ibid.

9. Ibid., 195–196.

10. Ibid., 198.

11. Marx, "Debates," 165, and see "Kölnische Zeitung," 196–197.

12. Marx, "Comments," 117. Marx's emphasis.

13. Ibid., 118, 125.

14. Ibid., 121.

15. Ibid., 122. Marx's emphasis.

16. Marx, "Debates," 143–144, 148.

17. Marx, "Debates on the Law on Thefts of Wood," *R.Z.*, no. 298 Supplement (25 October 1842), reprinted in *C.W.* 1:225 and passim. On the social context of the wood theft issue see Blasius, *Kriminalität*, 29–48, 103–126.

18. Ibid., 235–236.

19. Ibid., 242.

20. Ibid., 241, 253, 257.

21. Ibid., 253. Marx's emphasis.

22. Marx, "The Supplement to Nos. 335 and 336 of the Augsburg *Allgemeine Zeitung* on the Commission of the Estates in Prussia," *R.Z.*, no. 345 (11 December 1842), reprinted in *C.W.* 1:292. And see Marx, *C.W.* 1:221, 349.

23. Marx, "Marginal Notes to the Accusations of the Ministerial Rescript," *C.W.* 1:361–362.

24. Marx to Arnold Ruge, May 1843, *C.W.* 3:141. Also see Marx to Ruge, March 1843, *C.W.* 3:133; and Marx to Ruge, 25 January 1843, *C.W.* 1:397.

25. Marx to Ruge, September 1843, *C.W.* 3:142.

26. Avineri gives credit only to Feuerbach: see Shlomo Avineri, *The Social and Political Thought of Karl Marx*, (Cambridge, 1968), 10–12. But Zvi Rosen has convincingly argued that Bauer was also a major influence: see Zvi Rosen, *Bruno Bauer and Karl Marx*.

27. Marx, "Contribution to the Critique of Hegel's Philosophy of Law" (spring and summer 1843), *C.W.* 3:14. Hereafter cited as "Contribution." Also see Avineri, *Social and Political Thought*, 16.

28. Marx, "Contribution," 17–18.

29. Ibid.

30. Ibid., 39. Marx's emphasis.

31. Ibid., 33.

32. Ibid., 35–36.

33. Ibid., 63. Marx's emphasis.

34. Ibid., 32, 72; and see Marx, "On the Jewish Question" (hereafter cited as "J. Q."), *Deutsch-Französische Jahrbücher* 1 (1843), reprinted in *C.W.* 3:165–166.

35. Marx, "Contribution," 79–80.

36. Ibid., 80, and Marx, "J. Q.," 166.

37. Marx, "Contribution," 77.

38. Ibid. Marx's emphasis. And see Marx, "J. Q.," 154.

39. Marx, "Contribution," 45, 72.

40. Ibid., 46. And see Koselleck, *Preussen*, 388–393.

41. Marx, "Contribution," 64, 122–123.

42. Marx, ibid., 46–48.

43. Marx, ibid., 85, 88–89.

44. Marx, "J. Q.," 153.

45. Ibid., 155. Marx's emphasis.

46. Ibid., 149.

47. Ibid., 169–170.

48. Ibid., 171–172.

49. Ibid., 170–173.

50. See, for example, Avineri, *Social and Political Thought*, 30–31, 121; and Richard Hunt, *The Political Ideas of Marx and Engels* (Pittsburgh, 1974), 75–76.

51. Marx, "Contribution," 102, 109.

52. Marx to Arnold Ruge, September 1843, *C.W.* 3:143. Also see Marx to Ruge, 30 November 1842, *C.W.* 1:394; and Marx, "Communism and the Augsburg *Allgemeine Zeitung*," *R.Z.*, no. 289 (16 October 1842), reprinted in *C.W.* 1:220–221.

53. See Marx, "J. Q.," 174.

54. Marx, "Contribution," 30–32, 121.

55. Marx to Ruge, September 1843, *C.W.* 3:142.

56. Ibid.

57. See, for example, Marx's "Summary of Frederick Engels' Article 'Outlines of a Critique of Political Economy' Published in the *Deutsch-Französische Jahrbücher*," reprinted in *C.W.* 3:375–376.

58. McLellan estimates that in 1844 there were as many as a hundred thousand German workers in Paris. McLellan, 86–87.

59. Marx to Ludwig Feuerbach, 11 August 1844, *C.W.* 3:355.

60. Marx, "Contribution to the Critique of Hegel's Philosophy of Law: Introduction," *C.W.* 3:175. Marx's emphasis. Hereafter cited as "Introduction."

61. Ibid. Marx's emphasis.

62. Ibid.

63. Ibid., 176. Marx's emphasis.

64. Ibid.

65. Ibid.

66. Ibid., 179. The persistence of the ancien regime in Germany beyond its time appears to Marx as a "comedy" as opposed to the "tragic" fall of the old order in France (ibid., 178). Anachronisms in general seem comic to Marx. The most notable example of this is the famous opening of *The Eighteenth Brumaire of Louis Bonaparte.* For an interesting discussion of the problem of anachronism in that work see Siegel, *Marx's Fate,* 200 ff.

67. Marx, "Introduction," 180. Marx's emphasis.

68. Ibid. Marx's emphasis.

69. Ibid. Marx's emphasis.

70. Ibid., 181.

71. Ibid., 183, and see Marx, "Critical Marginal Notes on the Article 'King of Prussia and Social Reform by a Prussian,'" *Vorwärts!,* nos. 63 and 64 (7 and 8 August 1844), reprinted in *C.W.* 3:205.

72. Marx, "Introduction," 184. Marx's emphasis.

73. Ibid., 184.

74. Marx is not consistent in his use of terms. He freely interchanges *class* and *estate.*

75. Marx, "Introduction," 185. Marx's emphasis.

76. Ibid., 183.

77. Ibid., 186. Marx's emphasis.

78. Interpreters have generally overlooked this oscillation in the development of the young Marx's social and political theory. This has resulted in some confused controversy over the first appearance of the idea of a class-dominated state. See John Maguire, *Marx's Theory of Politics* (Cambridge, 1978), 10–12, which takes issue with Hunt, *Political Ideas,* 126, 59 ff.

Some commentators have attempted to combine the views of the "Contribution" with those of the "Introduction." Habermas, for example, argues that European society developed from the separation of state and society to the bourgeois-dominated state. To show how a depoliticized social group—the bourgeoisie—came to take over the state, Habermas employs the notion of "Öffentlichkeit" or, loosely translated, the "public." Öffentlichkeit is, on Habermas's theory, the agent that restores to private individuals a public and political identity. Habermas, *Öffentlichkeit*, 40 ff., 74, 88 ff.

79. Marx discussed the Silesian weavers' revolt in his article, "Critical Marginal Notes on the Article 'King of Prussia and Social Reform by a Prussian.'" The article was a refutation of Ruge's analysis of the revolt. Against Ruge's call for political reform to precede social reform, Marx asserted the primacy of the social. Workers, Marx argued, should first follow their direct sensuous needs (204). In the same article, the contrast in Marx's mind between philosophy as deceptive appearance and proletarian sensuousness as honest representation comes out very clearly. Marx displayed his outrage at how an English economist had dared to praise the clarity of modern political economy by applying to it what Bacon had said about philosophy. Marx denounced this as mystification by comparing it to proletarian reality. He first quoted Bacon, then added a scornful commentary:

"The man who, with true and untiring wisdom, suspends his judgement, who goes forward step by step, surmounting one after the other the obstacles which, like mountains, hinder the course of study, will eventually reach the summit of science, where peace and pure air may be enjoyed, where nature presents itself to the eye in all its beauty, and from where it is possible to descend by a comfortably sloping path to the last details of practice." Good *pure air*—the pestilential atmosphere of English cellar dwellings! Great *beauty of nature*— the fantastic rags worn by the English poor, and the flabby shrunken flesh of the women, undermined by labour and poverty; children crawling about in the dirt; deformity resulting from excessive labour in the monotonous mechanical operations of the factories! The most delightful *last details of practice*: prostitution, murder, and the gallows (193, Marx's emphasis).

Also see Marx and Engels, "The Holy Family," (1845), *C.W.* 4:53.

80. Marx, "Introduction," 187.

81. See, for example, George Lichtheim, *Marxism: An Historical and Critical Study* (New York, 1961), 56. Lichtheim calls Marx a "Jacobin" who favored the idea of a revolutionary proletariat "led by an intellectual vanguard."

82. Marx, "Introduction," 183.

83. Ibid., 182.

84. By linking the proletarian revolution to Germany's extraordinary historical backwardness, Marx seemed to imply that the proletariat was reserved for unusual historical circumstances.

85. Marx, "Economic and Philosophic Manuscripts of 1844," *C.W.* 3:231.

86. Ibid., 330–331.

87. Ibid.; and see Marx and Engels, "Holy Family," 57–61.

88. Marx, "Manuscripts," 339–341.

89. Ibid.; and Marx and Engels, "Holy Family," 192.

90. Marx, "Manuscripts," 339.

91. Ibid., 342.

92. Ibid., 339, 341, 343; and see Maguire, *Marx's Paris Writings: An Analysis* (Dublin, 1972), 86–91; Bhiku Parekh, *Marx's Theory of Ideology* (London, 1982), 73–99.

93. Moses Hess had been enlisted to write for *The German Ideology* a chapter attacking Ruge. The chapter was written but then left out of the book's final version. See note 7, *C.W.* 5:586.

94. Marx and Engels, "Holy Family," 7, 85, 193, and see 83; and "German Ideology," 27, 162, 184.

95. Marx and Engels, "Holy Family," 82–83, authors' emphasis. And see 11, 30, 53; and "German Ideology," 99, 109.

96. Marx and Engels, "Holy Family," 192.

97. Ibid., 158 ff.

98. See the first and sixth theses of Marx's "Theses on Feuerbach," *C.W.* 5:3–4; Marx and Engels, "German Ideology," 39.

99. Marx and Engels, "German Ideology," 39.

100. Marx, sixth thesis of "Theses," 4; Marx and Engels, "German Ideology," 39–41, 58.

101. Marx, first thesis of "Theses," 3; Marx and Engels, "German Ideology," 39.

102. Marx, ninth thesis of "Theses," 5. Marx's emphasis.

103. Marx and Engels, "German Ideology," 39.

104. Ibid., 41.

105. Ibid., 60, 128 ff., 215, 237, 287.

106. Ibid., 192.

107. Ibid., 130, and see 122.

108. Ibid., 293; and see Paterson, *The Nihilistic Egoist*, 115.

109. See Marx and Engels, "German Ideology," 420.

110. Ibid., 23.

111. Ibid., 193.

112. Ibid., 194.

113. Ibid., 195.

114. Ibid., 195–196. In the case of liberal philosophers such as Kant, this hidden relation to Germany's bad reality was reflected in the abstractness of their philosophy. Since their fragmented economic condition disqualified them from exercising political power, they could only give form to their political aspirations by converting them into philosophical concepts. Where the French bourgeoisie

transformed liberal principles into the reality of the July Revolution, the German bourgeoisie transformed them into "abstract ideas, principles valid in and for themselves, pious wishes and phrases, Kantian self-determinations of the will and of human beings as they ought to be." Consequently Germany's liberal thinkers perpetuated their impotence: "they exhibited a highly peculiar narrow-minded-ness [i.e., their disdain for reality] and remained unsuccessful in all their endeavors." Ibid., 196.

115. Ibid., 229.

116. Ibid., 217–219, 370.

117. Ibid., 314.

118. Ibid., 411.

119. Marx and Engels, "Holy Family," 119. Authors' emphasis.

120. Marx, "Preface" to "A Contribution to the Critique of Political Economy," (1859) reprinted in Robert C. Tucker, ed., The Marx-Engels Reader (New York, 1978), 5.

121. Marx and Engels, "German Ideology," 236.

122. Marx, "Manuscripts," 279–280, Marx's emphasis, and see Philip J. Kain, "Marx's Theory of Ideas," History and Theory. Beiheft 20: Studies in Marxist Historical Theory (1981):359.

123. Marx, "Manuscripts," 297, Marx's emphasis; and see 296.

124. Marx and Engels, "German Ideology," 236.

125. Ibid., 31. Helmut Fleischer, in Marxism and History (New York, 1973; first published in German in 1969), also points out that, in the 1844 Manuscripts, Marx spoke of "'the task of history',," of being "'in the service of history',," thereby rendering history a "metasubject" (Fleischer, 17). But after writing the Manuscripts, Marx self-consciously renounced such language and its idealist implications: "History does nothing, it 'possesses no immense wealth,' it 'wages no battles.' It is man, real living man who does all that, who possesses and fights; 'history' is not, as it were, a person apart using man as a means to achieve its own aims; history is nothing but the activity of man pursuing his aims" (Marx and Engels, "Holy Family," 93, authors' emphasis; and see Fleischer, 13).

126. Marx and Engels, "German Ideology," 31 ff., 41 ff., and for a less complete formulation, 64 ff. These formulations are mixed together with criticisms of Feuerbach. This disorderly arrangement of the text appears to give testimony to the struggle that was going on in Marx's mind. He alternates between detailed criticism of Feuerbach and detailed exposition of the evolution of sensuous human activity. It seems as if Marx, enveloped in the criticism of abstract theory, suddenly recognized his preoccupation with abstraction, drew himself out of it, and then, for relief, pressed his attention to the concrete data of sensuous reality, before his preoccupation once more took hold. Moreover, to reassure himself of the existence and importance of the sensuous world, to remind himself of the basic principles of historical materialism, he went over those principles repeatedly, articulating them again and again.

127. Marx and Engels, "German Ideology," 31.

128. Ibid., 31 ff., 41 ff.

129. Fleischer, *Marxism and History,* 13.

130. Marx and Engels, "German Ideology," 37.

131. Kain, "Marx's Theory of Ideas," 365.

132. Marx and Engels, "German Ideology," 35: "Empirical observation must in each separate instance bring out empirically, and without any mystification and speculation, the connection of the social and political structure with production." And see 31, 236; and Philip J. Kain, "Marx's Theory of Ideas," 359, 365.

133. Marx, second thesis, "Theses," 3.

134. Marx and Engels, "Holy Family," 53, 58 ff., authors' emphasis; and "German Ideology," 30.

135. Marx and Engels, "German Ideology," 236, my emphasis.

136. Marx and Engels, "German Ideology," 44.

137. Ibid.

138. Ibid.

139. Ibid., 45. Authors' emphasis.

140. Ibid., 46.

141. Ibid., 46–47.

142. Ibid., 47–48.

143. Ibid., 47; see 48–58.

144. According to Fleischer, Marx later developed the "pragmatological" view of history in *The German Ideology* into a "nomological view," found mainly in *Capital.* In the latter view, Marx emphasized the inexorable, autonomous logic of economic processes and hence seemed to render humanity incapable of contingent practice (Fleischer, *Marxism and History,* 29 ff.). Walter Adamson makes the important observation that the nomological view of *Capital* is already found in the pragmatological view of *The German Ideology.* Adamson also contends that Marx had a fourth view of history, that of the *Grundrisse* of 1857. In this fourth view, according to Adamson, Marx reintroduced the methodological use of abstraction prior to empirical observation. Adamson also makes an intriguing attempt to arrange Marx's four conceptions of history according to the literary categories given in Hayden White's *Metahistory.* Walter Adamson, "Marx's Four Histories: An Approach to his Intellectual Development," *History and Theory. Beiheft 20: Studies in Marxist Historical Theory* (1981), 384–385, 387–401; and see Kain, "Marx's Theory of Ideas," 366 ff. Marx's rehabilitation of abstraction after 1848 is discussed by Siegel in *Marx's Fate,* 194 ff., 293 ff.; and by Walter Adamson in *Marx and the Disillusionment of Marxism* (Berkeley, 1985), 54 ff.

Conclusion: The End of Philosophy

1. Mannheim, *Ideology,* 74 ff.

2. See Parekh, *Marx's Theory of Ideology,* 190.

3. As noted in chapter 8, note 144, with the failure of the 1848 Revolutions, Marx rehabilitated the use of abstraction prior to empirical observation. It was now also used prior to political practice. It was to be an autonomous "science." Parekh nicely demonstrates how such a science would operate, but wrongly assumes that it was a theory that Marx held consistently throughout his life (Parekh, *Marx's Theory of Ideology*, 186–210). Adamson considers how Marx's new notion of a science of society is related to a new view of proletarian practice. Adamson, *Marx and the Disillusionment of Marxism*, 67–74.

4. See Adamson, *Marx and the Disillusionment of Marxism*, 40–74, and Parekh, *Marx's Theory of Ideology*, 10 ff. Parekh's characterization of the shift in Marx's theory of ideology differs somewhat from that outlined above. Parekh sees a transition from the notion of ideology as "idealism"—that is, the belief that ideas are independent from society—to the notion of ideology as justification. He generally does not consider how the notion of compensation figured into the young Marx's thinking about ideology. The notion of ideological compensation reappears in Marx's *The Eighteenth Brumaire of Louis Bonaparte*. There Marx argues that the French bourgeoisie's appeal to a tradition of revolution is meant to conceal its fears and weaknesses, and Bonaparte's rise to power is a compensation for the inchoate organization of class interests in mid-nineteenth-century France.

5. See Adamson, *Karl Marx and the Disillusionment of Marxism*, 54 ff.

6. See Geertz, "Ideology as a Cultural System," 207 ff.; Edward Shils, "The Concept and Function of Ideology," in *International Encyclopedia of the Social Sciences* 7 (1968), 67; Mannheim, *Ideology*, 58, 78, 266; Dierse, "Ideologie," 161; Raymond Geuss, *The Idea of a Critical Theory: Habermas and the Frankfurt School* (Cambridge, 1981), 22 ff.; Lichtheim, "Concept," 185 ff.

7. Dierse, "Ideologie," 158 ff.; Martin Seliger, *The Marxist Conception of Ideology* (Cambridge, 1977), 182 ff. Mannheim has cogently pointed out that even the neutral theory of ideology contains a hidden evaluative aspect, for like the pejorative theory, the neutral and positive variations do not accept the traditional notion of the self-contained sovereignty of ideas. Like its pejorative counterpart, these variations assess ideas according to the function that they serve vis-à-vis the external, material world. This functional relation renders ideas dependent on the external world; a system of beliefs can thus always be assessed according to its relation to the world. Even a neutral or sympathetic sociologist can regard a people's set of ideas as bad if it is ill-adapted to the real world. See Mannheim, *Ideology*, 88 ff.

8. Geertz, however, wrongly suggests that Marx had no conception of this aspect of ideology. Geertz, "Ideology as a Cultural System," 203.

9. John Thompson has recently made an attempt to enhance the critical theory of ideology by bringing to it contemporary language theory. John B. Thompson, *Studies in the Theory of Ideology* (Berkeley, 1984).

10. See Fritz Ringer, *The Decline of the German Mandarins: The German Academic Community, 1890–1933* (Cambridge, Mass., 1969).

11. Mannheim, *Ideology*, 6 ff., and the introduction by Louis Wirth, xxv.

12. Mannheim, *Ideology*, 155 ff.

13. Ibid., 50.

Bibliography

Journals and Newspapers

Allgemeine Literatur-Zeitung. 1843–1844.
Deutsche Jahrbücher für Wissenschaft und Kritik. 1841–1843.
Deutsch-Französische Jahrbücher. 1844.
Einzundzwanzig Bogen aus der Schweiz. 1843.
Hallische Jahrbücher für deutsche Wissenschaft und Kritik. 1838–1841.
Norddeutsche Blätter für Kritik, Literatur und Unterhaltung. 1844–1845.
Rheinische Zeitung für Politik, Handel und Gewerbe. 1842–1843.
Vorwärts! January 1844–December 1844.

Articles found in these journals and newspapers are not cited individually below.

Primary Sources

Batscha, Zwi, and Jörn Garber, eds. *Von der ständischen zur bürgerlichen Gesellschaft: Politisch-soziale Theorien in Deutschland der zweiten Hälfte des 18. Jahrhunderts.* Frankfurt am Main: Suhrkamp, 1981.

Bauer, Bruno. "Bremisches Magazin für Wahrheit gegenüber dem modernen Pietismus." In *Anekdota zur neuesten deutschen Philosophie und Publicistik*, volume 2, edited by Arnold Ruge. Zurich: Verlag des literarischen Comptoirs, 1843.

———. *Die bürgerliche Revolution in Deutschland.* Berlin: Gustav Hempel Verlag, 1849; reprint ed., Darmstadt: Scientia Verlag, 1969.

———. "The Capacity of Present Day Jews to Become Free." *The Philosophical Forum* 2 (1978): 135–150. Originally appeared in *Einundzwanzig Bogen aus der Schweiz* 1 (1843).

———. "Charakteristik Ludwig Feuerbachs." *Wigands Vierteljahresschrift* 3 (1845): 86–147.

————. *Das entdeckte Christenthum.* Zurich: Verlag des literarischen Comptoirs. Reprinted in *Das entdeckte Christenthum in Vormärz: Bruno Bauers Kampf gegen Religion und Christenthum und Erstausgabe seiner Kampfschrift,* edited by Ernst Barnikol. Jena: Eugen Diedrichs, 1927.

————. *Feldzüge der reinen Kritik.* Edited and with an introduction by Hans-Martin Sass. Frankfurt am Main: Suhrkamp, 1968.

————. *Geschichte der Politik, Kultur und Aufklärung des 18. Jahrhunderts.* 4 parts in 2 volumes. Charlottenburg: Egbert Bauer Verlag, 1843–1845; reprint ed., Darmstadt: Scientia Verlag, 1965.

————. *Die gute Sache der Freiheit und meine eigene Angelegenheit.* Zurich: Verlag des literarischen Comptoirs, 1842.

————. *Hegels Lehre von der Religion und Kunst von dem Standpuncte des Glaubens aus beurteilt.* Leipzig: Otto Wigand, 1842.

————. *Herr Dr. Hengstenberg: Kritische Briefe über den Gegensatz des Gesetzes und das Evangelium.* Berlin: Ferdinand Dümmler, 1839.

————. *Die Judenfrage.* Braunschweig: F. Otto, 1843.

————. *Kritik der evangelischen Geschichte des Johannes.* Bremen: Verlag von Carl Schunemann, 1840.

————. *Kritik der evangelischen Geschichte der Synoptiker.* 3 volumes. Leipzig: Otto Wigand, 1841–1842.

————. *Die Landeskirche Preussens und die Wissenschaft.* Leipzig: Otto Wigand Verlag, 1840.

————. "Das Leben Jesu." *Jahrbücher für wissenschaftliche Kritik* 2 (1835): 879–912.

————. "Das Leben Jesu, Band II." *Jahrbücher für wissenschaftliche Kritik* 1 (1836): 681–704.

————. *Die Posaune des jüngsten Gerichts über Hegel den Atheisten und den Antichristen.* Leipzig: Otto Wigand, 1841.

————. *Die Religion des Alten Testaments in der geschichtlichen Entwickelung ihrer Principien.* 2 volumes. Berlin: Ferdinand Dümmler, 1838.

————. "Russland und Germanenthum" (1853). Reprinted in Karl Löwith, ed., *Die Hegelsche Linke.* Stuttgart: Friedrich Frommann, 1962.

————. "Streitschriften zur Vertheidigung meiner Schrift über das Leben Jesu und zur Charakteristik der gegenwärtigen Theologie." *Jahrbücher für wissenschaftliche Kritik* 1 (1838): 817–838.

————. *Der Untergang des Frankfurter Parlaments.* Berlin: Gerhard Verlag, 1849.

————. *Vollständige Geschichte der Partheikämpfe in Deutschland, 1842–1846.* 3 volumes. Charlottenburg: Egbert Bauer Verlag, 1847; reprint ed., Darmstadt: Scientia Verlag, 1964.

Bauer, Bruno, and Edgar Bauer. *Briefwechsel zwischen Bruno Bauer und Edgar Bauer, 1839–1842.* Charlottenburg: Verlag von Egbert Bauer, 1844.

Engels, Friedrich. *Ludwig Feuerbach and the Outcome of Classical German Philosophy*. New York: International Publishers, 1974; first published 1888.

Erdmann, Johann Eduard. *A History of Philosophy*. 3 volumes. Translated by W. S. Hough. New York: Macmillan, 1890–1892.

Feuerbach, Lugwig. *The Essence of Christianity*. Translated by George Eliot. New York: Harper and Row, 1957.

———. *The Fiery Brook: Selected Writings of Ludwig Feuerbach*. Translated by Zawar Hanfi. Garden City, N.Y.: Anchor Books, 1972.

Hegel, G. W. F. *Berliner Schriften, 1818–1831*. Edited by J. Hoffmeister. Hamburg: Felix Meiner, 1956.

———. *Briefe von und an Hegel*. 4 volumes. Edited by J. Hoffmeister. Hamburg: Felix Meiner, 1952–1960.

———. *Dokumente zu Hegels Entwicklung*. Edited by J. Hoffmeister. Stuttgart: Friedrich Frommann, 1974.

———. *Early Theological Writings*. Translated by T. M. Knox. Philadelphia: University of Pennsylvania Press, 1971.

———. *G. W. F. Hegel on Art, Religion and Philosophy*. Translated by Bernard Bosanquet and edited by J. Glenn Grey. New York: Harper and Row, 1970.

———. *Hegel's Political Writings*. Edited and translated by Z. A. Pelczynski. Oxford: Oxford University Press, 1964.

———. *Hegels Schriften zur Politik und Rechtsphilosophie*. Edited by Georg Lasson. Volume 7 of *Sämtliche Werke*. Leipzig: Felix Meiner, 1913.

———. *Natural Law*. Translated by T. M. Knox. Philadelphia: University of Pennsylvania Press, 1975.

———. *The Phenomenology of Spirit*. Translated by A. V. Miller. New York: Oxford University Press, 1979.

———. *Philosophy of History*. Translated by J. Sibree. New York: Dover Books, 1956.

———. *The Philosophy of Mind*. Translated by William Wallace. Oxford: Oxford University Press, 1971.

———. *The Philosophy of Right*. Translated by T. M. Knox. New York: Oxford University Press, 1973.

———. *Sämtliche Werke*. Edited by Hermann Glockner. Jubiläumsausgabe in 20 volumes. Stuttgart: Friedrich Frommann, 1949.

———. *Vorlesungen über Rechtsphilosophie, 1818–1831*. 4 volumes. Edited by Karl-Heinz Ilting. Stuttgart: Friedrich Frommann. 1973–1974.

Heine, Heinrich. *Beiträge zur deutschen Ideologie*. Edited and with an introduction by Hans Mayer. Frankfurt am Main: Verlag Ullstein, 1971.

Köppen, Carl Friedrich. *Friedrich der Grosse und seine Widersacher*. Leipzig: Otto Wigand Verlag, 1840.

Laufner, Richard, and Karl-Ludwig König, eds. *Bruno Bauer, Karl Marx und Trier: Ein unbekannter Brief von Bruno Bauer an Karl Marx und radikale*

Vormärzliteratur in der Stadtbibliothek Trier. Trier: Karl-Marx-Haus, 1978.

Leo, Heinrich. *Die Hegelingen.* Second and enlarged edition. Halle: Eduard Anton, 1839.

Löwith, Karl, ed. *Die Hegelsche Linke.* Stuttgart: Friedrich Frommann, 1962.

Lübbe, Hermann, ed. *Die Hegelsche Rechte.* Stuttgart: Friedrich Frommann, 1962.

Marx, Karl, and Friedrich Engels. *Collected Works.* New York: International Publishers, 1975–.

———. *Historisch-kritische Gesamtausgabe.* Edited by D. Rjazanov. Frankfurt-Berlin: Marx-Engels Archiv, 1927–1935.

———. *Werke.* Ergänzungsband 2. Berlin: Dietz, 1967.

Michelet, Karl Ludwig. *Geschichte der letzten Systeme der Philosophie in Deutschland von Kant bis Hegel.* 2 volumes. Berlin: Duncker und Humblot, 1837–1838.

Ruge, Arnold. *An's Volk und an Politiker.* Berlin: Verlag der Stuhrischen Buch- und Kunsthandlung, 1869.

———. *Aus früherer Zeit.* 4 volumes. Berlin: Verlag von Franz Duncker, 1862–1867.

———. *Briefwechsel und Tagebücher aus den Jahren 1825–1880.* 2 volumes. Edited by Paul Nerrlich. Berlin: Weidmann, 1886.

———. *Geschichte unsrer Zeit von dem Freiheitskriegen bis zum Ausbruch des deutsch-französischen Krieges.* Leipzig : C. F. Winter, 1881.

———. *Die Gründung der Demokratie in Deutschland oder der Volksstaat und der sozial-demokratische Freistaat.* Leipzig: Verlagsbureau, 1849.

———. "Die letzte Vorstellung gegen Censurgerichtsbarkeit und Bücherverbote in Deutschland." *Die Akademie* 1 (1848): 261–276.

———. "Neue Wendung der deutschen Philosophie." In *Anekdota zur neuesten deutschen Philosophie und Publicistik,* volume 2, edited by Arnold Ruge, 3–62. Zurich: Verlag des literarischen Comptoirs, 1843.

———. *New Germany: Its Modern History, Literature, Philosophy, Religion and Art.* London: Holyoake, 1854.

———. *Die preussische Revolution seit dem seibten September und die Contrerevolution seit dem zehnten November.* Leipzig: Verlagsbureau, 1848.

———. "Die Religion unserer Zeit." *Die Akademie* 1 (1848): 1–92.

———. *Sämtliche Werke.* 10 volumes. Second edition. Mannheim: Verlag von J. P. Grohe, 1847–1848.

———. "Was wird daraus werden: Ein politischer Brief an die Deutschen." *Die Akademie* 1 (1848): 191–226.

———, ed. *Anekdota zur neuesten deutschen Philosophie und Publicistik.* Zurich: Verlag des literarischen Comptoirs, 1843.

Stepelevich, Lawrence S., ed. *The Young Hegelians: An Anthology.* Cambridge: Cambridge University Press, 1983.

Stirner, Max. *The Ego and his Own.* Translated by Steven T. Byington. New York: Dover Publications, 1973.

———. *Der Einzige und sein Eigentum.* Stuttgart: Philipp Reclamm, 1972.

———. *Kleinere Schriften.* Edited by John Henry Mackay. Second and enlarged edition. Treptow bei Berlin: Bernhard Zacks Verlag, 1914.

Strauss, D. F. *The Life of Jesus Critically Examined.* Translated from the fourth German edition by George Eliot. Philadelphia: Fortress Press Reprint, 1972, of the 1892 publication.

———. *Streitschriften zur Verteidigung meiner Schrift über das Leben Jesu und zur Charakteristik der gegenwärtigen Theologie.* 3 volumes in 1. Tübingen: C. F. Osiander, 1837.

Wigard, Franz, ed. *Stenographischer Bericht über die Verhandlungen der deutschen constituirenden Nationalversammlung zu Frankfurt am Main und Stuttgart.* Volumes 1 and 2. Frankfurt am Main: J. D. Sauerlander, 1848–1850.

Secondary Sources

Abrams, M. H. *Natural Supernaturalism: Tradition and Revolution in Romantic Literature.* New York: W. W. Norton, 1971.

Adamson, Walter. *Marx and the Disillusionment of Marxism.* Berkeley, Los Angeles, and London: University of California Press, 1985.

———. "Marx's Four Histories: An Approach to his Intellectual Development." *History and Theory. Beiheft 20: Studies in Marxist Historical Theory* (1981): 379–403.

Avineri, Shlomo. *Hegel's Theory of the Modern State.* Cambridge: Cambridge University Press, 1972.

———. *The Social and Political Thought of Karl Marx.* Cambridge: Cambridge University Press, 1968.

Ball, Terence, and James Farr, eds. *After Marx.* Cambridge: Cambridge University Press, 1984.

Barnikol, Ernst. *Bruno Bauer: Studien und Materialien.* Edited by Peter Revmer and Hans-Martin Sass. Assen: Van Gorcum, 1972.

———. *Das entdeckte Christenthum im Vormärz: Bruno Bauers Kampf gegen Religion und Christenthum und Erstausgabe seiner Kampfschrift.* Jena: E. Diedrichs, 1927.

Barth, Hans. *Wahrheit und Ideologie.* Zurich: Manesee Verlag, 1945.

Benz, Ernst. "Hegels Religionsphilosophie und die Linkshegelianer." *Zeitschrift für Religions- und Geistesgeschichte* 8 (1955): 247–270.

Berlin, Isaiah. *Karl Marx: His Life and Environment.* 4th edition. Oxford: Oxford University Press, 1978. First published in 1939.

Bigler, Robert M. *The Politics of German Protestantism: The Rise of the Protes-*

tant Church Elite in Prussia, 1815–1848. Berkeley, Los Angeles, and London: University of California Press, 1972.

———. "The Social Status and Political Role of the Protestant Clergy in Pre-March Prussia." In *Sozialgeschichte Heute,* edited by H.-U. Wehler, 175–191. Göttingen: Vandenhoeck und Ruprecht, 1974.

Blasius, Dirk. *Bürgerliche Gesellschaft und Kriminalität.* Göttingen: Vandenhoeck und Ruprecht, 1976.

Blumenberg, Werner. *Karl Marx: An Illustrated Biography.* Translated by Douglas Scott. London: New Left Review Books, 1972.

Bramsted, Ernest K. *Aristocracy and the Middle Classes in Germany: Social Types in German Literature, 1830–1900.* Revised edition. Chicago: University of Chicago Press, 1964.

Brazil, William. *The Young Hegelians.* New Haven: Yale University Press, 1970.

Bruford, Walter H. *Culture and Society in Classical Weimar.* Cambridge: Cambridge University Press, 1962.

———. *The German Tradition of Self-Cultivation: "Bildung" from Humboldt to Thomas Mann.* Cambridge: Cambridge University Press, 1975.

———. *Germany in the Eighteenth Century: The Social Background of the Literary Revival.* Cambridge: Cambridge University Press, 1935.

Brunner, Otto. *Land und Herrschaft.* Second and revised edition. Vienna: Rudolf M. Rohrer Verlag, 1959.

———. *Neue Wege der Verfassungs- und Sozialgeschichte.* Second and enlarged edition. Göttingen: Vandenhoeck und Ruprecht, 1968.

Busch, Alexander. *Die Geschichte der Privatdozenten: Eine soziologische Studie zur grossbetrieblichen Entwicklung der deutschen Universitäten.* Stuttgart: Ferdinand Enke, 1959.

Campbell, Blair. "Thought and Political Action in Athenian Tradition: The Emergence of the Alienated Intellectual." *History of Political Thought* 5 (1984): 17–35.

Carlebach, Julius. *Karl Marx and the Radical Critique of Judaism.* London: Routledge and Kegan Paul, 1978.

Carlsnares, Walter. *The Concept of Ideology and Political Analysis: A Critical Examination of its Usage by Marx, Lenin, and Mannheim.* Westport, Connecticut: Greenwood, 1981.

Carr, Edward H. *Karl Marx: A Study in Fanaticism.* London: J. M. Dent, 1934.

Cohen, Gerald. *Karl Marx's Theory of History: A Defense.* Princeton: Princeton University Press, 1978.

Colletti, Lucio. *Marxism and Hegel.* London: New Left Review Books, 1979.

Conze, Werner. "Vom 'Pöbel' zum Proletariat: Sozialgeschichtliche Voraussetzungen für den Sozialismus in Deutschland." In Hans-Ulrich Wehler, ed., *Moderne deutsche Sozialgeschichte.* Köln: Verlag Kiepenhauer und Witsch, 1966.

————, ed. *Staat und Gesellschaft im deutschen Vormärz, 1815–1848.* Stuttgart: E. Klett, 1962.

Cook, Daniel J. "Marx's Critique of Philosophical Language." *Philosophy and Phenomenological Research* 42 (1982): 530–554.

Cornehl, Peter. *Die Zukunft der Versöhnung: Eschatologie und Emanzipation in der Aufklärung, bei Hegel und in der Hegelschen Schule.* Göttingen: Vandenhoeck und Ruprecht, 1971.

Cornu, Auguste. *Karl Marx et Friedrich Engels: leur vie et leur oeuvre.* 4 volumes. Paris: Presses universitaires de France, 1955–1970.

————. *Moses Hess et la gauche Hégélienne.* Paris: Presses universitaires de France, 1937.

Cristi, F. R. "The *Hegelsche Mitte* and Hegel's Monarch." *Political Theory* 11 (1983): 601–622.

Diefendorf, Jeffry M. *Businessmen and Politics in the Rhineland, 1789–1834.* Princeton: Princeton University Press, 1980.

Dierse, Ulrich. "Ideologie." In *Geschichtliche Grundbegriffe: Historisches Lexikon zur politischsozialen Sprache in Deutschland* 3, edited by Otto Brunner, Werner Conze, and Reinhart Koselleck, 131–169. Stuttgart: Klett-Cotta, 1982.

Dilthey, Wilhelm. *Gesammelte Schriften.* Volume 4, *Die Jugendgeschichte Hegels.* Göttingen: Vandenhoeck und Ruprecht, 1959.

Draper, Hal. *Karl Marx's Theory of Revolution.* 2 volumes. New York: Monthly Review Press, 1977.

Eyck, Frank. *The Frankfurt Parliament, 1848–1849.* New York: St. Martin's Press, 1968.

————. "Liberalismus und Katholizismus in der Zeit des deutschen Vormärz." In *Liberalismus in der Gesellschaft des deutschen Vormarz,* edited by Wolfgang Scheider, 133–146. Göttingen: Vandenhoeck und Ruprecht, 1982.

Epstein, Klaus. *The Genesis of German Conservatism.* Princeton: Princeton University Press, 1966.

Fackenhem, Emil L. *The Religious Dimension in Hegel's Thought.* Bloomington, Indiana: Indiana University Press, 1967.

Findlay, J. N. *Hegel: A Re-examination.* New York: Oxford University Press, 1976.

Fleischer, Helmut. *Marxism and History.* Translated by Eric Mosbacher. New York: Harper and Row, 1973, from the German edition of 1969.

Fraenkel, Hans. "Politische Gedanken und Strömungen in der Burschenschaft um 1821 bis 1824." In *Quellen und Darstellungen zur Geschichte der Burschenschaft und der deutschen Einheitsbewegung.* Heidelberg: C. Winter, 1966.

Friedrich, Manfred. *Philosophie und Ökonomie beim jungen Marx.* Berlin: Duncker und Humblot, 1960.

Gadamer, Hans-Georg. *Hegel's Dialectic: Five Hermeneutical Studies.* Translated and with an introduction by P. Christopher Smith. New Haven: Yale University Press, 1976.

Gebhardt, Jürgen. *Politik und Eschatologie: Studien zur Geschichte der Hegelschen Schule in den Jahren 1830–1840.* Munich: C. H. Beck, 1963.

Geertz, Clifford. *Interpretation of Cultures.* New York: Basic Books, 1973.

Gerth, Hans. *Bürgerliche Intelligenz um 1800: Zur Soziologie des deutschen Frühliberalismus.* Göttingen: Vandenhoeck und Ruprecht, 1976; first published in 1935.

Geuss, Raymond. *The Idea of a Critical Theory.* Cambridge: Cambridge University Press, 1981.

Gilbert, Alan. *Marx's Politics: Communists and Citizens.* New Brunswick, N.J.: Rutgers University Press.

Gilbert, Felix. "From Political to Social History: Lorenz von Stein and the Revolution of 1848." In *History: Choice and Commitment,* 411–423. Cambridge, Mass.: Harvard University Press, 1977.

Gillis, John. *The Prussian Bureaucracy in Crisis, 1841–1860.* Stanford: Stanford University Press, 1971.

Godechot, Jacques. *The Counter-Revolution: Doctrine and Action, 1789–1804.* Princeton: Princeton University Press, 1981.

Gould, Carol C. *Marx's Social Ontology: Individual and Community in Marx's Theory of Social Reality.* Cambridge, Mass.: The M.I.T. Press, 1978.

Gouldner, Alvin. *The Two Marxisms.* New York: Seabury Press, 1980.

Groh, Dieter. "Junghegelianer und noch kein Ende." *Der Staat* 3 (1964): 346–357.

Habermas, Jürgen. *Strukturwandel der Öffentlichkeit.* Darmstadt: Hermann Luchterhand, 1982; first published 1962.

———. *Theory and Practice.* Translated by John Viertel. Boston: Beacon Press, 1974.

Hahn, Manfred. *Bürgerlicher Optimismus im Niedergang: Studien zu Lorenz von Stein und Hegel.* Munich: Wilhelm Fink, 1969.

Haller, Michael. *System und Gesellschaft: Krise und Kritik der politischen Philosophie Hegels.* Stuttgart: Klett-Cotta, 1981.

Hamerow, Theodore. *Restoration, Revolution, Reaction: Economics and Politics in Germany, 1815–1871.* Princeton: Princeton University Press, 1958.

Hardtwig, Wolfgang. "Krise der Universität (1750–1819) und die Sozialisation der jugendlichen deutschen Bildungsschicht." *Geschichte und Gesellschaft* 11 (1985): 157–176.

Harris, H. S. "Hegel and the French Revolution." *Clio* 7 (1977): 5–18.

———. *Hegel's Development: Night Thoughts (Jena 1801–1806).* Oxford: Oxford University Press, 1983.

———. *Hegel's Development Toward the Sunlight, 1770–1801.* Oxford: Oxford University Press, 1972.

Haym, Rudolf. *Hegel und seine Zeit: Vorlesungen über die Entstehung und Entwickelung, Wesen und Werth der Hegelschen Philosophie.* Berlin: Verlag von Rudolph Gaertner, 1857; reprinted Hildesheim: Georg Olms Verlagsbuchhandlung, 1962.

Heinrich, Dieter. *Hegel im Kontext.* Frankfurt am Main: Suhrkamp, 1971.

Hertz-Eichenrode, Dieter. "Der Junghegelianer Bruno Bauer im Vormärz." Ph.D. dissertation, Berlin, 1959.

———. "'Massenpsychologie' bei dem Junghegelianern." *International Review of Social History* 7 (1962): 231–259.

Hillmann, Günther. *Marx und Hegel: Von der Spekulation zur Dialektik.* Frankfurt am Main: Europäische Verlagsanstalt, 1966.

Hinchman, Lewis B. *Hegel's Critique of the Enlightenment.* Gainesville: University Presses of Florida, 1981.

Hintze, Otto. *The Historical Essays of Otto Hintze.* Oxford: Oxford University Press, 1975.

Hirsch, Helmut. "Karl Friedrich Köppen: Der intimste Berliner Freund Marxens." *International Review of Social History* 1 (1936): 311–370.

Hočevar, Rolf K. *Hegel und der preussiche Staat.* Munich: Wilhelm Goldmann Verlag, 1973.

———. *Stände und Representation beim jungen Hegel.* Munich: C. H. Beck Verlag, 1968.

Holborn, Hajo. "German Idealism in the Light of Social History." In *Germany and Europe,* 1–33. Garden City, N.Y.: Doubleday, 1970.

———. *A History of Modern Germany.* 3 volumes. New York: Knopf, 1959–1969.

Hölzle, Erwin. *Idee und Ideologie: Eine Zeitkritik aus universal-historischer Sicht.* Bern: A. Francke Verlag, 1969.

Hook, Sidney. *From Hegel to Marx.* Second edition. Ann Arbor: Michigan University Press, 1962.

Horstmann, Rolf P. "Ist Hegels Rechtsphilosophie das Produkt der politischen Anpassung eines Liberalen?" *Hegel-Studien* 9 (1974): 241–252.

———. "Über die Rolle der bürgerlichen Gesellschaft." *Hegel-Studien* 9 (1974): 209–240.

Huber, Ernst Rudolf. *Deutsche Verfassungsgeschichte seit 1789.* 4 volumes. Stuttgart: W. Kohlhammer Verlag, 1957–1969.

Hunt, Richard. *The Political Ideas of Marx and Engels.* Pittsburgh: Pittsburgh University Press, 1974.

Hyppolite, Jean. *Genesis and Structure of Hegel's Phenomenology of Spirit.* Evanston, Illinois: Northwestern University Press, 1974.

———. *Studies on Marx and Hegel.* Translated by John O'Neill. New York: Basic Books, 1969.

Jacobson, Max. "Zur Geschichte der Hegelschen Philosophie an der preussischen

Universitäten in der Zeit von 1838 bis 1860." *Deutsche Revue* 30 (1905): 118–123.

Jaeschke, Walter. *Die Religionsphilosophie Hegels*. Darmstadt: Wissenschaftliche Buchgesellschaft, 1983.

———. "Urmenschheit und Monarchie. Eine politische Christologie der Hegelschen Rechten." *Hegel-Studien* 14 (1979): 73–108.

Jarusch, Konrad. "The Sources of German Student Unrest, 1815–1848." In Lawrence Stone, ed., *The University in Society*, volume 2, 533–569. Princeton: Princeton University Press, 1974.

Johnson, Harry M. "Ideology and the Social System." In *International Encyclopedia of the Social Sciences*, volume 7 (1968): 76–85.

Kägi, Paul. *Genesis des historischen Materialismus*. Vienna: Europa Verlag, 1965.

Kain, Philip J. "Marx's Dialectical Method." *History and Theory* 19 (1980): 294–312.

———. "Marx's Theory of Ideas." *History and Theory. Beiheft 20: Studies in Marxist Historical Theory* (1981): 357–378.

———. *Schiller, Hegel, and Marx: State, Society, and the Aesthetic Ideal of Ancient Greece*. Kingston and Montreal: McGill-Queen's University Press, 1982.

Kaltenbrunner, Gerd-Klaus, ed. *Hegel und die Folgen*. Freiburg: Verlag Rombach, 1970.

Kaufman, Walter. *Hegel: A Re-Interpretation*. Garden City, N.Y.: Anchor Books, 1965.

Kelly, George A. *Hegel's Retreat from Eleusis: Studies in Political Thought*. Princeton: Princeton University Press, 1978.

———. *Idealism, Politics, and History: Sources of Hegelian Thought*. Cambridge: Cambridge University Press, 1969.

Kempski, Jurgen. "Über Bruno Bauer: Eine Studie zum Ausgang des Hegelianismus." *Archiv für Philosophie* 11 (1961–1962): 223–245.

Kennedy, Emmett. "'Ideology' from Destutt de Tracy to Marx." *Journal of the History of Ideas* 40 (1979): 353–368.

Keohane, Nannerl. *Philosophy and the State in France: The Renaissance to the Enlightenment*. Princeton: Princeton University Press, 1980.

Kermode, Frank. *The Genesis of Secrecy*. Cambridge, Mass.: Harvard University Press, 1979.

Koch, Lothar, *Humanistischer Atheismus und gesellschaftliches Engagement: Bruno Bauers "Kritische Kritik."* Stuttgart: Verlag von Kohlhammer, 1971.

Koigen, David. *Zur Vorgeschichte des modernen philosophischen Sozialismus in Deutschland: Zur Geschichte der Philosophie und Sozialphilosophie des Junghegelianismus*. Bern: Druck von C. Sturzenegger, 1901.

Kojève, Alexander. *Introduction to the Reading to Hegel*. New York: Basic Books, 1969.

Kolakowski, Leszek. *Main Currents of Marxism: Its Origin, Growth and Dissolution.* 3 volumes. Oxford: Oxford University Press, 1981.

Kondylis, Ponajotis. *Die Entstehung der Dialektik: Eine Analyse der geistigen Entwicklung von Hölderlin, Schelling und Hegel bis 1802.* Stuttgart: Klett-Cotta, 1979.

Kors, Alan Charles. *D'Holbach's Coterie: An Enlightenment in Paris.* Princeton: Princeton University Press, 1976.

Koselleck, Reinhart. *Preussen zwischen Reform und Revolution.* Second edition. Stuttgart: E. Klett, 1975.

Köster, Udo. *Literarischer Radikalismus: Zeitbewusstsein und Geschichtsphilosophie in der Entwicklung vom jungen Deutschland zur Hegelschen Linke.* Frankfurt am Main: Athenaum Verlag, 1972.

Kramer, Lloyd S. "Exile and European Thought: Heine, Marx, and Mickiewicz in Paris." *Historical Reflections/Reflexions historiques* 11 (1984): 45–70.

Krieger, Leonard. *The German Idea of Freedom.* Chicago: University of Chicago Press, 1972; reprint of 1957 edition.

Künzli, Arnold. *Karl Marx: Eine Psychobiographie.* Vienna: Europa Verlag, 1966.

Larrain, Jorge. *The Concept of Ideology.* London: Hutchinson, 1979.

Lauer, Quentin. *Hegel's Concept of God.* Albany: State University of New York Press, 1982.

Lenz, Max. *Geschichte der königlichen Friedrich-Wilhelms-Universität zu Berlin,* volumes 1 and 2. Halle: Verlag der Buchhandlung des Waisenhaus, 1910.

Lichtheim, George. "The Concept of Ideology." *History and Theory* 4 (1965): 164–195.

———. *Marxism: An Historical and Critical Study.* New York: Praeger, 1961.

Lieblich, André. *Between Ideology and Utopia: The Politics and Philosophy of August Cieszkowski.* Dordrecht: D. Riedel, 1979.

Livergood, Norman D. *Activity in Marx's Philosophy.* The Hague: Martinus Nijhoff, 1967.

Lobkowicz, Nicholas. *Theory and Practice: History of a Concept from Aristotle to Marx.* Notre Dame, Indiana: University of Notre Dame Press, 1967.

Löwith, Karl. *From Hegel to Nietzsche: The Revolution in Nineteenth-Century Thought.* Translated by David E. Green. Garden City, N.Y.: Anchor Books, 1967; first published in German in 1941.

Lübbe, Hermann. *Politische Philosophie in Deutschland.* Basel und Stuttgart: B. Schwabe, 1963.

Lübbe-Wolff, Gertrude. "Hegels Staatsrecht als Stellungnahme in ersten preussischen Verfassungskampf." *Zeitschrift für philosophische Forschung* 35 (1981): 467–501.

Lutz, Rolland Ray, Jr. "The 'New Left' of Restoration Germany." *Journal of the History of Ideas* 31 (1970): 235–252.

Mackay, John Henry. *Max Stirner: Sein Leben und sein Werk.* Third edition.

Berlin: Selbstverlag des Verfassers, 1914.

Maguire, John. *Marx's Paris Writings: An Analysis.* Dublin: Gill and Macmillan, 1972.

———. *Marx's Theory of Politics.* Cambridge: Cambridge University Press, 1978.

Mannheim, Karl. *From Karl Mannheim.* Edited by Kurt H. Wolff. New York: Oxford University Press, 1971.

———. *Ideology and Utopia.* New York: Harcourt, Brace, and Jovanovich, n.d.; first published in English in 1936.

Marcus, Steven. *Engels, Manchester and the Working Class.* New York: Vintage Books, 1975.

Marcuse, Herbert. *Reason and Revolution.* Boston: Beacon, 1969.

Marquardt, Frederick. "Pauperism in Germany During the *Vormärz.*" *Central European History* 2 (1969): 76–88.

———. "Sozialer Aufstieg, sozialer Abstieg und die Entstehung der Berliner Arbeiterklasse, 1806–1808." *Geschichte und Gesellschaft* 1 (1975): 43–77.

———. "A Working Class in Berlin in the 1840s?" In *Sozialgeschichte Heute,* edited by Hans-Ulrich Wehler. Göttingen: Vandenhoeck und Ruprecht, 1974.

Massey, Marilyn Chapin. *Christ Unmasked: The Meaning of the "Life of Jesus" in German Politics.* Chapel Hill: The University of North Carolina Press, 1983.

Massey, James A. "The Hegelians, the Pietists and the Nature of Religion." *Journal of Religion* 58 (1978): 108–129.

Mayer, Gustav. "Die Anfänge des politischen Radikalismus im vormärzlichen Preussen." Reprinted in his *Radikalismus, Sozialismus und bürgerliche Demokratie.* Frankfurt am Main: Suhrkamp, 1969.

———. "Die Junghegelianer und der preussische Staat." *Historische Zeitschrift* 121 (1920): 413–440.

———. *Friedrich Engels: Eine Biographie.* 2 volumes. Frankfurt am Main: Verlag Ullstein, 1975.

McClelland, Charles E. *State, Society, and University in Germany, 1700–1914.* Cambridge: Cambridge University Press, 1980.

McLellan, David. *Karl Marx.* New York: Harper and Row, 1973.

———. *The Young Hegelians and Karl Marx.* London: Macmillan, 1969.

Mehlhausen, Joachim. "Dialektik, Selbstbewusstsein, und Offenbarung." Ph.D. dissertation, University of Bonn, 1965.

———. "Die religionsphilosophische Begründung der spekulativen Theologie Bruno Bauers." *Zeitschrift für Kirchengeschichte* 78 (1967): 102–129.

Mehring, Franz. *Karl Marx: The Story of his Life.* Translated by Edward Fitzgerald. New York: Covici and Friede Publishers, 1935; first published in German in 1918.

Meinecke, Friedrich. *The Age of German Liberation, 1795–1815.* Translated by Peter Paret. Berkeley, Los Angeles, and London: University of California Press, 1977.

Meist, Kurt Reiner. "Altenstein und Gans. Eine frühe politische Option für Hegels Rechtsphilosophie." *Hegel-Studien* 14 (1977): 39–72.

Merriman, John M., ed. *Consciousness and Class Experience in Nineteenth-Century Europe.* London: Holmes and Meier, 1979.

Mesmer-Strupp, Beatrix. *Arnold Ruges Plan einer Alliance intellectuelle zwischen Deutschen und Franzosen.* Bern: Verlag Herbert Lang, 1963.

Mészáros, István. *Marx's Theory of Alienation.* London: The Merlin Press, 1970.

Mill, John Stuart. *Autobiography.* New York: Bobbs-Merrill; first published in 1870.

Monz, Heinz. *Karl Marx: Grundlagen der Entwicklung zu Leben und Werk.* Trier: NCC-Verlag Neu, 1973; revised edition of *Karl Marx und Trier,* 1964.

Moog, Willy. *Hegel und die Hegelsche Schule.* Munich: E. Reinhardt, 1930.

Näf, Werner. "Frühformen des 'modernen Staates' im Spätmittelalter." *Historische Zeitschrift* 171 (1951): 225–243.

Nauen, Franz Gabriel. *Revolution, Idealism, and Human Freedom: Schelling, Hölderlin and Hegel and the Crisis of Early German Idealism.* The Hague: Martinus Nijhoff, 1971.

Neher, Walter. *Arnold Ruge als Politiker und politischer Schriftsteller.* Heidelberg: C. Winter, 1933.

Nicolaievsky, Boris, and Otto Maenchen-Helfen. *Karl Marx: Man and Fighter.* Translated by Gwenda David and Eric Mosbacher. London: Methuen and Co., n.d.; first published in 1936.

O'Boyle, Leonore. "Klassische Bildung und Soziale Struktur in Deutschland zwischen 1800 und 1848." *Historische Zeitschrift* 207 (1968): 584–608.

Oertel, Horst. "Zur Genesis des Ideologiebegriffs." *Deutsche Zeitschrift für Philosophie* 18 (1970): 206–211.

Ollmann, Bertell. *Alienation: Marx's Critique of Man in Capitalist Society.* Cambridge: Cambridge University Press, 1971.

O'Malley, J. J., et al., eds. *The Legacy of Hegel.* The Hague: Martinus Nijhoff, 1973.

Ottmann, Henning. "Hegels Rechtsphilosophie und das Problem der Akkommodation." *Zeitschrift für philosophische Forschung* 33 (1979): 227–243.

———. *Individuum und Gesellschaft bei Hegel,* volume 1. Berlin: Walter de Gruyter, 1977.

Padover, Saul K. *Karl Marx: An Intimate Biography.* New York: McGraw-Hill, 1978.

Parekh, Bhikhu. *Marx's Theory of Ideology.* London: Croom Helm, 1982.

Parkinson, G. H. R., ed. *Marx and Marxisms.* Cambridge: Cambridge University Press, 1982.

Paterson, R. W. K. *The Nihilistic Egoist: Max Stirner.* London: Oxford University Press, 1971.

Paulsen, Friedrich. *Geschichte des gelehrten Unterrichts auf den deutschen Schu-*

len und Universitäten vom Ausgang des Mittelalters bis zur Gegenwart, volume
2. Berlin: Walter de Gruyter, 1921.

Pelczynski, Z. A., ed. *Hegel's Political Philosophy.* Cambridge: Cambridge University Press, 1971.

————, ed. *The State and Civil Society: Studies in Hegel's Political Philosophy.* Cambridge: Cambridge University Press, 1984.

Pepperle, Ingrid. *Junghegelianische Geschichtsphilosophie und Kunsttheorie.* Berlin: Akademie Verlag, 1978.

Plamenatz, John. *Ideology.* New York: Praeger, 1970.

Plant, Raymond. "Hegel and Political Economy." *The New Left Review,* nos. 103–104 (1977): 79–92, 103–113.

————. *Hegel.* Bloomington, Indiana: Indiana University Press, 1973.

Pöggeler, Otto. *Hegel in Berlin: Preussische Kulturpolitik und idealistische Ästhetik zum 150. Todestag des Philosophen.* Berlin: Staatsbibliothek Preussischer Kulturbesitz, 1981.

————. *Hegels Idee einer Phänomenologie des Geistes.* Freiburg and Munich: Verlag Karl Alber, 1973.

Pöggeler, Otto, and Annemarie Gethmann-Siefert, eds. *Kunsterfahrung und Kulturpolitik im Berlin Hegels.* Beiheft 22 of *Hegel-Studien.* Bonn: Bouvier Verlag, 1983.

Popitz, Heinrich. *Der entfremdete Mensch: Zeitkritik und Geschichtsphilosophie des jungen Marx.* Frankfurt am Main: Europäische Verlagsanstalt, 1967.

Pradel, Hans. *Wie kam Karl Marx in Trier zum Sozialismus? Ein Beitrag zum Lebensbild des jungen Marx.* Boppard am Rhein: Harald Boldt Verlag, 1965.

Prawer, S. S. *Karl Marx and World Literature.* Oxford: Oxford University Press, 1976.

Pühle, Hans-Jurgen, and Hans-Ulrich Wehler. *Preussen im Rückblick.* Sonderheft 6 of *Geschichte und Gesellschaft.* Göttingen: Vandenhoeck und Ruprecht, 1980.

Raddatz, Fritz J. *Karl Marx: A Political Biography.* Translated by Richard Barry. London: Weidenfeld and Nicolson, 1979; first published in German in 1975.

Rader, Melvin. *Marx's Interpretation of History.* New York: Oxford University Press, 1979.

Rauh, Hans-Christopher. "Zur Herkunft, Vorgeschichte und ersten Verwendungsweise des Ideologiebegriffs bei Marx und Engels bis 1844." *Deutsche Zeitschrift für Philosophie* 18 (1970): 689–715.

Rawidowicz, Simon. *Ludwig Feuerbachs Philosophie: Ursprung und Schicksal.* Second edition. Berlin: Walter de Gruyter, 1964.

Riedel, Manfred. *Bürgerliche Gesellschaft und Staat: Grundproblem und Struktur des Hegelschen Rechtsphilosophie.* Neuwied: Leichterhand, 1970.

————. "Gesellschaft, bürgerliche." In *Geschichtliche Grundbegriffe. Historisches Lexikon zur politisch-sozialen Sprache in Deutschland,* volume 2, edited by Otto Brunner et al., 719–800. Stuttgart: Ernst Klett, 1975.

————. *Studien zu Hegels Rechtsphilosophie.* Frankfurt am Main: Suhrkamp, 1969.

————. *System und Geschichte: Studien zum historischen Standort von Hegels Philosophie.* Frankfurt am Main: Suhrkamp, 1973.

————. *Theorie und Praxis im Denken Hegels.* Stuttgart: W. Kohlhammer, 1965.

————, ed. *Materialien zu Hegels Rechtsphilosophie.* 2 volumes. Frankfurt am Main: Suhrkamp, 1974.

Rihs, Charles. *L'Ecole des jeunes Hegeliens et les penseurs socialistes français.* Paris: editions anthropos, 1978.

Ringer, Fritz Z. *The Decline of the German Mandarins: The German Academic Community, 1890–1933.* Cambridge, Mass.: Harvard University Press, 1969.

Ritter, Joachim. *Hegel und die französische Revolution.* Frankfurt am Main: Suhrkamp, 1965.

Roessler, Wilhelm. *Die Entstehung des modernen Erziehungswesens in Deutschlands.* Stuttgart: W. Kohlhammer Verlag, 1961.

Rose, Margaret A. *Reading the Young Marx and Engels: Poetry, Parody and the Censor.* Totowa, New Jersey: Rowman and Littlefield, 1978.

Rosen, Zvi. *Bruno Bauer and Karl Marx: The Influence of Bruno Bauer on Marx's Thought.* The Hague: Martinus Nijhoff, 1977.

Rosenberg, Hans. *Bureaucracy, Aristocracy, Autocracy: The Prussian Experience, 1660–1815.* Boston: Beacon, 1968; first published in 1958.

————. *Politische Denkströmungen im deutschen Vormärz.* Göttingen: Vandenhoeck und Ruprecht, 1972.

Rosenkranz, Karl. *Georg Wilhelm Friedrich Hegels Leben.* Darmstadt: Wissenschaftliche Buchgesellschaft, 1969; reprint of second Berlin edition, 1844.

Rosenzweig, Franz. *Hegel und der Staat.* 2 volumes in 1. Berlin: R. Oldenbourg, 1920; reprint ed., Aalen: Scientia Verlag, 1962.

Rubel, Maximilien. *Karl Marx: Essai de biographie intellectuelle.* Paris: Librairie Marcel Rivière et Cie, 1957.

Rühle, Otto. *Karl Marx: His Life and Work.* Translated by Eden and Cedar Paul. London: George Allen and Unwin, 1929.

Sammons, Jeffrey L. *Heinrich Heine: A Modern Biography.* Princeton: Princeton University Press, 1979.

Sass, Hans-Martin. "Bruno Bauers Idee der Rheinischen Zeitung." *Zeitschrift für Religions- und Geistesgeschichte* 19 (1967): 321–332.

————. "Untersuchungen zur Religionsphilosophie in der Hegelschule, 1830–1850." Ph.D. dissertation, University of Münster, 1963.

Sass, Hans-Martin, and Marx W. Wartofsky, eds. *The Philosophical Forum: Feuerbach, Marx, and the Left Hegelians* 8 (1978).

Schläger, E. "Bruno Bauer und seine Werke." *Internationale Monatsschrift* 1 (1882): 377–400.

Schlawe, Fritz. "Die junghegelsche Publizistik." *Die Welt als Geschichte* 20

(1960): 30–50.

Schmidt, Alfred. *The Concept of Nature in Marx*. Translated by B. Fowkes. London: New Left Review Books, 1971; first published in German in 1962.

Schmidt, James. "A *Paideia* for the 'Bürger als Bourgeois': The Concept of 'Civil Society' in Hegel's Political Thought." *History of Political Thought* 2 (1981): 469–493.

————. "Recent Hegel Literature: General Surveys and the Young Hegel." *Telos* 46 (Winter 1980–1981): 113–147.

Schnabel, Franz. *Deutsche Geschichte im neunzehnten Jahrhundert*. 4 volumes, second edition. Freiburg: Herder, 1929–1937.

Schuffenhauer, Werner. *Feuerbach und der junge Marx: Zur Entstehungsgeschichte der Marxistischen Weltanschauung*. Berlin: VEB Deutscher Verlag der Wissenschaften, 1965.

Schulz, Gerhard. "Die Entstehung der bürgerlichen Gesellschaft." In Gerhard A. Ritter, ed., *Entstehung und Wandel der modernen Gesellschaft*, 3–65. Berlin: Walter de Gruyter, 1970.

Schwarz, Joel. "Liberalism and the Jewish Connection: A Study of Spinoza and the Young Marx." *Political Theory* 13 (1985): 58–84.

Schweitzer, Albert. *The Quest of the Historical Jesus*. Translated by W. Montgomery. London: Adams and Charles Black, 1948, from the German edition of 1906.

Seliger, Martin. *The Marxist Conception of Ideology*. Cambridge: Cambridge University Press, 1977.

Sewell, William H., Jr. *Work and Revolution in France: The Language of Labor from the Old Regime to 1848*. Cambridge: Cambridge University Press, 1982.

Shaw, William. *Marx's Theory of History*. Stanford: Stanford University Press, 1978.

Shils, Edward. "The Concept and Function of Ideology." In *International Encyclopedia of the Social Sciences*, volume 7 (1968): 66–76.

Shklar, Judith. *Freedom and Independence*. Cambridge: Cambridge University Press, 1976.

Siegel, Jerrold. *Marx's Fate: The Shape of a Life*. Princeton: Princeton University Press, 1978.

Simon, Walter. *The Failure of the Prussian Reform Movement, 1807–1819*. Ithaca, N.Y.: Cornell University Press, 1955.

Stein, Lorenz von. *The History of the Social Movement in France, 1789–1850*. Translated by Kaethe Mengelberg. Totawa, New Jersey: The Bedminister Press, 1964.

Stepelevich, Lawrence S. "Max Stirner and Ludwig Feuerbach." *Journal of the History of Ideas* 39 (1978): 451–463.

————. "Max Stirner as Hegelian." *Journal of the History of Ideas* 46 (1985): 597–614.

Strauss, Herbert. "Zur sozial- und ideengeschichtlichen Einordnung Arnold Ruges." *Schweitzer Beiträge zur allgemeinen Geschichte* 12 (1954): 162–173.

Stuke, Horst. *Philosophie der Tat: Studien zur "Verwirklichung der Philosophie" bei den Junghegelianern und wahren Sozialisten.* Stuttgart: E. Klett, 1963.

Taylor, Charles. *Hegel.* Cambridge: Cambridge University Press, 1975.

Taylor, Mark C. *Journeys to Selfhood: Hegel and Kierkegaard.* Berkeley, Los Angeles, and London: University of California Press, 1980.

Teichgraeber, Richard. "Hegel on Property and Poverty." *Journal of the History of Ideas* 38 (1977): 47–64.

Thomas, Paul. *Karl Marx and the Anarchists.* London: Routledge and Kegan Paul, 1980.

Thompson, John B. *Studies in the Theory of Ideology.* Berkeley, Los Angeles, and London: University of California Press, 1984.

Tocqueville, Alexis de. *The Old Regime and the French Revolution.* Garden City, N.Y.: Anchor Books, 1955.

Toews, John. *Hegelianism: The Path Toward Dialectical Humanism, 1805–1841.* Cambridge: Cambridge University Press, 1981.

———. "The Innocence of the Self: Cultural Disinheritance and Cultural Liberation in the Thought of the Young Germans and Young Hegelians." 4 volumes. Ph.D. dissertation, Harvard University, 1973.

Treitschke, Heinrich von. *History of Germany in the Nineteenth Century.* 7 volumes. Translated by E. Paul and C. Paul. New York: McBride, Nast, and Co., 1915–1919.

Treue, Wilhelm. "Adam Smith in Deutschland: Zum Problem des 'politischen Professors' zwischen 1776 and 1810." In *Rothfels-Festschrift: Deutschland und Europa,* 101–133. Düsseldorf: n.p., 1951.

Trilling, Lionel. *Sincerity and Authenticity.* Cambridge, Mass.: Harvard University Press, 1971; paperback edition, 1978.

Tucker, Robert C. *Philosophy and Myth in Karl Marx.* Cambridge: Cambridge University Press, 1972.

Turner, R. Steven. "The *Bildungsbürgertum* and the Learned Professions in Prussia, 1770–1830: the Origins of a Class." *Historie social/Social History* 8 (1980): 105–136.

———. "The Growth of Professorial Research in Prussia, 1818 to 1848—Causes and Context." *Historical Studies in the Physical Sciences* 3 (1972): 137–182.

———. "University Reformers and Professorial Scholarship." In Lawrence Stone, ed., *The University in Society,* volume 2, 495–531. Princeton: Princeton University Press, 1974.

Valjavec, Fritz. *Die Entstehung der politischen Strömungen in Deutschland, 1770–1815.* Munich: R. Oldenbourg, 1951.

Varrentrapp, C. *Johannes Schulze und das höhere preussische Unterrichtswesen in seiner Zeit.* Leipzig: B. G. Teubner, 1889.

Vierhaus, Rudolf. "Politisches Bewusstsein in Deutschland vor 1789." *Staat* 6 (1967): 175–196.

————. "Ständewesen und Staatsverwaltung in Deutschland vom späten 18. Jahrhunderts." In R. Vierhaus and M. Botzenhart, eds., *Dauer und Wandel der Geschichte: Aspekte europäischer Vergangenheit.* Münster: Verlag Aschendorff, 1966.

Walker, Mack. *German Home Towns: Community, State and General Estate, 1648–1871.* Ithaca, N.Y.: Cornell University Press, 1971.

Wartofsky, Marx W. *Feuerbach.* Cambridge: Cambridge University Press, 1977.

Wehler, Hans-Ulrich. *Sozialgeschichte Heute.* Göttingen: Vandenhoeck und Ruprecht, 1974.

Weil, Eric. *Hegel et l'état.* Paris: Librairie Philosophique J. Vrin, 1950.

Wessell, Leonard P., Jr. *Karl Marx, Romantic Irony, and the Proletariat: The Mythopoetic Origins of Marxism.* Baton Rouge, Louisiana: Louisiana State University Press, 1979.

Wilson, Arthur. *Diderot.* New York: Oxford University Press, 1972.

Windelband, Wilhelm. *Die Philosophie in deutschen Geistesleben des XIX. Jahrhunderts.* Tübingen: Verlag von J. C. B. Mohr, 1909.

Wolfson, Murray. *Marx: Economist, Philosopher, Jew: Steps in the Development of a Doctrine.* London: Macmillan, 1982.

Wood, Allen W. *Karl Marx.* London: Routledge and Kegan Paul, 1981.

Index

299

251; financial problems of, 92, 93, 95; and French Revolution, 91, 103, 109; on German Liberation movement, 92, 94, 103; on idealism, 102–103, 255 n. 84; identification with phenomenology of spirit, 18–19, 90, 102, 104–106, 167, 218; "Karl Streckfuss und das Preussenthum," 114, 127; and Marx, 128–129, 130–131, 133, 194, 202–204; and "mass" society, 77, 131–133, 220, 222, 225; memoirs of, 89, 252 n. 1; and nature, 102–103; in Paris, 129–139; and Pietism, 108, 110, 112–115, 257 n. 15; on press and public opinion, 121; in prison, 96–98, 104; "Der protestantische Absolutismus," 122–126, 220; and Protestantism, 107, 109, 110, 127, 132, 134–136, 257 n. 31; on realism, 102, 105; reintegration into Prussian society, 98, 104–106; reinterpretation of Hegelian philosophy, 117–122, 134–136, 137, 221; residual loyalty to Hegelian philosophy, 115, 118–119, 121, 124–126, 132, 140; and Romanticism, 114–115, 126, 131, 135, 257 n. 15; and Saxon state, 116, 126–129, 136; schooling, 92–93, 103; and Stirner, 136–137, 206, 232 n. 16; and Strauss, 38, 107, 113, 126, 135; and theory of ideology, 2–3, 41–42, 118, 135, 137, 222, 226; at university, 93–96, 98, 103; "Unsre letzten zehn Jahre," 133–139, 221, 222

Saint-Simon, H., 264 n. 10
Savigny, Friedrich, 36
Schaller, Julius, 112
Schelling, Friedrich, 11, 12, 39
Schill, Major Ferdinand von, 97, 98, 111
Schlegel, Friedrich, 163
Schleiermacher, F., 46, 53, 55
Schulze, Johannes, 35, 111–112, 240 n. 76

Self-consciousness: anti-, 221; and Bruno Bauer, 50, 57–58, 73, 75, 83–84; as freedom, 12, 14, 16–17, 19, 49; and Marx, 167, 177, 203, 211; and Ruge, 105–106, 120–121, 167, 177
Simon, Eduard, 96
Skeptics, 172
Smith, A., 22
Socialism. See Communism
Socrates, 170–171
Sophocles, 97, 98, 111
Spiegel, Archbishop (of Cologne), 108
Spirit: definition of in Hegelian philosophy, 12; evolution as subject, 12–17; evolution as substance, 13, 25–26, 171; identification with individual philosopher, 17–19, 58, 90, 101–106, 166–168, 218
Sprewitz, Karl, 94
Stahl, F., 39
State: Hegel's view of, 25–27, 31–33, 189; Marx's view of, 188–189, 191–194, 198–199, 208, 215; Ruge's view of, 119–121; separation from civil society, 21–25, 188–189, 191–193, 237 n. 14; and Ständestaat, 21, 24, 25
Stein, Karl vom, 152
Stein, Lorenz von, 77
Stirner, Max: and Bauer, 76; and Marx, 203, 206–209; and Ruge, 136–137, 206, 232 n. 16
Stoicism, 101, 172
Stralow, 165–166
Strauss, D. F., 113; and Bauer, 45, 48, 54–55, 60–62, 75, 83; Life of Jesus and its consequences, 37, 47, 53, 169; and Marx, 169; relation to theory of ideology, 6, 232 n. 14; and Ruge, 38, 107, 113, 126, 135
Stuke, Horst, 84
Szeliga, 76

Tholuck, August, 48
Thucydides, 97

Designer: U.C. Press Staff
Compositor: Prestige Typography
Text: 10/13 Stempel Garamond
Display: Stempel Garamond
Printer: Malloy Lithographing, Inc.
Binder: John H. Dekker & Sons